*Books by Martin L. Gross*


THE BRAIN WATCHERS
THE DOCTORS
THE PSYCHOLOGICAL SOCIETY

# The Psychological Society

# THE PSYCHOLOGICAL SOCIETY

A Critical Analysis of Psychiatry,
Psychotherapy, Psychoanalysis
and the Psychological Revolution

## Martin L. Gross

Random House New York

Library of Congress Cataloging in Publication Data
Gross, Martin L.
The psychological society.

Includes index.
1. Psychiatry—Philosophy.   2. Psychology—
Philosophy.   3. Civilization, Modern—20th
century.   I.  Title.
RC437.5.G75        616.8'9'001        77–90288
ISBN 0–394–46233–5

Manufactured in the United States of America
1 2 4 6 8 9 7 5 3
First Edition

*To my wife,* ANITA, *then and now*

*A grateful acknowledgment to those psychiatrists and psychologists who gave of their time and knowledge to the author in the researching of this book.*

# Contents

# The Psychological Society

# *I*

---

# The
# *Psychological*
# *Society*

THIS BOOK IS ABOUT the most anxious, emotionally insecure and analyzed population in the history of man, the citizens of the contemporary Psychological Society. It is also about that Society's practitioners, the psychiatrists and psychologists who have built an elaborate professional structure to cater to our emotional needs.

Much has been said about the awesome *external* transformation in our modern world. These changes are obvious. But the *internal* shift in man's psyche has altered both our actions and expectations more than any technological force. This change in inner man has taken place quietly, yet it has altered the nature of our civilization beyond recognition.

*The major agent of change has been modern psychology.* At the time of Sigmund Freud's visit to Clark University in Massachusetts in 1909, psychology was an infant discipline. Today, psychology is an art, science, therapy, religion, moral code, life style, philosophy and cult. It sits at the very center of contemporary society as an international colossus whose professional minions number in the hundreds of thousands.

Its ranks include psychiatrists, psychoanalysts, clinical psychologists, psychotherapists, social workers, psychiatric nurses, school psychologists, guidance counselors, marriage and family therapists, educational psychologists, Sensitivity T-Group and Encounter leaders, and assorted lay therapists. Recently, it has added a number of newly hyphenated professionals including psycholinguists, bio-psychologists and psychobiographers.

Its experimental animals are an obliging, even grateful human race. We live in a civilization in which, as never before, man is preoccupied with *Self.* We have become fascinated with our madness, motivations and our endless, sometimes wearying search for normality. Modern psychology and psychiatry seek to satisfy that fascination by offering us a full range of systems, from the serious to the whimsical, with which we can understand our confused psyche, then seek to heal it.

The contemporary Psychological Society is the most vulnerable culture in history. Its citizen is a new model of Western man, one who is dependent on others for guidance as to what is real or false. In the unsure state of his mind, he is even doubtful of the authenticity of his own emotions. As the Protestant ethic has weakened in Western society, the confused citizen has turned to the only alternative he knows: the psychological expert who claims there is *a new scientific standard of behavior* to replace fading traditions.

In the 1950s, David Riesman spoke of the "other directed" man as receiving his life cues from outside sources. Today, we can see a new *psychologically directed* man in operation. His antennae are thrust continually outward for hints from experts who are handsomely paid to tell him what to make of himself and others, how best to live, even feel.

The citizen-patient has been told, and usually believes, that his tormenting doubts about love, sex, work, interpersonal relations, marriage and divorce, child raising, happiness, loneliness, even death, will yield to the new technology of the mind. Mouthing the holy name of *science,* the psychological expert claims to know all.

This new truth is fed to us continuously from birth to the grave. Childhood, once a hardy time of adventure, is now seen as a period of extreme psychological fragility. A U.S. Senate subcommittee warns us that premature emotional disturbance will strike one in ten of our children. The nation's child guidance clinics have trebled in number over the last twenty years. One physician, Dr. Arnold Hutschnecker, even suggests a grand scheme to screen all the nation's children to find those who need preventive psychotherapy.

The schoolhouse has become a vibrant psychological center, staffed not only by schoolteachers trained in "educational psychology" but by sixty thousand guidance workers and seven thousand school psychologists whose "counseling" borders on therapy. In one case, virtually an entire first-grade class at P.S. 198 in New York City has been given free psychotherapy at nearby Mount Sinai Hospital.

The need for psychological expertise follows us doggedly through life. Erik Erikson's *identity crisis* has become a symbol for millions of adolescents, an age group which is increasingly concerned about its psyche. A CBS-TV special on youth reported that uppermost in the minds of those interviewed were nagging doubts about mental health. The college-age population is also heavily into its psyches as "drop-in" counseling centers handle record numbers of anguished youth. Columbia University reports a threefold increase in student use of psychological services in a decade.

The adult is, of course, the mainstay of the new Society, for his anxieties are endless. The enormity of that need is only hinted at in a George Washington University study which showed that Americans ingest tons of psychochemicals, mainly minor tranquilizers, in a continuous search for tranquillity.

This frenetic quest is part of modern man's search for the elusive goal of normality. It is a state which Freud once called an *ideal fiction* and which society hopelessly confuses with happiness and peace of mind. "The quest for peace of mind—or good mental health, which is another name for it—is universal," the National Association of Mental Health informs an eager public.

Modern psychological-mindedness springs from many origins, one of which is the breakdown in the separation between health and sickness when applied to the mind. Historically, insanity was an affliction that struck the few. The remainder felt spared. They may have been mean, or unhappy, or even eccentric, but they were considered sane.

Today, that boundary between the well and the sick has been blurred by psychology and psychiatry. Emotional illness is now seen as an ugly but natural manifestation that strikes us all in varying degrees. "Now every normal person is only approximately normal," Freud reminded us shortly before his death. "His ego resembles that of the psychotic in one point or another, in a greater or lesser degree." In modern parlance, we are all, to some extent, *sick.*

Impressionable citizens of the Society have even falsely equated mental health with the usually unreachable *ideal* state which combines success, love and lack of anxiety. The Psychological Society thus creates its own self-fulfilling prophecy. *We are all sick, for normality is almost unattainable.*

This might be called *the theory of universal madness.* We have increasingly directed suspicion of mental instability against our friends, family and, eventually, ourselves. In New York City, a ten-year study, *Mental Health in the Metropolis,* claimed that approximately 80 percent of adults showed some symptoms of mental illness, with one in four actually impaired.

In 1977 the President's Commission on Mental Health confirmed these dire diagnoses. It concluded that the state of our psyches is worse than believed, and that one-quarter of all Americans suffer from severe emotional stress. They warn that up to 32 million Americans are in need of professional psychiatric help.

A National Institute of Mental Health psychologist even portrays universal madness as a statistical certainty. "Almost no family in the nation is entirely free of mental disorders," he stated in a recent federal study. The NIMH psychologist estimates that in addition to the 500,000 schizophrenics in hospitals, there are 1.75 million psychotics not hospitalized, and up to *60 million Americans who exhibit deviant mental behavior related to schizophrenia.* He speaks of the "psychological turbulence that is rampant in an American society that is confused, divided and concerned about its future."

Despite these warnings, mental illness has not increased significantly since 1955, when complete records first began. The annual mental hospitalization rate of 8.5 per 1000 population is remarkably steady and consistent throughout much of the developed world. What the Psychological Society has done is to redefine *normality.* It has taken the painful reactions to the normal vicissitudes of life—despair, anger, frustration—and labeled them as maladjustments.

The semantic trick is in equating happiness with normality. By permitting this, we have given up our simple right to be both *normal and suffering* at the same time. Instead, we have massively redefined ourselves as *neurotic,* even as incipient mental cases, particularly when life plays its negative tricks. It is a tendency which gives modern America, and increasingly much of the Western world, the tone of a giant psychiatric clinic.

This is only one legacy of modern psychology. Its pervasiveness in the fabric of our culture has become near total as it absorbs new disciplines each year. Armed with what it claims are the hidden truths about man's behavior, it has impressed its philosophical stamp on virtually all of contemporary life: mental health and illness, the arts, education, religion, medicine, the family, child care, business, the social sciences, history, government, language, advertising, law, crime and punishment, even architecture and economics.

Its most obvious impact is on what are now collectively called *the helping professions,* a mental health team that includes perhaps a dozen professionals headed by the psychiatrist. Much as the ministry did for years, the superprofessionals of psychology and psychiatry have now assumed the supreme watchdog role. Not only have we entrusted them with the care of so-called neurotics and our mentally ill, but delinquents, drug addicts, the low-achieving student, the stutterer, the confused collegian, the suicidal, the homosexual, the criminal, the alcoholic, even the aged and the poor are all considered their natural patients.

In the Psychological Society, human problems are no longer seen as normal variations or unseemly twists of fate. We now view them as the products of internal psychological maladjustments. We are even encouraged to believe that there would be no failure, no crime, no malevolence, no unhappiness if man could only understand his psyche, then set it for a metaphysical condition called *adjustment.* As more of us find that ideal state defeated by life's pressures, psychology offers its ultimate remedy—*psychotherapy.*

"The demand for psychotherapy is non-ending. It's unbelievable," states Dr. Donald M. Kaplan, a New York teaching and practicing psychologist-analyst. "Individual psychotherapy was once an elitist privilege, but it has now been democratized. The general population now feels entitled to it, and is seeking it out. In prior times, people would take care of ordinary life crises by themselves, or with the help of their families. Now they all want psychotherapy."

Millions receive psychotherapy each year in a multitude of forms, from psychoanalysis to simple supportive therapy, in groups or alone. Others seek the Nirvana in the new wave of *humanistic* therapies including scores of imaginative ideas from Gestalt Therapy to nude marathons. We are offered almost a hundred different psychotherapies for every healing taste. Each proclaims a somewhat different method, sworn to be the superior key.

The outpatient psychiatric clinics are busy sites of this new therapy rush. In 1955 they treated a total of 233,000 people. Since then, the number has risen dramatically to 2.4 million patients annually. This figure does not include another 1.5 million patients treated each year in the 570 federally supported Community Mental Health Centers.

The establishment bases of psychotherapy are the psychiatrists, the majority of whom see patients in their private offices, clinical psychologists and the psychiatric social workers (M.S.W. degree), the burgeoning third rung of the helping professions. Judging from a 1973 American Psychiatric Association study of private practice, and a more recent report on health services from the American Psychological Association, we can estimate that one and a half million Americans take their psychic repair in the private offices of these practitioners.

In all, some six million Americans each year receive psychotherapy in clinics and hospitals and from private therapists. To find the total number in therapy, however, we must also look at the growing legions of *lay therapists* who offer a psychological inventory from *est* to primal workshops and encounter. At least a million more Americans take their therapy from these sources, or a total of seven million who receive psychological intervention annually.

This balm is not evenly distributed, for the therapy professions have a geographic bias. Almost half the psychiatrists, for example, practice in New York, California, Illinois, Pennsylvania or Massachusetts. Nearly one-third are in New York and California alone. But the profession is expanding rapidly into the rest of the country. Once psychologically isolated Nebraska now boasts over a hundred psychiatrists.

Psychology is now an international movement which cuts across national and class boundaries. With the demise of the belief in immortality and the end of absolute morality, it is becoming the most generally accepted substitute. Its power level in each nation varies with how well its theme of magical human improvement matches the indigenous ethic.

It has not yet gained a strong hold in southern Europe, but its strength increases as one progresses northward into France, Germany, Holland, Scandinavia and Britain. Even the Soviet Union, a consistent critic of Western insight psychology, has begun to recant. In *Kommunist,* the official ideological journal, Soviet psychologists have recently called for more research into applications of the unseen *unconscious.*

America, however, has been the warm, natural host for modern psychology. It has nurtured the young colossus from its infancy to its current adulthood. In fact, the American sponsorship of psychology may be setting a pattern for world society as definitive as America's earlier leadership in industrial technology.

Psychology has taken hold in the Protestant world mainly because both the psychological and Protestant ethics insist that a method be found for the perfectibility of men. That perfectibility was once sought through the intervention of God, but is now accomplished by supposed scientific adjustment of the psyche. Long before the Psychological Society, the nineteenth-century social historian Alexis de Tocqueville saw this urgent need for perfectibility in the American character. "Aristocratic nations are liable to narrow the scope of human perfectibility; democratic nations to expand it beyond reason," he observed.

This democratic hope has encouraged our desperate search for psychic understanding and repair. Instead of increasing our stability as a culture, that search has paradoxically accelerated man's tendency toward anxiety and insecurity, shaking the very underpinnings of Western civilization. It is now apparent that the Judeo-Christian society in which psychology began its ascendancy is atrophying under the massive impact of several forces, particularly that of modern psychology. In its place stands a new culture of a troubled and confused citizenry, the Psychological Society.

For many, this Society has all the earmarks of a potent new religion. When educated man lost faith in formal religion, he required a substitute belief that would be as reputable in the last half of the twentieth century as Christianity was in the first. Psychology and psychiatry have now assumed that special role. They offer mass belief, a promise of a better future, opportunity for confession, unseen mystical workings and a trained priesthood of helping professionals devoted to servicing the paying-by-the-hour communicants.

Not only is the new Society attempting to fill the void left by Christianity, but it has created images that parallel older spiritual ones. The traditional religious idea of *sin* is becoming obsolete. But the medico-psychological concept of *sick* has replaced it almost intact. We now speak glibly of murderers, addicts, even the personality-distorted as being "sick" or "neurotic" as effortlessly as neighbors once gossiped about the sinfulness of the local alcoholic.

Even though psychology and psychiatry are at the core of this new Society, surprisingly they have been the least analyzed of all disciplines. While attention has been focused on their customers, psychology and psychiatry themselves have escaped outside scrutiny, leaving their extraordinary control over our lives less than understood.

This book hopes to correct that oversight and explain the psychologization of our culture. It will probe the Psychological Society, its operations, origins, claims, manifestations, customs, mores, shortcomings, validity, aspirations and ultimate significance. *This evalua-*

*tion has become essential, for not an idea, not a style, not a personal or cultural relationship exists which has not been drastically affected by the new supremacy of the Psychological Society.*

The intellectual root of much of this enormous activity is the supposed existence of the *Unconscious,* man's anticlerical equivalent of the *Soul.* In this dimension of man's mind is ostensibly hidden the secrets of human behavior which Sigmund Freud "won for science," as his British disciple, Ernest Jones, once boasted.

In his "Introductory Lectures on Psycho-Analysis," given at the University of Vienna, Freud speculated that there have been three decisive scientific blows to the confidence of the human species.

The first was the Copernican revolution, which burst man's illusion that his earth was the center of the universe. The second was the Darwinian theory, which undercut his belief in the Godly Creation of our species. Freud said that the third, or "most wounding blow," was the impact of psychological research on man's confidence in his conscious will. His work, Freud contended, "seeks to prove to the ego that it is not even master in its own house, but must content itself with scanty information of what is going on unconsciously in its mind."

The tantalizing challenge of the unconscious has dominated much modern thought and action, particularly in the last quarter-century. Using the unconscious as its battering ram, psychology and psychiatry have forced their influence into every facet of Western life, from business to art. In the arts, they have virtually shattered the traditional structures of creativity, making over the novel, drama, film, painting, even poetry in their own abstruse, anxious image.

Irish author James Joyce was one of the first to inject psychology into the arts. "In Ulysses, I have recorded simultaneously what a man says, sees, thinks, and what such seeing, thinking, saying does to what you Freudians call the subconscious," he reminded us. Since the publication of *Ulysses* in 1922, the storytelling function of the serious novel has virtually eroded. It has been replaced by a psychological thrust in which action is often more unconscious than overt. In painting, German abstractionist Paul Klee saw modern art as a psychological portrait of man's inner space rather than as an imitator of nature. "I am not here to reflect the surface," he said, "but must penetrate inside."

Whenever contemporary society seeks to examine any phenomenon in depth by asking the questions "Why?" or "How?" the ubiquitous psychological colossus raises its hand in youthful exuberance and shouts that it can provide the answers. Its purported insight into human behavior has produced a revolution in relationships, some of which seem more examined than lived.

Psychological awareness has redefined the joys and conflicts of marriage, sex and romance. It has altered the social contract between parent and child, sibling and sibling, friend and friend, even that of business acquaintances. The change may not be serving us well, for much of society's current strain may be a by-product of this psychologized self-consciousness in *interpersonal relationships.*

One of the most significant shifts has been between parent and child, a thirty-year-old psychological adventure which has spawned more recrimination than understanding. This generation of young adults was the first to be raised as the childhood "patient" of scientific parenting. It has created an epidemic of parental psychologizing and subsequent wails of guilt.

"Thousands of parents torture themselves unnecessarily by exaggerating the importance of minor cases of rather odd and seemingly inexplicable conduct that are all part of childhood," comments Dr. Donald J. Holmes, a former University of Michigan psychiatrist. He is concerned that his profession has taken advantage of the modern parent's awe of Freud and psychiatry. As a result, he says, "the tendency to see mental illness where none exists is one mistake which parents, teachers, and all the rest of us have made far too often."

Psychology has also moved swiftly to fill the power vacuums in such declining disciplines as the ministry. Freud's atheistic ideas have paradoxically been used to bulwark the dwindling belief in an anthropomorphic God. Ministers, priests and rabbis now flock to courses in *pastoral counseling,* making many members of the cloth seem more Freudian than Christian. The Union Theological Seminary, in collaboration with a New York growth center (G.R.O.W.), has offered a certified program in human relations education, a watered-down psychotherapy skill.

Crime and punishment, too, have become slavish servants to psychological technology. In the court of law the state traditionally asked "What?" The modern court also asks "Why?" calling on psychiatrists, psychologists, even probation officers for expertise. Each year the psychological *why* looms larger, establishing not only a criminal's ability to stand trial, the length of a prisoner's sentence, his parole or probation, but guilt and innocence itself.

Among the noncriminal mentally ill, psychology and psychiatry have seized even greater judicial power. It is a responsibility critics fear is sometimes abused. Outspoken libertarian Dr. Thomas S. Szasz insists that forced hospitalization based on psychiatric testimony is little different from imprisonment. Psychologist Russell P. Norman also complains: " . . . one sees individuals deprived of their freedom, their civil liberties, and their right to be heard in court because, it is alleged, they need 'treatment' for their mental condition and are unable to understand the true nature of their circumstances."

Mated academically with sociology and anthropology, psychology has broadened into the *behavioral sciences,* sometimes called the *human sciences.* Its catchall blandishment has enraptured the educated classes, much as theology dominated the mind of pre-Industrial man.

The applications seem infinite. At the City University of New York a doctoral degree has been granted in Environmental Psychology. Planners now speak of "psychological housing research." Even the behavioral aspect of architecture has been granted graduate status at the University of California. At New York University a four-year doctoral program in Human Relations promises expertise to those in government, business and administration.

During the mid-1970s the movie-industry ratings emanated from a code directed by a psychiatrist. The State Department has funded psychological studies on international problems, while Claremont College, in California, offers a graduate program in the psychology of public affairs.

Business has been a fervent user of psychology, for it was inevitable that modern management would subsidize any art that claimed special insight into people. Bell and Howell is one of many corporations who have used Sensitivity Training to trigger emotional revelations among their employees. That corporation stands out only because their Intimacy Encounter Program discontinued "toe-sucking" when complaints hinted at the similarity to fellatio. Clinical psychologist Harry Levinson, formerly of the Harvard Graduate School of Business, has applied Freudian theory to management problems, offering "organizational diagnosis" of a corporation's neuroses.

The federal government is very much a part of the Psychological Society. The Federal Aviation Administration has developed a secret "psychological profile" of hijackers which commercial airlines use to screen out potential sky pirates. Not only Head Start, the Peace Corps, various poverty programs, and the Office of Education, but the more impersonal Pentagon and C.I.A. are heavily involved in psychological stratagems.

Although the uses of psychology are diverse, the Society operates through one underlying, universal mechanism which permits it to move effortlessly from the treatment of emotional distress to the analysis of a novel. It is the Psychological Idea.

Like all historical systems, the Idea is deceptively simple. Much of its power lies in its refutation of traditional philosophies. It denies the organic view of the mind as a biochemical device with a relatively inflexible gene-determined inherited style, what we generally call one's *nature* or *temperament.* In this biological view, the environment is capable only of modifying one's inclinations. The person flourishes best when the environment and his nature are in fortunate juxtaposition.

The Psychological Idea has also haughtily replaced the Religious View, in which man is seen as a product of Creation. In this view, man's behavior was judged righteous or evil in accordance with a contract with God. In return for faith and obedience, God offered his healing power, which was proclaimed greater than that of man's. The Psychological Idea has been instrumental in the disintegration of this religious concept, what Freud in *The Future of an Illusion* termed "an infantile model."

The third denial involves the commonsense view, one which had survived for thousands of years. In this ancient pragmatic system, people see others as they appear to be: hateful, kind, friendly, strong, weak, evil, mature, childish or any combination thereof. One judged oneself and others by what one *did.* Each person was responsible for his own actions, which were more significant than one's supposed motives. In this view, there was little tolerance of experts, for behavior was self-evident, for all to see and judge.

The Psychological Idea, which is fast becoming the modern consensus, denies all three philosophies as superficial or erroneous. Man, it insists, knows little of himself and others. Things are usually not what they seem to be. (The confident businessman may be a frightened adult in unresolved childhood competition with his father.) Biologic temperament may exist, but man is basically an environmental animal whose personality was established during his childhood. "Man is equipped," said Freud, "with the most varied instinctual dispositions, whose ultimate course is determined by the experiences of early childhood."

Man may be impressed by his conscious thought and actions. But in the Psychological Idea, they are often seen as insignificant *secondary reactions.* What we see, what we think we feel, cannot be trusted.

They are only veils of ignorance disguising the psychological truth carefully hidden in our unconscious.

Only psychology, we are told, can divine our secret motivations and reveal the elusive "why" of the strange human animal. The rules of discovery require professional interpretation. Just as the clergy once mediated between man and his soul, so the psychiatric and psychological professional must now interpret the mind for man.

The popularity of the Idea is understandable. Never before has a general philosophical system so concerned itself with *Self.* Never before have we so revered self-indulgence. The Idea focuses directly on modern man's vulnerable psyche and newly acquired emotional rights. The lure is irresistible. To egocentric modern man, the prospect of *Self* instead of *God* seated at the center of a world philosophical system is exquisitely attractive.

The university has been invaluable in spreading the new gospel to millions of students. But to reach the public at large, the Idea required the cooperation of the popular communications industry, one which the media enthusiastically gave. Who wouldn't be intrigued by a system which claimed to tell you how to get along better with your son, improve your sex life or divine the inner motivations of a mass-killer?

The result has been the etching of millions of daily messages of psychology on the minds of hundreds of millions. A multitude of psychological how-to books are bought by people anxious for the surest scientific route to personal happiness, sexual gratification or marriages once made only in heaven. Dr. Joyce Brothers, who conveys the latest psychological generalizations to millions, has been voted "One of the Ten Most Influential Women in the World."

In such an environment, it was inevitable that the jargon of psychology would become the currency of an entire civilization: that *Psychespeak* would arrive before Orwellian *Newspeak.* The argot titillates millions in all generations and in every social class, filling in half-finished sentences in classrooms, cocktail parties and bedrooms with the new shorthand.

The word "psychological" has itself taken on symbolic overtones. Former President Nixon used the word several times in his 1972 State of the Union address. Political reporters constantly allude to a close defeat as a "psychological victory." A partner in a Stock Exchange firm commented that "the market is not going down because of economic reasons. It's strictly psychological."

Some psychological jargon infiltrated the language as early as forty years ago. Others are at the height of their fashionable ascent. *Identity crisis, projection, libido, defense mechanism, self-actualization, Oedipus complex, peak experiences, penis envy, interpersonal relationships, inferiority complex, sibling rivalry, feelings of inadequacy, compulsive personality, paranoiac, extrovert, trauma, phallic symbol, meaningful relationships, infantile sexuality, working through, human ecology, latent homosexuality, introvert, acting out, underachiever, castration complex, transference, sublimation, Freudian slip, pleasure principle, bisexuality, death wish, love-hate relationship,* and the Freudian structures of *id, ego, superego, conscious, preconscious* and *unconscious* are only a sampling of the psychological glossary.

Even the counterculture jargon of *do your own thing* was created by Gestalt psychologist Fritz Perls. The more contemporary "get my head together," or "get into my (or your) head," are derivatives of the same psychological jargon.

The Psychological Idea also insists that all of our thoughts and actions are "never the result of chance," as Freud said, but are shaped by our unconscious. The concept has gripped world imagination. Forgetting names and faces, coming late to work through bumper-to-bumper traffic, spilling drinks on a host's new couch, are considered *meaningful,* not random acts, in the Society.

This modern game has its origins in Freud's work, *The Psychopathology of Everyday Life,* published in 1901. When visiting a patient, he related, he would sometimes take out his own key. It was not just absent-mindedness, Freud said. It was "equivalent to the thought 'Here I feel I am at home.' " A mistake in reading or writing conceals a "repression" or an "insincerity," while the tunes we hum have a connection to the "subject that is occupying our minds," he told us.

Even physical accidents are denied as chance. Many of us, we are informed, are *accident prone.* Speaking of private plane accidents, Dr. Stanley Mohler of the Federal Aviation Administration believes that "most of these crashes are deliberate at the unconscious level," a phenomenon that has been dubbed *psychosomatic death.*

Through such symptomatic acts, including the classic Freudian slip, we reveal our true selves. The Psychological Society may be more forgiving of unorthodox social behavior than the Protestant one it has replaced. But it is the harshest of all in examining each person's statement and actions. *In this new culture, everything is psychologically on the record.*

These speculations of modern psychology promise insight into the most interesting of all animals: Oneself. But this was not enough to bring it power. It required another ingredient: *the reputation of science*. Without science, psychological theorems might be considered occult speculation not unlike the mysticism of Kabala. Psychiatrists and psychologists constantly strain to remind us of their scientific connection. As Dr. Franz G. Alexander boasted: ". . . the fact that psychology—the study of personality—can have the same cumulative and operational characteristics as the natural sciences was established."

*Self* and *science* have established a powerful psychological partnership. Its major products are its claims: truth and cure. Psychology's truth is in its thousands of *findings* about sex, marriage, mental health, personal attitudes, child raising, learning, aggression, which have been discovered by a professional. They cascade all around us in journals, newspapers, magazines, and on television, all labeled as "scientific evidence."

The claim of *cure* is made with equal enthusiasm. Psychiatrists answering a Group Health Insurance, Inc., survey of 923 patients claimed that 75 percent had recovered or improved. The Central Fact-Gathering Committee of the American Psychoanalytic Association reports that of those who "completed" treatment, over 96 percent "felt benefited."

Much of the public, and most professionals, accept these claims of cure. But, increasingly, outspoken psychiatrists and psychologists are becoming skeptical of some of the basic tenets of the Society. Dr. Alfred M. Freedman, former president of the American Psychiatric Association, raises one unsettling point. "It is possible that Freudian theory may be proven no more scientific than astrology or phrenology," he stated when interviewed at the New York Medical College, where he heads the psychiatry department.

Others fear that our excessive psychologizing is itself a *neurotic stimulus*. By focusing attention on inescapable human fears and disappointments which would be ignored in a less self-conscious civilization, we may be stimulating personal insecurity.

Prominent psychiatrist Dr. Jerome D. Frank, professor emeritus at Johns Hopkins University School of Medicine in Baltimore, even suggests that the mental health industry may be creating its own customers. "The greater the number of treatment facilities and the more widely they are known, the larger the number of persons seeking their services," he states. "Psychotherapy is the only form of treatment which, at least to some extent, appears to create the illness it treats."

These fears hardly represent general opinion in the Psychological Society. The public is awed. It is not only respectful, but usually unaware of internal strife within the professional colossus. Although the public may believe that certain "shrinks" are peculiar, the therapist's office is now the accepted, even enlightened, place to repair one's psyche or find solace.

It is all part of what psychiatrist Dr. John D. Vanderpool calls the *"quest for instant mental health."* It is an Americanization of the psyche that believes that the elimination of anxiety and being both normal and happy are not only rights but commodities that can be purchased from American technology.

The new Psychological Society is not an individualistic one. It is a conformist society in which we are taught not only what to think of ourselves and others, but *how to feel.* Natural emotions such as outrage, despair, grief, jealousy, suspicion, disappointment and passing depression are made to appear not only undesirable but abnormal. Our striving for psychological equanimity so violates human nature that the only defense against it is emotional blandness, a by-product of the new Society's conforming pressures.

The Psychological Society is also a talkative, even garrulous one in which privacy has become a serious victim. Americans are justly concerned about the invasion of privacy by data banks, credit checks, government agencies. Yet they are surprisingly willing to surrender their natural rights of privacy when a psychological rationale is offered. They will tell their life stories to professionals, paraprofessionals, even laymen who will listen. They will spill out their secret resentment, problems and sex lives to a dozen strangers called a *group.*

The new Society flourishes on the belief that human technology can remake man as effortlessly as a computerized assembly line. Santayana observed that life is a predicament. The Psychological Society seeks to repeal that truth by offering its techniques as the hope for a scientific Utopia.

This book will search out that technology and those who operate it. We will attempt to learn how and why it works, or fails. Only by examining it without awe can we learn how worthwhile, how scientific, how enlightened, or how false and debilitating the Psychological Society truly is.

# II

---

# The Fallacy
# of Psychotherapy

THE PSYCHIATRIC CLINIC AT THE KAISER Foundation Hospital in Oakland, California, could not accommodate everyone who applied for psychotherapy. Of 150 patients who sought help, all were first evaluated. Most were placed into therapy, but twenty-three had to wait six months before therapists were available to help them.

At the end of six months, doctors decided to check the patients to see how much better the treated had done than those who were still on the waiting list. When both groups were reevaluated psychiatrically, the researchers surprisingly found that the twenty-three who had waited had not only improved, but were doing essentially as well as those in therapy. "The therapy patients did not improve significantly more than did the waiting-list controls," the study authors report.

This disturbing experiment prompts two questions that are increasingly being posed by critics both within and outside the psychiatric and psychological professions. Is psychotherapy effective in treating neuroses and emotional disturbances? Or is the claim that psychology heals a modern fallacy?

These impertinent questions seem out-of-date seventy-five years after Freud and a therapy roster of some seven million patients a year. Their vote is that psychotherapy does work. It is a ballot symbolized by the more than $2 billion spent each year by citizens of the Psychological Society in search of the Holy Grail of psychic perfection, or at least relief from the pain of living.

But despite such public accolades, a sober, sometimes even bitter argument rages within the profession itself. Specifically, it is whether psychotherapy is a science or a superstition ennobled as a discipline. Are the emotionally distressed the recipients of the fruits of a true psychological revolution or the victims of a cheap psychic nostrum?

Two disparate case histories dramatize the opposing views of this long-heralded healing art. A thirty-one-year-old advertising executive with an M.B.A. degree and an $18,000-a-year salary sought out the services of a neo-Freudian practitioner in New York. He was having difficulty creating a permanent relationship with any girl, and was tired of the lack of satisfaction in his promiscuous sex life. In addition, his job had been dead-ended for almost two years. He was frequently depressed, slept poorly and was not eating properly. His concern was that the future would be a perpetuation of his meaningless treadmill.

He entered psychotherapy with the psychiatrist, and after eight months of treatment his life developed a new rhythm. At work, he met an attractive and sensitive girl, to whom he became engaged. Shortly after, a rival agency hired him as an account executive at $25,000 a year. Not long after that, he concluded his treatment, grateful to his therapist for the new insight which seemed to have miraculously altered his stalled existence.

The success of many such cases and their promotion by word-of-mouth and through the media has reinforced the reputation of psychotherapy as the modern boon for the pained and confused psyche.

But there is an obverse side to the therapy coin. This less attractive view is described by a prominent psychiatrist, Dr. Melitta Schmideberg, in the form of a case history. She tells of a colleague's patient, Miss R., a single woman in her thirties who lived with her sister and had worked in the same office job for ten years. The patient was sexually inhibited and had a passive personality. Miss R. sought out therapy because she thought it might help her to get married. In an attempt to solve her inhibitions, the therapist "tried to get out her aggression," Dr. Schmideberg reports in the *American Journal of Psychiatry.*

As a result of the therapy, the patient began to have difficulty with her sister, including violent domestic arguments. Simultaneously, the therapist tried to reduce Miss R.'s sexual inhibitions, after which she became "promiscuous and lost all self-respect," as Dr. Schmideberg says. Her new aggression also lost her the job she had held for ten years. She became depressed and agitated and was finally hospitalized for six months. She was no longer able to work and had to live on her brother's charity.

The debate as to whether psychotherapy is effective or a failure, science or shamanism, is a complex and heated one. But before we examine it more closely, we should look at its basic equation: *Who does what to whom,* as professionals coyly label it. First, who are the practitioners of this expensive contemporary exercise?

Three researchers—Henry, Sims and Spray—surveyed the therapy business in a study supported by the National Institute of Mental Health. They contacted all the accredited 6629 psychotherapists they could locate in the greater New York, Chicago and Los Angeles areas. The study covered psychiatrists (M.D.), psychoanalysts (M.D.), clinical psychologists (Ph.D.) and psychiatric social workers (M.S.W.)—what they collectively termed the *Fifth Profession,* the calling of psychotherapy.

Their study covered a sizable sample of the four groups that control the therapy profession. Of the 30,000 psychiatrists and psychoanalysts, almost all are involved in psychotherapy, either in private practice, or at hospitals. Of the 26,000 licensed psychologists, approximately 17,000 are doing psychotherapy, according to a study done by the American Psychological Association. The third major category, the clinical social worker (once called "psychiatric social worker"), is actually the largest therapist group, one which has silently achieved a new eminence in the last decade.

An estimated 35,000 social workers are doing psychotherapy in private practice, in mental hospitals and in the Community Mental Health Centers, for which they provide approximately half the manpower. Aping their worshiped psychiatrist model, the M.S.W. therapist is usually Freudian in his psychological outlook.

What does the proud member of the Fifth Profession look like? Seven in ten are male, the largest group is between forty and forty-nine years of age. Among psychiatrists, only 11 percent are women. But females predominate among social workers (57 percent). Three in four therapists have been in personal therapy, ranging from almost 100 percent of the psychoanalysts to 64 percent of social workers. Even multiple bouts on the couch are common: of therapists in therapy, half have had their psyches probed at least twice. Over 20 percent of the analysts have been back to the Freudian regimen *three times or more.*

Some seventy-five years after Freud, is the Viennese master still a model for modern psychotherapy? Apparently, he is. One study of 283 psychotherapists found that 60 percent declared themselves as "Freudian." Social scientist Arnold A. Rogow found that two of three psychiatrists practiced what they now termed "Freudian," "neo-Freudian," or the professionally fashionable *eclectic* psychotherapy.

In the flurry of new techniques from Transactional Analysis to Primal Scream, it is easy to lose sight of the fact that *psychodynamic therapy,* the offshoot of Freud and the neo-Freudians, still predominates as the prestigious, establishment therapy of the Psychological Society.

Unquestionably, more patients now scream, touch, feel, jump, play, strip and tickle their way toward emotional perfection. But the traditional *insight therapy* in which therapist and patient, at $20 to $100 an hour, try to struggle through childhood complexes and defense mechanisms to find out "why" is still what most people call psychotherapy.

Most therapists practice a mixture of various Freudian and neo-Freudian methods, what one New York psychiatrist calls the "American mishmash school of therapy." It is Sigmund Freud, metaphysically diluted, with less Oedipal emphasis and less infantile sexuality, and salted with the neo-Freudian culturalism of Harry Stack Sullivan or Karen Horney. It is as often conducted face-to-face in chairs as on the traditional therapy couch. Today, it may even include a patronizing acceptance of behavior modification therapy, particularly when faced with a phobic patient. (In Britain, most psychologists have an anti-Freudian and pro-behaviorist point of view.)

This pastiche of Freud, Sullivan, Horney, Adler, Hartmann, Rank, Stekel, Wilhelm Reich, and even such newcomers as the late Eric Berne *(Games People Play),* is put together somewhat differently by each practicing psychiatrist as his own psychotherapy, but always with the major debt to Freud.

"There is no doubt that psychoanalytically oriented psychotherapy is the core of most of the psychotherapy done by American psychiatrists today," Dr. Alfred Freedman, past president of the American Psychiatric Association, stated when interviewed.

"If I were to guess, I would say that the average mix of the average American private-practicing psychiatrist is sixty percent psychoanalytically oriented psychotherapy and forty percent other modalities, including psychochemotherapy, electroconvulsive shock treatment and behavioral therapy. The psychotherapy is itself a mixture with probably sixty percent either Freud or those closely identified with him, perhaps twenty-five percent Sullivan, Fromm and the William Alanson White School, ten percent Karen Horney, and bits from others."

Who does what to *whom?* The typical patient, according to a 1973 American Psychiatric Association report, is female (62 percent of all such patients), white (97 percent), middle-class, and "neurotic."

The truly sick, as we shall see, seldom receive the psychotherapeutic balm. More than two-thirds of the psychiatric patients were suffering from neuroticism, personality disorders or "transient situational disturbances." Fewer than one in four were seriously mentally ill. Overall, treatment averaged one visit a week. Of those who went beyond consultation, more than half received psychotherapy. Most were in individual therapy, but one in four was in a group. The usual fee for the 50-minute hour, says the APA, was $35, a figure which is now closer to $45, even $50.

To the believing public, this therapy often seems like the only remedy for emotional pain—a faith which has morally and financially supported the giant psychotherapy industry. But increasingly, researchers within the profession are raising significant doubts that psychotherapy is as effective as its practitioners, or its faithful customers, believe.

The first gauntlet thrown in therapy's proud face was by Hans J. Eysenck, Ph.D., of the Institute of Psychiatry, University of London. In a now historic 1952 monograph, he evaluated thirty years of reports on the effectiveness of psychotherapy. Eysenck's technique was to take the claims of psychotherapists' cures at face value, *but* to compare them with similar neurotic patients who had been given little or no therapy.

Eysenck collected reports on 7293 patients of eclectic psychotherapy from nineteen different professional studies. At first glance, the results looked promising to a confident profession: an average 64 percent of the psychotherapy patients showed improvement. But when Eysenck took the challenge one step further, the optimism fades. He compared these results with those of patients who had received little or no therapy and who had taken no medication. Surprisingly, one group of neurotic patients *showed a 72 percent improvement by the second year despite the absence of treatment* other than that given by their family doctors.

These surprisingly healthy untreated patients were 500 consecutive psychoneurotic disability claimants from Equitable Life Assurance Society files. Each had lost at least three months of work because of psychological illness. They were treated with sedatives and old-fashioned reassurance by their physicians, then followed up for at least five years. At the end of the first year the recovery rate was 45 percent, which rose to 90 percent in five years.

Eysenck's conclusions were revolutionary. The data showed, he says, that *"roughly two-thirds of a group of neurotic patients will recover or improve to a marked extent within about two years of the onset of their illness, whether they are treated by means of psychotherapy or not."*

Eysenck has been under continual professional fire for his opinion. Some critics have attacked his 1952 review of the literature as unfair, and less than rigorous. But few doubt that his early work was a now historic prod which stimulated his colleagues to take a closer look at psychotherapy.

Then in 1965, Eysenck released a more extensive survey of published studies, with still more damaging results for psychotherapy. He now claims that psychotherapy is a general failure by the very nature of its being unessential to the patient's recovery. "We have found that neurotic disorders tend to be self-limiting, that psychoanalysis is no more successful than any other method, and that in fact all methods of psychotherapy fail to improve on the recovery rate obtained through ordinary life-experiences and nonspecific treatment," Eysenck states.

The fervor of psychotherapists is not in question. In fact, the mere act of testing the art's effectiveness has raised a ground swell of anger within the profession. Eysenck warns that an "emotional feeling of considerable intensity" is aroused when therapy is challenged. One researcher was treated as a blasphemer by his colleagues when he broached the idea of scientific controls. It was "as if we were attempting a statistical test of the efficiency of prayer," Dr. Eysenck reports in the nonestablishment *International Journal of Psychiatry.*

This defensiveness is a professional trademark in the Psychological Society. A decade ago the reflex was near universal. Today, several professionals have opted for intellectual integrity, and are producing rigorous studies on whether therapy works and if not, why. If their research continues unabated, current psychological theorems will fall with the same unsuspecting suddenness as those toppled by the Freudians themselves a half-century ago.

The breakthrough in evaluating psychotherapy has come from the use of a simple scientific method, the *controlled study.* Therapy has built its inflated reputation on *clinical claims,* the anecdotal recounting of "cured" cases, which, like stories of early chiropractic "miracles," hypnotized an anxious society. Backed by a strident propaganda campaign, psychotherapy protested that it did not need studies to verify its beneficence.

But controlled studies are callous to public acclaim. By dividing a group in half, and giving treatment to one part while simply observing the other, a researcher can tell whether the treatment works better than nontreatment, and by how much. Whenever possible, it is best to use a *double-blind* study in which neither the impressionable doctor nor the patient knows who is receiving what. "The absence of serious controlled studies on therapy," says Dr. Eysenck, "is perhaps the most eloquent testimony for the failure of clinical psychologists and psychiatrists to take seriously their task of appraising the effects of the methods they use."

One of the earliest and most extensive attempts to validate or disprove the technique was performed decades ago in Massachusetts. The Cambridge-Somerville Youth Study placed on trial the accepted idea that psychological counseling could prevent delinquent behavior, an unproven theory that still flourishes.

The raw material was six hundred and fifty underprivileged boys, aged 6 to 10, believed to be potential delinquents. By a coin toss, half were assigned to a T (Treatment) group, the other half to a C (Control or Untreated) group. The treated children were turned over to counselors, who used either Freudian therapy methods, or the client-centered techniques of psychologist Carl Rogers. The experiment lasted eight years, after which time the youngsters were evaluated.

The statistical result unnerved the faithful. At first look, it has all the ingredients of a heart-warming psychological drama. Of 70 "likely" delinquents given preventive psychotherapy, only 23 had committed serious delinquent acts. The counselors reported two-thirds of the boys "substantially benefited."

The results were impressive until they checked the untreated control group. *The unpsychologized, uncounseled boys proved to have fewer delinquent episodes than their treated peers.* The treated boys were involved in 264 offenses, while the untreated committed only 218 offenses.

The Cambridge study was a pioneering one. Since then, courageous researchers have conducted scores of studies using control groups as careful barometers.

Quite by accident, society has created a ready-made laboratory in which we can test psychotherapy. It is the psychiatric-clinic *waiting list*. As we have witnessed in the Kaiser Hospital study, it is made up of a group of patients of the same type seeking the same psychological help from the very same place. Why not, researchers thought, compare how well the *treated* and the *waiting* do in solving their neurotic complaints?

Dr. Louis A. Gottschalk, of the University of California at Irvine, is one of the many psychiatrists who have tapped the research power of the waiting list. He evaluated two groups of applicants to an outpatient psychiatric clinic, a total of sixty-eight patients. One group received immediate *crisis intervention* treatment, a currently popular therapy. The others were put on the waiting list. At the end of six weeks Gottschalk's staff reevaluated both groups. They both had improved, with the sickest patients in each group improving least. But those who only waited did essentially as well as those who received psychotherapy.

How does Dr. Gottschalk explain his results? He believes it is because most neurotic complaints are self-limiting. As with the common cold, time is a splendid healer. "Most patients suffering from life crises recover spontaneously within six weeks regardless of the kind of care they receive," he says.

Dr. Norman Q. Brill, professor of psychiatry at U.C.L.A., suggests another explanation for the seemingly magical *power of waiting* for therapy. By no longer looking at himself as a patient, the person is forced to mobilize other life resources, he believes. "He stops thinking about certain things that bothered him, changes spontaneously take place in his life, other areas of interest replace the previous concerns that brought him to therapy," Dr. Brill stated when interviewed. "People follow a general rule: there is a tendency for the neurotic patient to improve."

What we are witnessing is probably the true miracle of the Psychological Society. *It is called spontaneous remission, the tendency of most emotional nonpsychotic complaints to improve without treatment.*

Since the human psyche constantly strains to repair itself, therapy often takes the credit for time itself. Psychotherapy may even be praised in cases where the patient really improves because of a fortunate change in life—a successful love affair, a better job, a good rest, or a pick-up in physical health. In one study, Freiss and Nelson examined 45 successful cases of psychotherapy and found that 33 had actually been the result of such external circumstances, not the therapy.

Spontaneous improvement without therapy even makes mathematical sense, suggests Dr. Jerome D. Frank, professor emeritus of psychiatry at Johns Hopkins University School of Medicine. He points out that "from a statistical standpoint, most people come to psychotherapy when they are in the throes of a crisis or recovering from one." Naturally, he explains, they will "be more distressed and incapacitated than they were a few months before or will be a few months later regardless of any intervention." Being sickest when they start, they tend to improve with or without help.

How can we know for sure that this prestigious technique of divining and repairing our psyches is not scientific after all? The best corroboration of this, and perhaps the most damaging evidence against psychotherapy, are tests in which psychoneurotic patients took pills containing nothing of known medical value, yet they recovered. This new research work in the seemingly miraculous effect of *placebo pills* is among the most important in the field.

The evidence is disquieting to therapists. Sugar placebo pills given to unsuspecting neurotic patients often do as well as psychotherapy treatments. As psychologists Allen E. Bergin and Sol Garfield, co-editors of the *Handbook of Psychotherapy and Behavior Change* state, placebos "too often yield improvement figures very close to therapy group figures." Between 50 and 76 percent of patients taking only placebos (Latin for "I shall please") showed improvement, about the same percentage showing positive results for psychotherapy.

Dr. Frank has put the sugar wafer directly up against psychotherapy, with poor results for the talking cure. Psychiatric outpatients were interviewed and tested on various measures, including a Mean Discomfort Score (MDS). They were then given what was called a "new pill, not yet on the market." They were also informed that it was known to be nontoxic and was believed to help patients with complaints similar to theirs.

The patients returned one week, then two weeks, later and were followed up periodically. *The placebo-takers improved more rapidly than the therapy patients.* They started with an MDS of 35, then dropped quickly to 15, rising to about 25 at the end of the three years. The psychotherapy patients, who took six months of treatment, had an MDS which started over 40, and never dropped below 25, an improvement which took five years. The result was that six months of psychotherapy failed to do better than the quick administration of "I Shall Please." "The difference between the two groups was not statistically significant," Dr. Frank explains.

Dr. Arthur K. Shapiro, clinical professor of psychiatry at Mount Sinai School of Medicine in New York, is a leader in placebo research, a subject he has written on extensively. At one institution, he conducted a series of experiments on the therapeutic process which illustrates the possible power of the placebo. Over a period of eight years, 1440 patients were first asked to fill out a long checklist of their symptoms. They were then given a harmless, psychologically inert dose of lactose sugar and told that "they should be helped by this psychotherapeutic medicine."

After the patients took their "medicine," they were asked to sit for an hour, and then record whether they felt better, the same or worse than before taking the placebo. "Fifty-five percent of the patients reported that they felt better within the hour of taking the placebo," Dr. Shapiro reported when interviewed. "Thirty percent said there was no change, and fifteen percent said they were worse. The placebo effect is a well-demonstrated one. As we have learned from studies, it can be a temporary one or not work at all, but it can also be powerful and pervasive."

What if the neurotic patient knows he is being fooled? It apparently makes little difference to his cure. Researchers L.C. Park and L. Covi candidly told patients they were receiving "sugar pills" with "no medicine in it at all." For the most gullible, they added a fillip: "I think this pill will help you as it helped so many others." Patients took their sugar pills three times a day for a week, then were psychiatrically reevaluated. Only one refused to participate in the seeming farce. Of the fourteen who took the pill, thirteen showed improvement on all criteria.

At the U.C.L.A. psychiatric clinic, Dr. Norman Q. Brill tested both placebo and the waiting list against psychotherapy, and even against minor medications. He conducted a controlled study of 299 outpatients and reported his upsetting results in the *Archives of General Psychiatry.*

Brill divided his patients into six groups. One group received psychotherapy for five months. Another was kept on the waiting list. A third was given a placebo. The three other groups received minor tranquilizers and sedative-hypnotic medication. When the patients were reevaluated by physicians at the conclusion of the experiment, most "felt" helped. But, points out Dr. Brill, there was "no statistically significant differences among the treatment groups." Both the waiting list and the placebo had performed basically as well as six months of historically touted psychotherapy.

"These findings were unexpected," states Dr. Brill. "They suggest that the widespread preference for the traditional outpatient psychotherapy is based as much on the physician's bias as on its proven greater effectiveness."

"What?" one might ask incredulously. What about the much heralded positive results of psychotherapy in everyday life? What of the work in child therapy, and in the treatment of alcoholism? Hasn't counseling been valuable on the college campus?

Modern psychotherapy has been proud of its work with children, viewing it as preventive medicine against mental illness at its source. As one psychiatrist puts it: "We had reasonable hope that dealing with the young was the ultimate solution to all of the nation's mental health problems." Begun in 1909 in a Chicago juvenile detention home, the movement is now burgeoning. *The New York Times* has headlined "Child Psychotherapy Is Increasing Rapidly," a phenomenon they referred to as "kiddie on the couch."

Child psychotherapy is epidemic in the Psychological Society. A National Institute of Mental Health survey showed that 772,000 youngsters under eighteen were in psychological care at some clinic facility. Added to private patients, the number rises to over one million. Parents who think therapy is the path to happiness routinely send their children to a psychiatrist or child guidance center for such complaints as school phobias, headaches, bed-wetting, truancy, behavior problems, aggressiveness, low school achievement, even the time-honored fear of animals. In some upper-middle-class circles, kiddie-on-the-couch provides the instant *psyche-chic* once awarded to adult patients in psychoanalysis.

But child psychotherapy now appears to have the same scientific failing as its adult counterpart. Psychologist Eugene E. Levitt, of the Indiana University School of Medicine, is the Eysenck of the child psychotherapy field. His studies show that despite the demand there is no proof that psychotherapy is of specific benefit to disturbed children. Levitt studied therapy reports on more than 9300 children over a thirty-five-year period. Just as Eysenck had learned about adults, Levitt found that two-thirds of the treated children had improved. But this in itself is not sufficient to test out child psychotherapy. What about *untreated* children with the same complaints? How many of them get better without psychological intervention?

Levitt conducted a carefully controlled study of child psychotherapy at the Institute for Juvenile Research in Chicago. He separated the youngsters whose parents had brought them in for treatment into two groups. One was the regular treatment group. The other was made up of those children who had gone through the diagnostic procedure and had been accepted as needing the treatment but who did not take it.

It was another startling case in spontaneous remission. *The improvement rate for the untreated children was the same as for the treated.* "Two-thirds of the patients examined at close during treatment and about three-quarters seen in follow-up have improved. Approximately the same percentages of improvement are found for comparable groups of untreated children," Levitt explains in the *Journal of Consulting Psychology.*

The confusion between the normal signs of *growing up* and the true symptoms of *emotional disturbance* seems to be at the heart of the controversy. "The many symptomatic manifestations in children who are basically normal tend to disappear in time as a function of development," says Dr. Levitt. He offers temper tantrums, sleep disturbances, enuresis (bed-wetting) and specific childhood fears as common examples.

"Apparently, there is some reality in the commonsense notion that children 'grow out' of symptomatic behavior," explains Dr. Levitt. "But an alarmed mother may bring a symptomatic child to the child guidance clinic, where developmental remission may be recorded as therapeutic success."

This *alarmed mother* is a key customer in the Psychological Society. In one revealing study, Dr. M. Sheperd found that children brought to clinics were, on the average, no more disturbed than other children. The emotional problem was more often the overpsychologized mother's nervous reaction to the child, he reports.

Seventy years after its enthusiastic beginning, the child psychotherapy movement is now shrouded in doubt. "Our hopes of preventing mental illness by mental health education and child guidance clinics have been disappointing, and there is no convincing evidence that anyone has ever been kept out of the state hospitals by such measures," observes Dr. R.C. Hunt.

In alcoholism the results of psychotherapy treatment have been particularly poor. Many disillusioned alcoholics have left the couch to return to such self-help groups as Alcoholics Anonymous. When researchers studied 400 alcoholics in state-supported outpatient psychotherapy clinics, they found that only 18 percent of those followed up had shown real improvement: they had been "dry" for at least one year. One in six was dead; one in ten had been institutionalized; the rest were unchanged. But of those who had improved, almost half had also relied on AA or had used similar methods.

On the college campus, the psychotherapy rush rivals the old Greek-letter craze. It is sustained by drop-in counseling houses, around-the-clock Crisis Centers and free Psychological Services units. On-campus advertising programs seduce collegians with promises that therapy is good for everything from test anxieties to broken love affairs. The guidance journals are swollen with praise for college counseling, even claiming that brief counseling of anxious freshmen can increase their grade averages.

These promotional claims are impressive until checked by careful research. Two psychologists, for example, destroyed the thesis that counseling makes for academic improvement. L.D. Goodstein and J.O. Crites, reporting in the *Journal of Counseling Psychology*, studied 33 academically poor students who took summer-session courses. They were split into three groups: one received psychological counseling; the second was contacted but did not seek counseling; the third was not even contacted. The results were, once again, professionally disturbing. *The uncontacted group did the best academically.*

Even if psychotherapy is not the panacea promoted by the profession, isn't it still possible, one might ask, that one particular therapy is superior to another?

The trumpeting of each therapy's virtues, and the poor-mouthing of its competitors, are a great professional pageant. As Dr. Morris Parloff, chief of the psychotherapy research section at NIMH, skeptically puts it: "No form of psychotherapy has ever been initiated without a claim that it has unique therapeutic advantages, and no form of psychotherapy has ever been abandoned because of its failure to live up to these claims."

Serious researchers ignore merchandising claims. "To be sure, practitioners of each method report successes with patients who had failed to respond to other methods, but since all can do this, the claims cancel each other," Dr. Frank reminds those patients who perpetually shop the therapy market.

In one comparative test, patients at the Institute for Psychoanalysis in Amsterdam were placed in three therapy groups by researcher

J.T. Barendregt. One group of 47 was treated with formal psycho-analysis at the institute. The second group of 79 patients received dynamic psychotherapy elsewhere. The third group of 74 patients was not treated at all. When they were followed up two and a half years later, none of the methods proved superior to any of the others.

To the chagrin of professionals, different forms of the same therapy also seem to produce the same results. Enthusiasts recite the glories of *group* over *individual* therapy and the superiority of *brief* over *intensive* therapy, and the other way around. The Phipps psychiatric clinic at Johns Hopkins tested some of these claims by giving one group of patients individual psychotherapy one hour a week. Another group was treated in group therapy one and a half hours a week. The third group was given *minimal contact therapy* a half-hour once every two weeks. The treatment lasted six months, after which they were evaluated, then followed up for five years.

The result? All three groups had performed equally well on symptom relief. Individual and group did the same on social effectiveness but better than minimal therapy. Eventually, however, minimal therapy caught up. *Attention* had proved essentially as good a healer as psychological technique.

Another professional shibboleth, *The longer the better,* has benefited the therapist's pocketbook. Freud, the impecunious healer, claimed to cure hysterics in months, sometimes even weeks. His wealthier followers have stretched out psychotherapy into an almost interminable process, which, like Parkinson's Law, fills the time available. At the University of Chicago counseling center, the average student therapy spanned six sessions in 1949. It had increased to forty-five sessions by 1970.

Does it at least help our psyches to see the therapist more often? Once again, the eager patient is scientifically frustrated. Researchers reporting in the *Journal of Abnormal and Social Psychology* studied veterans taking intensive psychotherapy in several clinics. Some patients were given therapy twice a week, others weekly and some only once every two weeks. On evaluation, no meaningful difference was found in their improvement.

Most practicing psychotherapists feel that *their* therapy works. But among the growing number of psychotherapy researchers, belief in the method varies from virtually none to the conclusion that therapy has only little, or modest healing powers. Dr. O. Hobart Mowrer, former president of the American Psychological Association, is among the skeptical. Like many of his colleagues after World

War II, the now retired research professor of psychology at the University of Illinois, had been in personal therapy and was excited about the possibility of the new psychodynamic approach.

"But over the years, I have become progressively disenchanted with results of psychotherapy and with the underlying theory itself," he explained when interviewed. "I am convinced that, in general, psychotherapy doesn't do patients very much good. Before he died, Freud himself admitted that the therapeutic effectiveness of psychotherapy is poor, and that it was mainly a research tool."

Dr. Eugene E. Levitt believes that psychotherapy is effective in approximately one in five cases. Dr. Paul E. Meehl, another former president of the American Psychological Association, believes that only a small percentage of patients benefit from therapy, stating that "our present power to help is in reality quite limited." Dr. Sol Garfield, a psychologist at Washington University, St. Louis, is one of the sophisticated researchers who believe *somewhat* in psychotherapy but whose enthusiasm is tempered by the new research data.

"The average effect of psychotherapy is not very powerful, but I believe there is some positive effect overall, although it is considerably less than most patients and therapists think," Dr. Garfield stated when interviewed. "In certain cases, therapy can be extremely helpful, in others it is of little or no value, and in still others it is rather damaging. It depends on the kind of therapist and patient. For example, an aggressive therapist who pushes a patient with a weak ego to face up to his deficiencies could produce a very damaging effect.

"I do not believe that behavior is primarily controlled by the Unconscious, or that most positive therapy results are created by insight, or psychodynamic understanding. They are not usually important. But increasingly, research shows that the things that used to be considered superficial and insignificant—such as faith in the therapist, the expectation of being helped, encouragement, suggestion—are among the important factors that lead to improvement. The things that were once dismissed as 'supportive' may be the ones that actually work in psychotherapy."

Practicing therapists are obviously more enthusiastic than these researchers. But what would a thorough search of the profession's own literature for pertinent controlled studies show? Dr. Allen Bergin, who is not a complete skeptic about psychotherapy, studied 52 of them. He then issued a box score which is less than encouraging for the profession. Twenty-two (22) of the studies showed *positive* results for therapy; fifteen (15) were *in doubt;* and fifteen (15) were *negative.*

Perhaps the most comprehensive overview has been conducted by psychologist Lester Luborsky and colleagues at the University of Pennsylvania. Dr. Luborsky reviewed the literature over the last two decades and published the results of more than a hundred psychotherapy studies.

The work is illuminating. Therapists often extol the advantage of one-to-one therapy over the cheaper group method. But Luborsky shows that in 13 studies, individual therapy did better in only 2. Group was better in 2, and they did equally well in 9. In tests of client-centered (Rogerian) versus psychodynamic therapy, the results were the same in 4 of 5 studies, with traditional therapy coming out ahead in 1. Behavior therapy performed as well as psychotherapy in 12 out of 18 studies, but was considered superior to psychotherapy in 6. In a test of drugs versus psychotherapy, drugs were better in 7 and tied in 1 study.

In a key test, Luborsky reviewed 33 studies which compared psychotherapy with the absence of psychotherapy, including waiting-list samples. Psychotherapy did better in 20, but the nontherapy patients did as well in 13 studies.

The Luborsky review is discouraging to therapy advocates. But the minor victory of therapy over the waiting list in 20 studies is heralded as offering *some* evidence that psychotherapy works. This is not necessarily true. The fact that the waiting list did as well as therapy in 13 studies actually casts doubt on the other 20. In the world of science, it is impossible for a treatment—say a specific antibiotic against a specific infection—to do better in 60 percent of the studies and fail to do as well as *nothing* in another 40 percent. Such inconsistency would force biological researchers back to the laboratory to find the error in their theory.

Although current theories are not solidly grounded, we do know that therapy—like any human intervention—can work *sometimes.* When it does, what is the mechanism? If it is not psychodynamic insight, what propels the anxious patient toward improvement?

Dr. Arthur Shapiro believes that it is the *placebo effect.* "Most therapists are convinced that it is their method and insight that produces patient improvement, but this is not true," Dr. Shapiro pointed out when interviewed. "Any improvement is probably the result of the placebo effect. In fact, the placebo was the underlying therapeutic factor in medicine until Pasteur laid the basis for effective medication. Modern psychotherapy claims to be a scientific treatment, but there is no evidence from controlled studies to support this. More likely, psychotherapy is still in its pre-Pasteur stage. It is a treatment whose major effect is that of the placebo."

"The placebo effect operates in various ways in psychotherapy: in the enthusiasm of the therapist, in his interest in and liking of the patient, in advice giving, in reenforcing the patient's desire to get well," Dr. Shapiro continued. "Most psychological explanations are nonsense, but it is another way to get at the placebo effect. If the patient is told about his unconscious Oedipus complex, the understanding can act as a placebo even if the theory is not true, which it isn't.

"In ancient times, the therapist would go into a bizarre dance in order to communicate with evil forces bedeviling his patient. He would speak in incantations, then spit out the bloody tissue of an animal. He would ask the spirits for relief for the patient, whose face would brighten with hope. Modern psychotherapy has magical trappings which are more appealing to the contemporary mind, but the underlying mechanism of both procedures is the same—mobilizing the power of the placebo."

What researchers are saying is that psychotherapy is *not* a science, or even a technology with a predictable outcome. It is a personal encounter between two people: a healer and a patient. Naturally, something has to take place during the interaction. If the *discipline* of psychotherapy is not involved, what is actually happening in the therapy room?

The answer to that question will shape psychotherapy's place in our society for some time to come. Succinctly stated, the answer now appears obvious. *Psychotherapy is a key ritual of our twentieth-century psychological religion.* In this ritual, the impressionable patient's hope and faith are coupled with the healer's belief in his own magical powers. The combination creates a persuasive setting of suspended reality. It is industrial society's sophisticated imitation of the witch doctor's primitive healing technique.

Dr. Shashi K. Pande, an Eastern psychiatrist trained in the West, is convinced that therapy is our equivalent of the "religious and ritualistic healings in the so-called primitive tribes." Because Western man considers *reason* the magical key to nature, he projects that image into the psychic healing room, says Pande. To the Easterner, the past, present and future merge almost into one, and magical ideas are openly accepted as such. But in our scientific-industrial West, everything must be explained by *reasons,* even if they later prove to be not so reasonable.

In the psychotherapeutic religion, as in all others, it is not validity that matters. It is *believability* that shapes the worshiper's faith. Dr. Pande explains that in insight therapy, supposedly "correct interpretations" provide the reasons why the patient is mentally disturbed.

Actually, says Pande, these explanations are a "magnificent ruse for fostering a long-term and intimate relationship" which provides the real potential for healing. The idea that the patient's sickness is caused by an unconscious childhood disturbance is only a disguise for an emotional involvement between patient and therapist.

Simple emotion is not accepted in the West, Pande reminds us. It must carry a more acceptable label, that of *scientific psychotherapy.* "This experience is difficult to have and to accept in an Anglo-Saxon setting, with its characteristic high ideals of self-sufficiency and responsibility for one's fate, except under the guise of 'sickness' and with the lofty Greek purpose of 'understanding.' "

It is now obvious that most tenets of the Psychological Society, including psychotherapy, are Western man's disguise for a new spirituality. It is the educated person's opportunity to practice religion under the cloak of science. It enables us to call on occult powers of healing while appeasing our Western need for a rational underpinning. It makes little difference that each of the psychotherapies has a different faith. *It is the faith itself, not the doctrine, that is the healing agent.*

Christianity advocated Faith, Hope and Charity. Psychotherapy is less candid, but its hidden theology also rests on Faith and Hope. The place of hope in psychotherapy is apparent. "Mobilization of patients' hope is a mainstay of all healing rituals in primitive societies and in faith healing in our own, and its importance has long been recognized by psychotherapists," says Dr. Jerome Frank.

The power of placebos has already been demonstrated, but Dr. Frank has taken hope one step further. In a controlled experiment, he demonstrated that the major reduction of symptoms occurred during the patient's preliminary psychological and physiological tests before the placebo was given. Just the prospect of therapy raised the patient's hope enough to make some improvement. Many of the patients saw the tests themselves as a form of therapy, Dr. Frank believes.

The "whys" of psychotherapy are intriguing. In learning why psychotherapy fails, and *why it sometimes does work,* the confused art becomes clearer to both its adherents and its critics.

One of the "whys" is apparently the age-old mechanism of faith healing. Psychiatrists and psychologists condescendingly point out the differences between modern psychotherapy and primitive healing. But the similarities are more striking, says psychologist Kenneth M. Calestro. Modern psychotherapy, he says, is "the bastard progeny of a long tradition of neo-religious and magical practices."

That psychotherapy is a modern faith-healing art is increasingly apparent. The primitive faith healer, like the modern psychotherapist, creates an aura of sacredness and belief. Again like the psychotherapist, the would-be shaman goes through an initiatory rite which grants him status and special powers of omnipotence and omniscience. His patients hold him in awe and share his assumptions about the affliction.

To make the "cure" possible, the patient and the healer must share a myth about the nature of the mind and the universe. In ancient Judea, the priestly Levites were the medical healers as well, purging illness through divine inspiration. In early Christianity, sickness was still a religious matter. One needed to share the Christian beliefs to partake of the healing power. The miracles of Lourdes, the evangelistic faith healer, the voodoo spiritualist all draw on the assumption that the healer and the patient are clued in to a special set of ideas.

The successful modern therapist, says Dr. Calestro, imitates the faith healer. He absorbs the *therapist's myth:* belief in a particular psychotherapy. "The therapist's beliefs regarding his efficiency as a curing agent generally derive from his training in and adoption of a particular school of psychotherapy," says Dr. Calestro.

The myth need not be consistent with others, nor need it be substantiated by scientific evidence. It is only necessary that both patient and healer believe in the same myth. A Moslem believer seeking religious help from a Catholic bishop is turned away by lack of faith. The same is true of a Freudian healer whose patient refuses to believe.

If faith heals, whether in psychotherapy or voodoo, how is it actually accomplished? The answer is that psychotherapy and primitive faith healing operate by the same secret mechanism. It is *suggestion,* the trick of directing a patient, or believer, without his knowing it.

*Suggestion, not science, is the method of psychotherapy.* "All forms of psychotherapy employ suggestion," says research psychologist Hans Strupp, of Vanderbilt University, and "the patient's suitability for psychotherapy is based on his potential openness to suggestion." The power of suggestion in psychotherapy even predates Freud. It was developed to its highest academic position by one of Freud's mentors, Dr. Hippolyte-Marie Bernheim, a French physician. Freud studied with him in Nancy, France, in 1889, and translated Bernheim's classic work, *Hypnotism and Suggestion in Psychotherapy* into German.

Bernheim believed that hypnotism gained its power from suggestion or autosuggestion, and that it is not a physiological process. He also felt that waking suggestion could be accomplished without hypnosis. Freud became a practitioner of suggestion, first through hypnotism, later through psychoanalysis. He consistently denied his debt to Bernheim, falsely claiming that analysis circumvented the prosaic power of suggestion.

Conforming to the therapist's suggestions is essential to the cure. The patient is typically a troubled, suggestible person anxious to be directed by an authority figure with impressive diplomas on his wall. The therapist, on his part, is dominated by the *therapist myth,* that a particular way of thinking and a particular systematic method of therapy will be curative for the patient. Through his training, the therapist has become Freudian, Adlerian, Jungian, Sullivanian or some eclectic mixture of several schools of psychological thought. This doctrine sustains him ideologically in his day-to-day work, providing a way for him to look at neurosis without professional anxiety.

One psychiatrist has labeled the patient's conformity to the therapist as *doctrinal compliance.* As the doctor's suggestions unfold through subtle clues, the patient conforms in the hope of getting well. He acts as if the therapist myth is true and produces appropriate memories, even emotions, to fit the therapist's psychological theories.

Studies show that the modern patient produces Freudian dreams for a Freudian analyst and Jungian dreams for followers of the Swiss prophet. "The underlying mechanism apparently involves a process of suggestion in which the patient responds to overt or covert suggestions by the therapist that certain phenomena will occur," Dr. Calestro explains.

Dr. Jerome Frank reminds us that patients typically "follow the therapist's unwitting leads." In an experiment conducted by R.M. Whitman and reported in the *Archives of General Psychiatry,* patients told their dreams to a researcher immediately after waking up. They later repeated their dreams to a psychiatrist during a professional interview. Whitman found that the dreamers only recalled those dreams they felt the psychiatrist would be pleased to receive.

Even the values of the impressionable patient involuntarily shift toward those of his therapist. The attitudes are successfully transmitted to the patient through the therapist's suggestions.

What about the therapist's supposed objectivity? He is seldom objective, even if unaware that he is foisting his biases onto an unsuspecting patient. Dr. Robert Rosenthal, of Harvard University, a leading researcher on *experimenter bias,* has conducted studies which strongly suggest that a word, nuance, inflection, interpretation or even silence can be a subtle signal from the experimenter to the subject.

In one experiment, Rosenthal demonstrated the enormous power of subtle suggestion. Experimenters were given a set of ten photographs of faces. They were told to test their subjects on whether they saw "success" or "failure" in the faces. The photos were preselected to cumulatively have no bias for success or failure. But experimenters were not told the truth. Instead, half were told that prior results had shown the pictures to be those of "successful" people; the other half were told that they were photographs of "failures." The experimenters then went to their subjects and asked them to grade the pictures. The results? *Two-thirds graded the picture with the same false bias as that passed on to the experimenters.*

This subjective modern therapist shares an embarrassing kinship with primitive shamanism and witch-doctoring. This is the view of Dr. E. Fuller Torrey, a psychiatrist-anthropologist who has studied several primitive cultures. He is convinced that all successful therapists use the same universal methods.

One of the secret therapy methods, he reports in the *American Journal of Orthopsychiatry,* is the "Rumpelstiltskin Principle," the importance of knowing the right word. The Yoruba *babalawo* ("father of mysteries") casts bones on the ground to identify offending spirits—such as those of a departed great-grandaunt—which have invaded the patient's mind. The modern therapist analyzes the patient's statements and memories to find the unconscious problem in his childhood.

Both are playing Rumpelstiltskin, the naming of the unknown, a game which convinces the patient that life's mysteries are being unraveled before his eyes. The modern and the ancient shaman are both suggesting that since the problem can be named and understood, it can also be cured.

Both systems rely on unseen spirits. One is a ghost from the past; the other, ghosts from an unconscious life in an unknown part of the mind. Within each subculture, it is the seeming plausibility which quiets the anxious mind.

In all cultures, the healer is granted status, which adds to the power of his suggestion. "The feelings of a Yoruba tribesman toward a *babalawo*," says Dr. Torrey, "have exact counterpart in the feelings of a cocktail party guest toward the psychiatrist in the room—attraction, awe, avoidance and fear."

Dr. Robert Bergman, former chief psychiatrist for an Indian Health Service in Arizona, describes how Navajo medicine men relieve anxiety with a nine-night Enemy Way dance. An Indian woman who had been hospitalized several times as a schizophrenic suddenly recovered after native treatment. When Bergman and a social worker visited her, she explained that after various futile Western psychiatric treatments, she had visited a medicine man, Tom Largewhiskers. She had gone to his camp, but he insisted on treating her at her home because this was where the illness had first struck. During the ceremony, the woman explained, "I felt my mind coming back to me."

The Navajo culture merges the psychiatrist and the minister into one. "In a Navajo ceremony, there is no way to tell what is healing and what is worship," says Dr. Bergman. "Everything is both."

In some spiritual ways, modern society does not serve us as well as these ancient cultures. Because of his agnosticism, the modern psychiatrist is not interested in the religious nature of healing. Ministers in the religious community are so awed by "scientific" psychotherapy that they have lost their dedication to the mysteries of theology. Psychiatry and the ministry have shaped a giant chasm into which nonspiritual neurotic modern man seems to have fallen.

Dr. Torrey rates the native healer as being as efficient as the Western psychotherapist. He concludes that "witch doctors get about the same therapeutic results as psychiatrists do." Canadian psychiatrist Raymond Prince studied the work of Yoruba African witch doctors for seventeen months and reported that although he found quacks as well as skilled therapists, "Western psychiatric techniques are not in my opinion demonstrably superior to many indigenous Yoruba practices."

In one of Dr. Prince's cases, a Yoruba man with psychosis-like symptoms failed to respond to chlorpromazine treatment. The *babalawo* doctor took the case and put the patient through a series of sacrifice sessions, followed by initiation into a worship cult. The patient recovered and had no relapses.

Modern psychiatry and native healing have even competed directly in a research test. Western-trained psychiatrists at the All-India Institute of Mental Health in Bangalore conducted a five-year study comparing the results of Ayurvedic native treatment and Western psychiatry on schizophrenics. The results of the two treatments were surprisingly similar.

The average "psychiatric" patient stayed 65.8 days and showed improvement in 85 percent of the cases, and partial improvement in 5 percent. The Ayurvedic patients stayed a shorter time, 59.6 days, and showed improvement in 75 percent of the cases, and partial improvement in 15 percent. "We should not be too surprised to find that therapists in other cultures are as effective as those in our own culture," Dr. Torrey states. "They can name the patient's disease and raise his expectations as well as we can."

Thus far, we have concentrated on whether or not the modern patient will improve in psychotherapy. We should also consider another probable, if uninviting, result. What about the possibility that the person seeking emotional help may be *harmed* by the confrontation of his suggestible psyche with that of the therapist's?

In the naïve religious faith of the Psychological Society, the patient seldom considers that he may become a *psychiatrogenic* victim of the art. But this unnerving realization is now attracting serious professional attention. "The evidence now available suggests that, on the average, psychotherapy may be harmful as often as helpful, with an average effect comparable to receiving no help," say researchers Charles B. Truax and Robert R. Carkhuff.

This *psychiatrogenic* (therapist-caused), or *psychonoxious,* damage produced by inept, if well-intentioned, therapists is the dark underside of modern psychotherapy. "Evidently there is something unique about psychotherapy which has the power to cause improvement beyond that occurring among controls," says Dr. Allen Bergin, "but equally evident is a contrary deteriorating impact which makes some cases worse than they were to begin with . . . In general, deterioration of various kinds is much too common to be ignored."

This *deterioration effect* was ignored for some time by a profession hypnotized by its own self-importance. "The good of psychotherapy has been evangelically proclaimed. Its possible dangers have been left unmentioned," warns Dr. Arthur H. Chapman, a former University of Kansas School of Medicine psychiatrist.

But the literature of psychonoxious psychotherapy is now expanding. Dr. Christian Astrup, a Norwegian psychiatrist, reports that of 2500 cases treated in the Gaustad Hospital, "we have collected a considerable number of functional psychoses where the psychotic breakdown appeared to be precipitated by intensive analytically oriented therapy."

What are the statistical chances that a patient will be harmed in psychotherapy? Is it the rare result of a callous or ignorant therapist, or is it a common product of the sanctified therapy room? Dr. Allen Bergin has attempted to estimate the probability by studying reports of therapy deterioration over a six-year period. He found that it ranged from only 1 percent in some studies, up to a devastating 36 percent. *Dr. Hans Strupp estimates that one in ten patients is a psychonoxious victim of psychotherapy.*

These are troublesome numbers, and individual cases such as the one described by Dr. Schmideberg can be tragic. Dr. Chapman warns of the possible eruption of psychosis in psychotherapy patients who have weak egos. Although it is a known side effect of psychotherapy, he says, we do not know "how frequent such adverse reactions are." Dr. Chapman warns that professionals who have tried to openly discuss such professional unmentionables have been insulted. They have had psychiatric diagnoses "thrown at them," he reveals.

Psychotherapy can also be dangerous to the patient's marriage, Dr. Chapman fears. As a result of the therapy of one mate, the family equilibrium can be shattered beyond repair, he says. He talks of a passive man influenced by his therapist to become aggressive, upsetting a balanced marriage in which the wife had been the aggressive partner. The opposite can also be true. The passive wife is now taught in therapy to "stand up" and become aggressive. While it can do wonders for the partners' self-image, the changes can also increase the divorce statistics.

Another deleterious effect of therapy may be dependence on the therapy itself. Psychotherapy may produce the increasingly common *therapy addict.* Harold D. Werner, a New Jersey psychiatric social worker, argues that psychodynamic therapy requires maximum involvement with the therapist. This can lower the patient's own self-sufficiency. The danger, he says, is "a breed of individuals . . . who cannot let go of treatment." These therapy addicts are always looking for more service, insisting they need lots of time to work problems out, he states.

One of the most popular contemporary techniques is family therapy, in which several members are treated simultaneously, usually by the same therapist. A Montreal psychiatrist and family therapist, Dr. Herta A. Guttman, warns that the technique can provoke explosive psychiatrogenic events. "While treating families before, during and after the hospitalization of one member—in each instance a young adult—I have been impressed by a number of cases in which family therapy seems to have precipitated or aggravated the psychotic breakdown of this member," she states in the *Archives of General Psychiatry.*

In 1976 Dr. Hans Strupp and Suzanne W. Hadley at Vanderbilt University surveyed 150 experienced therapists and researchers on the *negative effects* in psychotherapy. "There was virtual unanimity that there is a real problem of negative effects," the study authors report. Answers varied from an occasional dissent to the comment by Dr. Robert Spitzer of the New York Psychiatric Institute that "negative effects in long-term outpatient psychotherapy are extremely common."

Some respondents spoke of the common negative effects of insight therapy, including the weakening of the patient's will. Strupp and Hadley also point up the potential danger of deep psychological interpretations. "At a minimum, the misuse of interpretations may promote an unhealthy imbalance in the patient's life . . . At its worst, the misuse of interpretations and faulty efforts to produce 'insight' may be patently destructive of the patient's psychological well-being," they conclude.

Several therapists were concerned about therapy *worsening* the patient's symptoms, including depressive breakdown, destructive acting out, increases in anxiety and hostility, lower self-confidence, worsening of phobias—what one therapist called making "federal cases out of something simply treated."

One clinical psychologist, Anthony M. Graziano, of the State University of New York, Buffalo, suggests the ultimate psychonoxious theory: *that psychotherapy itself may be a major neurotic stimulus.* He is concerned that the mental health industry is creating its own customers. "It may be true that what we are really doing is convincing even greater numbers of persons that even minor anxieties might be symptoms of deeper and more severe problems," he says. "Might we not, in effect, be mobilizing our social power to convince more and more persons that they are mentally ill?"

Who is the agent of damage in psychonoxious accidents? Any therapist can cause one, but several researchers think it is mainly the work of the poor therapist. The fact that incompetence is common-place in the Fifth Profession is obvious to those patients who futilely shop therapists, but it still comes as a shock to many weaned on the psychological revolution.

Dr. Allen Bergin suggests that the disparity in therapist skill may be so great that "only a small proportion of therapists and patients" may account for all the positive effects of psychotherapy. Dr. Paul E. Meehl fears that this group of competent therapists is only one in four of those practicing. He is convinced that the patient entering the therapy chamber has begun his psychological adventure against heavily loaded statistics.

The patient population can be divided into three parts, says Dr. Meehl. The first is the minimally ill, who do not need therapy be-cause they "are going to get better whether they receive psychother-apy or not." The second group is the truly ill, the "schizotypes in varying degrees of decompensation," who do not benefit from ther-apy. Although they are temporarily "better compensated" from the therapeutic relationship, says Dr. Meehl, their basic illness is a "con-stitutional, neurological aberration" on which is superimposed a "largely irreversible set of aversive social learnings." When therapy is terminated, their situation is worsened, he feels. The third group, the "appropriate cases" for psychotherapy, includes only one in four of the present therapy population, he says. Since from his personal experience, he estimates that only one in four therapists is competent at his job, the therapeutic mix of therapists and patients is math-ematically discouraging. "Assuming an essentially random model of patient-therapist pairing, the joint probability of the suitable patient getting to a suitable therapist is around .06 [1 in 16], a very small tail to wag the statistical dog in an outcome study," Dr. Meehl instructs his colleagues.

If science and statistics are not on the side of psychotherapy, and if shamanism and witch doctoring do as well, what is holding up its inordinate prestige? As in other major unscientific movements, its true support is a *religious idea* which has captured the mass imagina-tion.

*One of the most powerful religious ideas of the second half of the twentieth century is the Great Unconscious.* All prior societies have looked toward external models of behavior. We have had the Es-thetic Greek Man, the Pragmatic Roman Man, the Guilty Christian Man, the Searching Scientific Man. Today's model is the believer in the Unconscious, the self-conscious Psychological Man.

Believers are constantly looking inward to the hidden psyche as their guide to life style and philosophy. The system revolves about the belief that there is a *true man* residing somewhere inside our mind, living a sequestered private life begrudgingly revealed to us in fleeting moments. Our Unconscious becomes real only after revelation by a therapist-priest who can explain the mysteries of the Unknown Us, as reasonably as the clergy once explained the secrets of the Unseen God.

In this religion of the Unconscious, our conscious mind is a second-class being. It is a mere puppet of the unknown true self which implacably and stubbornly dictates our life, our desires, our future, much as our Soul once did. We can control our present and our future, we are told, *only* if we learn the mysteries of psychology and psychiatry which can unlock the Unconscious. Like the primitive witch doctor, the modern therapist promises to do this in exchange for power and money.

Is there really an Unconscious? The question brings a resounding "Yes" from most educated modern men. Despite this glib affirmation, the question and its answer actually rank with the query "Is there a God?" Modern psychiatry denies the parallel, stating that we see proof of the unconscious in dreams, in slips of the tongue, in our failure to know our true selves. Such argument ranks with the theological argument which demands belief in a divine God because of the magnificence of nature.

Just as logically, there is no unconscious. In the Psychological Society, the Unconscious is seen as a second mind whose thinking and operation are mainly involved in unpleasant motivation and repressed thoughts purposely hidden from our consciousness. From a scientific point of view, it is a theological device which fills the gap in man's biological ignorance, just as Genesis once explained Creation. Man's true self could just as logically be a genetic code acted out during a lifetime against the pressures of society.

What we call the Unconscious may instead be a complex, gene-determined neurological-biochemical circuitry. It responds to stimuli, creating ideas and feelings to suit the DNA-coded needs of the particular human animal. Reactions to love, adventure, threat, sex, friendship may be partially learned, but they are also biologically hidden—not in the romantic Unconscious—but in thousands of protein-coded genes each of us has been endowed with since the moment of conception. This, not the mystical *Id, Ego* and *Superego,* may be the unknown psychology of man.

As we shall see, even the dream that supposedly proves the Unconscious may be another manifestation, without particular meaning, of the bioelectrical circuitry. By once again worshiping what he does not yet know, Psychological Man is repeating the history of his primitive ancestors.

Not all of this has been lost on the perceptive therapist. His intuition tells him that his work touches more on the magical and the mystical than on the framework of science. He also knows the power of the occult in all societies, and the godly aura that accompanies those who delve into its mysteries.

As a result, the modern therapist has sought the priestly power once granted to the clergy he is replacing. Many psychiatrists and therapists have developed what has been termed "the quest for omnipotence," the drive to be regarded as a magical figure by self and public.

"As psychiatry has gained in prestige and influence, interest has grown in the problem of the unrealistic exaggeration of the psychiatrist's therapeutic power," state Myron R. Sharaf and Daniel Levinson, who studied psychiatric residents in Boston. Dr. Judd Marmor, former president of the American Psychiatric Association, has called it simply "the feeling of superiority" which dominates many practicing psychiatrists. The young therapist uses his teachers as a model and imagines that like them he can become a magical, omnipotent figure—a modern medicine man.

If the therapist is not a scientist but a religious figure, then the therapist as a person must be all-important to his healing. What do we know of him as a person? Is he the superior being needed for this role? Is he wise and mature enough to be mentor to so many millions?

The therapist feels confident that he is. A University of California study of 421 therapists revealed that they feel irrepressibly superior. They fashioned a loving portrait of themselves as *dependable, capable, conscientious, intelligent, friendly, honest, adaptable, responsible, reasonable, considerate.*

Others have found the portrait less appealing. One concern among professionals, whispered within the establishment, is that it attracts people who are particularly anxious about their emotional stability.

One measure of instability is suicidal tendencies. Dr. Walter Freeman studied the records of his colleagues and concluded that psychiatrists tend in that direction. "Doctors of medicine are more prone to suicide than men in other occupations. Psychiatrists appear to be at the top of the list," Dr. Freeman reports in the *American Journal of Psychiatry.*

Dr. Freeman studied the obituary records from the *Journal of the American Medical Association* since 1895, plus official death certificates. He found that at least 203 psychiatrists have committed suicide, and that the rate is accelerating. In a recent five-year period, he says, 54 psychiatrists killed themselves, more than in any prior decade. Suicide is often the result of disillusionment in old age. In the case of psychiatrists, however, 81 psychiatrists took their own lives before the age of forty. The rate of suicide among psychiatrists is seven times that of the general population.

Some believe the high suicide rate is due to emotional pressure of the job. Others think it has a simpler cause: a case of the unstable seeking out psychiatry as a vocation. "Among the specialties, psychiatry appears to yield a disproportionate number of suicides," the *British Medical Journal* comments. "The explanation may lie in the choosing of the specialty rather than in meeting its demands, for some who take up psychiatry probably do so for morbid reasons," Dr. Freeman agrees. He puts some of the blame on personal therapy as a requirement for professional advancement. Not everyone can take such insistent probing, he says.

*Therapy for the therapist* is routine in the Psychological Society. Almost two-thirds of professionals undergo it, for it is supposed to make them more secure people and better therapists. The assumption has been investigated by Sol Garfield and Allen E. Bergin, who report back that the theory is not true. Studying eighteen therapists, *they found that therapy for the therapist may even be poor therapy for their patients.* The patients of four therapists who had not been through therapy had the greatest improvement. The patients of seven therapists with a limited amount of therapy (less than 175 hours) did next best. Patients of therapists who had been the most thoroughly treated showed the least improvement.

Early experience with mental illness in the therapist's life may also be a motivation for psychiatry. Dr. Walter N. Stone of the Cincinnati General Hospital studied the background of 55 psychiatric faculty members and residents and not only found that they had an I.Q. of 128, but that over one-third had contact with mental illness in childhood or adolescence. In half the cases, it was someone close to them. This experience, says Stone, is "a possible factor enticing them toward psychiatry."

The image of the emotionally weak therapist is discouraging to the educated public, whose logic would lead them to desire a more stable fraternity of healers. While admitting the emotional weakness among some in his profession, Dr. Arthur Shapiro takes the opposing view, arguing that it may be a helpful defect for the work.

"The therapist who is concerned about his own emotional short-comings may be the only type of person who could listen to other people's problems for hours. I think the more important defect in many psychotherapists is the lack of good judgment. Without it, the therapist will be afraid to offer sound advice to his patient, and by default will permit him to wreck his life. The therapist who has good judgment can help the patient who is in trouble to avoid the episodic calamities which eventually build up and create unsolvable difficulties."

But despite the scientific and personal shortcomings of the profession, many therapists are dedicated to their work and *some* patients obviously do improve in therapy. What is the equation that makes one therapeutic encounter a failure, even a danger, and another a success?

There is new evidence indicating that success in therapy may be determined by the same factors that help make for success in life. One research study shows that successful therapy may simply be the result of whether the doctor and patient found each other *likable* and *attractive.*

At the Westchester Community Mental Health Center, a team headed by Dr. Shapiro studied 13 therapists and 113 patients, 65 percent of whom were diagnosed as neurotic. After up to a year of treatment, they compared dozens of factors between therapist and patient and success and failure in psychotherapy. They found very little that made scientific sense, except for one factor. When the patient and therapist liked each other, thought each other good-looking, or respectively thought they were a good patient or a good therapist, the results were satisfactory.

The importance of *liking and being liked* is shown in the statistics. "If patient and therapist liked each other, their respective percent improvement varied between 77 and 96 percent," Dr. Shapiro reports. "However, if the therapist did not like the patient, the percent improvement reported by the therapist varied between 52 and 62 percent." *If the patient did not like his therapist, less than 25 percent reported themselves improved.*

If we assume that only a minority of therapists are competent, then the frustrated patient, who doggedly goes from therapist to therapist seeking the right one, has to eventually ask, "What makes a good therapist?"

There seems to be almost no criteria, either academic or personal, that the patient can rely on. But Dr. Allen Bergin thinks that he has an answer. *He believes psychotherapy is a talent, not unlike music or painting.* Training may enhance the talent if it exists, but it cannot create it.

"Unfortunately, only a small percentage of professionals have the talent and those are the ones who get the big effects in therapy," Dr. Bergin stated when interviewed. "The average untrained therapist does as well as the average trained one—although I believe training is good for those who have the talent. Our problem is that we select therapists on academic credentials instead of on their personality. Academic work is almost irrelevant to the situation. The only way to select people for this field is to put them in a real-life situation and see how they work. Either they can do it or they can't. Surprisingly, in our experiments with college students as therapists, we found that English majors made the best therapists."

Dr. Bergin believes there must be a revolution in the selection of psychotherapists. "Generally the people who go into psychology and psychiatry are more anxious, and appear to be more neurotic," he says. "Some therapists are using their careers to act out conflicts in their own personality. Since the therapist is the agent of healing, the effect is to reduce the number of people who are truly effective. The answer is to attract and then select more mature, stable people into the field."

What of the patient? Is it possible that some people make better subjects for therapy, and have a better chance for improvement? The answer is an unequivocal "Yes." Even more than the therapist, a certain type of neurotic patient is ideally suited for the modern psychotherapeutic experience.

The ideal patient must be *suggestible.* He should be able to easily absorb dogma and ideas of the most abstract, even outlandish dimension. He should be philosophically adaptable and able to ape the therapist's value system and biases. The more he agrees with the therapist, the better his chances of being helped. This conditioning process is at the core of all faith healing, magic and religion.

Psychologist David Rosenthal checked out the connection between improvement and value-conditioning in psychotherapy. He found that those rated as "improved" had changed their moral values in sex, aggression and authority in the direction of the therapist's own prejudices. Those who had been rated "unimproved" had tended to hold out.

Dr. W.M. Mendel, professor of psychiatry at the University of Southern California, conducted a study which showed how common, and important, patient suggestibility can be. In an ingenious experiment, he demonstrated both the general *gullibility* of psychotherapy patients and the fact that *belief* is more important than the content of a psychological interpretation.

Dr. Mendel concocted a series of incorrect interpretations, then offered them to a group of his patients as true individual statements about them. The supposed insight was in the form of such horoscope-like clichés as "You seem to live your life as though you were apologizing all the time." Of the twenty-four interpretations, patients agreed with the invented statements twenty times, Dr. Mendel reported in the *American Journal of Psychoanalysis.* The patients even experienced a drop in anxiety following the experiment. "This demonstrates that the process of interpretation, rather than its content, lowers the level of patient anxiety," he stated when interviewed.

What does the superior patient look like to the therapist? Surprisingly, he is both an extraordinary person and *not very sick.* Two psychologists at the University of California, at Berkeley, asked 421 psychotherapists to check adjectives that best described their "preferred patients." The good patient profile more resembled a Nobel peace prize candidate than a distraught neurotic seeking help.

The adjectives most frequently checked were *intelligent, alert, adaptable, frank, cooperative, sincere, sensitive, curious.* The only commonly chosen negative word was "anxious." Those adjectives which portrayed man in need of help—*despondent, high-strung, hostile, suspicious, unstable*—were checked by less than a fourth of the therapists. "In fact, if anxious were removed from the list of the 25 most descriptive adjectives, the preferred patient would appear to be an unusually productive and creative person," say the study authors.

In *Psychotherapy,* Dr. Alvin R. Mahrer describes this ideal patient as psychologically minded, reasonably intelligent, anxious, verbal, and once again, *not very sick.* He has a strong desire to reveal his feelings and has a high need for self-understanding. He should be able to achieve a warm, homophilic relationship with the therapist. The inferior patient, who does not improve much, is less intelligent, more severely disturbed, less introspective and more action-oriented.

The therapist's prejudice against the sick and unimaginative patient is so pronounced that a professional acronym has been created for the ideal subject. It is the YAVIS syndrome—Young, Attractive, Verbal, Intelligent, Successful. Because of this, one suspects that most psychotherapy may not be a treatment for emotional illness at all. It may instead be a cultural, symbolic ritual of the newly sophisticated middle and upper-middle classes for whom it is a mystical corroboration that one is indeed a YAVIS.

Education is the catalyst which moves patients toward psychotherapy. The behavioral sciences have convinced most educated people that there are "experts" who understand human behavior better than they do. The frenetic search for paid psychological expertise is the product of that belief.

The more years of schooling one has, the more one is apt to seek out therapy. The poorer and less well educated, saddled with problems of survival, have less belief in the abstract workings of psychology and seek out therapy less. *The paradox of the Psychological Society is that its most successful citizens feel the most inadequate emotionally and crave repair the most.*

Psychotherapy is healing by conversation. The patient is therefore drawn to his therapist by social class, and vice versa. Studies even show that the patient's education rises and falls directly along with his therapist's. In a study of 377 patients, Dr. William Schofield found that half the patients of psychiatrists had college degrees. At the next level of professional prestige, the clinical pscyhologist, the number of college-educated patients dropped to 35 percent. Among social-worker therapists, only 5 percent of the patients were college-educated.

The therapist bias is clear: the good patient who can be helped in therapy has achieved, or was born into, a good social class. In fact, therapists see social class as a hallmark of mental health. This was cleverly demonstrated by two psychologists at the University of Oklahoma. They trained an actor to portray a man of exceptional mental health. He enjoyed life, was happily married, was warm, relaxed and the proud possessor of a happy childhood. He admitted to only minor complaints: he disagreed with his wife on churchgoing and on some aspects of child raising. The researchers tape-recorded a psychiatric interview with the man, then played the tape to four groups of ten psychiatric residents.

The first group of psychiatrists was told that the patient worked in a wholesale market for $85 a week. Another group heard him described as a man with a $14,000 home, who was an office-supply salesman making $9,000 a year. The third group was told a story of gilded munificence: he had two homes, one in

Tulsa, another in San Francisco. He was an executive in his wealthy family's industrial concern, attended private school and did graduate work at Stanford University. The fourth group was told nothing of his background.

Unfortunately, psychiatrists performed as expected. Diagnosis was not by psychopathology, but by social class. The group which heard the low socioeconomic story diagnosed him as being mentally ill with a relatively poor prognosis. Those who heard the "wealthy" fabrication diagnosed him as quite normal. The groups who heard the middle-class story and those who had been told nothing, gave psychiatric diagnoses in between. When the hoax was admitted to the psychiatrists, they were incredulous at their performance.

Snobbery may be one reason therapists choose patients of their own social class. But it is also because the sophisticated therapist is an astute bet hedger. He knows the patient must be sufficiently educated to share his modern myths.

Psychiatrists and psychologists claim that *psychodynamics* are universal, cross-cultural ideas. This is not true. A Park Avenue therapist would have difficulty explaining to an Asian villager that an American young adult who had relatively concerned parents, color TV and vacations abroad as a child has suffered "maternal deprivation" and is now reaping its neurotic harvest. If psychotherapy is viewed as Morse code, then only those who know the code can be helped.

To avoid falling into a cross-cultural trap, the therapist discourages poorer, nonverbal patients. He thus carefully keeps the nonpsychological-minded from sampling his wares. In the *American Sociological Review* Meyers and Schaffer report that even in a clinic setting, patient social class fixes the level of therapist who is assigned. The best-educated patients tended to be seen by the staff psychiatrist. The middle-level patients are treated by the psychiatric resident, while the poorer, less verbal patients are learning tools for medical students.

The private-practice therapist who earns his living by the hour is even more careful in screening out the sick and the socially disoriented. A study in the *American Journal of Psychiatry* reveals that among private-practice psychiatrists in Boston, 20 to 50 percent refused to treat those suffering from various ailments, including alcoholism, drug addiction or even adolescent behavior problems.

Dr. Martin T. Orne, of the University of Pennsylvania, offers a theory why psychotherapy success is so often related to life success, instead of the other way around. He believes it is because psychotherapy is a "self-perpetuating process" that requires societal success to give it follow-through.

"This may help to explain why the patients who are most successfully treated are the ones who appear to require the least help; that is, they have the wherewithal so that they can almost achieve their goals without help," says Dr. Orne. "If an individual does not have, or acquire, the resources to enable him to ultimately 'make it' in real life, the mechanism described here cannot become self-perpetuating, and the results of psychotherapeutic help, if any, are typically transient."

This knotty correlation between life success and psychotherapy success has become a dilemma for those charged with treating the poor. Some clinic officials in poorer areas are looking for substitutes to replace the "well-trained" therapist. "It has been our experience and that of others, that most mental health professionals are not prepared, experientially or attitudinally, to treat effectively that segment of the mentally ill population who do not meet the verbal, intellectual and motivational requirements of dynamic and insight-oriented psychotherapy," state spokesmen at the Temple University Community Mental Health Center in Philadelphia. The center decided to train eighteen local people, some even without high school diplomas, as therapists. Working with over 250 patients, these *peer-group therapists* have reportedly cut hospitalization cases by 50 percent.

The idea that untrained laymen may do as well at psychotherapy as trained psychiatrists and psychologists is upsetting to the field. What can it say about all the esoteric material and involved training, if laymen without a day's professional experience are just as competent as they?

Several researchers have investigated this thesis, and their results have shocked their colleagues. *Several studies show that untrained laymen do as well as psychiatrists or clinical psychologists.* One mental hospital, which uses hospital aides to perform outpatient psychotherapy with discharged schizophrenics, compared the aides' performance with that of psychiatrists on the staff who offered the same service to other patients. "The treatment results of the nonprofessional personnel compared favorably with the results of the psychiatrists," the study authors report in the *Archives of Psychiatry.*

In another study, E.G. Poser pressed college students into service as group therapy leaders at a mental hospital and compared their results with those of psychiatrists and social workers running similar groups at the hospitals. *The college students achieved better results than did the professionals.*

The most recent work in this area is the unpublished study of Dr. Hans Strupp at Vanderbilt University. It involved twelve therapists: five of the most experienced psychiatrists and psychologists on the university hospital staff, and seven members of the college faculty without any training in the field. The college professors—teachers in English, history, philosophy and mathematics—were selected because they were student-oriented and well liked on campus. The patients were all male college students, single, who presented symptoms of shy, bashful, withdrawn behavior and were anxious or depressed.

Fifteen of the student-patients were treated by the professionals, three psychiatrists and two psychologists. The other fifteen were treated by the college professors. The teachers were simply asked to meet with the students, and told to do what comes naturally in attempting to help them. "There were up to twenty-five hours of individual therapy in each of the groups—twice a week for three or four months," Dr. Strupp explained. "The patients were evaluated at intake, at termination of the therapy and a year later." The results? Overall they were the same for the trained and untrained therapists.

What, we might ask, is at the heart of psychotherapy's scientific problem? Dr. Allen Bergin hazards a guess. "Psychology is still a primitive discipline, in its pre-Galilean stage awaiting a breakthrough that will bring it closer to science," he suggests. "The problem, I believe, is that psychology skipped its naturalistic, descriptive phase. It jumped into experimentation without first going through its job of simple observation. Perhaps before theorizing and experimenting, we should have talked to grandmothers and mothers, watched children and adults and simply described them. Biology did that for hundreds of years, drawing human bodies, animals and plants before it advanced. It is still possible that psychology's Messiah will come. Some say Freud was our Isaac Newton, but I don't think so."

Until the Newton of psychology arrives, the emotionally troubled patient may still feel the need for aid or understanding from another human being. The Psychological Society has appointed the psychiatrist, the clinical psychologist and the psychiatric social worker as the ones to see if we need psychotherapy. In what circumstances will someone get better by visiting these professionally trained, modern faith healers?

Dr. Lester Luborsky of the University of Pennsylvania tried to unravel this conundrum by studying 166 research studies on psychotherapy. He has arrived at dozens of conclusions, including the following:

• The type of therapy is of no significance. There are no measurable differences in results.

• The more severe the ailment, the less improvement can be expected.

• Patients of higher intelligence do better.

• Anxious patients improve the most.

• The match between therapist and patient in values and social class is important to success.

• People concerned about their physical health (including the sick) do less well.

• Those who are human relations–oriented have a better prognosis.

• The higher the patient's social achievement, the better his chance to improve his psyche in therapy.

In summing up his findings, Dr. Luborsky still offers a skeptical view of the talking cure. "It cannot be determined whether the type of individual who profits most would also have profited from another form of treatment or from change-inducing experiences which usually are not designated as psychotherapy—or indeed from nothing more than the mysterious change attributed to the passage of time," he says.

It has been over three-quarters of a century since Freud's original work. During this era, psychotherapy has been dignified as a philosophy, a science and a technology. Its philosophical implications are still reverberating in our culture. As researchers have gained the courage to dissect it, they have concluded that it fails to fulfill its extravagant promise.

"Our profession has too long operated on the *belief* that it was doing a good job for the public," says Dr. Shapiro. "It is time that we forget about our exaggerated claims, about the theories of Sigmund Freud and our mystical shibboleths of the Unconscious and start doing the solid research necessary for a profession with integrity."

Until that time comes, if it can, psychotherapy will remain one of the significant religions of the educated classes in the second half of the twentieth century, a modern reproduction of faith healing and shamanism.

# III

---

# The New Seers

WHEN *JAWS* SET OFF EDDIES of fear throughout the nation, it prompted several psychiatrists and psychologists to offer professional opinions on why the movie's box office gross exceeded even that of *The Godfather.*

One Atlanta psychiatrist, Dr. Alfred A. Messer, viewed the contest between man and the shark as a metaphor for the "helplessness and powerlessness" that we feel in our everyday lives. But some of his colleagues suggested a more guilty motive. The audience did not identify with the bloodied victims, they said, but with the savage of the sea. The shark had become a symbolic substitute for the movie viewer's own ferocious, pent-up aggressions.

This habit of judging, explaining, exploring and divining the behavior of individuals and groups in the second half of the twentieth century has become the exclusive province of a group of new seers, the psychiatrists and psychologists. By offering us the *hidden truth* behind virtually every act of our waking hours, they have effectively seized the role society once divided among the clergy, philosophers and statesmen—and in earlier times among oracles, prophets, even magicians.

Whenever man has been unable to understand a vital phenomenon —whether love, war, death or a natural or national catastrophe—he has called on an omnipotent expert to clear the clouded ethos.

Today, the M.D. psychiatrist and his first cousin, the Ph.D. psychologist, have appointed themselves the undisputed Solomons of our era, the sages of the Psychological Society. Their expertise covers an infinite variety of subjects that affect modern man: homosexuality, crime, sexual habits, marriage and divorce, psychosomatics, education, international relations, politics, child-parent relations and psychobiography.

Aggression and violence are prime subjects for the new seer. After the 1968 Chicago Democratic convention in which forces of radicalism, political frustration and rapid social change emptied into the streets, one prominent member of the American Psychiatric Association immodestly suggested that his profession had the answer all along. "If we had been asked, we could easily have told the Chicago Police Department some of the factors involved in the outbreak of violence and could have suggested measures to enable them to prevent it," he said.

Today, after every assassination, mass murder or act of mayhem, the public immediately turns to a psychiatrist for the revealed word. The answer is so quick in coming that one is tempted to believe that the opinion is less than reasoned. Following closely on the murder of Martin Luther King, Jr., an Oklahoma psychiatrist said that the assailant *unconsciously* reasoned: It is not I who slay my father, rape the family womenfolk, devastate the community and destroy my own society, whose taboos and frustrating restrictions so infuriated me when I was a child. It is not I, it is the stranger. I must be sure he remains a stranger so that I cannot find out the truth about myself.

Some psychiatrists and psychologists tend to exploit the public interest in violent crime by offering sensational diagnoses to the press. This rash professional tendency has prompted an annoyed editorial, "The Psychiatrist as a Commentator on Acts of Violence," in the *American Journal of Psychiatry.* After a murder, psychiatrists too often rush into print with unsupported comment, the editorial warns. Dr. Dana L. Farnsworth, the writer, suggests that his colleagues show moderation when approached by the press. "To refuse to make any comment at all may be construed as abnegating a professional responsibility," he states. "After all, who is supposed to be an expert on these matters?" But, he advises: "If in doubt, do not comment at all. If you decide to comment, then do it thoughtfully."

The wisdom of the new seer is dispensed in many forms, one of which is the *psychological finding,* a supposedly scientific study which fills the professional journals and is dispensed to us daily through the media, in self-help books, in school classrooms, during therapy and even at the newly psychologized Sunday church sermons. Some of these generalizations about human behavior are meant to be universe-shaking, others are trivial, but they all clearly show that modern life must be interpreted for us by the new expertise.

Most findings capitalize on originality, offering us intriguing alternatives to the layman's commonplace thought. We would think that the *more stable* of unwed young mothers would be more likely to keep and raise their offspring. "No," says Boston psychologist David Haughey. He finds that it is the *least stable* ones who cling to their infants. It is not out of love, he says, but out of anger at their life predicament.

The popular image of the *macho* skyjacker is also highly inaccurate, insists another psychological finding. Dallas psychiatrist David G. Hubbard believes that the typical skyjacker is not the supposed all-male bad guy, but actually an *effeminate* individual who is emotionally immature.

The new seer delivers his pronouncements with the infallible air of a papal bull, a stance which intimidates even the most confident of laymen. When a *touch* of identification is added, it can be mesmerizing. We have long been told, for example, that adolescence and old age were mankind's major problem areas. Now we are informed by a New Jersey psychologist that the relatively benign *thirties* may actually be the most traumatic decade of life. He says that a study of 1700 people in the United States and England showed that during the thirties decade, with half of life over, adults face the threatening questions: "Who am I?" "Where am I going?" "What does it all add up to?" This, he insists, can be crippling.

The *finding* is a versatile tool that can be applied to any phenomenon, for it need not begin with considered thought or a hypothesis. The seer need only take a psychological survey of a handful of people and extrapolate his result as a working generalization onto all of an unsuspecting, and often trusting, humanity.

The seer has applied his techniques to every arena of life, including the common denominator of sex:

• Two California psychologists studied one hundred rapists and found them to be more timid than other criminals and to have a *lower sex drive*.

• The lower-class male lover, heralded in literature from Lady Chatterley's days on, has been exposed as a myth by psychologists studying sex satisfaction. Middle-class married couples have greater sexual satisfaction than lower-class males, a researcher contends in the *Journal of Social Issues.*

• Stripteasers, report two Case Western Reserve behavioral scientists, are generally firstborn girls seeking the love from their male audiences which their fathers never provided.

• Young victims of sexual assault usually do not suffer trauma from the maddened rapist, says one psychologist. The problem is the child's parents, who on learning of the assault, behave in a way which traumatizes the innocent young girl.

• Even the bullfighter is sexually examined, and revealed to be less than his *macho* legend. Spanish psychiatrist Enrique Guarner, who has psychoanalyzed prominent bullfighters, believes that by abandoning or ignoring him, the father has left the matador with feelings of sexual impotence. In the bullring, the animal is symbolic of the matador's father. To dominate the bull is to transform impotence into omnipotence. Guarner also points out that the bullfighter's movements have hidden sexual implications: the matador assumes feminine poses, bites horns, waves his buttocks in front of the bull, and even has the animal pass close to his genitals.

The power of the psychological finding rests on two stanchions: the public's need to believe and the veneer of science that surrounds the activity. The citizen of the Psychological Society is more vulnerable and unsure of his own judgments than members of any prior civilization. He has been educated to believe that there is an *expert methodology of life* and that he can learn what is true, right, even useful from these new seers. The thought is provocative: that universal truths which have escaped man for thousands of years are now being regularly discovered by psychological professionals.

The reputation of science is also used to convert tenuous concepts into "fact." We are regularly reminded that truths unearthed by psychology and psychiatry belong to the general grouping of the *social sciences,* or, as they are more recently called, the *human sciences.* This boast has been accepted at face value by millions, making the psychological *finding* seem as proven as a balanced equation in chemistry.

The applications of the psychological finding are infinite, touching every aspect of the human drama. Here is a short glossary of findings which illustrate why the new seer has so captured society's imagination:

• Children consider male smiles more friendly than female ones, state three University of California psychologists. Middle-class mothers, they add, smile more than lower-class mothers, but their smiles represent middle-class insecurity about the role of motherhood.

• The common opinion that loving parents help stimulate a child's creativity has been challenged. An educational psychologist at City College in New York surveyed 418 students, and found that those with the strongest creative potential had parents who were *rejecting* rather than loving and supportive.

• A psychiatrist and a social scientist at Columbia University have studied the motivation of female smokers, and have come up with extraordinary results. Sixty percent of women who identified with their fathers' personality smoked compared to only 48 percent who related to Mom. This, they theorized, places the fiery cigarette in the same category as the penis, a phallic symbol of the Oedipal conflict between father and daughter. It involves "far larger and deeper issues than have hitherto been grasped," they hint.

• Women who fight with their husbands run the risk of developing rheumatoid arthritis. The husband who gets involved in marital conflict is more apt to develop a peptic ulcer, a University of Michigan Institute for Social Research study concludes.

• Common opinion holds that people in big cities are inhospitable and inconsiderate. Not so, says a New York psychology doctoral candidate. He found that New York pedestrians were generally considerate about orderly passage across streets. Similarly, Columbia University psychologists, aided by students, found that the supposed desert of human compassion, the New York subway, was actually an oasis of humanity peopled by underground Samaritans.

Is all this seemingly profound activity *scientific?* Hardly. Knowledge of human behavior is not that easy to come by. In fact, critics are convinced that the psychological finding is riddled with scientific, statistical and philosophical errors. In most cases, we are dealing with the seer's own personal opinion which is elevated to fact through his exaggerated status in the Psychological Society.

The late Gordon W. Allport, a prominent Harvard University psychologist, warned his colleagues to beware of constructing theories about human behavior based on small samples of people. Allport labeled this unscientific tendency as "galloping empiricism," and was convinced that it is an "occupational disease" of psychologists.

In the hard sciences of physics and chemistry, which operate within the strict logic of natural law, the leap from small sample to giant theory is often possible. But this is not true in human behavior. People and laboratory conditions can seldom be duplicated, and the human animal has proven a most elusive guinea pig. "Too often researchers overgeneralize from a specific study in a way that may not only mislead but deteriorates our habits of consecutive thought," Allport warned.

Dr. Allport offered an example of such failure. He cited surveys which "show conclusively that, on the broad average, church attenders harbor more ethnic prejudice than non-attenders." He points out the opposite is also true: that many ardent workers for civil rights, from Christ to Gandhi (and Martin Luther King, Jr.) were religiously motivated. When presented with life paradoxes that run counter to their statistics, Dr. Allport suggests that researchers forget the statistics and consider a new theory.

Psychiatrists and psychologists are not offering false prophecies to the public for monetary gain. But there is a basic fallacy in modern seerdom. *It is that their speculations are mainly metaphysical.* They provide a seemingly modern but theoretically invalid reference system, which, like ancient religions, makes us believe that unlike the animal, we understand our true nature.

The inconsistency of human behavior and the inability of the new seer to properly control his laboratory animal is shown in the *contradictory finding.* As the study at City College in New York revealed, "rejecting," not "loving," parents tended to produce creative children. But a similar study by the National Institute of Mental Health says something quite different.

The Institute psychologists divided young Westinghouse Science scholars into two groups of more and of less creative boys based on their projects' originality. The researchers learned that the creative boys, unlike the City College group, thought their mothers were "less rejecting." In this study, parental *acceptance* seemed the key. Both the creative and noncreative groups thought their parents were non-rejecting.

Contradictory psychological studies are commonplace, if unpublicized. In two studies on the character of smokers, for example, the results brilliantly refuted one another. A behavioral scientist at the University of Wisconsin studied men smokers and came away with a disheartening opinion of the Marlboro Man. Male smokers tend to be less masculine than nonsmokers, claims Dr. John Pflaum. A similar study in England indicates just the opposite: that the cigarette is a burning symbol of youthful virility. The Central Council for

Health and Education studied 1900 teenage boys and found that half the boys who smoked heavily were already sexually experienced.

Modern seers are convinced that smoking is related to emotional instability, an opinion regularly stated in psychological literature. An English study in *Lancet* refutes even this simple psychological prejudice. Over 1400 individuals in southeast London were given a health screening that included a psychiatric evaluation and a report on smoking habits. Despite "previous evidence to the contrary," say the study authors, comparison of smokers and nonsmokers showed that formal psychiatric disorder is not related to smoking.

Unlike Gordon Allport, most modern seers try not to wash their psychological linen in public. As a result, study findings are presented as fact even though contradictory information has already been found by colleagues. The discrepancies are left quietly ensconced in yellowing professional journals.

To their credit, some psychologists do violate the unwritten law against public controversy. Dr. David B. Vinson, of Houston, is one who plays devil's advocate. "Many psychologists and others have put forth the concept that racing drivers have a death wish," he stated at a national conference. "I would like to go on record as questioning this; really, I think they are preoccupied with living." Dr. Vinson studied racing drivers before, during and after short races and concluded that they were no more neurotic than anyone else.

Freely offered psychiatric opinion is often just as inconsistent and contradictory as the finding. One subject which attracts psychiatric seerdom like a grisly magnet is the mass killer. A U.C.L.A. psychiatrist commented on the murder of twenty-seven young boys in Houston's homosexual-torture killings, suggesting that sexual perversion is at the unruly core of mass killing. "Almost invariably, mass murderers have a sexual motivation," he stated. "Such persons are turned on by inflicting pain on others."

The opinion that sex is at the base of violent crime is a common one among the new seers. One Galveston, Texas, psychiatrist claims that 25 percent of the young murderers he studied engaged in sexual acts, often perverted, right after committing the murder.

But like many psychological "facts," this one is refuted by other professionals. Dr. Harry Kozol, formerly of the Center for the Diagnosis and Treatment of Dangerous Persons in Massachusetts, states that although homosexual mass murders receive great attention, their incidence is small. "Sex does not seem to be the motivation in most mass murders," he has said.

Dr. S. Frazier, a Harvard psychiatrist, is another dissenter who believes that there is little connection between homosexuality and mass murder. He studied Charles Whitman, who killed thirteen people from an Austin, Texas, tower in 1966. From his study, Frazier concludes that perverted sex has never played an important role in such crimes. Frazier has candidly stated that his profession cannot predict either who is going to commit murder or who will commit single or multiple murders.

A tragic illustration of this psychiatric inability was demonstrated in upstate New York in 1975. Daniel Jones, a twenty-one-year-old mental patient described as not being "a troublesome boy," was released on a weekend pass from the Willard Psychiatric Center. When he returned home, he shot and killed his mother and three sisters and set fire to the house.

The psychiatrist and psychologist have recently entered a new area of seerdom, *politics and international affairs,* where the power stakes are high. The goal is to intrude their expertise into this glamorous arena and demonstrate that psychiatric wisdom can, and perhaps should, replace citizen awareness and traditional political rights.

The mail-order psychiatric diagnosis of Barry Goldwater is a caricature in point. The conservative 1964 Republican presidential candidate was the subject of a questionnaire sent to members of the American Psychiatric Association by *Fact* magazine. The magazine blatantly asked psychiatrists for their professional opinion of Goldwater's mental stability. Many psychiatrists immaturely took the political bait and offered psychiatric diagnoses of Goldwater without ever meeting the candidate.

According to *Fact,* 1846 psychiatrists sent in usable replies, 150 of which were printed by the magazine. Most defamed Goldwater. The *American Journal of Psychiatry* attacked the action of their colleagues as "Diagnosis by Mail," reporting dejectedly that some newspapers had asked: "Is psychiatry merely a guessing game?"

In 1968 the magazine *Avant Garde* undertook a similar mail-order survey of psychiatrists. This time former President Lyndon Johnson was the subject. The magazine reported receiving such blind medical diagnoses as "The subject is dangerous to civilization and unfit" and comments that Johnson was "a paranoid personality." One psychiatrist said that Johnson manifests "continued distortion of reality to suit his illusions."

"Is it possible that these psychiatrists really believe that their diagnostic labels sent by mail have any scientific validity?" Dr. Wal-

ter E. Barton, in the *American Journal of Psychiatry,* asked incredulously. "If so—and we doubt it—it behooves their peers to find some
effective way of disabusing them of their belief."

The faith of psychiatrists and psychologists that their professions
hold the panacea for man's political ills is unsophisticated. They
appeal to a segment of society frustrated in peace-making and seeking any way to explain human failure in international affairs. One
Mayo Clinic psychiatrist plays on this weakness in his article "Psychiatry and Foreign Affairs," in which he asks for a psychiatrically
"audacious course" to heal a "sick" world society.

Dr. George H. Stevenson, former president of the American Psychiatric Association, has called war a *public health problem* with its
roots in "psychological and psychopathological factors" that require
preventive psychiatry. Another psychiatrist, Dr. Bryant Wedge, has
even suggested training psychiatrists for international relations
work, ostensibly to produce Freudian-oriented Kissingers as adept
at unconscious symbolism as at jet-age diplomacy.

"Psychiatry cannot solve all the problems of international relations," Dr. Wedge modestly states, then adds: "But it can contribute
to better understanding of the nonrational, often unconscious and
unrecognized factors that influence international outlooks . . . "

Although such advice is still untested, perhaps even dangerously
false, one prominent psychologist has outlined a specific plan for the
psychologization of world affairs. Civil rights advocate Kenneth
Clark, former president of the American Psychological Association,
stepped out of his usually judicious character to call for the use of
*psychotechnology* to halt man's aggressive instincts in high places. In
his plan, professionally appointed savants would administer antiag-
gression psychochemicals to world political leaders to temper their
ambitions. The superdrugs would block the "animalistic, barbaric
and primitive propensities in men," and lead us to the "uniquely
human moral and ethical characteristics of love, kindness, empathy," Dr. Clark assures us.

Another entry in the world psychological sweepstakes is Abraham
Zaleznik, professor of social psychology management at the Harvard
Business School, who introduced his unique theory before the
American Psychoanalytic Association. World politics would be
more clearly understood, he claims, if we could but see political
leaders as one of two basic types: Minimum Man and Maximum
Man. The first is a bureaucratic type seeking coalition and consensus,
exemplified by such American leaders as Johnson, Eisenhower and

Nixon. The Maximum Man, who holds more strongly to principle, is exemplified by Charles de Gaulle. Both types ostensibly have their origin in childhood parental experience. Minimum Man is the product of a strong mother; Maximum Man is an ideal blend of the mother and father image.

This type of finding, so glibly bandied about in the Psychological Society, is promoted as the contemporary symbol of revealed truth. Unfortunately, it rests on two slender foundations. One is the bias of the researcher, who has distorted or ignored the scientific method to create an aura of authenticity. The other is less ignoble but equally dangerous. It is the unsophisticated use of both logic and statistics to make their hypothetical statements sound like fact.

*Statistical correlations* are the basis of most psychological findings. It is a rather simple connection of factors. For example, one study found that women with arthritis are more likely to come from high-status-stress families. The association here is between arthritis and high-status stress. It is the statistical correlation between the two factors that makes the psychological finding.

The correlation is not an absolute statement. It is based on the semantic generality *more likely*. This is usually less impressive statistically than seers would have us believe. Although it refers to numbers which psychologists call *statistically significant,* it often includes percentages of difference which laymen would consider *less than significant.* Some are only a few percentage points higher than simple chance.

"The word 'significant' is itself misleading, since its nontechnical meaning connotes 'consequential,' 'important,' 'large,' or 'meaningful,' " researchers Robert L. Spitzer and Jacob Cohen remind us. "None of these connotations applies to its meaning in the phrase 'statistically significant.' "

One common correlation is *birth order.* Hundreds of papers have been written on the difference between first-, second- and last-born children. According to studies, the first-born child is more likely to be of high intelligence, to attend college and achieve eminence.

This correlation was first noticed in 1874 by Sir Francis Galton. He studied birth order and life success using criteria such as being a Fellow in the Royal Society. He found that first-born or only children were more likely to gain recognition. William Altus, professor of psychology at the University of California, Santa Barbara, has found that first-born and only children are overrepresented in the nation's elite colleges. Other studies, including reviews of *Who's*

*Who,* seem to confirm the finding. So did a survey of the Mercury astronauts, all seven of whom were first-born or eldest in their family.

But other studies remarkably show another result: that these same first-born are more likely to be scarred psychologically, and may perform *less well.* Robert Helmreich, University of Texas psychologist, reports that the first-born among the Sealab aquanauts performed less well than their later-born colleagues. Stanley Schachter, of Columbia, found this equally true of Korean War fighter pilots. Later-born, not first-born, were more likely to achieve "ace" status. Other psychological studies, including some by Dr. Helmreich, show that first-born and only children have *less confidence* in their ability than do their younger siblings.

The first-born literature is large, but not necessarily convincing. Two psychiatrists at Michael Reese Hospital, Chicago, reporting in the *Archives of General Psychiatry,* are dubious. "These studies [on first-born children], however, have produced conflicting results, and many have come to regard such correlations with a great deal of skepticism," they state.

One of these skeptics is Dr. E.H. Hare of the famed Maudsley Hospital in England. In the *International Journal of Psychiatry,* he says that although some of these associations may exist, the relationships are *trivial* rather than important. He also believes that many of these experiments may not have been carefully designed. The skeptical Dr. Hare then warns against making too many psychological conclusions about first-borns before checking other biological variables, including the fact that the parents were relatively young when the children were born. "Unless the contrary has been shown," he says, "it is not unreasonable to attribute the pre-eminence of the first-born to the biological advantages of maternal and perhaps also paternal youth."

An unspoken factor in the game of seerdom is the gullibility of both the public and the scientists themselves. This was illustrated by a charming, carefully staged hoax by *The Sciences* magazine staff writer Harry Atkins. He penned a pseudo-scientific paper entitled *Freud Eggs* which was replete with all the accouterments of a professional article: control groups, statistical evidence, citations from other learned publications and abstruse clinical terms, such as *frustration-tolerance.*

The article's thesis was to prove "the relationship between eating habits and personality traits." The material was so blatantly concocted that the hoax seemed painfully transparent. For example, the author drew a portrait of a neurotic asparagus eater: "Subjects who spontaneously attack and eat the tip first are likely to be immature, fearful and dependent, unable to defer gratification even briefly." But many readers, raised on contemporary seerdom, were taken in. The piece elicited calls from eager doctors and scientists who believed "Freud Eggs" and wanted to know more. It was a poignant reminder of the subjectivity that passes for science in the Psychological Society.

Seerdom has no bounds. The new seer believes his expertise can be applied to any facet of life, past or present. One of his most intriguing excursions involves *psychohistory* or *psychobiography,* the psychological investigation of the lives of prominent persons, living or dead. Unlike conventional biographies, which draw conclusions from events in the subject's life, this technique makes psychological assumptions upon which the author builds a superstructure of personality. Unfortunately, such historic castles in the air can tumble if the tenuous psychological assumptions are not correct.

It all started with Sigmund Freud's psychobiography of Leonardo da Vinci. Since then, many of mankind's most prominent citizens have been subjected to this modern probe of the unconscious motives which supposedly propelled them onto the world stage. Napoleon, Joseph Conrad, Trotsky, Lenin, Gandhi, Van Gogh, Martin Luther, Whittaker Chambers and Alger Hiss, and most recently, John F. Kennedy, Lyndon Johnson, Richard Nixon, and even the peripatetic Kissinger, have become unwilling psychiatric patients on the couch of history. And more analytic histories are being published each month.

In this psychoanalytically based rewriting of history, not battles and issues or men and their mistresses, but *mother, father* and *siblings* emerge as the shapers of world history.

Even a newcomer to the historical stage, Jimmy Carter, has already been subjected to the psychobiographical couch. In 1977, five psychohistorians analyzed the thirty-ninth President in the volume *Jimmy Carter and American Fantasy.* Lloyd deMause, chairman of the International Psychohistory Association, is convinced that the psychic damage done in the Georgian's childhood will result in havoc for the world. "Our conclusion is that Jimmy Carter—for reasons rooted in his own personality and in the powerful emotional demands of American fantasy—is very likely to lead us into a new war by 1979."

The villain, as in many psychohistories, is the mother, Lillian Carter. The psychobiographic group, which includes four Ph.D.s, is unanimous in its opinion that Miss Lillian was a "distancing" and unloving mother who penalized her son's psyche. The mothers of Presidents, says deMause, must be "good enough" to give their offspring the ego needed to reach that high office. But at the same time their general coolness gives their children "a deep hole of loneliness in the pit of their stomachs, a hole which they feel driven to fill with the needs and the adulation of large masses of people." Lillian, says deMause, often worked and did not believe children should spend much time with their mothers.

David R. Beisel, a member of that psychohistory team, claims that Jimmy Carter does not view his mother realistically. Instead, he has "turned whatever anger he feels toward her into a fantasy vision of the perfect mother." In reality, he says, Carter harbors hostility against her because she worked as a nurse during his formative years of childhood. In order to obtain the love of this busy, emotionally distant mother, Jimmy had no recourse but to become *like her*—hard-driving and success-oriented, says Beisel.

Numerous psychohistories of Carter are inevitable. But surpassing him in analytic attention is Richard Nixon, whose style provides a rich psychic lode for psychobiographic investigators. Even the late Stewart Alsop, usually a hard idea-and-fact man, made an excursion into the now glutted world of Nixon *Freudiana.* In a 1968 *Newsweek* column, he explained Nixon's appeal to psychohistorians as being related both to his *hateability* and to Nixon's attempt to put psychological distance between himself and others. "Nixon had always been a favorite subject for amateur psychoanalysts," said Alsop. "There is something hidden and mysterious about the man." Alsop then immersed himself in the swift, uncertain waters of psychobiography. Nixon, he said, is Irish on both sides. His black hair and heavy beard show that Nixon was "Black Irish," and therefore the possessor of Iberian blood, the Spanish having invaded the west coast of Ireland. Nixon's father, Alsop stated, was described as "cantankerous" and "pugnacious." In this mother-father view of history, the other side of Nixon was that of the gentle moralist inherited from his Quaker mother.

One Nixon psychobiography, *In Search of Nixon,* was written by M.I.T. history professor Bruce Mazlish. Mazlish's study suggests that Nixon is dominated by "death fears" brought on by the premature death of two brothers. To confront these fears, says Mazlish, the author of *Six Crises* may subconsciously seek out crises which he can then defeat.

A newer psychohistory, *President Nixon's Psychiatric Profile,* by psychiatrist Eli S. Chesen, offers another version of the emotional sickness of the failed President. What does Dr. Chesen believe are the psychological flaws that culminated in the Watergate debacle? Chesen offers two: (1) the psychic imprint of dominant mother Hannah Nixon's hard-fisted Fundamentalist religion and (2) psychic traumas Nixon experienced as a boy. At the age of three, Chesen tells us, Nixon was nearly killed in a buggy accident. At the age of four, he nearly died of pneumonia. "Trauma and illness are frightening at any age; at the ages of three and four respectively, they take on considerably greater significance," Chesen states.

*Mother* is an essential ingredient of the new psychohistory. In these psychologically lurid biographies of the famous, it is often the Freudian caricature of an overbearing mother who unconsciously forces the child-man into seeking world attention, sometimes by seeking to dominate and emasculate him.

Latent homosexuality, and its lay cousin, the fear of being a "sissy," turns up in many psychobiographies, including those of Nixon. Chesen speaks of young Nixon's overconcern with "proving himself manly." Although Nixon willingly helped his mother with domestic chores, Chesen tells us he "would draw the blinds tight to shut the world out from his humiliation."

To Chesen, Nixon is the quintessential dominated male who overcompensates by exaggerating his manliness. "A profound fear of being feminine (weak, submissive, sissyfied) best explains his excessive concern over being humiliated . . ." Chesen concludes: "Unconsciously, he is helpless, dominated and weak."

Nixon was in a psychological double bind which culminated in his failure, says Chesen. "If he emulates strength and domination, he is in fact emulating his mother, a woman. In other words, to be strong is to be womanlike," Chesen claims.

Psychobiographers are masters of the isolated reason. Nixon's domination by his mother plus his view of women as being strong supposedly destroyed him. In this anecdotal reasoning, contradictory examples are avoided for fear the thin thesis will crack under its own weight. What about *strong* Presidents who yielded to dominating mothers and wives?

Franklin Roosevelt, whom historians almost unanimously rate as a great President, lived socially and emotionally in the shadow of his matriarchal mother, Sara Delano Roosevelt. Harry Truman, a rival for FDR's crown of greatness, was later to reveal that the "buck" did not really stop at his desk. It was passed upstairs every evening to Bess Truman, a strong, perhaps dominating wife-mother figure.

Columbia University scholar Jacques Barzun is one of several academicians and historians who have looked at the new psychohistory and come away skeptical. He derides the mindless extrapolation of minor points made without evidence. He offers the case of a Cleveland analyst who had been told about an anecdote in Rousseau's autobiography, *Confessions.* The French intellectual traveling in Venice was passionately taken by a beautiful girl, but lost his passion when he saw that one of her breasts was missing its nipple. Rousseau attributed his loss of ardor to the malformed breast. "No," says the Cleveland analyst-turned-psychohistorian. He remembered reading that Rousseau suffered from enuresis (bed-wetting) and from a sexual malformation, hypospadias. The analyst quickly offered his Freudian recast of history. Rousseau had projected his sexual defect upon the girl, and saw one nipple even though she really had two! Barzun complains that the technique is unrealistic. He points out that the professional historian "is not content to accept as proved fact the *possibility* that Rousseau 'projected' and saw single where he should have seen double."

The danger, says Barzun, is the tendency to turn *surmise* into *fact.* He offers a simple example: in handling the relationship between poet William Wordsworth and his sister Dorothy, one psychobiographer turns a strong affection between them into an incestuous love. The biographer did this "on no additional evidence," says Barzun.

The conversion of hunch into evidence is the Merlin-like tool of the new historians. At a conference on psychology and history at the City University of New York, Herbert Feis made the telling point: that we must know "how adequate psychological knowledge is, how stable it is, how precise it is, and how agreed it is."

Prominent historian Daniel Boorstin, who spoke at that same conference and who is now the Librarian of Congress, is concerned about the accuracy of posthumous psychoanalyzing. He was quoted as asking his colleagues to show greater concern with the conscious rather than unconscious aspects of history. "I know this is a radical suggestion, especially since it is so firmly rooted in common sense," he said.

When interviewed, Dr. Boorstin elaborated: "I'm in favor of experiments in the exploration of history. But I think it is difficult to draw conclusions about the unconscious of people who are still alive and could be put on the couch for endless hours. How much more perilous it must be to draw conclusions about the unconscious of people who are dead," he says.

Gertrude Himmelfarb, professor of history at the City University of New York, attacks psychohistory as an ill-formed discipline. "Psychohistory derives its 'facts' not from history, but from psychoanalysis, and deduces its theories not from this or that instance but from a view of human nature that transcends history," she states in *Commentary*. "It denies the basic criterion of historical evidence: that the evidence be publicly accessible to, and therefore assessable by, all historians."

Professor Himmelfarb offers an example of such capriciousness. A psychobiographer writing in the *History of Childhood Quarterly* traced Hitler's murder of the Jews and his specific use of gas chambers to early psychoanalytic material. A Jewish physician, Dr. Bloch, had operated on Hitler's mother for breast cancer. Bloch removed the breast, but when the cancer recurred he tried to arrest it with iodoform. Hitler, says the author, unconsciously blamed the doctor for his mother's death and for the huge medical bill he had to pay on Christmas Eve.

When Hitler was gassed in World War I, the gas burned through his skin, "just like iodoform." He therefore associated his condition with his mother's. After Germany's defeat, he felt called upon to avenge his country, which, says the analyst, was "transparently his mother." His use of the gas chambers as a murder weapon was associated with the iodoform experience and his own gassing. This neatly completed the "psychological continuum," as the psychohistorian sees it.

It is difficult to engage such interpretation in intelligent argument. Hitler's mother did die of breast cancer. She did have a Jewish doctor. Hitler was gassed in World War I. But the *associations,* those creative leaps of intellectual fancy, are the analyst's own. Even though he cannot prove them, his arrogant stance is "You can't disprove it!"

Not only is analytic whimsy under attack, but in some psychohistories, the entire psychological case rests on a factual error. The most serious offender in this charade was the Master himself, Sigmund Freud, the author of three psychobiographies.

The first work of psychobiography was Freud's *Leonardo Da Vinci, and a Memory of His Childhood*. His thesis was based on a childhood memory which Da Vinci had recorded in a scientific notebook. Speaking about the flight of a vulture, Da Vinci interrupts himself with an early memory:

> It seems that it had been destined before that I should occupy myself
> so thoroughly with the vulture, for it comes to my mind as a very early

memory, when I was still in the cradle, a vulture came down to me, opened my mouth with his tail and struck me many times with his tail against my lips.

Freud translated the memory into sexual terms. The bird's tail (*coda* in Italian) refers to the male organ, he says. Da Vinci's early memory obviously involves oral sex, says Freud. The artist's fantasy "resembles certain dreams and fantasies of women and of passive homosexuals," the first psychobiographer claimed.

Freud then comments on fellatio: "The desire to take the male member into the mouth and suck it, which is commonly considered as one of the most disgusting of sexual perversions, is nevertheless a frequent occurrence among women of our time—and as shown in old sculptures was the same in earlier times—and in the state of being in love seems to lose entirely its disgusting character."

Freud's interpretation of Da Vinci is classically analytic. The fantasy is a homosexual one, he says. Its origin is in Leonardo's love for his true mother. She was not married to his father, Ser Piero da Vinci, who later married the prominent Donna Albiera during the year of Leonardo's birth. Da Vinci was taken from his mother to live in his father's house at the age of five, but his overwhelming love for his natural mother produced an unresolved Oedipus complex.

Freud quotes Da Vinci's unconscious: "Through the erotic relations to my mother I became a homosexual." Freud hastens to explain that there is no proof that Da Vinci actually practiced sexual inversion. During Leonardo's apprenticeship with Verrocchio, he was accused of having homosexual relations with a young boy, but was acquitted.

The vulture in the dream is a vital clue in Freud's analytic detective story. In ancient Egyptian hieroglyphics, the mother is symbolized by a picture of the vulture. The Egyptians, he adds, also worshiped a "motherly deity," "Mut," one of whose heads was vulturelike. The reading of Egyptian hieroglyphics tells us, says Freud, that the vulture was a symbol of motherhood. The Egyptians falsely believed the species had no males.

From this, Freud reconstructs Da Vinci's early psychohistory. The image of the vulture's tail in his dream replaces the early memory of his sucking at his true mother's breast. But the *coda,* or vulture's tail, represents the male penis. How did the vulture-breast become a penis? Freud returns to mythology. The vulture-headed godness Mut was pictured with a feminine body, but "its breast also bore the masculine member in a state of erection," Freud reminds us. Freud believed that this myth was related to the "mother-penis" concept. The boy child thinks that everyone, particularly the woman he loves—his mother—has a penis just as he does.

According to Freud, Leonardo never properly resolved his Oedipal anger against his father. After being deserted by the boy's father, Da Vinci's mother "thus took her little son in place of her husband and robbed him of part of his virility by maturing too early his erotic life," we are told.

It is a beautiful Freudian tale. But the vulture theme Freud used to explain Da Vinci's homosexuality has only one problem. *It is the result of faulty translation from the original Italian.* In describing his fantasy, Leonardo never mentioned a vulture. He used the word *nibio* (modern Italian: *nibbio*), which means a *kite,* a small predator bird with a wing span only one-fourth as long as a vulture's. Freud had been grievously misled by German translations of the Italian. He had predicated much of his theory on a mistranslated word.

*Thomas Woodrow Wilson: a Psychological Study* is a work the psychoanalytic world would prefer to forget. It was published twenty-eight years after Freud's death to the great embarrassment of Wilson's heirs and Freud's followers. Freud's collaborator was the American statesman William C. Bullitt, who had been appointed to the American Peace Commission in Paris in 1919 by President Wilson.

Freud's work is a classic of historical distortion. Freud even admitted that he was not being objective. "I must, however, commence by contribution to this psychological study of Thomas Woodrow Wilson with the confession that the figure of the American president . . . was from the beginning unsympathetic to me, and that this aversion increased in the course of years the more I learned about him . . ."

Most unflattering psychobiographies are dominated by a towering mother figure. In Wilson's case, it was a father fixation that was the destructive subconscious drive. The Reverend Joseph Ruggles Wilson was an upper-class Presbyterian minister, for whom son Woodrow Wilson felt a "dominant passion," claims Freud. "My precious son," "My beloved father," "Darling boy," they wrote to each other. "They invariably kissed emotionally when they met," Freud explains. He describes Wilson's mother as the antithesis of this healthy, handsome, positive, vigorous man. While Minister Wilson "talked, joked, punned," Mrs. Jessie Woodrow Wilson, his mother, was "silent, solemn, dutiful, negative."

Wilson was a sickly youth whose mother coddled him, we are told. Although he was laughed at as a "mama's boy," she was not his model. Says Freud: "He regretted that he had inherited her feeble body, weak eyes and shyness." Instead, Wilson sought to emulate his father. Until after he was forty, claimed Freud, Wilson "never made an important decision of any kind without first seeking his father's advice."

Modeling oneself after a strong father is usually considered admirable. Now it became the root cause of Wilson's international failures, as Freud saw them. It was *the father* which eventually produced what American-hating Sigmund Freud considered Wilson's impertinent meddling in European affairs.

Freud's psychohistory was once again based on the ravages of the Oedipus complex. It was Wilson's failure to resolve his natural Oedipal hostility toward his father which resulted in a repressed unconscious hatred of him. This internal fault eventually erupted into international chaos, Freud claims.

Freud makes a giant psychological leap from an unresolved Oedipus complex to World War II. Wilson's abnormal passivity to his father was at the root of his personality problem, Freud believed. Wilson had a weak, feminine approach to life and world affairs which culminated in his supposed inability to deal with "father representatives." Freud was convinced that this resulted in Wilson's weak handling of postwar affairs, creating a divisive Europe, which in turn brought on the war in 1939.

The publication of *Thomas Woodrow Wilson: A Psychological Study* had been held up at Freud's request until the death of the second Mrs. Wilson. When published in 1967, it was greeted with an embarrassed apology from the psychological community. Robert Sussman Stewart, a historian of Freud, reviewed it negatively in *The New York Times*. He called it a "regrettable collaboration" of two men who had only one thing in common: a dislike of Wilson.

Bullitt had been sent by Wilson on a special mission to Russia after the revolution, but when he returned with Lenin's proposals, Wilson refused to see him. Joined by enmity for Wilson, Bullitt and Freud used history and psychoanalysis—now fused into psychohistory—to defame their subject. Says historian Barbara Tuchman about the work: "This seemingly bizarre combination has produced a fascinating but distorted book . . . the authors have allowed emotional bias to direct their inquiry, which has led to undisciplined reasoning, wild overstatement and false conclusions."

In the coming years, we can anticipate a flood of psychobiographies, including several on John Fitzgerald Kennedy, at least one of which has already been published. *The Kennedy Neurosis: A Psychological Portrait of the American Dynasty,* by Nancy Gager Clinch, was reviewed by Harvard University psychiatrist Robert Coles as "an exercise in nastiness." He adds: "It is an instructive lesson in how psychological words and phrases, presented as a means of scientific exposition, can become in certain hands instruments of moral condemnation, and even malicious abuse." In one paragraph, psychohistorian Clinch traced Kennedy's failure in Vietnam to his distrust of women.

> Kennedy essentially disliked and distrusted women. Therefore his strong emotional need for support and approval led him to follow the counsel of male authority figures. Unfortunately, a large number of these authority figures—such as McNamara, Rusk, Acheson, Taylor, Bundy and Rostow were as confused and misguided as Kennedy about national values and priorities. The 1971 publication of the Pentagon Papers clearly revealed this about their Vietnam policy.

Such nonsense is more rule than exception as psychohistorians seek to emulate the Master. But just as he failed, so do their theory and methodology fall short. The art of psychobiography is neither modern nor incisive, but is merely another inaccurate tool of the Psychological Society.

Harvard psychiatrist Robert Coles makes perhaps the most telling argument against psychohistory in speaking of its tendency to be *pejorative.* "There is also a stinginess of spirit in some of the descriptions psychiatrists and psychologists (and those who follow their lead in other disciplines) give to individuals of the most obvious attainments," he says. "Will the application of psychological 'insight' to history or the arts be done in such a way as to produce caricatures of human beings . . . ?"

It is obvious that psychiatric and psychological seerdom surrounds us. But in no area of contemporary life has the new seer been as omnipresent as in the court of law. Crime and punishment has now been partially transformed into an appendage of psychiatric opinion. Guilt or innocence no longer determines the outcome of the court's deliberation. Increasingly the judge and jury are being influenced by the psychiatrist's diagnosis of whether a defendant is mentally fit to stand trial or whether the accused was sane at the time of his crime. Even the psychiatric state of the obviously guilty person influences the sentence itself.

The psychiatrist (and by recent ruling the clinical psychologist as well) has come to the bar as magisterially as any robed member of the court. "When you find a guy with a smoking gun standing over a dead body you immediately call a psychiatrist," says Selwyn Ross, a psychiatrist and law professor at Loyola University in Los Angeles. The truth of his statement is verified by the involvement of psychiatrists in such prominent cases as Jack Ruby, the killer of Oswald; David Berkowitz, the "Son of Sam"; the failed insanity plea of Sirhan B. Sirhan, the assassin of Robert Kennedy; the elaborate psychiatric diagnosis of "Squeaky" Fromme and Sara Jane Moore, the two who attempted to kill President Gerald Ford; and the trial of Patty Hearst. Even the Nazi Rudolf Hess sought clemency from the war crimes court at Nuremberg by pretending to be insane, a ploy he later confessed to a fellow prisoner.

The Sirhan B. Sirhan case brought psychiatric testimony in the courtroom to the fore. The defense admitted that Sirhan fired the shots that killed Robert Kennedy, but pleaded that he suffered from inability to control his acts at the time. The defense marshaled the testimony of half a dozen expert witnesses, psychiatrists and psychologists, all of whom felt he was insane. One witness, a clinical psychologist, described Sirhan as "paranoid," with tendencies toward schizophrenia. He contended that Sirhan killed Kennedy as a substitute for his father, presumably the hatred rival of the Oedipal argument.

The assistant district attorney, now judge, David N. Fitts told the court that there was a problem with that defense. It was that much of the psychologist's testimony was taken from a psychiatric textbook, and "cribbed or copied or variously changed to suit his purpose." The text, *Casebook of a Crime Psychiatrist,* was written by Dr. James A. Brussel. The similarity of his text and the defense psychologist's report was challenged by the prosecution.

"The Sirhan defense was in a shambles right from the beginning," Stephen S. Trott, acting chief deputy district attorney of Los Angeles County, recalled when interviewed. "Although they had six or seven expert witnesses to testify that Sirhan was insane when he shot Robert Kennedy, the very first one was caught cribbing his testimony from a psychiatric description of the Mad Bomber case from a textbook. We had only one witness, Dr. Seymour Pollack of the University of Southern California, to testify that Sirhan was sane, and he was believed by the jury. Sirhan was convicted of first degree murder and received the death sentence, later changed to life imprisonment."

Trott believes that psychiatric testimony in court is often "way out of balance," that it is part of a battle of psychiatrists who tend to disagree with each other. "I get the impression that some of the expert witnesses write their reports on the basis of who's paying for it—the prosecution or the defense."

Two attorneys, writing in *The California Law Review,* have also challenged the accuracy of court psychiatrists. They believe they are "less accurate than the flip of a coin" in predicting dangerous behavior. Bruce J. Ennis, legal director of the American Civil Liberties Union, and Thomas R. Litwack, an associate professor of psychology at John Jay College of Criminal Justice, found that psychiatric diagnoses are "quite unreliable." They conclude that "it is more likely than not" that another psychiatrist would disagree with the diagnosis of his colleague.

The idea that the mental state of a criminal should be considered in his punishment is a British concept dating back to the mid-nineteenth century. "The Anglo-Saxons have an obsession with insanity as a legal issue," states Leon Radzinowicz, former director of the Institute of Criminology at Cambridge University.

The "obsession" began in 1843 with the case of Daniel M'Naghten, who killed the private secretary to the Prime Minister, Sir Robert Peel. M'Naghten believed he was being persecuted by the Tories and he took his anger out on someone in authority. After medical evidence was introduced that he suffered from "morbid delusions," he was declared not guilty on grounds of insanity.

This single decision became a linchpin of British and American common law. It has often turned the courtroom into more of a chamber of wizardry than a place for dispassionate examination of the facts. The popular phrase used to express the M'Naghten ruling is "temporary insanity." It refers to the court's conclusion that *at the time of committing the act,* the accused was suffering from "a defect of reason, from a disease of the mind, as not to know the nature and quality of the act he was doing or, if he did know it, that he did not know that what he was doing was wrong." The crime was considered, as the court said, "a delusion."

Under the M'Naghten rule the basic question was: At the time of the crime, did the criminal know right from wrong? The M'Naghten ruling held from 1843 until recently, when two new decisions have changed the definition of the insanity plea. But it has not changed the basic, confusing dilemma of relying on psychiatry to decide guilt and punishment.

In 1959 the psychic state of the defendant became even more important than before, sometimes overshadowing the crime itself. In the Durham case the federal appellate court for the District of Columbia broadened the concept by ruling that *a person was not criminally responsible "if his unlawful act was the product of either a mental disease or a mental defect."* It has created a courtroom guessing game in which opposing psychiatrists argue the defendant's mental state like trial lawyers in a television drama.

In 1962, in the McDonald case, the court decided to give mental illness a legal definition, which many now believe to be a hopeless task. In 1972, in the case of *U.S.* v. *Brawner,* the federal court adopted the Model Penal Code of the American Law Institute. It reads: "A person is not responsible for criminal conduct if at the time of such conduct as a result of mental disease or defect he lacks substantial capacity to appreciate the wrongfulness of his conduct or to conform his conduct to the requirements of the law."

The reality is that none of the rulings have changed the irrational mixture of justice and psychiatry that exists in the Psychological Society. Chief Judge David L. Bazelon of the U.S. Court of Appeals, who personally wrote the Durham decision, now acknowledges both the failure and the fruitlessness of the new ruling. It will still put the dominant role in the hands of supposed experts, he says.

The pessimism of those involved with courtroom psychology and psychiatry is growing. A judge in Washington, D.C., Alexander Holtzoff, even refused to honor the release of a larceny convict acquitted for reasons of insanity. He believes that the psychological interpretation of crime is an "open escape hatch" for the accused.

That escape hatch is not always negotiated. But there have been many cases where the death sentence or long imprisonment has been avoided by the plea of insanity. One of the most successful uses of the insanity law has been to exercise it twice in a row. The person is acquitted of the crime for being *insane at the time,* then hospitalized for insanity. He is then freed from hospital confinement by proving the opposite: that he is *no longer insane.*

One man in his thirties had been committed to asylums many times. In between commitments he stole cars. In 1965 he was picked up for stealing a car, but entered an insanity defense. He was acquitted on the basis of being insane at the time of the crime. He was sent to a psychiatric hospital for treatment but, once there, filed a *habeas corpus* writ. He argued that just because he was insane at the time of the theft, it did not mean that he was still insane.

He felt he should have the same rights as other people, which would include a hearing on his sanity. The U.S. Court of Appeals for Washington, D.C., reviewed his case, and agreed. The insanity plea, the court stated, "is neither an express nor an implied admission of present illness, and acquittal rests only on a reasonable doubt of sanity at the time of the offense."

In 1966 a businessman was indicted for underreporting his income tax. A defense psychiatrist testified that he was "suffering from a psychotic reactive depression." Despite the insanity plea, he was convicted and given a six-month sentence. The decision to use the American Law Institute's model of insanity was handed down while he was out on bail. The Appellate Court reversed his conviction. It ordered a new trial where he could seek acquittal based on the new insanity model.

Many psychiatrists, flushed with victory in other areas of life, would like to see jurisprudence increasingly in their hands. Dr. Samuel B. Guze, head of the Department of Psychiatry at Washington University School of Medicine in St. Louis, warns against that. "Until psychiatry proves that it has something to offer these people, the better model is the legal one, the one that has stood the test of time," he says.

Judges are becoming more sophisticated and increasingly doubtful of the value of psychiatric testimony in court. Dr. Seymour Pollack, in a government mental health report, concludes that judges have little use for psychiatric testimony bearing on the credibility of witnesses and the capacity of a witness to testify. The judges who were queried also felt that psychiatric testimony was *frequently colored with personal bias.*

What can be done to make the psychiatrist better suit the courtroom? Harvard Law professor Alan Dershowitz believes that current legal definitions of insanity are inadequate, and that "every attempt at change has backfired."

It is now obvious that to improve the situation it is necessary to eliminate psychiatry and psychology from the courtroom in determining matters of guilt or innocence. Dr. L.K. Berryhill of Fort Dodge, Iowa, offers such a plan. A psychiatrist should be called to testify whether the patient is well enough to stand trial, and if not, to treat the accused until he is. But, he adds: "When an individual faces trial, the psychiatrist would have nothing to do with deciding whether he is guilty or innocent. . . . In this way, the plea of not guilty by reason of insanity would be removed, and psychiatrists would no longer be pitted against each other by lawyers in courtroom dramas like pawns in a chess game."

In the world of seerdom, power stems from making the unknown become known. No human phenomenon lends itself better to this than homosexuality, a mysterious deviation from normal sexual preference. Derived from the Greek *homo* (same as) and not from the Latin *homo* (man), it has been the subject of both curiosity and inquisition since the beginning of civilization.

Oscar Wilde was jailed for his preference. Dozens of the great, particularly in the arts, have been homosexuals. Marcel Proust, André Gide, Tennessee Williams, Michelangelo, Noel Coward, Walt Whitman, Somerset Maugham are some of the prominent men who have reportedly practiced *sexual inversion,* as psychiatrists often term homosexuality. (Some believe that the homosexual roster included Marlowe, Frederick the Great, Beethoven, Goethe, Tchaikovsky and Hart Crane.)

The obverse of the proud homosexual coin is the fleeting, almost anonymous sexual encounter in men's rooms, the sleazy gay bar pickup, the trying double life of appearing "straight" for conventional society, the guilt that drives so many homosexuals into psychotherapy for either a "cure" or the courage to face their sexual preference without shame.

Approximately 1 to 2 percent of all adult men are believed to be exclusively homosexual. Kinsey reported that a considerably higher percentage of men sampled had reached orgasm in some homosexual experience. In any case, the question of homosexuality is of increasing societal interest as this sexual preference becomes more open.

What causes homosexuality? The query has confounded man for thousands of years, but once again the modern seer claims to know. He has answered with confidence: "It is born in the bosom of the family." The villain? The parents, with the mother usually cast as the psychic devil.

Freud and many of his modern successors saw homosexuality as the penalty for the boy child's failure to win the Oedipal battle against a seductive, overbearing, over-affectionate mother—the classic Mrs. Portnoy. Instead of finally identifying with the hated father at the resolution of the Oedipal rivalry, the child identifies with the mother. Thereafter, the now homosexual male seeks other men as his love object. Freud has outlined the process many times, the clearest being in his volume on Leonardo da Vinci:

> In all our male homosexuals there was a very intensive erotic attach-ment to a feminine person, as a rule to the mother, which was manifest in the very first period of childhood and later entirely forgotten by the individual. This attachment was produced or favored by too much love from the mother herself, but was also furthered by the retirement or absence of the father during the childhood period . . .
>
> The love of the mother cannot continue to develop consciously so that it merges into repression. The boy represses the love for the mother by putting himself in her place, by identifying himself with her and by taking his own person as a model through the similarity of which he is guided in the selection of his love object. He thus becomes a homosexual . . .

In the Freudian homosexual model, the *penis-adoring child also shows disgust for the penisless woman.* This is coupled with his castra-tion fear at the hands of an angry father-rival. Although this is the dominant theory, there have been analytic subtheories, ranging from Dr. Edmund Bergler's *psychic masochism* as the cause of homosexu-ality to the common Freudian concept of sibling rivalry.

Author Tennessee Williams apparently has been told that rivalry with his younger brother had helped trigger his homosexuality. In his autobiography, *Memoirs,* Williams describes days spent as a psychiatric patient in Barnes Hospital in St. Louis.

> I am walking very, very slowly down a corridor toward a lighted room and I am chanting a poem.
>
> The recurrent line of each verse is "Redemption, redemption." And I am performing, as I move slowly down the corridor, a mincing exaggeration of the walk of a drag-queen. What am I chanting about? About the birth of my brother Dakin when I was eight and my first sight of him, suckling the bare breast of my mother in the St. Louis hospital.
>
> Redemption from what. A never-before-spoken sibling rivalry with him, I suppose. And also a redemption from the "crime" of my love-life with boys and young men . . .

Psychoanalysts often speak of the homosexual-producing mother as being dominant, what Freudian disciple Isador Sadger called a "man-woman." In the *Comprehensive Textbook of Psychiatry,* Dr. Irving Bieber, the dean of psychoanalytic homosexuality, wrote what can be considered the establishment view of homosexuality. Said Bieber: "Thus, the parental constellation most likely to produce a homosexual or a heterosexual with severe homosexual problems was a detached, hostile father and a close-binding, overly intimate, seductive mother who dominated and minimized her husband."

Like most Freudian theories, this one is pseudoscientific. It can apply *sometimes,* not unlike the correlation between human personality and the Zodiac chart. Bieber tells us it was true in a "majority" of cases in analysis. There were exceptions, we are told. Some mothers of homosexuals were not overly close, but actually "detached, disinterested, and even explicitly hostile." In other cases, the father was not typically detached. "Some of the fathers were overly-close," he admits. But he is quick to add that they were also "minimizing and demeaning."

At the present level of knowledge, no one truly understands the etiology of this extraordinary, yet widespread, phenomenon. But there is some evidence, both modern and historical, that the modern seer has once again exceeded the bounds of his competence.

Early psychiatrists and psychologists seemed to have an intuitive grasp of the subject, an understanding that escapes many modern seers. The famed sex researcher Dr. Richard von Krafft-Ebing, who was Freud's contemporary at the University of Vienna, expressed his opinion in the work *Psychopathia Sexualis* (1886). Krafft-Ebing saw homosexuality as either a congenital condition or an acquired one, brought on accidentally among those people who have a *genetic disposition* for it. Says Krafft-Ebing:

> This perverse sexuality appears spontaneously with the developing sexual life, without external causes, as the individual manifestation of an abnormal modification of the *vita sexualis,* and must then be regarded as a congenital phenomenon; or it develops as a result of special injurious influences working on a sexuality which had at first been normal, and must then be regarded as an acquired phenomenon.
>
> On what this mysterious phenomenon, the acquired homosexual instinct, may rest, at present entirely escapes exploration, and belongs to the hypothesis. It is possible, from the careful investigation of so-called acquired cases, that the pre-disposition here consists in a latent homosexuality, or, at least, bisexuality, which requires for its manifestation the operation of accidental causes to awaken it from its slumber.

The famed English sex researcher, Havelock Ellis, showed that homosexuality generally makes its presence known early in life, an indication of genetic disposition. Of 43 cases of homosexuality which Havelock Ellis investigated, in 39 the "abnormal instinct" was manifested early. In 24 cases, it showed itself before puberty. In many instances, Ellis noted a sexual precocity which he believed helps to encourage the inversion when it exists.

As researchers do today, Ellis faced the eternal question about homosexuality. Is it inborn or acquired, a question of nature or nurture? Ellis believed that it was basically inborn:

> The first point that impresses me is that we must regard sexual inversion as largely a congenital phenomenon, or to speak more accurately, as a phenomenon which is based on congenital conditions . . . There are at the present day two streams of tendency in the views regarding sexual inversion: one seeking to enlarge the sphere of the acquired (represented by Binet—who, however, recognizes pre-disposition—Schrenk-Notzing and others), the other seeking to enlarge the sphere of the congenital (represented by Krafft-Ebing, Moll, Fere, and others). There is, as usually happens, truth in both these views. But inasmuch as those who represent the acquired view often emphatically deny any congenital element, I think we are specially called upon to emphasize this congenital element.

Evidence from other cultures shows that homosexuality is found in most. This is verified by a study, *Patterns of Sexual Behavior,* which showed that in 76 societies observed, homosexuality in some form was acknowledged in two-thirds of the cultures.

In the majority of cultures where homosexuality is acknowledged, attitudes toward it vary. Years ago, George Devereux, of the University of Pennsylvania, studied the sex practices of the Mohave Indians, and found that although it was considered socially inferior to be a male homosexual, there was a method of adapting it within the tribe.

Mohaves believed that homosexuals were born that way. Young boys who seemed more feminine than masculine were voluntarily initiated into the tribe as an *alyha,* a person whose sex was informally changed and could thereafter marry a man, and be excused from hunting and warfare.

What is known about homosexuality in our Western culture? Theories abound. The reverse of the Freudian-Oedipal cause is the biological theory, which had considerable credence before Freud, and is gaining new currency in some psychiatric circles. In 1971, Dr. Robert C. Kolodny, of Washington University, St. Louis, in collaboration with famed sex researcher Dr. William H. Masters, conducted experiments which indicate a possible hormonal difference between heterosexuals and homosexuals. Their studies indicate that homosexuals have a different endocrine chemistry and that their male hormone and sperm counts are lower than in heterosexual men.

Dr. Sidney Margolese, a Los Angeles endocrinologist, believes that homosexuality is associated with an imbalance of two chemicals related to the male hormone, *testosterone.* When testosterone is broken down by the body it produces the chemicals *etiocholanolone* and *andresterone.* Studying fourteen heterosexuals and ten homosexuals, Margolese found that in normal men the amount of andresterone was invariably greater than the amount of etiocholanolone. In homosexuals the ratio was reversed.

When Dr. Oscar Janiger, a psychiatrist at the University of California at Irvine, heard about the experiment, he asked Dr. Margolese to locate the homosexuals among a mixed group of ten men by examining their urine. Margolese identified every case correctly, Janiger says.

Drs. Janiger and Margolese have since replicated their study with the help of an NIMH grant and have published their results in the *British Medical Journal.* "I think there is an increasing acceptance of the idea that biology plays a more important part in the creation of homosexuality than we had once thought," Dr. Janiger stated when interviewed. "A German researcher, G. Dörner, has shown that a race of homosexual rats could be created by altering the hormonal concentration in the fetal sac. Other researchers speak of the 'sexualization of the brain,' an imprinting pattern that is fixed in the earliest period of life. Some homosexual behavior is apparently the result of situational stress or conditioning, but I believe that in the case of *obligatory homosexuals,* those who have always shown a preference for members of their own sex, that homosexuality has a constitutional base. In such cases, we have probably exaggerated the importance of environment."

Although it is now fashionable to believe that homosexuality is a psychological rather than a biological condition, contradictory evidence had also been offered by the late Dr. Franz Kallmann of Columbia Medical Center. Dr. Kallmann did extensive studies on monozygotic (identical) and dizygotic (fraternal) twins, and compared them for homosexuality.

Dr. Kallmann worked with sets of twins in which at least one of them was homosexual. Among the 26 pairs of dizygotic, or fraternal, twins, who come from two separate eggs in the mother's uterus, the concordance rate (both twins shared the attribute for homosexuality) was somewhat higher than among the general population, but not significantly.

But among the 37 pairs of identical twins, who come from one split human egg, the agreement rate was *100* percent. In every set, both of the twins were homosexual. The Kallmann statistics have been criticized, first by those who claim that both youngsters had similar upbringing, and by others who cite other twin studies in which there was less agreement for homosexuality.

Researchers L. L. Heston and James Shields surveyed the twin studies on homosexuality and concluded: "Though Kallmann's study overestimated the resemblance generally found in MA pairs, it appears from the literature that MZ twins are significantly more alike as regards male homosexuality than are DZ pairs. There is therefore prima facie evidence of the relevance of genetic factors."

The question is far from settled, but we do seem to know a few things about homosexuality. It is often, if not always, related to feminine behavior and attitudes. It generally has an early onset, and there seems to be a sexual precocity connected to it. Bieber reports that of his 106 homosexuals studied, 60 percent remembered having erotic responses to males by the age of twelve. By the age of fourteen, more than half of his sample had had genital homosexual contact, as opposed to only 10 percent of heterosexual males.

The onset of feminine manners in boys, often a precursor of homosexuality, is usually seen early in childhood, another sign of constitutional disposition. At U.C.L.A., a Gender Identity Research Treatment Program tries to help effeminate boys between the ages of four and a half and ten to avoid some of the social pain of their behavior. Many of the youngsters already walk with a "mince," and some would prefer to be girls, researchers report.

Homosexuality is as old as man, and will probably exist eternally. It may someday yield more of its secrets than it has thus far. There is also growing evidence that the new information will be mainly biological. But the theory of modern psychology and psychiatry that the universal, age-old practice of homosexuality is the product of a poorly resolved Oedipus complex and an over-erotic, dominating mother can be laid to rest with other superstitions of the Psychological Society.

The new seer gains his strength by offering his wizardry to explain away man's gnawing uncertainties. In no area is uncertainty more telling than in the matters of life and death, sickness and health. Wherever science has learned the cause of illness and its control, as in bacterial infection and the use of antibiotics, psychology has little to say. But whenever medicine is uncertain, psychiatry and psychology proudly fill the gap. They insist that the scourge is *psychosomatic,* an illness strongly influenced by, or caused by, human emotions.

The fact that the mind and body interact is ancient wisdom. It is fortified each day by observing how emotions may help healing in certain situations. The most obvious is the value of an understanding, warm environment for a sick patient. Most educated laymen are also aware of the research of Dr. Hans Selye, who has shown that adrenal and other hormonal and endocrine changes can cause harm to the body when the person is under physical or mental stress.

The new seers have catapulted this reality to near fantasy. And they have taken the gullible public and the medical profession along. Not only laymen but physicians in the Psychological Society have been tutored that anywhere from 40 to 80 percent of the complaints presented by patients are *functional* or "emotionally based." Even a host of serious organic ailments, including asthma, high blood pressure, heart disease and duodenal ulcer, are claimed to be *psychosomatic.*

The list of ailments with uncertain cause that psychiatrists and psychologists believe are psychosomatic is growing. Dr. Gerald F. Powell says that psychological factors may be more important than genes in the creation of dwarfs. Even the scourge of cancer has been labeled as psychosomatic by the overenthusiastic. Psychologist Claus Bahnson, of the Eastern Pennsylvania Psychiatric Institute, believes the cancer patient is a specific personality type.

The cancer type is the Freudian caricature of the unhappy youngster who suffered from lack of affection from his parents. This unrequited love is not only a neurotic stimulus, we are told, but can actually be a death sentence by causing cancer. The possible cure for cancer? Dr. Bahnson suggests psychiatric treatment. "Psychotherapy may be one of several ways one can influence the malignant process," he says.

The best-known psychosomatic ailment is the duodenal ulcer. The connection is so common that people are described as *ulcer-prone,* or the *ulcerous type,* if they are apparently nervous. High-pressure jobs in management and advertising are typically characterized as *ulcer-producing.* In novels and motion pictures, the man under stress is often portrayed in a single effective vignette. He is shown popping an antacid pill into his mouth to quiet an incipient ulcer. In many medical schools, peptic ulcer is considered one of the seven major psychosomatic or *psychogenic* illnesses. The others are bronchial asthma, hypertension, hyperthyroidism, neurodermatitis, rheumatoid arthritis and ulcerative colitis.

So ingrained is this theory that at the Chicago Institute of Psychoanalysis, researchers proudly reported that in 41 percent of the cases they could tell the specific disease solely from the patient's psychological make-up. What were the hidden profiles? They report in the text *Psychosomatics:* "Clear patterns of motivation have emerged, among them: Duodenal ulcer patients have a characteristic conflict about dependency needs. Asthma sufferers frequently fear losing their mothers and have difficulty crying. Trouble in handling hostile impulses appears again and again in people suffering from hypertension. Neurodermatitis victims intensely crave physical closeness."

Such cookbook personality formulas are irresistible to untutored patients, doctors and the lay public. But mythology about psychosomatics, including the connection between emotions and ulcers, is rampant. Even though many doctors believe the fashionable psychosomatic explanation about ulcers, several ulcer experts are convinced that it is a tale with little or no scientific base.

One of America's leading surgeons, Dr. Francis D. Moore of Boston, considers the psychosomatic ulcer a medical myth. From his years of experience, he has come to believe that ulcers attack the human body irrespective of emotional make-up. "For the great majority of patients with ulcers, at the present time, the only thing that sets them apart from his fellow man, either physiologically or biochemically, is the fact that he does indeed have an ulcer," he states. "Factors of psychology, adrenocortical function, environmental stress, may all be present in the background, but they exist to an equal degree in other patients who do not have duodenal ulcers."

World-famed gastroenterologist Dr. Thomas C. Hunt, of London, author of the text *Pathophysiology of Peptic Ulcer,* explodes the notion that modern stress has increased the number of ulcer cases, a statistic necessary to uphold the psychogenic ulcer theory. "The view that civilization has brought with it such an increase in general anxiety that it has led to a high incidence of duodenal ulcer is not confirmed on critical examination," he states. "Many fail to show any correlation between ulcer incidence and stressful situations in a world survey of forty countries."

In a study of 61 of his own patients, Dr. Hunt confirmed this failure of psychosomatic theory. He found that there were "neurotics" and "non-neurotics" alike among the ulcer patients, with the "non-neurotics" in the majority. He believes only 15 of the 49 male ulcer victims and only 4 of the 12 female patients could be described as "neurotic."

Dr. Basil I. Hirschowitz, of the Medical College of Alabama, is another psychosomatic skeptic. "While much is written about the personality of duodenal ulcer patients, there is no common ground between the successful hard-driving executives who are supposedly characteristic and the poorest workers in India, Nigeria and other areas who show a great prevalence of duodenal ulcer," he states. Because of its supposed psychosomatic base, many doctors prescribe tranquilizers and sedatives for ulcer patients, but the remedy may be more beneficial for the anxious doctor than for the ulcer patient. "Neither type of drug has any pharmacologic effect on the stomach," says Dr. Hirschowitz.

Another dramatic image of the Psychological Society is the heart victim whose fatal attack is brought on by his "emotions." We have been convinced that the heart attack strikes mainly those with a "coronary personality." Not just smoking, overweight and high serum cholesterol levels, but psychological defects can bring on heart disease, we are told.

The *coronary personality* has become almost legendary in psychiatric circles. In *Psychosomatic Medicine,* Dr. F. Dunbar has described that person as having many characteristics including inadequate sexual adjustment. There is a tendency to present a distinguished appearance, but it is only a surface calm which conceals an underlying aggression and resentment, Dr. Dunbar stated. These victims of coronary artery disease are typically portrayed as stereotyped compulsives: hard workers who are excessively competitive and determined to get to the top. It is the profile of the modern uptight, ever-striving man.

Prominent psychoanalyst Jacob Arlow even sees the adult heart-attack victim in the infant psychological profile, the child being father to the coronary. "The usual story of the patient with coronary artery disease is that of a stubborn, self-willed child, who early entered into competitive relationship with a much-feared and envied parent," he states. "Through hard work, self-discipline, and compulsive devotion to the termination of the task he assigns himself, the patient keeps driving himself to success . . ."

These theories are highly attractive, particularly to a society weaned on the potency of psychology. But extensive study of the research—a job accomplished by Arnold M. Mordkoff, Ph.D., and Oscar A. Parsons, Ph.D.—indicates that the coronary personality is probably a false stereotype. The evidence showed that the search for a unique personality portrait associated with heart attack "has been disappointingly unproductive."

Heart-attack victims are "more similar to the population strata from which they are drawn" than to other heart-attack patients, they believe. The two Ph.D.s quote a study by H.H.W. Miles from *Psychosomatic Medicine.* Miles took one hundred male coronary patients and compared them with a control group without heart disease. The evaluation failed to show a pattern of compulsive striving, hard work or self-discipline among the heart patients. *In fact, less than one in four of the patients fit that psychological stereotype.* "We found no convincing evidence that the personality differences exhibited by the coronary patients, as compared to the control subjects, could be implicated as significant factors in the genesis of coronary artery atherosclerosis," Mordkoff and Parkson conclude.

Two other researchers, D.D. O'Connell and R.M. Lundy, reporting in the *Journal of Consulting Psychology,* actually came up with results almost opposite to the current heart-attack personality theory. When they compared a group of atherosclerotic heart disease patients with a group of hypertensives, they found that hypertensives set their life goals very high so as to ensure failure. Heart-disease patients—unlike the high-striving stereotype—set their goals *purposely low* so as to ensure success, they discovered.

Researchers Mordkoff and Parsons believe that stress may be involved in heart disease, but not in terms of the cliché coronary personality. But how? They offer a theory of hereditary disposition. It involves increased vulnerability to atherosclerosis because of several factors including hereditary cholesterol and lipid-making systems, and the anatomy of the coronary artery tree. "It is most probable that the well-established hereditary determination of CAD (coronary artery disease) and socio-cultural factors will be the vehicles through which the contribution of personality to disease of the coronary artery will eventually be understood," they report.

The link between heart disease and personality has not proven accurate, but it is not as fanciful as some psychosomatic excursions. One psychoanalytically oriented dentist believes that tension influences periodontal disease involving bleeding gums and infection of the bones beneath the gums. "We have come to realize the mouth is one of the most erotic areas of the body," he told *The New York Times.* "It represents virility. It acts as a barometer of the personality set of the individual."

Dr. Lawrence LeShan claims he has found the missing personality equation in cancer itself. There is, he told the Conference of Psychophysiological Aspects of Cancer, a characteristic type of cancer-prone personality: what others consider "a good, decent or benign person."

Such simplism is part of the appeal of the Psychological Society. It is the near-childish reduction of complex biological and human equations to formulas with an almost religious appeal. A Harvard Medical School pediatrician reports that a family crisis can precipitate strep throat in children. Two psychiatrists at the Mental Research Institute in Palo Alto report that the families of eight young ulcerative colitis patients had the same personality constellation: rigidity, discouragement of humor and creativity, quiet and expressionless voice tones, the avoidance of argument.

One Harvard psychiatrist is convinced that emotions are so related to physical illness that dreams can prefigure disease. He recounts the case of a woman who dreamt of riding in a red car with a German shepherd dog. Soon after, she broke out in German measles with the familiar red rash. In another case, a professor who had a bad sexual relationship with his wife became a voyeur. Because of his guilt, and because he wished for the death of his father, who had serious eye problems, the professor had turned his own eyes into "target organs" for disease. His eyes would ache whenever he read pornography or attended a sex exhibition. The result? The professor is now blind in both eyes from detached retinas.

Most psychiatrists and psychologists, are enthusiasts of the modern psychosomatic theory. But some psychiatrists are doubtful of cookbook psychosomatics, as was the late Dr. Lawrence S. Kubie.

Dr. Kubie examined patients suffering from such psychogenic diseases as migraines, ulcerative colitis and heart disease. He found no consistent personality types involved. "I have been impressed by the dissimilarities at least as vividly as by the similarities among the individuals in each group," Kubie reported. "Indeed I could not convince myself that the similarities were greater than those which obtain among any heterogeneous group of neurotic patients."

The psychosomatic idea has become increasingly popular with the medical profession, with deleterious results. It has made it easier for both regular physicians and psychiatrists to overlook serious disease, both physical and mental. Dr. Arthur K. Shapiro, clinical professor of psychiatry at Mount Sinai School of Medicine, warns of "the clinical dangers of psychological theorizing" about diseases with unknown causes.

Shapiro is an authority on Gilles de la Tourette's Syndrome, a pathology of the central nervous system. The symptoms of this strange ailment include severe tics of the head, neck and shoulder, bizarre movements, frequent throat clearings followed by the uttering of sounds such as *heh, heh, ha, ha* and even of extreme obscenities.

Psychiatrists often diagnose such patients as suffering from a psychogenic illness. It is then treated with long-term psychotherapy, Shapiro reports. He believes such treatment is useless and that the psychological symptoms of Gilles de la Tourette's Syndrome are the result of an organic pathology which is treatable with a drug, haloperidol.

He describes the case of a male patient who first showed symptoms of eye blinking and eye closing at age thirteen. At fourteen he began to shake his head, then at fifteen the first involuntary sounds began. In his twenties the symptoms became more severe: he began to make spitting sounds and repeatedly struck his forehead with his hand or a kitchen utensil. He was treated with extensive weekly psychotherapy, but all therapies failed. Fourteen treatments of electroconvulsive therapy helped, but only briefly.

Coprolalia, or the involuntary uttering of obscenities, began at age thirty-six. They were emitted on the average of one barrage every three minutes. "The first words were 'cunt, prick, fuck,' followed by 'son-of-a-bitch, cocksucker and motherfucker,' and finally long phrases such as 'fuck you, you cock-sucking cunt, son-of-a-bitch motherfucker,' and so on," Shapiro reports. Since the syndrome is so antisocial, victims often rush to a nearby toilet to unburden themselves of both the tic and the involuntary stream of obscenities.

Shapiro laments the overzealous psychologizing of such cases. He recalls a psychologist's report on the case. It describes the patient as an "infantile and regressed personality . . . unable to recognize or accept in any way his own hostile aggressive and power-striving impulses . . . The tic itself expresses all of these elements in a dramatic fashion . . ."

At age forty-six, after thirty-three years of suffering, the patient was finally hospitalized and treated with haloperidol. After a month, reports Shapiro, "the coprolalia, coughing, barking, and clearing of the throat disappeared . . . Four months later, the only symptom was one tic every three or four days."

The modern tendency to report illnesses as psychosomatic has spilled over into another harmful area in the Psychological Society. It is the false labeling of patients who are organically ill as being psychoneurotic. That is, they are accused of having imaginary illnesses invented by the burdened mind. These supposed hypochondriacs jam doctor's offices with functional ailments which many doctors believe require psychiatric, not medical, attention. As millions have been told by their physicians: "It's all in your head."

Sending such patients to psychiatrists distresses some physicians, who are concerned that it is more often a sign of poor medical diagnosis than of patient psychoneurosis. This warning is issued by Dr. William F. Sheeley in the *American Journal of Psychiatry*. He tells physicians that they are exposing their patients to needless suffering and death itself by mistakenly labeling real organic illness as being "mental" in origin.

Dr. Phillip L. Rossman of Los Angeles, an internist, has the same fear. "Too often the doctors put the cart before the horse," he stated when interviewed. "They fail to realize that people often appear to be, or are, neurotic because they are physically sick."

Rossman's comprehensive study of this phenomenon is eye-opening. He collected the case histories of 115 patients who had been described by their doctors as being psychoneurotic. They had been sent to a psychiatrist for a mental checkup instead of receiving proper organic attention. Every one of Rossman's cases—compiled from his own files, from colleagues, and from others who learned of his study—involved patients who proved to be seriously organically ill.

The diagnosis was missed by the original doctor and incorrectly blamed on emotional causes. Of the 115 "neurotics," thirty-one died of organic illness, including twenty-five from cancer. Of eight patients who were given electroshock for their "mental" disturbance, three proved to have hyperthyroidism, while the others had brucellosis (undulant fever), chronic pelvic inflammatory disease, drug intoxication, glioblastoma multiforme (tumor of the central nervous system), aortic aneurysm (balloonlike tumor of the main heart artery). "Frequently such a patient's complaints go unheeded until a catastrophe occurs," warns Dr. Rossman.

The new seer has enlarged his professional status to include virtually every manifestation of modern life. He has done so brashly, using the tools of modern communications to reinforce his claims. He has been at fault in exaggerating, even inventing, an expertise that does not exist. But the public, in accepting him, has been not only gullible but equally culpable.

In this last quarter of the twentieth century, we have elected the seer of the Psychological Society as our interpreter of the unknown. He has been permitted, even encouraged, to cast the mysteries of life, love, health and happiness into a psychological form which entertains and ostensibly informs us.

By offering the seeming structure of science wedded to mystical insight, the psychological and psychiatric seer successfully masquerades as a modern oracle. He can only be countered if we learn how to strenuously seek the truth from more reliable and responsible sources.

# IV

## Insanity in the Psychological Society: The Schizophrenic Failure

"MANY FORMS OF INSANITY are unquestionably the external manifestations of the effects upon the brain substance of poisons fermented within the body . . . These poisons we shall, I have no doubt, be able to isolate after we know the normal chemistry to its uttermost detail."

This biochemical view of insanity, including what we now call *schizophrenia,* was written in 1884. It was twenty years before the beginnings of the Freudian psychological revolution, a movement which many critics believe has helped to retard true research into the mind and its diseases for two generations.

The author of the now forgotten quote on "poisons" in the brain was J.W. Thudichum, a Britisher and a founder of modern neurochemistry. His book, *A Treatise on the Chemical Constitution of the Brain,* helped solidify the suspicions of pre-Freudian doctors that madness was mainly biological and chemical in origin.

Since then, many psychologists and psychiatrists have convinced millions in the Psychological Society that the origin of this dreaded ailment is not in the biology of the brain but in the psychological bosom of the family. Distorted relations, particularly between the mother and child, are at the core of insanity, we have repeatedly been warned.

Insanity has lived under many names over the centuries. The

contemporary term for the condition is *psychosis,* with *schizophrenia* as one of its chief subdivisions. Schizophrenia's macabre symptoms and personality deterioration strike almost 1 in 100 persons throughout the world, an onslaught that has been with us since the human condition first began.

*New York Post* columnist James Wechsler is one of the millions of modern innocents whose lives have been touched by schizophrenia and by the philosophical battle over its mysterious cause. Wechsler has written a sensitive volume, *In a Darkness,* about the sickness and suicide of his twenty-seven-year-old schizophrenic son, Michael. It was an illness for which Wechsler, as father of the schizophrenic, was to feel the psychic whiplash of an angered, if unknowing, psychiatric profession.

"During his long battle, Michael was treated for varying intervals by eight therapists over a period of nine years, as well as by innumerable interns whom he encountered during periods of hospitalization that began in 1964," Wechsler recounts. "He spent more than twenty-six months in five institutions . . . It was in one of these hospitals that he wrote these lines:

" 'It is a feeling of hopelessness, creeping, casual but sure,
How much more, Dr. Freud, can I endure?' "

The story is a tragic reminder of how little we know about the scourge of mental illness and, conversely, how much the Psychological Society claims to know.

"In an angry moment, Michael once exclaimed, 'You know, Dad, I wasn't *born* this way,' " his father relates. Wechsler then painfully adds: "The accusation against me required no elaboration. He was saying what he—and others—were later to say in one way or another in many family therapy sessions we attended: that their illness could be traced to some parental failure or neglect."

This blame is one of the modern curses of schizophrenia. It is an extra burden of psychological guilt placed on those closest to the sick person. Each story of mental illness has its own special poignancy. But there is that deadly repetition of *blame.* Louise Wilson, who wrote about her schizophrenic son, Tony, in *This Stranger, My Son,* recalls that first shock of parental guilt. She told her doctor that she did not believe there was anything wrong in the family environment, or in her relations with her husband, that could have made Tony so sick. "Dr. Maxwell looked steadily at me," she recounts. Then her doctor said: "Nothing wrong that you are aware of. But no child is born with problems. It is always something in the home. In some way he has been damaged in your home."

This theory of the parent as the cause of schizophrenia and all insanity is increasingly debated within the profession. The argument is carried on daily within the psychiatric and psychological professions in professional journals, at symposia, or at cocktail parties. The tone is polite, but underneath is a sometimes bitter contest between opposing camps over the true etiology of schizophrenia and all mental illness. Are they biologic, organic diseases not unlike cancer or diabetes? Or is mental illness a psychogenic punishment for a twisted childhood existence? On the answer to these questions rests the possible liberation of millions of schizophrenics now living, and the hope of hundreds of millions yet to be born.

Two psychiatrists who disagree on schizophrenia dramatize this growing conflict, even unrest, within the field. Dr. Silvano Arieti, clinical professor of psychiatry at the New York Medical College, expresses the psychoanalytic—Freudian and neo-Freudian—viewpoint. The schizophrenic, he says, is born in a distorted family environment. The future schizophrenic invariably lives in a family "so constituted as not to be able to offer him a modicum of security or basic trust," says Dr. Arieti. "The early interpersonal relations are characterized by intense anxiety, devastating hostility, or false detachment, or a combination of these feelings."

This family-damaged youngster struggles along in childhood with a "patched self-image" and an overdeveloped fantasy life, says Arieti. But as a young adult he experiences *schizophrenic panic,* in which the repressed urges of his early life come back to confront him. "These obscure forces, generally silent but now reemerging with destructive clamor, are the repressed early experiences of the first stage," Arieti explains. In this theory, the young adult's only defense against these inexorable unconscious drives is schizophrenia.

Dr. Donald F. Klein, director of research at the New York State Psychiatric Institute at Columbia Medical Center, sees schizophrenia and mental illness in a more biologic and less poetic manner. "I have seen too many families in which there is nothing very damaging going on, yet one of the children becomes schizophrenic, while the others seem perfectly all right," Dr. Klein stated when interviewed. "At times there seems to be an environmental precipitant for a schizophrenic episode, but to elevate this into an adequate cause seems unwarranted. I believe that the cause of schizophrenia will turn out to be mainly biological as it will be for the other major psychosis, manic-depressive affective disease."

Before we examine the evidence evolving from new scientific research, we should look at schizophrenia as it is today. How common is the ailment? How does a schizophrenic act? What separates him from others who are mentally ill?

As we have seen, there are 1,800,000 annual hospitalizations for mental illness in the United States, or 8.5 per every 1000 persons. A National Institute of Mental Health study of state and county mental hospitals for 1975 shows that schizophrenia is the most commonly diagnosed ailment of *hospitalized* mental patients. Of more than a dozen types of patients, almost half (48.7 percent) were labeled as "schizophrenic." Among the psychotic cases, the overwhelming majority were schizophrenics.

Psychiatrists use the term *schizophrenia* as if it were a clearly defined disease. It is not. It is more probable that schizophrenia is a spectrum of diseases resting nervously under the semantic umbrella created in 1911 by Dr. Eugen Bleuler, director of the famed Burghölzli Asylum in Zurich, Switzerland, and an early admirer of Sigmund Freud.

The exact definition of schizophrenia has mystified observers for thousands of years. Yet there is a type of psychotic behavior that trained physicians can call "schizophrenic." Bleuler saw it as a failure of coherence in the patient's personality. It is a disruption of *associations* which makes it impossible for the schizophrenic to think and to feel as other people do. His world becomes disordered. Simple connectives in thought and feeling which make it possible for others to survive are now jumbled, as in a specially coded phone call.

"From clinical experience and patients' own accounts," say Drs. Fredrick C. Redlich and Daniel X. Freedman, "we are inclined to see the cardinal disturbance as a disorder in the organization of communications, resulting in a profound alteration of the patient's self-experience and his experience of the world."

The schizophrenic's illogical thoughts and feelings make communication both with himself and with the outside world almost impossible. As in *Alice in Wonderland,* words begin to mean only what the sick person believes they mean, a type of Jabberwocky. One schizophrenic patient told his psychiatrist that "the world and everyone in it had a rhythm." The patient complained that he was having trouble "getting his rhythm to oscillate" in time with others'.

Schizophrenics are driven to mental disorganization by a painful, overwhelming force they cannot control. As a result, the language of the schizophrenic becomes a private undecipherable code. It is not meaningful in itself, but in its distorted logic, it is typically schizophrenic. By breaking down the codes and symbols of conventional communication, the schizophrenic builds a new language that reveals the disorder that dominates his mind.

Dr. David Shakow illustrates this with an anecdote. A patient refused to eat his meal because the menu listed soup. The idea of soup disgusted him, he said. It made him think of urine. He reminded the doctor that it was spelled s-o-u-*p*.

One psychiatrist at New York University Medical Center recalls a schizophrenic patient who exhibited this same classical distortion of meaning. A patient stared at a sign, "Admitting Office" which had been placed over a door. He turned to his doctor and asked, "Is this where I go to *admit* my sins?"

Perhaps the best way to understand schizophrenia is to make the simple analogy between the dream of a normal person and the mind of a schizophrenic. When we dream, we suspend normal thought and illogical fantasy takes over. In the normal person the dream operates as a kind of nighttime schizophrenia, which may actually have a purging, curative effect. As we sleep, our reality is invaded by strange hallucinations and delusions, which we usually forget within minutes after waking.

But in the schizophrenic, daytime life often has the frightening feeling of living in a dream, with its maddening method of communications. Dr. Otto Pötzl has stated that schizophrenia is a disease in which the dream penetrates existence like a malignant tumor. Carl Gustav Jung drew a word picture of a healthy dreamer who would be able to both speak the lines of his dream and act out the script. Jung believed that this portrait of a dreamer would be indistinguishable from the schizophrenic.

The schizophrenic suffers from *delusions.* With his distortion of logic, he takes the ordinary concerns of normal people and exaggerates them into delusionary patterns. Society may be worried about crime and Communist China. But the schizophrenic patient, one psychiatrist explains, may be convinced that God has appointed him to destroy the Mafia. A psychiatrist recalls a patient who told him, "Every time I clench my teeth, thirty thousand Chinese die!"

Schizophrenics may have disturbing visual hallucinations, but auditory hallucinations are more common. In fact, they are almost a trademark of the disease. "Many schizophrenics will hear well-formed voices, which he may engage in a two- or three-way conversation," one psychiatrist explains. "If asked who the voices are, he may say St. Paul, or Marie Antoinette, or perhaps answer that he doesn't know who it is. Sometimes the voices do not trouble him, but other times he will be displeased with the hallucination. I remember one patient who had a three-way conversation with himself about a tie. The first voice said, 'It's an ugly tie.' The second voice answered, 'It's not so ugly.' Finally, the patient dismissed the voices by calling, 'Both of you, get out of here!'"

Schizophrenics may also have olfactory hallucinations in which things smell rotten, as well as taste sensations which do not jibe with the food eaten. However, psychiatrists suggest that distortion of smell, taste and vision are signs that the patient should be checked for possible organic damage. Many schizophrenics do have tactile, or *haptic,* hallucinations, in which they claim to feel things which are not there. One patient was convinced that someone was walking on his body. A female schizophrenic said she felt that her vagina was closing up.

An English psychiatrist, the late Dr. F.J. Fish, has put the unrealistic symptoms of schizophrenia into eight categories. Each of them, he says, are telltale "first rank" signs of the disease: (1) hearing one's voice or one's thoughts spoken aloud; (2) hallucinating voices in the form of a statement and replies so that the patient hears voices speaking about him in the third person; (3) hallucinating voices in the form of a running commentary; (4) bodily hallucinations, that is, the patient has sensations in his body that he knows are produced by external agencies; (5) thought withdrawal, thought insertion and other influences of thought; (6) thought broadcasting; (7) delusion perception; (8) all events in the spheres of feeling, drive and volition that are experienced as made or influenced by others.

The schizophrenic both *misperceives* and *misevaluates.* The actions of others are often misinterpreted, for the patient reads a "message" into the ordinary behavior of those around him. His view of the environment is highly personalized. He is convinced that people are paying special attention to him. As one psychiatrist explains about this false belief: "These may range from the belief that others are looking at the patient or talking about him to the belief that all surrounding individuals are involved in a play in which every action is undertaken for its effect upon the patient."

Not all schizophrenics who are victims of this false-belief system feel persecuted. But when they do, they invent a host of delusionary enemies, from God to the F.B.I., and are diagnosed as *paranoid schizophrenics.*

Schizophrenic delusions are the most creative inventions of the distorted psyche. They often appear humorous in their bizarre nature, but they are signs of grave internal torture. One twenty-five-year-old man, married with one child, told his wife that he might be God. When admitted to the hospital, he told the psychiatrist that he was God, the Holy Ghost or the Son of God, and that he could kill everyone, or help them. He had powerful visions and wanted to speak to the President.

One forty-three-year-old divorced man, who was living alone, told hospital psychiatrists that he was being used in an electronic experiment to manipulate the sphincter muscles of his rectum. A sixteen-year-old girl who broke down not long after friends accused her of being pregnant suddenly stopped eating, refused to go to school and begged for forgiveness for her sins. She was sure that she was being poisoned and was going to die. She heard voices and claimed that she had been transformed into the Virgin Mary. A thirty-two-year-old female patient was convinced that the voices she heard were the result of ventriloquism and that microphones had been placed in her room to record her conversations.

Several of the emotional reactions of the schizophrenic—whether anger, fear or depression—are found in other mentally ill patients. But in the schizophrenic there is also a flattening out of emotion, a blunting that is not appropriate to the stimulus.

There are few physical signs that distinguish schizophrenia, except for some forms of *motor retardation* involving inappropriate posture and gestures. Some schizophrenics will show an awkward, even bizarre posture, and strange grimacing and inappropriate smiling. Diagnostically, these signs are not exact, for others who are mentally ill—including some with organic disturbances—also show motor problems. Surprisingly, these signs were frequently reported a hundred years ago, but are seen much less today except in chronic, deteriorated cases.

It is a cruel disease, generally resistant to cure. Schizophrenia might be seen as a large-screen, daytime dream, rich with hallucinations, coded language, delusions, inappropriate response and emotions, and frightening threats to identity and survival. It deprives the victim more of himself than does a cancer. Consciousness is man's only tool in dealing with his threatening environment. Schizophrenia twists and distorts that consciousness, weakening him more than would the loss of an arm or a leg.

Schizophrenia is also a stubborn ailment, jealously guarding its origin. But this mystery of the mind has never stopped mankind from *inventing* the cause of madness. It has been a mystical age-old pursuit which has occupied philosophers—from pre-Biblical oracles up to the nineteenth-century seer, Sigmund Freud.

The Assipu priest-physicians of ancient Mesopotamia preached that mental illness was generated by devils within the body. They could only be exorcised by religious magic, including incantations which bear remarkable resemblance to modern psychotherapy. Medical historian Henry Sigerist speaks of this Mesopotamian psychological magic: "The rites performed and the words spoken by the incantation priest had a profound suggestive power."

The Hebrews added theology to the shrouded cause of mental illness. The one God, Yahweh, was the creator and arbiter of health and disease. Mental illness was one manifestation of his wrath, his punishment for man's sins. In *Deuteronomy,* it is written: "The Lord will smite thee with madness," a threat which God enforced against King Saul, who suffered a depression which ended in suicide. The belief in the religious nature of mental illness was so inviolate among Hebrews that when lay physicians finally won the healing power from priests, the treatment of insanity was still reserved for the religious class.

The early Hellenes viewed insanity much as did the Hebrews, as punishment for having offended the gods. But their treatment had more natural, physical overtones. Aesculapian healing temples were constructed on beautiful sites, adorned with gardens and offering luxurious baths. The patients received instruction in cleanliness and simple diet, and would receive dream instructions, a form of psychological suggestion. Like most modern psychotherapists, the Aesculapian priests turned away those too ill to be helped by their innocuous methods.

Hippocratic physicians in Greece were the first to discard the supernatural or theological origin of insanity. They organized mental illness on a rational, even if primitive, basis. They accurately described the symptoms of depression, which they believed was caused by an accumulation of black bile.

The Greeks organized mental illness into a reasonable *schema* that still makes some sense. It included the classification of epilepsy, mania, melancholia and paranoia, which, to them, meant mental deterioration. In terms of cause, the Greek system was ill-conceived scientifically. But in its descriptive approach, it was a forerunner of modern psychiatry.

Psychiatry is a relatively new discipline, stemming from European medicine of the nineteenth century. In the last hundred and fifty years, it has made abrupt swings in opinion in trying to shake age-old superstitions, which at various times viewed insanity as a curse, a moral plague, the product of devils, or the result of poverty or ill-fortune in life or love. In the early 1800s frustration about finding the cause of insanity had turned a number of physicians to what has been called *Romantic speculations.* They attributed madness to environment and mystical sources, a movement not unlike the current psychological one.

Moritz Romberg, a University of Berlin neurologist, was among the first modern psychiatrists. In 1840 his book, *Lehrbuch der Nervenkrankheiten,* established medicine of the mind as a specialty. His successor at the university, Wilhelm Griesinger, who was given the newly conceived title of professor of psychiatry and neurology, outlined his historic descriptions of mental illness before he was thirty years old. Griesinger attempted to root out speculations from psychiatry.

Researchers had already found pathological brain lesions in paresis, the insanity caused by syphilis. Griesinger became convinced that all mental illness was basically physical, rather than psychological in origin. He theorized that insanity involved anatomical brain changes, although he admitted they could not then be seen.

Henry Maudsley, an English psychiatrist, echoed Griesinger's organic theory. So did the giant of this period, Emil Kraepelin, a German physician. Kraepelin was sure that in *Wissenschaft* (science), rather than in philosophy, would be found the secret of insanity. In 1883, at the age of twenty-eight, he wrote his textbook describing the various forms of mental illness, a volume he continually updated. The Kraepelinian system was completed in 1899, and became the descriptive compendium of the diseases of the mind, one which is still professionally invaluable.

Kraepelin divided mental illness into two large categories: *dementia praecox* and *manic-depressive* psychoses. Each, he said, is predetermined with its own course of symptoms and effects. The subjective aspect of the patient's illness—his life conditions and his thoughts—are less important than its predetermined biological course, Kraepelin explained. The manic-depressive psychoses run a cyclical course of attacks of elation and deep depression. Between attacks the patient usually recovers and goes through a normal interval. This type of patient could recover naturally, Kraepelin felt.

But Kraepelin was pessimistic about the *dementia praecox* patient. That disease generally strikes in early adulthood and is characterized by bizarre actions, auditory hallucinations and often a feeling of being persecuted, he explained. The patient runs a natural course of mental deterioration, does not recover and eventually becomes one of the permanently insane—those who filled our mental hospitals before the psychochemical revolution.

Kraepelin found that dementia praecox struck in three forms: *catatonia,* for patients who fluctuate between mute, vegetable-like states, then suddenly erupt into violent behavior; *hebephrenia,* for those who exhibit a silly and inappropriate behavior; and *paranoia.* Today, it is known as *paranoid schizophrenia,* characterized by feelings of persecution. Kraepelin was convinced that all three forms had a biological, physical cause and were not the result of environmental or psychological pressures.

Kraepelin's prognosis of insanity was sometimes overstated. Some dementia praecox patients do recover, and other manic-depressives do not. But he did thoroughly wring the mysticism and theology out of mental illness. He saw it as an objective group of diseases which could be described without calling on the subjective thoughts and feelings of the sick person. He focused our attention on insanity as an illness no different from cancer or heart disease. The difference was that it made its symptoms known through our brain, an arena whose unfathomable mysteries have made all types of witchcraft successful throughout the ages.

The next insight into insanity was a strange amalgam of Kraepelin's view and a return to the Romanticism of the early eighteenth century. It is an amorphous, confusing blend of medicine and arcane philosophy which has characterized American psychiatry in the last forty years. The mysticism was contributed by Sigmund Freud, the academic psychiatry by Eugen Bleuler, the Swiss psychiatrist who invented the now common misnomer, *schizophrenia.*

Blueler felt that the subjective feelings of the insane were important and that their illness could be approached psychologically. He had been drawn to the work of Sigmund Freud in Vienna. Soon he and his colleague, Carl Gustav Jung, had joined the embryonic psychoanalytic movement, and offered the Burghölzli as a training site for psychoanalytic psychiatrists.

Bleuler agreed with Kraepelin that the disease probably had an organic origin. But he paradoxically sought to explain its symptoms as the products of psychological events and human motivations. Bleuler and Jung did not agree with Kraepelin that dementia praecox ultimately led to incurable insanity. Bleuler felt that the main feature of the illness was a *split in the personality,* a condition supposedly brought about by morbid thought processes.

The idea of a split suggested the term *schizophrenia,* a poetic and nonmedical concept. It is now considered inaccurate psychiatrically, but the exotic name has stuck. It has succeeded in confusing millions of educated people about a disease which needs no further obfuscation.

The unfortunate misnomer has spawned hundreds of false dramatic novels, plays and movies involving tales of split personality— of seemingly normal people suddenly exhibiting an insane side. But anyone exposed to the disease, directly or indirectly, knows that its symptomatology is much less romantic. It does not split the personality, it *destroys* it.

Another unfortunate aspect of the term schizophrenia was its creation as a catchall. Its euphonious name was destined to replace all forms of Kraepelin's dementia praecox and several other psychotic states, a bewildering task for one ill-conceived word. In fact, Bleuler spoke of the "group of schizophrenias," adding collective power to the confusion. Just as Kraepelin tried to place mental illness in the descriptive structure of other diseases, Bleuler and Freud purposely increased its symbolic and speculative power, forcing it further from the realm of science.

Freud had explained neurotic symptoms in psychological terms, mainly as a failure of the sex or pleasure instinct *(libido)* at various stages of infant development. Bleuler tried to extend this semantic method to mental illness. He used Freud's concepts of unconscious symbolism, particularly primitive thought processes, which he called *autistic thinking.* They do not follow logic, or the laws of reality, but are characterized by the kind of thinking we experience in our dreams, Bleuler said.

Traditionally, there has been a dividing line between the sane and the insane. But Bleuler liked Freud's new concept of a continuum that connects the psychology of the normal, the neurotic and the psychotic. The unconscious ideas which caused neurosis could now also shape madness. Bleuler knew of Freud's work in love-hate relationships and he theorized that these opposing emotions were more intense in schizophrenics. He called it *ambivalence,* a now common psychological term.

Freud and Bleuler were a good team: Freud a philosopher with few establishment followers; Bleuler an academic psychiatrist with credentials. Together they had brought back discarded nineteenth-century Romantic thought to psychiatry, virtually halting scientific investigation into the diseases of the mind.

No one could see Freud's frustrated infantile libido. Nor could a doctor see *ambivalence* in his patients. He could observe Kraepelin's manic-depressive cycles, catatonia, hebephrenia and paranoia. But at the turn of the century Freudian psychology seemed to promise something that Kraepelin could not offer: *hope.* If the condition was psychological and one could learn to understand it through unconscious symbolism, perhaps there would be a nonmedical, philosophical, even magical, breakthrough.

From this early psychoanalytic environment in Vienna—where Freud and his colleagues met every Wednesday in his house at Berggasse 19—and in Zurich at the Burghölzli came the theories of schizophrenia which have dominated much of psychiatry for two generations. Although now weakening before scientific experimentation, their metaphysical influence is still potent worldwide.

From Freud to today, this view of mental illness as *psychogenic,* or psychologically caused, has been greeted as the sign of a new Enlightened Age. Insanity has been seen as a disease caused by emotions and feelings, rather than as a biochemical and genetic disease which in turn created distorted emotions and feelings. The patient was no longer seen as an organically ill person for whom there was no medical cure. The schizophrenic was someone whose psychosis was, in many ways, an extension of commonplace neuroses.

This era might be seen as the Dark Age of psychiatry. It has been a time during which psychiatry has been oriented in the wrong direction. Rather than concentrating their medical treatment on the sick and on their research in the institutions to seek the cause and cure of schizophrenia, the best talents opened private offices where they could cater to the emotional needs of the affluent sane, now called neurotic.

This period formally ran from the Freud-Bleuler partnership of 1911 until the common use of anti-psychotic drugs in the 1960s. But it is still very much alive in many parts of the psychiatric profession and among the public itself. It is a time history will remember as one in which the truly sick were ignored, and the "neurotic" sane were seduced by a psychiatric profession more involved in metaphysics than in medicine.

Psychiatry's failure was not only in giving insufficient attention to the sick, but in falsely claiming that the psychological therapy could actually cure mental illness. Of all the schizophrenic failures, the false promise of psychotherapy as a tool against mental illness stands out as the most telling.

"From the 1930s through the 1960s, a whole generation of psychiatrists were taught to believe that psychotherapy was the only way to help, even cure, schizophrenia," Dr. Philip May, chief of research and development at the Veterans Administration Hospital in Los Angeles and professor of psychiatry at U.C.L.A., stated when interviewed. "In actuality, psychotherapy has proven to be a very poor treatment for the acute phase of schizophrenia. Both patients and psychiatrists have been victims of psychotherapy's greatly inflated claims. For years, psychiatric residents were taught that psychotherapy was the only possible treatment for mental illness. If it did not work with the patient then something was supposedly wrong with the young psychiatrist."

Dr. May's definitive research on psychotherapy has proven its failure in treating the mentally ill. A team of psychiatrists, psychologists and nurses headed by Dr. May conducted a study on 228 schizophrenic patients who had their first admission to Camarillo State Hospital in California. The patients were selected for their "average" prognosis for improvement. They were each assigned to one of five treatment groups. The first received only individual psychotherapy. The second group was given only phenothiazine, or anti-schizophrenic, drugs. The third group received the drugs plus psychotherapy. The fourth group received electroconvulsive shock treatment, ECT. The fifth group, the control, was labeled "milieu," and given none of the these four special treatments.

The results were promising for phenothiazine drugs, and discouraging for those who believe psychotherapy alters the psychic mechanism. "Psychotherapy alone and milieu [no special treatment] were clearly the least effective and most expensive forms of treatment with little to choose between them," states Dr. May. He stresses the success of the drugs, which "had a powerful and extremely significant effect in increasing the number of successful releases and, even despite the increased number, a highly significant effect in reducing the average stay and cost for those released." He adds: "By contrast, the *psychotherapy* has no appreciable effect on release rate, and it did seem to increase the length of time that a patient will be kept in treatment in the hospital . . ."

The numbers dramatize Dr. May's conclusion. Those schizophrenics treated with drugs alone stayed in the hospital the shortest time, an average of 130 days. *Those given only psychotherapy stayed 185 days, three weeks longer than those who had been given no specific treatment.* Of the 228 patients, 95 percent of those under drug treatment were released. But only 65 percent of those with psychotherapy were released. This rate was also considerably lower than the release rate of 79 percent for those treated with electric shock. Even when the psychotherapy was added to the drugs, as in the second group, there was no improvement over treatment by phenothiazines alone.

"All in all, it is difficult to dismiss the impression that this study has dealt the use of psychotherapy, as an essential modality of treatment for hospitalized schizophrenics, a hard blow," says Dr. Milton Greenblatt, professor of psychiatry at U.C.L.A.

The failure of psychotherapy and the relative success of the phenothiazine drugs raises strong questions about the supposed psychological cause of mental illness. How could an illness caused by an emotional malfunction in the family environment be vastly improved by a drug, while *psychodynamic insight* into the problem seems to do no good, even possible harm?

Dr. Donald F. Klein believes that the anti-schizophrenic action of the phenothiazines is a pharmacological sign that the disease is organic, not psychological, in origin. "Some medication has the same effect on everyone. Gelusil, for example, seems to lower stomach acidity in everyone, whether their stomach is sick or not," Dr. Klein explains. "The effect of such a drug is like a rheostat. It pushes things up and down regardless of the patient. Aspirin, on the other hand, acts like a thermostat. It lowers a fever temperature, but it does not bring the temperature down below normal. And if someone has a normal temperature, it does not lower it. The same thing is true of digitalis. It normalizes a deranged heartbeat, but nothing happens when it is given to a person with a normal heart.

"The anti-psychotics act in the same thermostatic manner," he continues. "They have an enormous effect on the mentally ill. But if they are given to a normal person, nothing happens. Prolixin is one hundred times more powerful than chlorpromazine as an anti-psychotic, but they both have the same effect—slight sedation—on a person who is not psychotic. Because the anti-psychotics work this way, there must be a biological derangement in the major psychoses."

Dr. Klein, and scores of his colleagues, also point to the growing body of genetic evidence which shows the biological base of mental illness. How can we prove that without isolating its cause? The first step is to show that it is an *inherited* disturbance passed on from parent to child through the gene system.

All studies show that schizophrenic parents produce more schizophrenic children than would be expected in the general population by a factor of 10 to 1, or more. Dr. E. James Anthony, of Washington University, St. Louis, studied 220 families in which one parent suffered from either schizophrenia or manic-depressive psychosis. He found that 15 percent of their offspring eventually became psychotic. Equally tragic was the fact that 40 to 50 percent of the other children later developed antisocial behavior.

The schizophrenic connection has also been established in sibling-to-sibling studies. They generally show that brothers and sisters of schizophrenics have approximately eight times the chance of developing the disease as do the general population: an 8 percent incidence of schizophrenia compared with 1 percent for people at random.

Dr. T. Lidz studied 24 brothers and sisters of young adult schizophrenics hospitalized at the Yale Psychiatric Institute. He not only found schizophrenia more common among siblings, but uncovered a spectrum of other personality disorders among brothers and sisters of the sick. Three (12 percent) were clinically schizophrenic: seven (29 percent) were borderline psychotics; eight (33 percent) were emotionally disturbed. Only six (25 percent) were considered adjusted.

A Finnish researcher, Dr. Y.O. Alanen, conducted a similar study with similar results. Of 49 siblings of schizophrenics, 8 percent were found to be schizophrenic. Another 12 percent were nonschizophrenic but psychotic. As a check, Alanen examined a group of 40 siblings of controls. None of them proved to be schizophrenic or psychotic.

At Hillside Hospital on Long Island, researchers examined 64 siblings of schizophrenic patients. They found that five (8 percent) of the siblings had the disease, and 34 percent more had some emotional disturbance. The study had one optimistic note: 58 percent of the siblings were normal.

What do these studies prove? They make it abundantly clear that schizophrenia is "transmitted" within the family. What was not clear is whether that contagion is environmental or genetic. Do young people "catch" schizophrenia because of the distorted family environment that surrounds, then eventually destroys, them? Or is the schizophrenic contagion genetic? Is it a time bomb built into the inherited DNA and RNA family code?

There are two life laboratories that can help us learn the solution to this Solomonesque riddle. One is the identical, or monozygotic, twin who shares virtually the same biology as the sibling. It is a scientific convenience provided by nature by splitting one fertilized human egg into two fetuses with the same genetic structure.

The other laboratory is the foster home, which helps to separate the genetic effect from the environment. In the foster home the child has his true parent's biology, but lives in an environment composed of biologic strangers. If the sick parent does not raise the child but the offspring still "catches" schizophrenia in a normal environment, the case for heredity is strengthened.

These two laboratories have been successful in revealing the truth about schizophrenia. It is a truth which shows that the disease is heavily genetically based, or, as the vernacular would have it, that blood tells.

Minnesota psychiatrist L.L. Heston reported in the *British Journal of Psychiatry* on 47 children who had schizophrenic mothers, but who had been reared by normal foster parents. He compared their eventual mental health with an equal number of foster-reared children whose mothers had not been schizophrenic.

If environment were the trigger for the disease, both groups would have approximately the same amount of schizophrenia. But it did not work out that way. *There was over ten times the normal incidence of schizophrenia among the foster children whose biologic parents were schizophrenic. There was not a single case of schizophrenia among the other group.* Despite being reared away from their schizophrenic-prone family, the biologically prone children contracted the disease in relatively large numbers.

The growing evidence that schizophrenia is genetically based and inherited prompted an editorial in the *American Journal of Psychiatry*. It presents a view which infuriates environment-biased psychiatrists and psychologists who believe that parents' behavior, not their genes, creates schizophrenia. "We are only beginning to comprehend how widespread the genetic influence of schizophrenia may be," states Dr. Barbara Fish, former director of child psychiatry at the New York University Medical Center. She quotes one study which shows that 50 percent of the offspring of schizophrenic mothers suffered from significant psychiatric handicaps, *even though they were separated from their mothers at birth.*

Perhaps the most impressive research in this area is the work of Dr. Seymour S. Kety, professor of psychiatry at Harvard medical school, and colleagues, Drs. Paul H. Wender, David Rosenthal and Fini Schulsinger. "Adopted children, who receive their genetic endowment from one family and their environmental interactions from another, constitute a uniquely useful population for disentangling these two groups of variables in the transmission of schizophrenia," the researchers state.

Their laboratory was Denmark. Through the Danish government, they obtained the complete file of adoption records of Copenhagen between the years of 1924 and 1948. It showed the adoptions by all persons not biologically related to the child.

The researchers decided to check the "adopted-away" offspring of schizophrenic parents. Would their mental health match the biology of their parents or the environment of their new home? They found 5500 adoptees, and traced 10,000 of their parents. (They failed to find about 1000 of the fathers.) Through a central psychiatric registry, they learned which of the parents had mental illness, defined as schizophrenia, manic-depressive disease or borderline schizophrenia.

From these, they selected mentally ill "index" parents. They then examined the mental health of their offspring, all of whom had been raised by someone else. Despite the better environment, almost 32 percent of the adopted children were found to have had some mental disorder. "The evidence supports the theory that heredity plays a significant role in the etiology of schizophrenic spectrum disorders," report the study authors.

In another study, Kety and his colleagues located 33 Danish adoptees whose psychiatric history warranted a diagnosis of schizophrenia. He then took 33 adoptees with no history of mental illness for comparison. In each group he located approximately 150 biological relatives—parents, siblings or half-siblings—of the adopted children. Their records were then checked for mental illness.

The results? Of the biological relatives of the sick adopted children, there were "schizophrenic spectrum disorders" in 13 percent of the cases. In the control group there was illness in 3 percent of the cases. As a double check, the researchers compared the adopted relatives of both groups. Environment seemed to play little part. They both had approximately the same incidence of mental illness typical of the general population.

Since the genetics of identical twins is the same, one can also gain information about the genetic base of schizophrenia by learning if monozygotic, or identical, twins share schizophrenia more often than do fraternal, or dizygotic (two eggs), twins. These dizygotic twins are no more biologically alike than ordinary brothers and sisters. If schizophrenia is genetically based, identical twins would contract the disease together more often than do fraternal twins.

At the Maudsley Hospital in London, in a study conducted by Drs. Irving I. Gottesman, of the University of Minnesota, and James Shields, of Maudsley, seven diagnosticians studied the psychiatric histories of 114 twins of whom at least one member of each pair was schizophrenic. The psychiatric team was an international one, composed of doctors from the United States, Japan, Sweden and the United Kingdom. It was an attempt to do away with the national biases as to what schizophrenia actually is. For example, it is diagnosed more often in the United States than in Britain.

The 57 pairs of twins (114 people) were culled from 45,000 psychiatric patients admitted to Maudsley over a period of sixteen years. The results were startling. The fraternal twins both had schizophrenia in only 9 percent of the cases. This ratio is similar to that in most studies of ordinary brothers and sisters. But the consensus of the judges was that the *identical twins both had schizophrenia in 50 percent of the cases.* Since schizophrenia is distributed in the general population about 1 percent of the time, *this one-egg sample shows a more than 50 times higher schizophrenia rate.* It is dramatic evidence that the disease is basically both genetic and inherited, and not subject to the psychodynamic theories that have controlled so much of American psychiatric thought.

Other identical-twin reports support the Maudsley work. Studies since 1953 show a concordance ranging from 35 percent to 76 percent. In studies including the Maudsley series, researchers have estimated an average concordance for schizophrenia in 46 percent of monozygotic twins. This compared with an average of 14 percent concordance for mental illness in fraternal twins, who neither look nor act alike. Both figures show that schizophrenia runs in families. But there is more than three times as much schizophrenia in the identical, or biologically alike, twins. It is clear evidence that unknown genes are at the core of this mystery of mental illness.

The first large-scale identical-twin study of schizophrenia was conducted in 1946 by Dr. Franz J. Kallmann at Columbia Medical Center. Kallmann reported on almost 700 twin pairs, showing an 86 percent concordance for schizophrenia in the identical twins, against only 10 to 15 percent concordance in the fraternal twins.

The Kallmann study is considered at the high end of probability. A newer study is probably at the low end. In 1969 Dr. William Pollin, of the National Institute of Mental Health, reported on 15,909 twins who had served in the armed forces. Using their health records only, he located those who had either schizophrenia or manic-depressive illness, then checked the records of their twins. Of 80 pairs of identical twins the concordance was 15.5 percent, versus only 4.4 percent in 145 pairs of fraternal twins.

The relationship between the two types of twins was typical, but the 15.5 percent rate for identical twins was the lowest yet found. A revised study of the same sample based on a review of the Veterans Administration claim folders has brought these figures up somewhat: 27.4 percent in monozygotic twins versus only 4.8 percent in fraternal twins. Even these higher figures have been attacked as too low for a simple reason. The twins were selected for *health*. Both were well enough to have served in the armed forces, a situation which is quite atypical for schizophrenics.

What does all this mean? If schizophrenia is basically a genetic, inherited disease, why doesn't every identical twin become mentally ill if his twin does? If concordance among identical twins averages 50 percent, does this mean that schizophrenia is half genetic, half environmental?

Firstly, the 50–50 concept is oversimplistic mathematics. If approximately 1 percent of the general population is schizophrenic (.085 is the figure often assumed in Western European countries), then only 1 percent of identical twins should both have the disease. As we have shown, a 50 percent concordance is *fifty times, or 5000 percent, higher than chance.*

Critics of the genetic theory claim that identical twins have a very similar environment, and suffer the same psychological blows. Therefore, why shouldn't they share schizophrenia? This argument is refuted by Dr. Kety's work. By showing that adopted children of schizophrenic parents—totally removed from the environment that ostensibly spawns the illness—still produced as much schizophrenia, the environmental argument is shown to be fallacious.

If identical twins and adopted-away children are good laboratories, what about combining the two? What about identical twins who have been reared apart? Unfortunately, there are only a small number of such cases. But those few strongly point to heredity. *Of seventeen cases of identical twins separated at birth or in childhood and reared apart, eleven sets of twins both developed schizophrenia.* In one telling study, conducted in Japan in 1967, H. Mitsuda even showed that a group of identical twins had a similar rate of schizophrenic concordance whether they were reared together or apart.

Then why, the skeptic might ask, don't all identical twins get identical schizophrenia? Firstly, identical twins are not exactly identical. They may have the same gene system, but their *constitutional* factors vary. One twin may develop somewhat differently because of conditions in the mother's uterus. One of the identical twins often has a lighter birth weight and an early pattern of poorer sleeping and feeding behavior.

In a study of 15 pairs of identical twins, selected because only one of each pair was schizophrenic, the Center for Studies of Schizophrenia found that 11 of the schizophrenic twins were weaker biologically at birth. Two others had severe childhood illness: one contracted cyanosis due to a heating-gas accident during infancy; the other had serious Rocky Mountain spotted fever at age three and a half. They also found that the twin who developed schizophrenia tended to show early neurological abnormalities.

If schizophrenia is indeed transmitted through the genes, how can it be charted? How can we tell who will inherit the disease and who will not? Unfortunately for science and those affected, the genetics of schizophrenia is confusing.

*Schizophrenia does not breed true.* It is not a simple genetic disease like some whose course can be predicted. For example, PKU, a type of mental deficiency found in children, is caused by recessive genes. As a rule, 25 percent of the children of a carrier are affected. Huntington's chorea is another inherited disease of clearer proportions. If one parent has the disease, 50 percent of the children should eventually develop it.

But schizophrenia has an elusive heredity. Drs. Gottesman and Shields compare it with diabetes, which they call a "geneticist's nightmare." Like schizophrenia, diabetes strikes about 1 in 10 children of the ill. But where and how is unknown. They propose a *polygenic* theory to explain schizophrenia. In this theory there is "the simultaneous occurrence of many small discontinuities." Rather than being the effect on one major gene, schizophrenia is probably the result of the cumulative effect of less potent multiple genes, or polygenes.

The polygenes of either schizophrenia or diabetes act differently from the dominant and recessive Mendelian genes. In the polygene theory, when one goes from first- to second-degree relatives, there is a sharp drop in the number of those affected. In polygene heredity, the more severe the case, the greater the risk to relatives. And the risk increases as the number of other family members affected by it increases.

What is the chance that a particular relative of a schizophrenic will be affected? In 1967 a German researcher, E. Zerbin-Rudin, put together a comprehensive chart culled from some 35,000 relatives of schizophrenics. She found that children of a schizophrenic had a 13.8 (approximately 1 in 7) chance of becoming schizophrenic. Brothers and sisters of a schizophrenic had 10.2 percent chance (1 in 10), which increased to 17.2 (1 in 6) if a parent was also mentally ill. There was a frightening 46.3 chance (almost 1 in 2) in the child of two schizophrenics who mate. There was only a 3 percent chance of schizophrenia—or three times normal—in more distant relatives, including half-siblings, uncles, aunts, nephews, nieces, grandchildren and first cousins.

Dr. C. Peter Rosenbaum, of Stanford University Medical Center, concludes that "the closer in consanguinity [blood] to a schizophrenic patient a person is, the greater is the likelihood that he will develop schizophrenia." He adds that "the likelihood is slightly increased if one is of the same sex as the index patient, or if the index patient is a female."

His statistics generally confirm the schizophrenic "odds" offered by Zerbin-Rudin, but they are somewhat higher. For a full brother or sister, the risk varies from 12 to 16 percent, according to Dr. Rosenbaum. For the child of a schizophrenic mother the chance is 16 to 17 percent; for a half-sibling it is approximately 7 percent.

In contrast to this careful work in probing schizophrenia's mystery, the Freudian explanations for mental illness now seem puerile. They are a combination of metaphysical symbolism and inaccuracies which has been passed on to modern psychiatry as absolute confusion.

Freud was not initially clear in distinguishing neurosis from psychosis. Neurosis, he said, was caused by a disturbance in infantile psychosexual development. In 1914 he finally offered a psychological explanation for psychosis. Unfortunately, it is one which illuminates little for the mentally ill. In his essay *On Narcissism,* Freud separated neurosis from psychosis in terms of the sex-pleasure drive, the libido. The psychotic breaks with reality, Freud said, by regressing to the infant stage. His libido is withdrawn from the outside world and affixed to his own ego. He returns to the stage of infant self-love, or narcissism. The neurotic, on the other hand, still retains a mental image of objects from the outside world and thus avoids psychosis.

Unlike some of his followers, Freud was pessimistic that his "science" of psychoanalysis could cure psychosis. The reason, he said, was that the psychotic's narcissistic self-love kept him from transferring his libido to the psychoanalyst. Without this *transference love,* there could be no cure.

But in his clinical practice, Freud was often unclear as to whether his patients were neurotic or psychotic. Several critics have since commented that whenever Freud diagnosed a patient as a severe neurotic, we should assume that the patient was either borderline-psychotic or frankly insane.

This seems to be true about his patient, the so-called Wolf Man, a Russian emigré in Vienna whom Freud started to analyze in 1910. The patient had already been hospitalized several times as a manic-depressive, but Freud diagnosed him as a severe case of *obsessional neurosis.* During the first interview the Wolf Man offered to submit to anal intercourse with Freud and to defecate on his head. Later, learning that Freud had undergone an operation on his mouth, the Wolf Man started to masturbate compulsively.

Freud made only one diagnosis of psychosis. The patient was analyzed not in person, but from a book Freud had read. The "patient" was a former hospitalized psychotic, Daniel Paul Schreber, who had been president of the Court of Appeals of Saxony. His book, *Memoirs of My Nervous Illness,* described his thirteen years in a mental institution. During that time, Schreber experienced painful body experiences which he thought were "miracles" God had performed through "rays" focused on his body.

Freud analyzed that the "basis of Schreber's illness was an outbreak of homosexual feeling" toward his physician, Flechsig, a father surrogate. Freud believed that Schreber, "as a means of warding off a homosexual wish-fantasy, reacted precisely with delusions of persecution."

Freud's long-distance deductions about Schreber were to lead to a false psychiatric opinion which has dogged the profession for over a half-century. Freud's conclusion that Schreber was suffering from paranoid feelings of persecution due to *repressed homosexual feelings* became his sample of one. From it he extrapolated that *paranoid schizophrenia* was caused by repressed homosexuality.

This Freudian theory was taught as scientific truth to psychiatrists, patients and the public for decades. Even though it is now being revealed as another superstition, it is still believed by sizable numbers of people in the healing professions.

Schreber's "delusions" of persecution have since been investigated by another psychiatrist, Dr. Morton Schatzman. Schatzman agrees that the insane judge may have been delusionary, but he points out that Schreber *was actually persecuted by his father.*

Daniel Paul Schreber's father was a physician and a teacher who had developed cruel methods of training children. Schreber, the son, believed that the painful body experiences he endured during his years in a mental institution were miracles. "One of the most horrifying miracles was the so-called compression-of-the-chest miracle," said the psychotic son. "It consisted in the whole chest wall being compressed, so that a state of oppression caused by the lack of breath was transmitted to my whole body."

Dr. Schatzman examined the father's writings on child rearing and found that the "delusion" had actually taken place. The father had invented a device called *Schrebersche Geradhalter* (Schreber's straight holder), which he used on his own son. An iron crossbar was pressed against the child's collarbone and the front of the shoulder to prevent forward movements or crooked posture. Schreber, senior, also tied to the bed a belt which crossed the child's chest so that his young body remained straight while sleeping.

Schreber also suffered from the delusion that a device on his head was causing uninterrupted headaches. In reality, his father had forced him to wear a *Kopfhalter,* a head-holding device to prevent the child's head from falling forward or sideways.

Dr. Otto A. Will, Jr., in evaluating Schatzman's work, warns his colleagues not to fall into Freud's error. "It is well for each of us to be reminded . . . that our data are frequently scant and difficult to decipher and evaluate. Our theories . . . must ever be exposed to data which may require their change or even abandonment . . ."

Some analytically oriented psychiatrists and psychologists still stick doggedly to the Freudian superstition that paranoid schizophrenia is closely related to repressed homosexuality. But Robert Spitzer, clinical professor of psychiatry at Columbia Medical Center who heads the American Psychiatric Association's task force to revamp the profession's diagnostic manual, speaks for the enlightened portion of the profession in discarding such mythology. "The Freudian idea that repressed homosexuality plays a decisive role in the cause of paranoid schizophrenia is no longer a widely held theory. In the next edition of the APA manual, it is not mentioned as a predisposing factor in the disease. But the new edition of the manual does mention that there is a familial, genetic relationship in schizophrenia."

Those who believe in the psychological cause of insanity generally avoid the scientific method. Instead, the theory of the psychological cause of neurosis and insanity is simply stated, then repeated in thousands of prestigious books and journal articles. The arguments are couched in a historic method of verisimilitude: scientific-sounding but mainly philsophical concepts supported by anecdote and artistry.

There are exceptions, for a handful of supposedly scientific attempts have been made to prove Freudian theory. But when the theory is submitted to the laboratory, the method and results often seem ludicrous. In the *Journal of Nervous and Mental Disease,* a team which included two Ph.D.s from the Laboratory of Psychology of the National Institute of Mental Health tried to prove the Freudian theory of insanity by examining the *sucking power* of schizophrenics.

The experiment was based on the psychological damage that a negligent or uncaring mother is supposed to inflict on a child in the weaning stage. J. Rickman studied the literature of three decades of psychoanalysis, then summarized the Freudian opinion: Dementia praecox is associated with a disturbance in the early oral phase of libido development, the period when the child gains his sexual pleasure from sucking on the mother's nipple.

Manic-depressive disease, Rickman also concluded from his survey, was a product of a disturbance in the late oral phase when the child angrily bites the mother's nipple in sadistic defiance. As one psychoanalyst poetically states about insanity: "Psychotics live immediately under the shadow of the breast."

This breast theory of insanity appears even more occult when subjected to experimentation. The sucking study conducted by NIMH psychologists is entitled "Oral Functions in Schizophrenia." The subjects were 55 schizophrenics from two public institutions who were subjected to several tests: (1) Single Suck, (2) Multiple Sucking, (3) Lifting Liquids, (4) Swallowing, (5) Biting, (6) Blowing.

If their theory was correct, schizophrenics should not suck as well as normal subjects, the government psychologists stated. The outcome was as the psychologists hoped: "The results of the two experiments suggest that schizophrenics, as compared to normal controls, are impaired in their sucking capacity. Since sucking is the early oral function *par excellence,* the results can be considered as partially supporting the original hypothesis of a connection between schizophrenia and a disturbance in the early oral phase."

The conclusion is, of course, less than significant. Numerous studies show that hospitalized schizophrenics do less well than normal controls on a host of psychomotor activities.

Sucking deficiency as a cause of mental illness sounds like an archaic idea to many educated patients. Modern Freudians and neo-Freudians have been revising the *psychogenic,* or emotionally caused, theory of schizophrenia to make it sound more plausible to the contemporary mind. The latest theory is the *double-bind* concept developed by Dr. Gregory Bateson. Like traditional Freudianism, it once again implicates the parents, charging that schizophrenia is born in the bosom of the home. But in this new concept, schizophrenia supposedly starts with an immature mother who speaks to her child in a set of contradictory equations, a Freudian forked tongue.

Bateson describes one of these conflicting situations: "A young man who had fairly well recovered from an acute schizophrenic episode was visited in the hospital by his mother. He was glad to see her and impulsively put his arm around her shoulders, whereupon she stiffened. He withdrew his arm, and she asked, 'Don't you love me any more?' He then blushed, and she said, 'Dear, you must not be so easily embarrassed and afraid of your feelings.' "

This is a classic *double bind,* a damned-if-you-do-and-damned-if-you-don't situation. It sets up a conflicting set of messages which ostensibly puts the child in an impossible dilemma from which there is no escape, except schizophrenia. The psychological message is: "If I am to keep my tie to my mother I must not show her that I love her, but if I do not show her that I love her, then I will lose her."

"We are investigating the hypothesis that schizophrenic communication is learned and becomes habitual as a result of continual traumata of this kind," Bateson states. His disciples speak of "family interaction processes" as being *schizophrenic,* as bringing on the disease.

As a contemporary psychological theory, Bateson's idea is both novel and plausible. Everyone knows of such cases of psychological manipulation. But as a theory of how schizophrenia is born, it is almost as abstruse as classical Freudianism. As we have seen, children of schizophrenic parents brought up outside their own homes have virtually the same rate of mental illness as those who stayed at home and were supposedly subjected to the double bind.

The cause of schizophrenia is obviously more complex than insufficient sucking, the double bind, or any unseen mechanism in the child-parent relationship. The suspicion that early family environment did not trigger schizophrenia started when a handful of professionals and parents of schizophrenics saw that their other children, who grew up in the same home environment, were perfectly normal.

This skepticism is being substantiated by astute psychologists and psychiatrists. The late Dr. Carl Fenichel, then the director of a New York State school for emotionally disturbed children, observed that the brothers and sisters of his patients were often quite normal. Speaking of his young patients, he said: "We saw evidence that these kids were different from the very first weeks of life. These kids rejected the parents, not vice versa. These kids didn't respond to love, to cuddling, to games."

Dr. Lauretta Bender, prominent child psychiatrist who headed the children's ward at Bellevue Psychiatric Hospital in New York for years, is one of the psychiatrists who have turned away from the idea that schizophrenia is an environmental, parent-caused disease.

Dr. Bender is one of the *grandes dames* of child psychiatry, who began her career almost forty-five years ago. She has seen changes in treatments and fads in psychiatry, and has come virtually full circle from her early psychoanalytic days. In the *International Journal of Psychiatry* she reminds us that treatment in those days consisted solely of group activities and psychoanalytic therapy.

The results, she recalls, were negative. Analysts hoped that child psychoanalysis would reveal the traumas that caused the schizophrenia, but they were disappointed. "Psychoanalysis had not discovered such factors in adults. . . . Work with children, whether by Melanie Klein or in our own group, had also been very disappointing," she states.

The truth about childhood schizophrenia did not come from Freudian theory, Dr. Bender points out. It came from biology in the form of the work of pediatrician Dr. Arnold Gesell. In his book, *The Embryology of Behavior,* Dr. Gesell showed the similarity between the behavior of the fetus and the body movement of schizophrenic children.

Dr. Bender is now convinced that childhood schizophrenia is an organic disease, probably with an inherited vulnerability. The disease is shaped during pregnancy in the fetus, she feels. "In childhood schizophrenia I have found the stress or environmental factor to be an organic one . . . The defect occurs in the mother's uterus, during and just before birth, and in early childhood."

Dr. Bender studied 100 schizophrenic children at Bellevue Hospital from 1935 to 1952. When she followed them up as adults in 1973, her study showed both the severity of the disease and its organic base. Thirty-seven were still in the community, but almost two-thirds had been chronically institutionalized. Eight had convulsions and several had died in early adulthood of convulsions or inadequate cardiac function.

In all, says Dr. Bender, *"seventy percent* of the total group had histories of clinical evidence of organicity affecting the brain that accounted for the onset of an early schizophrenic decompensation."

Their heredity was also heavily tainted, or *genetically loaded,* with schizophrenia. Thirty-four of the former patients now had forty-eight schizophrenic or personality-disordered children of their own. "The recent genetic studies," states Dr. Bender, "accept Kallman's estimate. . . . of forty-five percent of each class of first-degree relatives as being in the 'schizophrenic spectrum.' "

Dr. Bender believes that a warm relationship with a therapist can be helpful for a schizophrenic child. But she is worried that the therapist may take his psychological theories too seriously. "I have found that it is very harmful if schizophrenic children are given interpretative psychoanalysis in adolescence," Dr. Bender stated when interviewed. "The young patient only learns the vocabulary and gives back the words, but in a paranoid form. The youngster can get more out of the human relationship than from the supposed psychological insight.

"Many therapists also get the false idea that a child schizophrenic is cured by their therapy," Dr. Bender continued. "Actually, childhood schizophrenics go into natural remission for several years. But the child then becomes sick again during or after puberty. I do not have as much experience with adult schizophrenics, but in my opinion that ailment is also due to organic conditions."

Another childhood psychosis smeared with the psychological brush of parental guilt is *autism.* In this crippling condition, the child is emotionally defective, reacting very little to normal stimuli and living in a private and desperately lonely world. Autism strikes 1 in every 15,000 children, making it about one-fourth as common as childhood schizophrenia.

At a U.C.L.A. program for autistic children, one child endlessly occupies herself staring at her hands. Eleven-year-old Tina has been pounding her head against the sharp end of furniture since she was three. Others just rock back and forth for hours, or repeat meaningless phrases. They are neither blind nor deaf, but they seem unaware of stimuli. They are indifferent to their parents and to their brothers and sisters, who are usually normal children. Most important, they seem incapable of love. Surprisingly, some test normally on an I.Q. test. Others are subnormal or even retarded.

Autism has become a cause célèbre for the psychologically minded who see it as visible proof of unseen traumas inflicted on the child. "The autistic condition in a child is directly consequent to the wish of the mother that the child did not exist," says Dr. Bruno Bettelheim, University of Chicago psychologist. Bettelheim's theory has been made internationally prominent by his book, *The Empty Fortress,* in which parents of autistic children are cast as villains.

Bettelheim treats his autistic patients with psychoanalytic therapy, but only nature seems to determine the fate of these unfortunate children. After autistic children reach the age of five, their behavior moves toward other malfunctioning groups. Some become like the retarded, or like those with organic brain disease. Still others end up schizophrenic. There is a fourth and happier course: a near normalcy hampered only by an oddness of character and a lack of empathy for others.

Psychologist Bernard Rimland, of the Stanford Center for Advanced Study in Behavioral Sciences, is the father of an autistic child. Along with an increasing number of observers, he is convinced that the damage is organic, not psychological. Genetic studies show that the male Y chromosome of some autistic boys, and their fathers, has an unusually long arm. This is particularly interesting because the ratio of autistic boys to girls is high: 3.5 to 1.

Dr. Lorna Wing, a British physician, and the mother of an autistic child, also believes that autism will eventually prove to have an organic origin. She thinks certain illnesses in pregnancy—such as measles and measles encephalitis—increase the chance of autism.

A group of parents have formed the National Society for Autistic Children to help their children and to fight the Bettelheim school of thought. "Bettelheim obviously thinks women are idiots," Ruth Sullivan, the organization's former president, has stated. "Anyone who ever saw the deadpan face of an autistic child in his most severe stage of withdrawal could not possibly say that he was emotionally disordered. They don't have any emotions."

It was once thought that better-educated parents produced more autistic children. These families supposedly suffered from obsessive meticulousness and emotional "refrigeration." But later research reported by Drs. Ritvo and Ornitz, of the Division of Child Psychiatry at U.C.L.A., exposes that as another psychological myth. "These children come from every socioeconomic class and the parents may, or may not be, professionally employed," they state. "While some of the parents are reported to be cold, isolated or refrigerated individuals, others have proven to be quite warm, loving."

This U.C.L.A. team also reports vital evidence that shows the genetic base of autism. They showed that in a study of identical twins, with only one exception, both twins were autistic. Meanwhile, the fraternal twins were discordant for autism.

Behavioral geneticist Irving I. Gottesman, of the University of Minnesota, agrees that autism is biologically, and not psychologically, based. But he believes that the ailment is probably caused by damage during the period of pregnancy and birth, and is not inherited.

Fortunately, childhood schizophrenia and autism are not typical among psychotics. *Most schizophrenics do not break down in childhood.* They survive that period and typically become ill in late adolescence or early adulthood. Are these youngsters any different from others during their childhood?

Within the riddle of adolescence and its connection to adult schizophrenia may lie the answer to those questions. The connection between puberty and mental illness is obscure, but it obviously exists. Dr. Bender reminds us that even in childhood schizophrenia there is a remission beginning with the latency period—at age eight in girls and age ten in boys. The child temporarily improves *until* the body's hormonal storm begins at puberty.

Kraepelin's dementia praecox was considered a "precocious" schizophrenia brought on by puberty and adolescence. Kraepelin had a dim view of recovery in such cases, believing that only 4 percent get better. Recovery is now somewhat better, but Kraepelin was correct in thinking that adolescent and postadolescent schizophrenias are virtually incurable ailments, at least with our current remedies.

Recovery in schizophrenia is inversely related to age of onset. *The older one is when schizophrenia strikes, the better the chances of recovery.* At Hillside Hospital, Long Island, researchers followed up 81 well-educated, intensively treated schizophrenic patients three years after their discharge. They found that only 7 percent of the adolescents (under twenty at first hospitalization) showed "excellent" or "good" results three years later. Only 12 percent of the young adults (twenty to twenty-nine when first hospitalized) had the same good performance. But 45 percent, or almost half the older adults, showed strong improvement.

What are the dangerous early signs of schizophrenic breakdown? Unfortunately, no one sign is truly predictive. The best clue to date is a tendency to be *socially isolated* prior to the sickness. Harriet Field studied 122 males treated in childhood or adolescence at a Boston guidance center. Sixty of the group were schizophrenic. She found that those who became schizophrenic had shown "a greater tendency to withdraw" during their youth.

The Hillside Hospital researchers also found that *pre-morbid* (prior to sickness) social adjustment, and grades in school, affected the final outcome. Those who had been socially withdrawn and who had school difficulty had the least improvement. The brightest seemed to do the best. Those with "very poor" results had a mean I.Q. of 100 (average), while the "good" and "excellent" prospects had closer to a 120 I.Q.

The disease called schizophrenia obviously encompasses several emotional aberrations. As Professor K. Leonard of the Clinic for Nervous Diseases in Berlin states, "I am convinced that there is not one but several or perhaps even many dominant hereditary schizophrenias and several recessive ones."

Labeling *the schizophrenias* is a problem in itself. The classic, advanced types defined by Kraepelin are seen less today, perhaps because of the swift intervention of anti-psychotic medication. Dr. M. Straker, a U.C.L.A. psychiatrist, comments on the "increasing rarity of simple hebephrenic and catatonic schizophrenias." He points out that most schizophrenias are now "classified as either paranoid or undifferentiated."

There is also a third modern type that is increasingly diagnosed: *schizo-affective schizophrenia,* a cross of the two Kraepelin plagues of the mind. The patients may be either manic or depressed, and also suffer from certain symptoms of schizophrenia, including delusions and persecutory hallucinations. Because this ailment has one foot in the affective diseases, it apparently offers more hope for the patient than clear-cut schizophrenia.

As Dr. Klein states, "This schizophrenic subgroup benefits most from psychotropic agents and has the best long-term outcome." The treatment for schizo-affective patients is the same as for regular schizophrenics: the phenothiazines. But Klein believes that antidepressants offer "some beneficial effects" for this type of patient.

What about schizophrenia caused by traumatic events? Don't some people actually become insane in extreme situations? Yes, life can bring on a psychotic episode in some people. It is often referred to as *reactive schizophrenia,* but there is disagreement over whether it is a true schizophrenia. Although its symptoms are similar, its course is quite different.

Swiss psychiatrist Manfred Bleuler, son of Freud's colleague Eugen Bleuler, explains the types of shock that can bring it on. "For instance, they are to be found in some prisoners, or in somebody whose negligence was to blame for the death of a parent, or in a young girl after sexual trauma, or in a woman surprised by a daughter in an adulterous act," he reports.

Reactive schizophrenia has been ennobled in novels and Hollywood films, but too often it has become the public's distorted idea of mental illness. Its symptoms accurately mimic those of schizophrenia, but unlike the real disease, they recede in time. While true schizophrenia is undoubtedly the product of brain biochemical imbalance, the reactive psychosis is the result of a temporary, and not inbuilt, distortion.

Manfred Bleuler believes that even those who succumb to life-shock schizophrenia may have *some* genetic disposition to schizophrenia. "Among the relatives of patients with reactive schizophrenia, we found more schizophrenics than in the average population, but less than among the relatives of schizophrenics," Bleuler reports.

These emotional breakdowns produced by life traumas are not as common as many believe. In fact, Dr. Eli Ginzberg of Columbia University found that even war produced fewer psychoses than expected in soldiers who were supposedly susceptible to mental illness. In his documented volume, *The Lost Divisions,* Ginzberg studied men who had been exempt from service for psychiatric reasons during World War II. Many of them were suddenly called up and put into action after the Battle of the Bulge. Their breakdown rate? No different from other GIs', Dr. Ginzberg informs us.

Schizophrenia in its various forms takes its toll on 1 in every 100 persons. But perhaps as many more people are affected by the *borderline states* of mental illness. Most do not end up in mental hospitals, but they are half crippled by the distorted thinking and feeling.

One of the most common borderline groupings has been called both *pseudoneurotic schizophrenia* and *pseudoschizophrenic neurosis.*

Drs. Redlich and Freedman speak of such patients as "having few or mild schizophrenic symptoms." They suffer from severe anxiety and from a variety of other neurotic symptoms and perversions. Phobias, compulsions and depression are common in this group.

What is the prognosis for the borderline sick? Fortunately, much better than for regular schizophrenics. Dr. Roy R. Grinker, Sr., of Chicago refers to the borderline state of schizophrenia as "stable instability." The borderline sick learn to live within their environment, much as the lame learn to walk. Unlike true schizophrenics, they generally do not get worse, even if they do not usually recover. The condition seems to be a stable purgatory between the relative heaven of mental health and the hell of schizophrenia.

The borderline states are part of the schizophrenic picture, but psychiatry is also dealing with the phenomenon of *pseudoschizophrenia*—what appears to be schizophrenia, but is not. In such cases, symptoms similar to those of schizophrenia confuse the psychiatrist and set off a serious misdiagnosis.

Dr. Straker of U.C.L.A. warns that other organic and psychiatric ailments can masquerade as schizophrenia. Relying solely on symptoms such as hallucinations or distorted thinking, he says, "cannot differentiate schizophrenia from an hallucinogenic 'bad trip,' a 'silent' cerebral infarct, an early brain tumor, or Huntington's chorea."

In one study reported by Straker, twenty-six psychotics diagnosed as schizophrenics were reexamined. *Eventually, only one patient satisfied the criteria for the disease.* Thirteen of the patients were rediagnosed as manics. "There is an unusual readiness to diagnose (or misdiagnose) schizophrenia in the United States because insufficient attention is paid to the basic steps in psychiatric history-taking and examination procedures," Dr. Straker charges.

Several psychiatrists believe that some patients labeled as schizophrenics may actually have one of the *affective* diseases—either mania or depression, or manic-depressive disease. Their emotional panic mimics schizophrenia, but in such cases the phenothiazine treatment may be insufficient or even ill-advised.

Dr. A.A. Reid has outlined several diseases which "closely mimic schizophrenia," fooling both patient and doctor. He lists twenty-one conditions, beginning with an increasingly common one, the temporary psychosis brought on by amphetamine drugs.

Dr. Reid explains that drug-induced psychosis is complete with delusions of persecution and hallucinations, and "is often indistinguishable from an acute or paranoid schizophrenic illness." Many young adult schizophrenics have supposedly been "cured" in the past decade, but the cure was possible because they were not true schizophrenics. They were suffering the temporary psychotic effects of an amphetamine "bad trip." Even bromides can produce delusions of persecution not unlike those of paranoid schizophrenia.

Physical diseases can also produce the symptoms of mental illness. Acute porphyria, myxedema, toxoplasmosis, post-encephalitic condition, adrenal hyperfunction, Klinefelter's Syndrome and other organic ailments can mimic schizophrenia and confuse the psychiatrist.

Epilepsy and schizophrenia are separate diseases. But some organic relation may explain why epileptics are sometimes labeled schizophrenic by mistake. In one study of sixty epileptics, six patients suffered classical schizophrenic delusions. Dr. Reid describes a conversation with an epileptic girl which dramatizes her schizophrenia-like symptoms:

> The patient maintained that her epilepsy was in some ways caused by the moon, and that her "periods" were controlled by some outside agency. She also maintained that recently she had been observed by her mother to have new arms and had developed these new ones "immediately like a flash."

Although schizophrenia undoubtedly has an organic cause, there is professional frustration over the lack of a clear-cut diagnosis, or even an understanding of what makes someone schizophrenic. We know that diabetes is generally inherited, and is caused by a deficiency of the pancreas in making insulin. What chemical, hormone or nervous-system error is responsible for schizophrenia?

There are scores of theories, but most have failed to gain acceptance. One theory is based on the molecular similarity of the amino-acid brain-chemical *epinephrine* and the hallucination-producing *mescaline.*

Two doctors, Freidhoff and Van Winkler, have isolated a compound, DMPEA, which is a depressant on the central nervous system. They claim it was found in the urine in 67 percent of schizophrenics. Conversely, it is present in only 2 percent of normal people.

Dr. Robert G. Heath, of Tulane University, has fractionated a protein substance, *taraxein,* from the blood of schizophrenics. When injected into volunteers, taraxein supposedly produces a temporary psychotic state. Later studies by Heath led to the theory that schizophrenia is an autoimmune disorder with taraxein as an antibody. Unfortunately, attempts to replicate his work have not succeeded.

Russian researchers are now working on a theory that schizophrenia is caused by a viral infection. It has even been suggested that body type is related to the disease. Body shapes are roughly divided into three groups: *ectomorphic* (tall and slender), *mesomorphic* (stocky and muscular) and *endomorphic* (chubby and rounded). Researchers have suggested that the ectomorphic body type—tall and thin—is related to schizophrenia.

These theories have stimulated hope, but most of it has been premature. They have proved to be disappointing to both psychiatrists and patients.

Into this morass of frustration, one new idea has stimulated the psychiatric community to debate, if not to full acceptance. It is the relatively new *dopamine* theory of schizophrenia. The theory is based on both the beneficial and harmful effects of such phenothiazine drugs as chlorpromazine and thioridazine.

The phenothiazines have revolutionized the treatment of schizophrenics throughout the world. These chemicals are not merely sedatives but specific anti-schizophrenics which act on the fundamental symptoms of the disease. They activate withdrawn patients and calm hyperactive ones. The second reaction to the phenothiazines is a negative one, the *extrapyramidal* side effects on the central nervous system. This includes Parkinson's syndrome, characterized by muscular rigidity, alterations of posture and tremors.

Both effects provide clues for the dopamine theory of schizophrenia. Dopamine is one of the several brain *neurotransmitters* released by the nerves to speed communication among the billions of brain cells. Some of the neurotransmitters excite us, others are inhibitors. It is also possible, researchers believe, that some neurotransmitters communicate feelings, while others deal only with thinking.

"The dopamine theory explains a lot about schizophrenia," Dr. Solomon Snyder, professor of psychiatry and pharmacology at Johns Hopkins Medical School, said when interviewed. "Phenothiazines act on the brain by blocking the effects of dopamine. We also know that the treatment for Parkinson's Disease is l-dopa, an amino acid which is converted into dopamine by the brain. Since the main side effect of phenothiazine is a Parkinson-like syndrome, it is obvious that dopamine is involved in both cases—first in the phenothiazine's ability to relieve schizophrenic symptoms, then in creating a Parkinson-like syndrome. Research has also shown us that amphetamines and l-dopa, which release dopamine in the brain, can cause schizophrenia-like symptoms. In my opinion, the majority of psychiatrists in biochemical research today consider the dopamine theory of schizophrenia to be the most plausible one."

Some researchers reject the dopamine theory, but many prominent scientists, including Dr. Seymour Kety, professor of psychiatry at Harvard Medical School, believe that although it is far from proven, it offers substantial insight. "The involvement of dopamine in the action of anti-schizophrenic drugs is very clear," Dr. Kety stated when interviewed. "However, the possibility that disturbances in the dopamine system in the brain are involved in the cause of schizophrenia is simply a hypothesis at the present time. But it is a plausible hypothesis which deserves further evaluation."

Dr. Kety stresses that there are several other plausible theories, including the possibility that some forms of schizophrenia are the result of viruses. The *herpes simplex* virus, he explains, can affect the central nervous system and produce a psychosis not unlike schizophrenia. "There is a good bit of evidence available to construct a theory that some forms of schizophrenia are caused by viruses," Dr. Kety continued. "After all, we are probably not dealing with a single disease in schizophrenia. There may be several diseases with several causes."

The newest research in mental illness was begun in the summer of 1977, and is described by Lasker Award–winning psychiatrist Nathan Kline "as the most exciting thing I have witnessed in my more than twenty-five years of work in the field." Dr. Kline, who is director of the Rockland Research Institute in New York, has been honored twice for his work in mental illness: first in 1957 for research in treatment with the tranquilizer reserpine, and again in 1964 for research on the use of antidepressants.

The new research activity centers on a substance found normally in everyone and produced in small amounts by the pituitary gland. Dr. Kline and his colleague, Dr. Heinz Lehmann, professor of psychiatry at McGill University—who introduced the use of Thorazine into North America—have been using a new substance, *beta-endorphin*, in treating both schizophrenia and manic-depressive disease.

Surprisingly, the link to mental illness came through research in painkillers. In 1964 Dr. C. H. Li, a biochemist at the Hormone Research Laboratory at the University of California, San Francisco, isolated the human growth hormone and simultaneously discovered a substance, *beta-lipotropin*, produced by the anterior pituitary. It is a 91 amino acid polypeptide, which indicates that it is a chain made up of 91 amino acids.

Several researchers in Europe and America, including Dr. Solomon Snyder at Johns Hopkins, discovered that certain cells in the brain acted as receptors for the painkilling opiates, which include opium, codeine and morphine. Other researchers, particularly John Hughes and Hans Kosterlitz in Scotland, isolated *enkephalin,* a natural pentapeptide made up of five amino acids, which appeared to go to these brain receptors as well. It reduced pain, but only for a few minutes.

Then a researcher noted that enkephalin had the same sequence of amino acids as the beta-lipotropin discovered by C.H. Li. This started Li thinking that perhaps the beta-lipotropin, which had many more amino acids, might be a natural painkiller. He asked himself: Which animal seems the most resistant to pain? He decided it might be the camel, which travels for days through the desert heat without water. Dr. Li and a graduate student examined the pituitary gland of many camels and found that of the 91-chain amino acid the segment from 61 to 91 seemed to give the camel his greater resistance to pain. This segment was isolated by C.H. Li and was named beta-endorphin.

"The next step took place in 1977," Dr. Kline recounted when interviewed. "C.H. Li had developed a method of synthesizing the beta-endorphin and of purifying it. I had the idea of using it experimentally with the mentally ill. I know Li, and I asked for some of the substance to use on my patients in my private practice in New York City. There is some logic in the idea. It seems that the brain area, the amygdala, which is related to emotional disturbance, also has receptors which receive the painkillers.

"I began the work with Dr. Lehmann in my private practice in June 1977. Since then, we have given over fifty injections of beta-endorphin to eighteen patients with the most unusual results. When it was given to severely depressed patients, it had a positive effect within five to ten minutes. They started to become less depressed and more lively. The effect of one injection lasts about five hours. When placebos were given to these same patients, it had no effect.

"Beta-endorphin seems to work in schizophrenia as well. There is no major effect for twenty-four to seventy-two hours, then we see what appears to be relief from auditory hallucinations. There is more coherent thinking, and even some restoration of former personality. The effect lasts from two to three days. One schizophrenic patient has received six injections and has been much improved for four months. The beta-endorphin may be starting a process in which self-healing of the personality takes place. The substance seems to work in other mental conditions as well, including obsessive-compulsive illness and severe anxiety states, including agoraphobia, the fear of open spaces. The results are so surprising that I would have doubted my own observations. But Dr. Lehmann confirms it and we have video-taped some of the earlier patients." Dr. Kline is enthusiastic, but he stresses that his results have to be confirmed by other researchers.

Is beta-endorphin safe? Dr. Kline feels that this is one of its greatest assets. "It seems quite safe," he says. "The only side effect we have noticed is a little flushing, and there is no evidence that it is addictive." Researchers using beta-endorphin on animals showed that it produced severe convulsions, but Dr. Kline points out that they were using 1500-milligram doses, while his patients have been receiving only 10 milligrams of the substance.

At present, beta-endorphin is manufactured only in experimental doses by Dr. Li and costs $3000 per 10-milligram injection. However, the same substance is commercially manufactured for use in animals by two drug companies, and Dr. Li is now trying to persuade a pharmaceutical house to produce it in sufficient quantities for extensive clinical trials.

Why should beta-endorphin work, if indeed it does? Dr. Kline thinks it reduces the general anxiety level of the brain and increases gratification. It also seems related to the brain neurotransmittters and is compatible with the dopamine theory of schizophrenia.

"Dr. Kline's research is exciting, and it has some basis in psychiatric theory, but we must be cautious until it is confirmed," says Dr. Solomon Snyder, a pioneer in opiate brain receptor work. "In the long history of psychiatric research, we have often gone astray because the research was not double-blind. In a double-blind study, the researcher does not know which of his patients are receiving the active drug and which are being given the placebo. Because of the small amount of beta-endorphin available, Dr. Kline could not do that. So we must wait and see if his work is later confirmed in double-blind studies."

Dr. Snyder is cautious about the work, but he does feel there may be scientific logic in the effect of beta-endorphin on the mentally ill. "Firstly, its action may be similar to that of morphine—it makes you feel good and the depressive and schizophrenic symptoms are lessened," he says. "In fact, the opiates were a major treatment for mental disorders until we learned that they were dangerously addictive, and that it required more and more of the same opiate to get a beneficial effect. Secondly, we do know that there is a lot of dopamine in the amygdala, which is the brain's emotional center. In fact, dopamine neurons are concentrated in the central nucleus of this area. The enkephalin and opiate receptors are also concentrated here. The beta-endorphin might be going directly to the amygdala, being picked up by the receptors and producing a distinct positive change in feeling."

Dr. Snyder points out that there is another possible problem: the question of addiction. Beta-endorphin was shown to be addictive in animals, he says. Thus far, Dr. Kline has not seen addiction in humans, and since beta-endorphin is also a human body product, it might not be addictive. But this, Dr. Snyder stresses, has yet to be proven.

The need to understand and conquer mental illness is vital. *Psychotic disorder* refers to all serious emotional disorders, of which schizophrenia represents the largest subgroup of hospitalized patients. Rivaling schizophrenia in destructive power are the *affective diseases:* mania, depression and the manic-depressive disorders.

As we have seen, Kraepelin divided mental illness into two categories: dementia praecox, characterized by an unfavorable course, and the manic-depressive psychoses with their more favorable outcome. Affective cases do show the most recovery, but manic-depressives do not always run a favorable course. In fact, many suicides take place in the depressive stages of the disease.

No one can avoid feelings of periodic depression. But this is not psychotic behavior. Psychotic or *retarded depression* is not just reaction to grief, or unhappiness produced by an unrewarding life or unsuccessful search for love. These come from external stimuli, while severe depression is more often *endogenous,* from within.

Psychotic depression is an insidious biologically based ailment which affects both the mind and the body. It creates a general slowdown in psychomotor activity. In some cases the onset is hormonal. It may be triggered by a postpartum psychosis, which strikes susceptible women after childbirth. Or it may be set off by the hormonal change of menopause. Or it may come on spontaneously without any apparent stimulus.

This biochemical despair is part of a disease state which, like cancer or diabetes, affects every organ of the body. There is a loss of appetite, an irregularity of sleep patterns, a lessening of sexual drive. An added punishment is an apparent blockage of the thinking process, making the depressed person seem less "bright" than before. Delusions of sin, guilt, poverty and unworthiness are common.

Researchers at Washington University School of Medicine in St. Louis have set ten simple criteria for depression. They include: poor appetite, weight loss, sleep difficulty, loss of energy, agitation, constipation, decreased sexual drive, loss of concentration, slowed thinking and thoughts of suicide. If a person has six of the ten, they are considered "depressed."

The depressed person's existence might seem reasonable, even excellent to an observer. But no amount of talking will usually change the depressed person's pessimistic view. If the depressed state does not end in suicide or slip over into psychotic behavior, it will generally lift, only to be followed by another attack, weeks, months or years later.

The obverse side of the psychic coin is *mania,* a state of euphoria and excitability in which the person's psychomotor activity is speeded up. The crude analogy with a movie camera is not inappropriate. If depression is life in slow motion, mania is a speeded-up camera image with all the distortions of a Keystone Kops movie. The mind seems to operate at optimum speed, but judgment is usually lost in the haste. There is flight of ideas, a grandiose self-image and often a desire for extravagant spending.

It has been said that many successful business and creative people are somewhat manic. This may be true, for a heightened psychomotor activity is invaluable in competitive society. However, such people are usually spared acute mania or the reverse—deep depression.

Psychiatrists now believe there are two subgroups within *primary affective disorders.* One is *unipolar,* in which the only malfunction is depression. The other is *bipolar,* or manic-depressive, disease. In that crippling ailment, the person moves from mania to depression and back.

Like schizophrenia, affective disorders run in families. Dr. George Winokur studied the parents and siblings of 325 patients with either manic or depressive disorders at the Iowa Psychopathic Hospital. Of the 1187 relatives, 160 had some form of the disease, a morbidity risk of 13.5 percent—or 1 in 7.

Evidence is mounting that the affective diseases are also genetically based and inherited. Once again, we look at twin studies for corroboration. In six separate studies of manic-depressive diseases,

92 sets of twins were examined. *In almost three-fourths of the cases, the other identical twin also had manic-depressive disease.* For comparison, the investigators also studied fraternal twins, both of whom had manic-depressive disease only 19 percent of the time.

Dr. Elliot S. Gershon, of the National Institute of Mental Health, believes the genetic base of depression and manic-depressive disease has been proven. "Genetic factors are of great importance in determining who will manifest affective illness. Whatever the major etiologic factors are, they are largely heritable," he states.

Suicide is the main threat in affective disorders. At the worst point of the depressive cycle, life is so painful that suicide seems almost reasonable. Researchers estimate that the mortality among such cases is 15 percent: one in every seven kills himself. The rate is about the same whether it is a case of unipolar depression or manic-depressive disease.

The suicide rate among relatives of the ill is also abnormally high. Of 1187 parents and siblings of sick patients in the Iowa study, 36 (3 percent) had committed suicide. This figure is much higher than the national average, and three times higher than the suicide rate of relatives of schizophrenics.

How common are depression and manic-depressive disease? George Winokur and Ferris N. Pitts estimate that approximately 2 percent of the population have some form of affective disease. This would make it twice as prevalent as schizophrenia.

Some studies estimate the damage as even greater. A population study of Iceland done by Dr. T. Helgason showed that *5 percent* of the females and *3 percent* of the males had serious affective disorders. Even at the 2 percent level, we are dealing with a disease that will strike almost 5 million Americans now living, and 70 million people worldwide. To this we must add the havoc caused among hundreds of millions of their children, spouses and parents.

The spread of all mental illness is unchecked. As the new psychochemical intervention saves millions from deterioration, they marry and have children, enlarging the gene pool of mental illness. Only by finding the method of genetic transmission and the brain chemistry involved will we be able to understand and conquer it. As we have seen, psychiatry's half-century-old flirtation with psychological efforts to treat mental illness and its attempt to understand it in psychological terms have been useless.

A major genetic discovery may have taken place in the last five years. Dr. Ronald R. Fieve, professor of clinical psychiatry at Columbia Presbyterian Medical Center, and colleagues at the New York State Psychiatric Institute believe they have uncovered a link in the genetic transmission of manic-depressive disease. Their sample was 120 patients referred to their Lithium Clinic.

They think the genetic carrier is the X, or female, sex chromosome. On each of the forty-six chromosomes are located thousands of the genes which shape the human being, both physically and mentally. The exact location on the X chromosome for the gene for manic-depressive disease is not known, but Fieve reports that he has connected several factors that may eventually pinpoint it.

The technique is an ingenious one called *genetic linkage*. We tend to inherit several unrelated traits merely because the genes are closely located on one of the chromosomes. The closer the genes are to each other, the better the chances their traits will be passed on together. By using markers, geneticists have been able to "map" several genes, including the ones for red-green color blindness, and another for a blood group.

Researchers, including Dr. Winokur, had previously found a measurable, but not consistent, linkage between red-green color blindness and manic-depression. Then in 1972 Fieve reported that a linkage exists between manic-depressive illness and the Xg blood group. Fieve found six patients whose families showed a correlation between Xg blood group and manic-depressive disease in three successive generations. This double gene correlation, Fieve believes, indicates that the X chromosome may be the manic-depressive carrier we have been searching for. But Fieve stresses that not everyone who has either Xg blood type or color blindness is necessarily susceptible to manic-depressive disease.

Dr. Fieve hopes to pinpoint the specific manic-depressive gene. Data published in the *American Journal of Human Genetics* by Remwick and Schulze showed that Xg blood group and color blindness are far apart on the chromosome. "Our results are consistent with their report," Fieve says. "The loci for manic-depressive illness appear to lie between the Xg locus and the color blindness loci, although they may be closer to the latter."

Six years after his report there is considerable controversy over Fieve's genetic research. Some investigators have found a similar linkage, but others have been unable to replicate it. "I believe that at least one subtype of manic-depressive disease will prove to be X chromosome–linked," Dr. Fieve stated when interviewed.

Scientific opinion is divided on how affective disorders are actually inherited. At Washington University, St. Louis, researchers used a computational model to analyze the family tree of one hundred psychiatric outpatients. They conclude that unipolar depression is probably passed on through several polygenes rather than through a single, dominant gene. However, one of the study authors points out that there are possibly several types of psychotic depression, each with its own method of genetic transmission.

As in schizophrenia, there is a biochemical theory that describes how depression may be created in the brain of certain patients, particularly those with severe endogenous depression. The major chemicals involved in mood changes are believed to be the *neurotransmitters*—a group of biogenic amines which include norepinephrine, dopamine, serotonin and others. When these are in some unknown balance at the key points—the nerve cell synapses—a normal, or moderate, mood is maintained in the brain.

Naturally, there will be periods of elation and depression in us all, but the extremes of mania and severe depression will not take place in those without a disorder. In the amphetamine ("speed") user, for example, there is a quick discharge of norepinephrine and dopamine resulting in the "high." Conversely, the brain chemical serotonin seems to be related to sleep and depression. According to the serotonin theory, some severely depressed people have a low level of serotonin, or the neurotransmitter is not acting properly within the brain.

The theory is debated within psychiatry, but some experiments, including one performed in Stockholm, seem to substantiate that there are lower levels of serotonin in some severely depressed patients. Swedish researcher Marie Asberg measured the spinal fluid of severely depressed patients who had attempted suicide and found that a metabolic product of serotonin was lower than normal in these patients, indicating a deficiency of the vital neurotransmitter.

Why then, we might ask, don't we give serotonin as an effective remedy for depression? Unfortunately, like some chemicals, serotonin will not pass through the brain's membrane barrier. Recently, a Dutch researcher, Herman van Praag, has sought to get around this obstacle by giving patients a metabolic precursor of serotonin, 5HTP, as a treatment. He found that the patients' depression improved significantly.

Such research is encouraging but still not confirmed. But at New York University Medical School, Dr. Samuel Gershon has conducted an experiment which adds further credibility to the serotonin hypothesis. Depressed patients were placed in two groups and given either of the two popular antidepressants, Tofranil or an MAO inhibitor. Those who showed some initial improvement were again divided into two groups, each of which received an additional medication.

One group was given AMPT, which blocks the manufacture of norepinephrine, while the other group received PCPA, a chemical that blocks the manufacture of serotonin. "We found that the improvement stopped in those patients who had received the PCPA," Dr. Gershon explained when interviewed. "Then, when the PCPA was withdrawn, the improvement continued unabated. The work still has to be confirmed, but it does help to substantiate the serotonin theory."

If lack of serotonin is at the base of much serious depression, then antidepressants might be developed that tend to increase serotonin availability in the brain. One such drug, chlorimipramine (Anafranil) is used in Europe, but has not yet been approved for use in America. Dr. Asberg in Sweden has found it valuable both against depression and in helping patients with obsessive-compulsive rituals.

Whatever its exact cause, there is little doubt that psychotic depression is biological in origin. This was reinforced by the discovery of chemicals that could change the depressive mood. It was a work of serendipity. In the early 1950s, patients in a tubercular sanatorium in New York were being treated with an anti-tubercular drug, iproniazid. In addition to the effect on T.B., it seemed to lift the spirits of depressed tubercular patients.

The medication was subsequently found to be a *monoamine oxidase inhibitor,* a drug that blocks the action of the monoamine oxidase, the enzyme that makes some of the neurotransmitters ineffective. In 1957 a Swiss psychiatrist developed the second generation of mood drugs, the *tricyclic antidepressants,* the most common of which are *imipramine* and *amitriptyline,* known to most by their trade names of Tofranil and Elavil.

Unfortunately, the tricyclic antidepressants take a long time to work, sometimes as much as four weeks. During this time the patient is often severely depressed and may be suicide-prone. Norwich Hospital in Connecticut studied the response of twenty-one acutely depressed patients who were given imipramine. Fifteen responded to treatment, while six did not. The first patient responded in seven days, but one patient did not respond until the twenty-sixth day of treatment. It took two weeks on the average for the medication to work, and it helped 74 percent of the patients.

Researchers have been trying to eliminate this dangerous delay. University of North Carolina researchers treated twenty depressed patients with the antidepressant plus a thyroid hormone, T-3, and found that it quickened the antidepressant effect. They point out that "the omnipresent danger of suicide makes speed of treatment a prime consideration." There may be difficult side effects from the thyroid, but in severe cases, speed may be vital.

Who is subject to severe depression? As we have seen, family history of the disease is important. But what about psychodynamic theory? If a child has had a traumatic early life, wouldn't that predispose him to later depression?

Evidence indicates that the answer is "no." A British psychiatrist, Dr. K.L. Granville-Grossman, studied the childhood experiences of adult depressives. He made a comprehensive review of the literature looking for obvious injuries to childhood psyche: divorce of their parents, death of a parent or a sibling, severe conflict between parents, illegitimacy, broken homes. The result? Granville-Grossman states that these studies do not support "the view that early environment is of etiological importance in the affective disorders."

Although childhood experience is probably not important, the sex of the person apparently is. Women seem to become the victims of severe depression much more than men. In one study at New York State Psychiatric Institute, 168 of 203 depressed patients were women. In another study of 555 depressed patients conducted by Allen Raskin of the National Institute of Mental Health, 71 percent of the patients were women. A report on 115 manic-depressed patients at the Barnes Hospital in St. Louis showed that 74 percent were women, a figure that substantiates the approximately 3–1 female-to-male ratio in both depression and other affective disorders.

Severe depression is also related to age: it increases as we get older. Although young people can become severely depressed, the median age for unipolar (depressed only) patients is forty-five years. By contrast, the manic-depressive patient (bipolar) is first struck at a median age of only thirty.

The theory that both women and older people are more prone to severe depression received corroboration from a University of Vermont College of Medicine study. Researchers speculated that since MAO inhibitors blocked depression, monoamine oxidase was probably implicated in the creation of depression. They studied the MAO blood levels in 113 volunteers ranging in age from twenty-one to eighty-four, and also checked the MAO activity directly in the brain during twenty-six autopsies. They found that MAO activity was higher in older people, and that women had significantly higher MAO blood activity than men.

What is the best treatment for severe depression? A consensus of organically oriented psychiatrists feels it is fourfold: (1) the tricyclic antidepressants, (2) electroconvulsive therapy (ECT), (3) monoamine oxidase inhibitors and (4) lithium when manic-depressive illness is involved. Surprisingly, the most seriously ill—those who have an *endogenous, retarded* or *severe* depression—respond best. It is probably an indication that their ailments are biological, not psychological, in origin.

As in schizophrenia, psychotherapy is of no significant value. Dr. Joseph Schildkraut, of Harvard Medical School, notes that both psychotherapy and placebos are inadequate in treating these serious depressions. An experiment at Johns Hopkins School of Medicine confirmed this failure. Depressed women outpatients were given one of three medications, and sent to either weekly group psythotherapy sessions or only brief biweekly contact at a clinic. As the report states: *"No advantage for group therapy was detected."* There was, however, a marked therapeutic advantage for imipramine drug treatment.

The placebo is of no significant value, either, in mental illness, but it plays a part in treatment of *less severe* depressions. The reason is simple. The placebo does nothing biochemically, but it permits the minor depression to do what nature intended: get better by itself.

At Camarillo State Hospital in California, investigators treated 74 depressed patients with either a placebo or a tricyclic antidepressant. Of those on antidepressants, 77 percent were either completely better or moderately improved after treatment. Of those who had been given the placebo instead, 52 percent showed the same gain. Surprisingly, those with *neurotic* or *reactive* depressions did as well on the placebo as they did on the drug. But those who had severe *endogenous* depression did much better on the antidepressant drug.

Donald F. Klein and J.M. Davis pooled the results of 36 studies on depression treatment with both placebo and imipramine antidepressant. The results showed that placebo had a 39 percent improvement rate, while the antidepressant showed a 70 percent improvement.

Several facts emerge from these studies. First, many cases of depression are self-curing. Secondly, we are probably dealing with two depressive diseases. One depression is a reaction to life stress and thus called psychoneurotic or *reactive depression.* The second is a severe *endogenous* or *retarded depression* with its basis in an unbalanced body chemistry, probably a result of genetic inheritance.

This distinction between these two depressions is made by several psychiatrists, including Drs. Winokur and Pitts, who have studied the personalities of people who were later struck with severe depression. *They found that unlike neurotics, those who become psychotically depressed had relatively stable and non-neurotic personalities before the onset of the disease.* The only hint of their future breakdown was in their family history.

Electroconvulsive therapy (ECT) is an effective treatment for serious depressions. Dr. Jonathan O. Cole, of McLean Hospital in Massachusetts, calls ECT a "safe, effective, and remunerative treatment for depression," adding that the ECT treatment works "very frequently."

But antidepressants are generally the treatment of choice, mainly because of their ease of administration. Unfortunately, the chemical cure can sometimes have negative effects. Dr. Allen Raskin, of the National Institute of Mental Health, warns that imipramine can activate psychotic, manic and hostile behavior in certain people. He suggests that this may be a clue that the patient is actually manic-depressive and not merely depressed.

The antidepressants have other unwelcome side effects. The MAO inhibitors have triggered serious hypertensive and vascular accidents in some patients. The problem proved to be foods such as cheese, beer, chicken liver which had a high *tyramine* level and were dangerous when mixed with MAO inhibitors. Patients on the drug must be careful not to eat the implicated foods. The tricyclic antidepressants do not react in this way, but the MAO inhibitors are sometimes necessary in treatment.

Manic-depressive disease presents a more difficult problem, for it involves both mania and depression. What is needed is *one* drug to handle that maddening psychosis and prevent its recurrence.

That drug may be lithium carbonate. In 1949 Australian psychiatrist J. Cade reported that lithium salts seemed to reduce the excitation of psychotic mania. Since then, the psychiatric community has found lithium carbonate a valuable medication. "The effectiveness of lithium carbonate in the treatment and prevention of manic-depressive psychoses, manic type, has been documented," write Drs. Douglas R. Bey and Robert E. Chapman. *But,* these psychiatrists stress, its role in preventing depression and in treating schizo-affective disorders is less clear.

Its best performance to date has been in curbing mania. Dr. Christiaan Van der Velde, research psychiatrist at Norwich (Connecticut) Hospital, tested lithium carbonate on 75 manic-depressive patients who were in their manic stage. They were followed up for a period of three years. Fifty-five of the patients (73 percent) responded well to the lithium, showing a "marked reduction of their acute manic symptoms" within fourteen days after taking the drug.

In addition to its power in curbing acute mania, lithium is considered useful in preventing recurring bouts of the manic-depressive cycle. Between 1967 and 1975 Dr. Ronald Fieve comprehensively studied the preventive power of lithium on approximately one hundred patients at the New York Psychiatric Institute. Some of the patients received lithium while others were given a sugar placebo. "In terms of all indices—hospitalization, well time at the clinic, rating of intensity of depressive relapse and the frequency of needing additional antidepressant medication—the lithium heavily outperformed the placebo," says Dr. Fieve. "I found lithium to be three times as effective as the placebo—eighty percent versus twenty-eight percent—in the prevention of further episodes."

Another study was done by the Veterans Administration with 205 hospitalized manic-depressives in eighteen hospitals. After their discharge, they were treated with either lithium carbonate or a placebo, then followed up two years later. The results showed that 67 percent of the placebo patients had serious relapses, against only 31 percent of the lithium carbonate patients.

Researchers hoped that lithium's seeming miraculous powers might extend to treating depression, but the results have been very mixed. When Dr. Ronald Fieve treated acutely depressed manic-depressive patients with lithium, he concluded that it was only a "mild" antidepressant.

What are some of the negative factors against this inexpensive, readily available drug? There are several, but lithium's strongest drawback is that it is a poison when it reaches high levels in the blood. Psychiatrists at the University of Rochester warn that "almost 80 percent of our patients have experienced some kind of adverse side effects" with lithium, although most of them are minor.

The amount of lithium in the blood is monitored regularly during treatment to keep it at safe levels. Drs. Bey and Chapman, who run a lithium clinic in Illinois, show that the initial side effects are often an upset stomach (including nausea and loose stools), thirst, a dazed feeling, muscular weakness and a fine resting tremor. But these signs generally disappear after a few weeks, they add optimistically.

The toxic effects of lithium that patients must watch out for are sluggishness, drowsiness, slurred speech, coarse tremor, muscular twitching, vomiting and diarrhea. When these signs appear, the lithium should be stopped until the blood levels are checked and the dosage adjusted.

During the last decade, there has been more progress made in understanding and treating mental illness than during the still-potent half-century reign of Freudian superstition. But the psychological input into insanity is still a detrimental factor, both as a confusing method of understanding its cause, and as a false system of treatment.

There are still psychoanalytically oriented psychiatrists who refuse to use the new medication. Or if they do, it is done grudgingly. They claim the medication will mask the patient's symptoms and will make psychotherapy more difficult. Dr. Donald Klein attacks this attitude as one of professional vanity. "Not infrequently," Dr. Klein says, "this belief masks a Messianic attitude that the patient's improvement should be entirely attributed to the inspired personal impact of the therapist."

The intrusion of psychotherapy and abstruse Freudian theory into the serious business of medical psychiatry has been an American excess. In England, psychotherapy is almost totally divorced from treatment of the ill. Dr. Hugh Freeman, a Manchester, England, psychiatrist and one of the early researchers in injectable prolixin, is convinced that America's Freudian involvement has done serious damage. "America's enchantment with psychoanalytic psychotherapy has done more to retard psychiatry in America than any other factor," he stated when interviewed.

The English divorcement of psychiatry from Freudian psychological theory is obvious. At Springfield Hospital, a state institution in a London suburb, patients live in a cheerful, sympathetic atmosphere. They come in desperately ill, and are given the same medical treatments as in American hospitals. They leave greatly improved *without* having received psychological intervention, either in the form of psychotherapy or as extensive probing to find the supposed childhood cause of the illness.

American psychiatry is torn between the new stirrings of the biological sciences and its twentieth-century history of religious Freudianism. It lives and works with one foot in science and the other in mysticism. This schism is represented by a continual internecine battle between the Freudian and neo-Freudians in one camp, and the scientifically oriented psychiatrists in the other. The fight rages within institutions and between them.

As heads of psychiatric departments change, institutions move from one camp to another, hiring those who represent their point of view. Columbia Medical Center, which had traditionally been psychoanalytically oriented, is now moving rapidly into the scientific fold. Other institutions which had been organically based are moving backwards into the arcane mysteries of the Viennese seer.

The split between mysticism and science is even apparent in American patients. Most are now treated with new medication, but are often simultaneously indoctrinated in Freudian psychoanalytic theory. One twenty-eight-year-old New York single woman suffered from deep depression. She was hospitalized for six months, during which time she was treated with an MAO inhibitor. The change was extraordinary. Her depression lifted, she has returned to work and an active life.

How does she account for her sickness? Despite the success of the medication, she has been convinced that her depression was the result of sibling rivalry against her sister, and of her unresolved competition with an unloving father. The patient, like most in the Psychological Society, failed to connect cause and cure. Her father is still ostensibly unloving, but the depression has lifted.

Events move quickly in the psychiatric world, but one fact is indisputable. As scientific advance continues in finding the cause of schizophrenia and the affective psychoses, and new treatments are developed to cure these scourges, the primitive, cultist views of the Freudian revolution will recede as effectively as did the centuries-old theory of "humors" causing sickness within the human body.

# The
# Psychoanalytic
# Ritual

A SENIOR ANALYST AT THE St. Louis Psychoanalytic Foundation greeted his patient, a tall, attractive twenty-six-year-old housewife and mother of two small children. In pre-analytic interviews, she had been diagnosed as suffering from "a mixed psychoneurosis with phobic conversion and depression symptoms and free-floating anxiety."

She began her preliminary analytic session in a chair facing her analyst, who carefully explained *free association* to her. She was to say whatever came into her mind, no matter how repulsive, irrelevant or painful. Nothing was to block her thoughts, memories or the retelling of her dreams. The analyst would not interrupt unless she was being unproductive, or he felt a deep analytic *interpretation* was called for.

The patient then moved to the couch. In addition to the trivia of everyday life, much of which bores analysts, the St. Louis housewife soon unfolded an esoteric, stylized narration that exists nowhere except in the sanctuary of the analytic room:

Analyst: You feel as if you're a bug and your father is a snake. What comes to your mind?
Patient: It's all vicious. The snake eats the bug. It's horrible!—It's so hard to believe that little girls can have thoughts like this.—

Analyst: How do you mean?

Patient: That they can think about penises—... Now I think about my father's penis inside of me, but it's all too adult. It makes me so nervous and it's so ugly. I feel so depressed and like it's the end of the world.

Analyst: Let's try to follow the thought about your father's penis being inside of you. Then what happens?

Patient: Now I can picture myself growing bigger. The penis is inside of me. It gets bigger and bigger and now I'm it!— It's the same old thing. Ugh! I become the penis and I am inside my mother.

Analyst: Let's go on—You're the penis and you're inside of Mother. Now what comes to mind?

Patient: —It's all so dark!— ... Now I go into Mother ... I'll destroy her and I'll destroy the baby up there.—I'm going to tear everything up!—Who is that baby? Is it me or is it my sister?—Now I feel so mad! Good God!—I want to go in there and I want to be born again and this time be born with a penis!

We have not eavesdropped on a psychotic episode. This bizarre dialogue, later published as part of a full analysis by her psychoanalyst, is a near-perfect exposition of psychoanalytic theory. The patient had reached an elevated level of fantasy, and in one explosive burst she relived three of the most telling Freudian theories. She had unconsciously experienced intercourse with her father in a replay of the *Oedipus complex;* she had found the beloved penis which would dispel female *penis envy;* she had even considered violent murder of her embryonic sister, a reenactment of Freud's hostile *sibling rivalry.*

This ritual of classical psychoanalysis is the esoteric core of the entire Psychological Society. For in the hierarchy of that Society, the classical psychoanalyst is the high priest and the prophet, while the patient—the *analysand*—is considered the recipient of the purest form of psychic repair.

No profession has influenced modern society more than Freudian psychoanalysis, and no professional has been so exalted. No discipline is more gossiped about and discussed, yet none is as little understood. Excessive praise, half-truths, distortions, cocktail-party popularizations of analysis are common. Yet in our heavily psychologized civilization, the intimate truths about psychoanalysis and psychoanalysts are secreted just as strenuously as its message is propagated into the mainstream.

Psychoanalysis has been touched with magic; few phenomena have so intrigued modern man. Statistically, only 1 in 7 psychiatrists and 1 in 50 patients are involved in actual psychoanalysis. Yet this elite theory and therapy dominates medical psychiatry in America and psychotherapy worldwide.

To the majority of psychological and psychiatric professionals, it holds the exalted position of *the* explanation of the mind. Some therapists like to flaunt their differences with Freudian analysis, or even to disparage it. Yet virtually all—from the neo-Freudians to "I'm OK, you're OK" advocates—have been spawned from this psychoanlytic art, or *science,* as its practitioners happily call it.

In the authoritative *Psychological Issues,* psychologists David Shakow and David Rapaport point up analysis' professional power. Freud, they say, "is the fountainhead of dynamic psychology in general, and of psychology's present-day conceptions of motivations and of the unconscious in particular."

Ever since Freud first used the term "Psycho-Analysis" in a French essay on March 30, 1896, it has changed the inner vocabulary of millions. We have learned to view our emotional instability, even our normal behavior, through the semantic prism of Freudian dogma. We now openly ruminate about our sexual repressions, psychosomatic rumblings, ambivalent love-and-hate relationships, hidden motivations and the psychopathology of our everyday slips.

So prestigious is psychoanalysis that most people purposely confuse it with less expensive, briefer psychotherapies. Many who bare their psyche to a "shrink," a "doctor," "therapist," "counselor," "psychologist," "psychiatric social worker" or "psychiatrist" boast that they have been "psychoanalyzed." Others who are not aware of the difference between analysis and psychotherapy believe that they too have been, or are, in analysis.

Even opposing therapies are often mislabeled as psychoanalysis. New York psychologist Andrew Salter, a prominent practitioner of anti-analytic behavior therapy, recalls that a former patient, actress Dyan Cannon, spoke glowingly in a women's magazine article about her "psychoanalysis" with him.

The power of Freudian psychoanalysis stems from a mystique unequaled in the Western world. It creates a new level of believability in arcane phenomena. Its sexual theories are titillating, even shocking, to a public not moved by popular obscenity. Its complexity intrigues the intellectually oriented, for whom its intrapsychic revelations hold an endless fascination.

Psychoanalysis became a significant entity with Freud's turn-of-the-century cures of conversion hysteria. It has since transformed the analyst's office into a hushed sanctuary where his successors are expected to repeat the miracles of the Viennese master.

Its greatest victory worldwide has been its ascendancy in American psychiatry. Dr. Alfred M. Freedman, past president of the American Psychiatric Association, drew the Freudian shape of that profession when interviewed at the New York Medical College. "Psychoanalysis has been incorporated into American psychiatry through our leading teaching hospitals and medical schools," he explained. "Psychiatrists in training are heavily indoctrinated in analytic notions, and their psychotherapy training is psychoanalytically oriented. Their supervisors are usually oriented in the same direction, and even if the resident does not take formal analytic training, his mind is full of Freudian theories. In our institution, for example, the principal supervisors of psychotherapy training are psychoanalysts."

Both the enemies and the adherents of psychoanalysis agree that the marriage of medicine and the Freudian unconscious has been a potent one. Prominent English psychiatrist Dr. William Sargant, former head of psychiatry at St. Thomas Hospital, bemoans the power of psychoanalysis in American psychiatry. When interviewed at his London home, he repeated a previous indictment that he is "bewildered at the way direction and control of American psychiatry has been taken over since World War Two by psychoanalysis."

Dr. Sargant's observations are statistically verifiable. Over half the departments of psychiatry of American medical schools are headed by psychoanalysts. This power has not been lost on ambitious young psychiatrists. "Most of our psychiatric teachers are psychoanalysts who trained in analysis after World War Two," a chief psychiatric resident at a large Eastern hospital explains. "They are appealing models, both for intellectual and practical reasons. Most residents do not intend to become full-time psychoanalysts, but most of us are being analyzed as part of our training. When we first began residency, thirty percent to forty percent were in analysis, but by the time we completed training, at least eighty percent were being psychoanalyzed either as patients or in training analysis as part of psychoanalytic preparation."

At Mount Sinai Hospital in New York, a professor of psychiatry estimates that at least two-thirds of the psychiatric residents are already in personal psychoanalysis. The figure is as high at Columbia University, which maintains its own analytic institute. Although Freudian influence is less dominant outside metropolitan areas, it is still a thriving psychiatric power coast-to-coast. One psychiatrist trained at a Southwestern medical school recalls that only two students were then in psychoanalysis. By the time they finished residencies throughout the country, more than half had been analyzed.

Accurate tales of spending ten, even fifteen years or more on the couch astound the public. Psychoanalysis was once a brief process in which Freud treated most of his patients in a matter of weeks or months. Freud relates the case of a young woman who could not walk because of an acute pain in her legs. "After an analysis lasting nine months, the trouble disappeared and the patient, whose character was truly sound and estimable, was able once more to take her place in life," he explains.

Today's patient would welcome a return to Freud's nine-month cure. Bringing the patient to *genital maturity* (or to be a "mensch," as professionals say) now requires more and more horizontal time on the couch. In the 1972 *Biographical-Professional Survey,* analysts answered that the typical length of their last completed analyses was five to six years. Only 2 percent lasted less than two years, and some 30 percent between three to four years. Almost 1 in 5 patients had spent more than seven years in analysis.

This increase in couch time is corroborated by the training analyses of *candidates,* young psychiatrists studying the calling. In 1946–47, the typical one took 609 hours, or three years; by 1968, it had gone to 899 hours. A recent American Psychoanalytic Association (APsaA) study shows it is now 1000 hours, or five years, and rising. Eventually, psychoanalysis may become, as Freud hinted in 1937, a lifelong activity for the devoted.

With cheaper, briefer psychotherapies now available, who seeks out this lengthy procedure, and why? Analysands are surprisingly few in number: currently only 30,000 patients in the United States, perhaps 40,000 worldwide. But they represent a cross section of the upper-echelon neurotic population of the Psychological Society. When Drs. H. Aronson and Walter Weintraub, of the University of Maryland, surveyed 144 analytic patients, they found they were typically high-income and highly educated individuals. "My patients are the same kind of people I meet in my social set," comments one Washington, D.C., psychoanalyst.

Analysis is the therapy for high-status individuals. In the five-level Hollingshead scale of social position, almost all (94 percent) of the Maryland analytic patients were in the highest two categories, as opposed to a normal 10 percent. Their educational level was extraordinary: 50 percent had completed graduate school; 83 percent were at least college graduates. Thirty percent were working minions of the Society, members of the psychological helping professions.

Therapists are drawn to analysis not only because they hope to gain personal insight, but because "being analyzed" has become a psychic badge of prestige that helps professional advancement. "The high proportion of patients in the 'helping' areas may partially explain the fact that the knowledge of analysis is much broader in modern psychiatry than the actual number of patients would warrant," say the Maryland surveyors.

Analysis is also a therapy of the relatively young. More than half the patients were in their thirties; only 3 percent were fifty or over. There was a strong representation of Jewish patients, a tendency possibly related to the large number of Jewish analysts, a tradition begun by Freud and his disciples.

In the Maryland study, 40 percent of the patients were Jewish; 33 percent, Protestant; 13 percent, Catholic; and 12 percent, without affiliation. An American Psychoanalytic Association study generally confirms these figures. They report 45.2 Jewish patients, 43.6 Protestant and 10.1 percent Catholic.

Some patients are drawn to analysis by the hope of a psychological miracle, *a structural personality change* instead of the supposedly "cheap and dirty" symptom cures of quicker therapies. The educated and intellectually pretentious seek out analysis because of its verbal interplay and the creative input required of the patient. For them, the analysis becomes an emotionally and sexually lurid novel of their psychic life.

A full-scale psychoanalysis has another unspoken attraction: prestige. It provides the only direct link, only one or two generations removed, to the prophet Freud. It is as if one could absorb the glories of Christianity today at the foot of Peter. "Among the dynamic therapies analysis ranks high in prestige for the analysand," state the Maryland researchers. "A patient who 'possesses' an analyst is much in the position of a man who owns a handmade violin."

The analysand is more than a patient. In some peculiar way, he is initiated into the analytic guild as a junior member who is expected to propagate the faith. In the 1920s–1950s, it was the analyzed artists, writers, intellectuals, societal leaders, even status-hungry Hollywood stars, who brought psychoanalysis to public attention. Marshall Field and other members of the status community of the thirties and forties found relief on the couch of such stellar analysts as Gregory Zilboorg. They passed the word to the new postwar sub-elite through books, novels, plays and Hollywood-fabricated psychological films.

Possessing the "handmade" instrument of analysis is expensive. Analysis is a dollar-consuming regimen. A dollar a minute—$50 for fifty minutes—is standard in analytic center, the island of Manhattan. But many analysts are now charging $60 an hour. A young New York analyst may settle for $40, the going rate in such smaller centers as Seattle. Analytic stars can command outlandishly high rates; one aging New York analyst who studied with Freud charges $100 an hour.

The most common frequency is four sessions a week. Using a modest $40-an-hour mean, the average analysis costs $8000 a year, or a total of $44,000. At a not uncommon $50 an hour, five days a week, it rises to $62,500. For the 1 in 7 whose couch time is seven years, the analytic bill will be a most impressive $84,000.

Less expensive analysis is available to the public at institute clinics, where patients are analyzed by student candidates. At the prestigious New York Psychoanalytic Institute Clinic on East 82nd Street, the maximum charge is $25 an hour.

The psychoanalytic process that supports this entire establishment has been at the center of a raging debate for seventy-five years, a controversy that is now accelerating. Unfortunately, much of the argument is based on misinformation about the art, for psychoanalysis is mired in distortion. This confusion is often inevitable, for psychoanalysis operates as a semisecret vocation under the aegis of a suspicious guild. With the same fervor with which it seeks converts, the profession conceals the details of what actually goes on behind its closed analytic doors.

To effectively peer behind those doors and put the modern analyst, his theories and practices on the sociological couch, we have called upon all sources—friendly, heretical and antagonistic. But in defining psychoanalysis, we have relied upon authentic Freudian authority. Otherwise, the overview is vulnerable to acerbic, even personal, comment by supersensitive Freudians.

We hope to avoid such recriminations, if possible. It will be done not by shunning controversy or criticism, but by drawing on its most authoritative spokesmen, its superior texts and journals. Freud can be a reliable source, but the Master often contradicted himself. Some of his theories, such as the death instinct of Thanatos, are not accepted. Other modern dogma goes beyond Freud's original views.

Since psychoanalysis has mistakenly become a generic term, it is necessary to separate it from its less rigorous offspring. Classical analysis has four *musts:* (1) the use of the couch; (2) the length of treatment; (3) the frequency of sessions; (4) treatment by a well-defined psychoanalyst.

Analysis is synonymous with the couch, which has evolved from the overstuffed Viennese sofa bed to the austere foam-rubber slab with skimpy, often triangular pillow. It is a key analytic tool. The couch invites free association. It stimulates the patient to enter the never-never land of fantasy. It keeps the patient from viewing the analyst's reactions. The couch also has a personal value to the analyst. "I cannot bear to be gazed at for eight hours a day (or more)," Freud confessed.

We have seen that Freudian analysis averages five to six years, compared with perhaps a year for ordinary psychodynamic therapy. Another rule that separates "the pure gold of psychoanalysis," as Freud called it, from the dross of suggestion, which is supposedly the basis of all other methods, is the number of sessions per week. "I work with my patients every day, except Sundays and public holidays, that is, usually six days a week," Freud said. The six sessions a week first eroded to five, now to four among many analysts. "At present, four analytic sessions a week is considered the minimum," a prominent Freudian declares. "If it were less than that I would not consider it classical psychoanalysis."

Most analysts agree. Three-quarters reported that they saw analytic patients four or five times a week. Only 22 percent felt treatment could still be called "psychoanalysis" at three sessions per week or less. (The fifty-minute hour is now being cut to forty-five minutes by some time-pressured analysts.)

We now come to a crucial question: Who is qualified to conduct a psychoanalysis? The word "psychoanalysis" has no legal definition. Anyone with sufficient psychotherapeutic gall can use it. But the American Psychoanalytic Association, the rock on which Freud inadvertently built his church, defines who is and who is not a classical Freudian analyst both for the profession and for the society.

"Up until 1972, to be eligible for membership in the American Psychoanalytic Association," explained Dr. Edward D. Joseph, former president of the group, "one had to be an M.D., licensed to practice medicine in at least one state, have completed at least two years of psychiatric residency and be a graduate of one of our twenty-one approved psychoanalytic institutions. He must have completed a personal psychoanalysis conducted by one of our training analysts, and have analyzed at least three patients under the supervision of a supervising analyst, completing at least one of the analyses."

In addition, the American Psychoanalytic Association has sought to open its membership by adding two additional categories: affiliate membership for its candidates and an associate membership for advanced students and recent graduates. But the most significant trend in recent years has been the acknowledgment that *a classical Freudian analyst need not be a medical doctor or a psychiatrist*—the status rock on which the whole American profession was founded. "It is still generally true that an analyst is a licensed doctor," Dr. Joseph continued, "but in the last few years more nonmedical people are being trained and acquiring full status within our association."

The connection between medicine and psychoanalysis in America has been a trademark of the profession, a symbol of confidence for the patient that the man or woman on the other side of the couch is a *doctor.* But despite its inordinate prestige, psychoanalysis is not a medical specialty, nor even a subdivision of psychiatry. Of the members of the American Psychoanalytic Association, forty-eight do not have medical degrees. Thirty-nine are Ph.D psychologists, and nine are laymen whose background varies from social work to college teaching. The most prominent *lay analysts* are an American, Erik Erikson, and an Englishwoman, Anna Freud, the prophet's daughter. Helen Ross, a retired psychoanalyst and life member of the APsaA, holds only a bachelor's degree in education from the University of Missouri. Now eighty-seven, she took her personal psychoanalysis with one of Freud's students, Dr. Helene Deutsch, in Vienna. She then practiced psychoanalysis in America for years without academic or medical credentials.

Considering its potency in the psychological professions, the roster of American analysts is small. The American Psychoanalytic Association has approximately 2500 members, plus 450 nonmember graduates of approved analytic institutes. If we add the 700 analysts in training, we arrive at 3650 American psychiatrists (and 48 nonpsychiatrists) who maintain the American wing of the Freudian or "kosher" school of analytic therapy, as it is informally called by analysts.

The psychoanalytic community is even more geographically clustered than are the general psychiatrists. The two major analytic capitals are almost three thousand miles apart: Manhattan and Los Angeles. One California suburb, Beverly Hills, boasts 63 classical analysts, a number exceeded only by a handful of states. A New York suburb, Great Neck, has as many analysts as the entire state of Florida. Washington, D.C., the center of political anxiety, is serviced by over 150 classical psychoanalysts.

The analytic center of the world is obviously Manhattan, where almost one in fifteen American analysts practices. The analytic population is spread throughout the fashionable East Side (mainly Park, Madison and Fifth, from 60th to 96th streets), and on, or closely off, Central Park West. If one had to choose analytic "ground zero," it would be Fifth Avenue at 96th Street. A few feet from its corner, two buildings—1148 Fifth Avenue and 9 East 96th Street—house a phenomenal number of 21 classical Freudian analysts. Including its neighbor buildings at 1140 and 1143 Fifth Avenue and 8 East 96th Street, that one city corner flies the Freudian pennant as the home of as many classical psychoanalysts as Minnesota, Oregon, Delaware, Oklahoma, Vermont, Wisconsin and Tennessee *combined*.

Eleven states have resisted the blandishments of Freud, and do not have a single member of the American Psychoanalytic Association. These holdouts include Alaska, Idaho, Iowa, Kentucky, Montana, Nebraska, South Dakota, Utah, West Virginia and Wyoming.

Wherever it is geographically, the analytic community is tightly knit, blocking out interlopers. They have even rejected their philosophical first cousins, the neo-Freudian analysts. "The traditional Freudians maintain an elitist outlook and would like to exclude everyone else from the profession," complains Dr. John P. Briggs, of the 850-member rival American Academy of Psychoanalysis.

The Academy is the intellectual watering hole of several varieties of neo-Freudian psychiatrists. Its members are mainly graduates of four nonorthodox institutions: the Karen Horney Institute in New York founded by the creator of "feminine psychology"; the William Alanson White Institute in New York, the spiritual home of Harry Stack Sullivan's "interpersonal relationships"; the New York Medical College's eclectic training center; and the Tulane University Comprehensive Course in Psychoanalysis.

It requires a complex mental chart to sort out the opposing analytic theories and groups, a controversy that is carefully hidden from patients, for whom an analyst is an analyst is an analyst.

"There is a variety of analytic opinion among our members, but in general our dispute is with the rigidity and dogma of the orthodox Freudian establishment," Dr. John Briggs explained. "We are Freudians and we believe in the concepts of infantile sexuality, including the Oedipus complex. It is just that we do not consider them the centerpiece in the creation of neurosis. We utilize intrapsychic phenomena, but we don't want to exclude—as orthodox Freudians do—the importance of cultural values, of the here and now, of the person in society. Neither do we believe you need to see a patient five times a week. I personally think two or three sessions a week is usually sufficient for an analysis."

By adding these 850 apostates, we estimate that there are about 4500 psychiatrists now practicing or training in psychoanalysis in the United States—approximately 1 in 7 psychiatrists. No one can, of course, divine the number of other psychoanalyzed psychiatrists who do "pick up" psychoanalysis in the privacy of their offices.

Internationally, psychoanalysis is relatively small, but its status is rising as other Western nations experience the early pangs of modern psychologization. There are an estimated 1000 psychoanalysts outside the United States, with the second largest base in the United Kingdom, specifically in London. Although analysis and psychotherapy are not used much in treating the mentally ill in Britain, the British Psycho-Analytical Society, with a membership of over 300, is the prominent influence in British psychotherapy.

British psychoanalysis is mainly purchased by the upper classes on Harley and Upper Wimpole streets' analytic couches. It is also available through some National Health Insurance clinics, especially the Tavistock Clinic in suburban Swiss Cottage, close to the last home of Freud and the current residence of his daughter, Anna.

To the patient, whether in London or New York, the subtleties of the analytic room are shrouded in mystery. Many patients go into analysis expecting a warm, supportive therapy, an atmosphere of *Gemütlichkeit* in which the analyst is the quintessential $50-an-hour Jewish mother.

Nothing could be further from the truth. Classical analysis is a hard, disciplined engagement. Dr. Ralph Greenson, of the Los Angeles Psychoanalytic Institute, describes analysis as a "painful" and "uneven" arrangement which is uniquely artificial. It not only "runs counter to the way human beings usually relate to one another," he says, but is "a one-sided demeaning experience for the patient."

Many analysts admit that analysis is punishing. The necessity to reveal all and to take direction like a child makes it "a humiliating experience" for sensitive people, as one analyst says. It can also be emotionally anguishing. "Some of my patients cry during difficult sessions," a New York analyst explains. "They are reliving painfully sad situations from their childhood, and recalling old affects that accompany those memories."

In this contrived setting, reality is played down and the stage set for a virtual séance of fantasy. The patient lies on a couch, seeing only a portion of the room. He deals with an analyst whom he sees only fleetingly when he enters and leaves the room. The analyst may say little or nothing for minutes, even days or weeks. When he does speak to the patient the analyst's voice can seem like an ethereal offstage direction.

The patient is stimulated to put aside his real world for fifty minutes and enter what one analytic authority calls a "state of reverie" not unlike sleeping or dreaming. The late Freudian theoretician Dr. Robert Waelder has described it as an "artificial, partial and controlled regression for the purpose of a study of inner conflicts." During this regression, the submissive patient drops his adult manner and reverts to a childlike stance.

The couch becomes a foam-rubber springboard back to supposed childhood desires, generally of an erotic nature. "The nonreality of the analytic situation is purposely enhanced to facilitate fantasy and transference," says a prominent member of the American Psychoanalytic Association. "In an almost laboratory way, we can undertake a study of the patient's early life and the roles played by early family figures in the patient's infantile conflicts."

It is obvious that the real and the unreal can fuse in seconds during the analytic ritual. "At a single instance on the couch, there can be total nonreality," one analyst at New York's 96th Street and Fifth Avenue explains. "The patient cannot see me, but she hears me smoking my pipe. She thinks I am moving my mouth and coming over to the couch to kiss her. The next instant she returns to reality and realizes that I am just smoking my pipe."

This unreality can be magnified by the analyst's pregnant silence. Like the wordless Dr. Spielvogel in Philip Roth's *Portnoy's Complaint,* the silent therapist has become a Freudian caricature. Yet it does have a base in reality. One patient, the late Dr. Carney Landis, estimated that his psychoanalyst spoke only 2 percent of the time.

Analytic silence was born when Frau Elizabeth von R. admonished Freud to keep still so she could tell him what was on her mind. At that moment, Freud had discovered free association, and the analyst's silence with which it is often met. When Dr. Edward Glover, the late prominent British analyst, surveyed his colleagues, he found that most "talked little" during the session.

Silence is not an accident. It is deliberately delivered in large doses, when the patient is speaking and even when he is silent. The silence helps to let the analyst's presence recede into the background, enhancing the patient's fantasy production, according to Dr. Ralph Greenson. Analyst silence is also used to confront analysand silence, producing the "silent combat" of the analytic chamber.

A training analyst from Downstate Medical Center in Brooklyn sees the analyst's silence as a chance for the patient "to unfold his buried inner life." He recalls a case in which after a half-hour of silence, a patient turned around to look at him. "When I asked why, he told me he thought I was dead. The patient's father, I know, had died of a heart attack. He thought the same thing had happened to his analytic father," he explained.

At $50 an hour, extended silence can become a minor trauma even for the sophisticated analysand. One New York psychiatrist recalls that his own analyst was once silent for three weeks. "When weeks went by without his saying a word, I thought I would go nuts," he recounts. "I felt unworthy. I thought that what I had to say was not worthwhile. But as far as he was concerned, the more silence the better as long as I was free-associating."

"Nothing can be more active than silence," an officer of the American Psychoanalytic Association argues. "It puts tremendous pressure on the patient to work. In some sessions, I may say nothing at all. The good analytic patient doesn't take umbrage. The patient who doesn't understand may get annoyed. He thinks 'You're not giving me enough help. I'm struggling with this thing and you're not doing a darn thing.'"

The analytic ritual is not only artificial but eccentric. It includes two other unusual Freudian rules: *abstinence* and *incognito.*

The classical analyst has a reputation for aloofness. He has been likened to the surgeon, dissecting the psyche without involving himself. The stereotype is sometimes overdrawn, but it does rest on the analytic rule of *abstinence.* Abstinence is an unbreakable analytic code which denies the patient the very love he came to buy. Unlike most therapists, the analyst is not permitted to play the "sympathetic mother" who gratifies the patient's needs. He is not to give advice, make small talk or comfort the anxious patient.

The theory is simple: the warm-hearted analyst is an analytic ogre.

His TLC (tender, loving care) will seem to cure the neurotic as the patient's symptoms disappear through a premature *flight into health.* For a true, permanent cure, analysts insist the patient must be maintained in a state of psychic suffering, perhaps for years.

Sigmund Freud, as usual, expressed it best. "Analytic treatment should be carried through, as far as possible under privation—in a state of abstinence. Harsh though it may sound, we must see to it that the patient's sufferings, to a degree that is in some way or other effective, do not come to an end prematurely," said the Master.

Analysts object to the heartless stereotype, insisting there is a place for sympathy, *if* it is handled without excess emotion. One analyst even outlines the permissible quotient of sympathy. "If the patient comes to analysis for love, he'll be disappointed. There are other forms of therapy that will give him that," he explained. "We cannot gratify the patient's desires in concrete ways, but we must be human. If, for example, there is a death in the family, the analyst should mention that he knows about it and is sorry. But of course, he shouldn't go too far. If the patient is struggling with angry feelings toward the parent, too much sympathy—even at the parent's death —would hurt the purpose."

Abstinence can disrupt the patient's personal life. Patients are expected not to begin new love affairs, not to travel excessively for pleasure and not to become too absorbed in hobbies. These are all contraindicated "symptom substitute gratification."

Contrary to public belief that the analyst is a YMCA counselor in Freudian disguise, analytic dogma does not permit direct repair of the patient's life. No matter how banal or deadly is the life style that the patient brings to analysis, it is to be painfully maintained during the years on the couch. As researcher Dr. Edward Glover has advised, "No important changes should be made affecting his occupational or emotional life."

The proper analyst is also scrupulously *neutral.* He should not approve or disapprove of the patient's actions or motives. He is not to inject his own value system into the unconscious engagement. In theory, the analytic room is the last place one should try to buy advice by the hour. Almost all analysts refuse to answer the common plea: "What do you think I should do about . . . ?" "Many patients ask us: 'For God's sake, tell me what to do,' but we can't help them that way. That's the job of psychotherapy, not psychoanalysis," says one Brooklyn analyst.

Analysts often parry questions with another: "Why do you think you asked me that question?" Some even stubbornly refuse to explain their refusal to answer. One analyst recalls that a patient came to him from such a colleague in a tearful state, describing the degradation he felt when his first analyst failed to respond or explain.

The image of the absolutely neutral analyst is, of course, idealized. The flesh-and-blood doctor often finds that his prejudices do intrude. One Berkeley, California, analyst confesses that although he usually restrains himself, one day, after listening to a patient describe the hash he had made of his life, he blurted out, "You're a schmuck!"

The proper analyst is not only detached, he is symbolically invisible. He assumes his *incognito,* a carefully nourished secretive stance designed to keep him totally anonymous to the patient. As Freud admonished his successors: "The physician should be impenetrable to the patient, and, like a mirror, reflect nothing but what is shown to him."

This analyst-patient *apartheid* is rigidly enforced. Psychoanalysts divulge little about themselves and scrupulously eschew social contact with patients. "My contact with patients outside the office is practically nonexistent. I seldom even receive phone calls from them," says one married analyst who works in his apartment. "I tell my analytic patients nothing about my personal life. In fact, one of my female patients is convinced that I have no family at all."

One analyst who is married and has three children explains how he parries patient curiosity. "When they ask about my personal life, I ask them: 'What comes to your mind?' Some of them may imagine that I am unmarried or even a wife beater. But our anonymity is vital. We must be a neutral, screenlike figure, a mirror to their mind." An analyst recounts that he often meets patients on the street. "I just say 'Hello' and walk right on."

Some patients are driven by curiosity to try to break their analyst's incognito. They look up their analysts in medical directories, ask other patients and psychiatrists what they know about him. In fact, a survey of analysts showed they believed that most patients eventually "read" the analyst's unconscious.

Anonymity is part of the cure, for, as one analyst says, "it enables the patient to project onto us any image he wants." The process is called *transference,* a foundation stone of modern psychoanalysis. The official *Glossary* of the American Psychoanalytic Association defines transference as "the displacement of patterns of feelings and behavior, originally experienced with significant figures of one's childhood, to individuals in one's current relationships." In analysis that individual is the analyst.

In transference, the patient does not see his analyst as flesh-and-blood. Instead, Freud tells us, "the person of the analyst replaces some earlier person" in the patient's childhood. Transference is one of analysis' high dramas, the theater of the past replayed in the present. Without actually remembering the repressed past, the patient relives it through a new person. Emotions once felt toward parents, for example, are now ostensibly felt toward the analyst. By analyzing the transference, analysts believe they can uncover clues to the neurosis-producing childhood.

Does the patient in transference actually believe the analyst is his parent? The answer is typically analytic: *he knows the analyst is not his parent, yet he reacts as if he is.* One analyst offers the case of a female patient who had been kept waiting in his outer office. She started to cry because she felt she was being ignored. Analysis revealed that it was a case of transference involving the analyst as her father. As a child, she was frustrated each night at bedtime. She waited for her father to first say good night to her younger sister before he came to see her.

The *analytic situation* is a "living redramatization of the distorting influences of the past," states Dr. Harold P. Blum. The key redramatization is the unresolved Oedipus complex, the child's incestuous longing for the parent of the opposite sex. Until that ancient conflict is resolved, says theory, the patient cannot be cured.

One analyst relates the case of a patient, Mrs. A., a pleasant young married woman. In a dream she stole an object whose color was the same as that of her analyst's necktie. She wanted to steal his penis, the analyst suggested. As an adolescent, Mrs. A. would go into the bathroom after her mother had coitus and pick up her mother's used douche bag. She masturbated with the nozzle, a representation of her wish for her father's penis. She was now reliving this infantile wish through her transference desire for the analyst's penis.

The all-important transference may be *positive* or *negative*. The patient can express either the love or the hate felt in infancy. Positive transference is felt by both sexes but in different forms. Among sexually normal men, the love sought from a male analyst is closer to affection or respect, the same love ideally sought from one's father.

When patients and doctors are of the opposite sex, however, analysis can develop an erotic *transference love.* Many women are content to express that love unconsciously, but some female patients experience a heated sexual transference. Although theoretically based on a childhood wish, it more than passes for the real thing. Speaking of two female patients, one analyst says, "They were ready for action."

Is it analytic gossip or do female patients actually fall in love with their analysts? The eroticized transference is not inevitable, but neither is it rare. Freud discovered transference love when a female patient suddenly threw her arms around him. Freud describes it plainly as a case "in which a woman or girl patient shows by unmistakable allusions or openly avows that she has fallen in love, like any other mortal woman, with the physician who is analyzing her." (Homosexual patients may also "fall in love" with their male analysts.)

Freud warned self-deluded analysts that this heightened sexuality is a by-product of analysis and not "the charms of his person." He also advises against *countertransference,* analyst love for the patient, as being unethical. The female patient may be in an exaggerated "readiness for sexual surrender," he explains, while "the younger men especially, who are not bound by a permanent tie, may find it a hard task" to resist.

There are no statistics on how well Freud's concern is honored. Most analysts avoid sexual encounters with patients, but some do marry former patients, and still others have been known to transgress. Dr. Martin Shepard, a maverick psychiatrist, has written *The Love Treatment* which discusses sexual indulgence with patients, a concept his colleagues find outrageous.

One analyst believes that falling in love with the analyst is a "regular occurrence." Because of a painful life, he says, the female neurotic is in a state of transference readiness. Some patients are even intellectually primed. He speaks of the pseudo-sophisticated patient who asks, "Doctor, when am I supposed to fall in love with you?"

Patients may even become obsessed by their love for the analyst. They dream about him and think about him all the time, even during intercourse. One woman threw her arms around a distinguished West Coast analyst and passionately said, "Let's stop wasting time and let's have sex." The physician related how he handled her coolly: "Mrs. Jones, I want to help you and I can do that by working. So let's work together and stop wasting time."

There is also transference hate, the *negative transference* through which the patient relives his childhood aggressive instincts. Like love, hostility is essential in psychoanalysis. Its absence may even be a sign that the patient is unconsciously stifling his or her anger. The patient is holding up the cure by not showing aggressive feelings which can be put through the analytic mill.

The transference relationship is so powerful that analysts believe it creates a new neurotic sickness, the *transference neurosis*. It is a strange product of the ritual that can only be cured by its cause, the analysis itself. Freud called it "a new edition or facsimile" of the original childhood illness.

"The creation and dissolution of the transference neurosis classically distinguishes psychoanalysis from all other types of psychotherapy," Dr. Harold Blum explains. Once the new neurosis has been cured and the transference dissolved, the analyst becomes *internalized*. He lives forever in the grateful patient's unconscious as a more accepting image than the original biological parents.

In this hothouse environment, does the analysis really emerge as a powerful factor in the patient's life? The answer is that during the years on the couch the committed analysand often evaluates life not by how well he or she is doing in love or on the job, but by how well the analysis is going. In the *Journal of the American Psychoanalytic Association* (*JAPA*), an analyst describes a thirty-six-year-old wife and mother in analysis for whom "vacation, holidays and weekends were seen as interruptions to a pleasant relationship" with the analyst.

The outsize role of analysis is heightened by the rigid, no-nonsense regulation that governs psychoanalysis. A dramatic example is the unwritten contract covering time and money, two ingredients about which the profession is never silent.

The key is what Freud called *hire by the hour*. "A certain hour of my available working day is appointed to each patient; it is his, and he is liable for it, even if he does not make use of it," Freud wrote in 1913. (Freud evolved most of the analytic technique in his papers of 1910–1915.) Under a "less stringent regime," he feared that "accidental hindrances" and "intercurrent illnesses" would jeopardize the analyst's "material existence."

Does this mean that a patient whose car breaks down must pay for the missed hour? As disconsolate patients have learned, the answer is generally "yes." One analyst even shows how the patient will suffer psychologically if he escapes paying for missed appointments: (1) by excusing payment for canceled sessions, the analyst is committing an "act of love," which could be anti-therapeutic, (2) by charging for canceled sessions the analyst creates resentment and helps bring on the necessary negative transference.

"Paying the fee" is a brilliant Freudian maneuver which modern analysts are happy to duplicate. Freud suggested that it was neurotic to discuss either money or sex with circumspection. To avoid such neurosis, Freud recommended handling the patient's fees "with the same matter-of-course frankness that he wishes to induce in them toward matters relating to sexual life."

He even offered practical money advice. Bills should be presented once a month and not allowed to accumulate. He advised against "gratuitous treatment" (professional courtesy), pointing out that analysts do not earn as much as other medical specialists. (They are, of course, not penurious. The typical analyst grosses between $60,-000 and $100,000 a year.)

Freud ingeniously tied the fee to results. If the fee is very low, he warned, the value of the treatment will be denigrated in the patient's eyes. Free treatment is an analytic disaster, he insisted. Without the "corrective influence" of money, the patient is supposedly deprived of a "useful incentive to exert himself to bring the cure to an end."

Only in a few areas does modern analysis so slavishly follow Freud. The bill for the month's analysis (some $1000 at $50 an hour) is not mailed. It is presented, eyeball-to-psyche, to the patient at the end of the month. If payment is not forthcoming in time, there is an automatic reminder in the next bill. The next stop is medicine's most effective collection system: the analyst injects the unpaid bill into the analytic work to find the unconscious reason for the *resistance*.

"There is generally a psychological reason for a patient either coming late, missing appointments or failing to pay his bill," says a New York analyst. One analyst proposes that the patient who forgets to pay is really seeking the analyst's love. By not paying, he is denying that the relationship needs money to sustain it. (In one professional joke, the patient loses out no matter how he handles his analytic appointments. If he comes early he is displaying *anxiety*. If he is late he is offering *resistance*. If he regularly comes on time, he is *compulsive*.)

With inexpensive clinics for some and increased insurance, are money and cure still intertwined? Analyst Eugene Halpert believes that analytic money still talks. The use of insurance to pay for analysis, he says in *JAPA* "serves as a source of resistance." The patient develops an unconscious sexual fantasy: "I am protected by the insurance against loss of my penis and my body contents. I am in control and need not fear the analyst." In cases of anal fixation, Halpert adds, patients whose entire fee is paid by insurance or Medicaid may be rendered totally unanalyzable.

*Analyzability* is a curious term. It compares with the unlikely medical doctor who screens patients before mending their broken legs. The analytic patient is selected with more care by the suspicious doctor than is the analyst by the unknowing, trustful analysand. Instead of asking "How good is the psychoanalyst?" the analytic profession perpetually asks, "Is this patient analyzable?"

Who is analyzable? Screening patients is done through either an interview or a few weeks' *trial analysis.* One reason why some patients fail is a modern psychiatric paradox. *The analyst fears that the patient is mentally ill.* Since psychoanalysis is designed to treat neurotics and those with character disorders, most analysts scrupulously avoid the seriously mentally ill.

In Freudian theory, psychotics are fixated at the primitive *narcissistic,* or self-love, stage, and cannot develop the necessary transference relationship. In the APsaA Biographical-Professional Survey, 747 analysts reported treating a total of only 80 psychotic patients. Drug addicts, juveniles with behavior problems, sociopaths and alcoholics are also generally excluded from the privileged ranks of analysands.

This exclusivity dovetails with analysts' negative attitude toward modern psychochemical therapy. Most analysts avoid tranquilizers, antidepressants and anti-schizophrenic drugs in analytic cases, believing they "mask" symptoms and block ferreting out the root cause.

Although the good patient must be psychologically minded, analysts fear the patient who is too easily influenced. A New York analyst stood below the diploma of the prestigious New York Psychoanalytic Institute with Freud's portrait gazing sternly into the room. "First, we must believe the patient will not lose contact with reality on the couch," he explained. "The couch is a very effective instrument for stimulating fantasy. The patient only sees me when he comes in and when he leaves. During free association, some people feel as if they are floating. Some patients may even go wild.

"One patient, hearing my European accent, developed the idea that I was a Nazi—in fact, the commandant of Auschwitz. It was not just a fantasy; he believed it," he continued. "I immediately removed him from the couch, discontinued the analysis and used face-to-face psychotherapy. It is also essential that the person have sufficient ego strength to handle psychoanalysis. His ego must tolerate the pressures of unconscious fantasies and conflicts which emerge in analysis. There is a danger that a borderline patient without this ego strength might have a psychotic experience. Of course, a certain amount of psychological-mindedness is very helpful in a patient.

However, these days the majority of people who come to analytic offices are already very psychologically minded."

The suspicion emerges that the ideal analyzable patient is not only not very sick but relatively healthy. Dr. Ralph Greenson has developed a trait roster for the analyzable patient that seems better suited for screening candidates for an Order of the British Empire than a troubled soul seeking to spend $50,000 for psychic repair. The *good* analytic patient should have the following qualifications:

- The ability to endure waiting, frustration and hardship.
- Since the patient must reveal his innermost secrets, it requires a person of honesty and integrity of purpose.
- He should be "verbal" and have the ability to communicate intelligibly about subtle mixes of emotions.
- He should have excellent emotional flexibility: to regress to the childlike state, then bounce back as a co-worker of the analyst.
- He should not be physically sick. A severe illness will deplete the energy needed for his analytic work.
- He should not be in the midst of an exciting love affair.
- He should not have a combative or angry husband, wife or parent who interferes with the analyst.

The obvious suspicion that the best patients are relatively healthy was confirmed by the Boston Psychoanalytic Institute. Seeking patients for their analysts in training, they turned away people who had serious psychosomatic complaints, psychotic trends and adverse life situations. Those admitted expressed *warmth,* were *frank, honest* and *sincere* and *related well* to the psychiatrist. The institute admitted that the general criteria in selecting patients were "relative youthfulness and absence of severe neurotic disorders."

The good patient is also docile. He must be willing to accept psychological abuse and drop any pretense of privacy. "By saying everything that is in his mind, the patient is doing something no reasonable adult ever does," Dr. Edward Glover has reminded us. "Within the analytic hour he has to do what he is told without appeal or redress . . . He is frequently told and generally made to feel that he doesn't know what he is talking about . . ."

The truly good patient must also have the ability to talk dirty, or the willingness to learn how to. "I was surprised at my analyst's language," one embarrassed female relates. "He uses all the four-letter words and encourages me to do the same." At one point her doctor commented that this patient "had her head up her ass."

The patient's use of euphemistic sex terms is an attempt to hide their real emotions about sexual acts, analysts say. When patients use the term "making love," one analyst asks if they don't mean "f-u-c-k." Another doctor presses patients who say "fellatio" or "oral love" to talk straightforwardly about putting a penis in the mouth and sucking on it. Despite this, many sensitive analysts try to refute the common charge that analysts consider sex the be-all of psychic life. They passionately point out that *ego psychology* and its *defense mechanisms* tap other areas of man's unconscious. But even the dullest of patients quickly learn that psychoanalysis is a highly sexualized psychology.

At an American Psychoanalytic Association all-day seminar, psychoanalysis was presented as being as sexually innocent as a Victorian garden party. To test this, we conducted a simple experiment. We examined the official publication, the *Journal of the American Psychoanalytic Association* for six consecutive quarterly issues. In all, some forty case histories were presented by analysts, either in detail or in a cursory way.

Approximately 90 percent of them could be described as sexual. In the first anecdote, an eight-year-old girl's opening and closing of her eyes are compared to her "anal-vaginal contractions." In one short case history, the word "penis" appears at least eleven times. These six issues of *JAPA,* including the following cases, make erotic reading:

- Oedipal striving for the acquisition of father's penis.
- Seduction by a sister in mutual masturbation.
- Female pubic hair seen as a phallic symbol.
- Concern about urinating in front of father for fear of castration.
- Feminine identification, including fantasy of impregnating his sister with feces.
- Dreams of castration wishes against sibling.
- Dream of fellatio on father's catheterized penis.
- Remembrance of masturbating in front of mother.
- Unconscious homosexual fantasies about the analyst.
- Dreams of incest with mother.
- Jealousy of wife due to latent homosexuality.
- Sexual trauma for repeated exposure to parental intercourse, the classic *primal scene.*

Psychoanalytic power undoubtedly stems from its sexual titillation. But it is equally based on its reputation as a miracle cure. The first psychoanalytic miracle was the *talking cure*, or *catharsis*, performed on Fräulein Anna O. in the 1880s. By recalling the past and reliving the repressed emotion in the present, her neurotic symptoms reportedly disappeared quickly. It was in the tradition of Jesus returning sight to the blinded, or the first chiropractic cure of deafness. This Eureka model of analytic cure has since been discarded, but it became the plot spring of hundreds of psychological films and novels, and has captivated the public by its awesomeness.

If we were to isolate the beginning of the modern Psychological Society, it would be the striving of an unsuccessful *Privatdozent* in neuropathology in Vienna in the 1890s. His hope was to find a method of treating both his own "very considerable psychoneurosis" (as disciple Ernest Jones called it) and those of his *haute bourgeoise* Viennese patients.

The consulting room of Dr. Sigmund Freud at Berggasse 19 in an unfashionable section of Vienna was the site of the overstuffed analytic couch on which Freud's first formal "Psychical Analysis," as he then called it, was performed on Fräulein Elizabeth von R. in 1892. In the mind of the philosopher-physician were the seeds of a mystical, yet apparently irresistible revolution against the Christian middle-class society of pre–World War I.

Freud's *Mitteleuropa* was the perfect setting for the performance of psychological miracles. In Vienna a fashionable entity known as *hysteria* affected a number of upper-class women who filled the waiting rooms of nerve specialists such as Freud. The most dramatic cases suffered from what Freud later called *conversion hysteria*. They showed such symptoms as paralysis of limbs, fits, trances, loss of memory, double vision (diplopia), facial tics, loss of voice (aphonia), and even blindness and deafness. The illness was considered to be either simulation or a womb disorder, which some doctors tried to cure by removing the innocent organ.

The "miracle" came in 1895 with the publication of the now famed *Studies on Hysteria* by Freud and his mentor, Dr. Josef Breuer. The miracle was embryonic psychoanalysis, then called *catharsis*, a technique in which hypnosis was used to find the hidden secret which caused the hysteria. Once exposed and talked out, the lame would walk and the deaf hear.

To believers, the miracles of Breuer and Freud were only a little less sensational than the Christian cures at Lourdes. Their work was either ignored in Vienna or labeled as charlatanism, but it forcefully struck later generations throughout the world. The illness of conversion hysteria is now rarely seen among educated Western people, but the miracle has survived the disease.

The first case of Anna O., whose real name was Bertha Pappenheim, was conducted entirely by Breuer in 1881, when Freud was still a struggling research assistant. Anna was an attractive twenty-one-year-old puritanical Jewish girl who developed a bizarre set of symptoms, including paralysis of the neck and most of her limbs, and loss of speech for two weeks. When she regained her voice she could not speak in her native German, but had to converse in English, one of the languages in which she was fluent. Breuer would hypnotize her and Anna would talk out the memories and hallucinations. It was a method she herself labeled the "talking cure," or "chimney sweeping."

The Freud-Breuer theory, simply stated, was: "Hysterics suffer mainly from reminiscences." The memories were of traumas which had not been *abreacted,* or expressed with proper emotion at the time. In most cases the memories involved "things which the patient wished to forget, and therefore intentionally repressed."

This was the origin of *repression* and the emergence of the Freudian unconscious. When the doctors brought back the forgotten trauma which had provoked the ailment, they found, as they said, "to our great surprise at first, that each individual symptom immediately and permanently disappeared."

Unfortunately, Breuer's patient had reportedly fallen in love with him. His wife insisted he drop Anna O. as a patient. When Breuer made an emergency visit and found Anna in the throes of a false "hysterical childbirth," he fled in a cold sweat. He never again practiced the *talking cure,* leaving the legacy to Freud.

Having inherited the quasi-analytic theory, Freud transformed it. Under his guidance, sex now became the unruly base of repressed memories. Each of the four cases in the *Studies* handled exclusively by Freud was typical Victorian primness played out on a stage of nineteenth-century psychology. In one, the entire therapy was a single conversation with Katharina, a shapely eighteen-year-old girl with an "unhappy look." The girl, ostensibly a niece of the owner of a mountain inn where Freud was staying, suffered from severe attacks of shortness of breath. During the attacks, an awful, unrecognizable face glared at her.

With what he called a "lucky guess," Freud suggested that Katharina had seen something which had embarrassed her. Two years before, peering in a cabin window, she had seen her uncle "lying on" her young cousin, Franziska, a scene that "disgusted" her. Freud pushed Katharina to reveal that her uncle had once come into her bed and pressed his body against hers. "What part of his body was it you felt that night?" Freud asked, getting an embarrassed smile in response.

Freud performed an instant miracle. It was not the cabin scene which had disgusted her, he told Katharina. Rather, the face that haunted her was her uncle's, Freud revealed. Thirty years later, Freud added a startling footnote: "Katharina was not the niece, but the daughter of the landlady. The girl fell ill, therefore, as a result of sexual attempts on the part of her father." It was the first insight into Freud's obsessive views on incest and its place in the psychological family circle.

Freud's observations on sexuality abounded. In "Sexuality in the Aetiology of the Neurosis," he stated his conviction that "factors arising in sexual life represent the nearest and practically the most momentous causes of every single case of nervous illness." He had a grand design to destroy neurosis: it was *massive fornication.* In a letter to his Berlin confidant, Dr. Wilhelm Fliess, Freud outlined his scheme but warned that those who gave up masturbation for intercourse might contact venereal disease from prostitutes. But he had another vision: sex with respectable girls.

"The only alternative would be free sexual intercourse between young males and respectable girls; but this could only be resorted to if there were innocuous [birth] preventive methods," he speculated. Freud was pessimistic, for condoms were neither safe nor tolerable for many, he said. "In the absence of such a solution, society seems doomed to fall a victim to incurable neuroses . . . ," Freud gloomily prophesied.

Freud proved to be a poor sex prophet. Modern society has presented us with a living Freudian laboratory complete with birth control pills and respectable young women at the sexual ready. But neurosis is unabated, even increased, side by side with free and frequent copulation. As psychological counselors at universities can testify, the quest for emotional stability through orgasm has been a failure.

Freud's ideas on fornication and cure through catharsis are now analytically archaic. He eventually dropped adult sex as his villain and shifted to early-childhood sexuality. On May 2, 1896, he proposed that anxiety hysteria was created by sex at an inopportune age. His analysis of cases convinced him that every one of his neurotic patients had been a victim of childhood seduction, from as early as one year of age up to puberty. The seduction, he was sure, had caused the hysteria.

In females, the villain had generally been the father or elder brother. The seducers of boys were typically nursemaids, servants or teachers. These childhood seductions, Freud explained, consisted of "coitus-like" acts, including manipulation of the genitals by the older partner, use of the anus, mouth and, in some cases, what appeared to be regular intercourse.

One child who was forced to stimulate an adult woman's genitals with her feet later developed hysteria paralysis in both legs. Another female patient suffering from hysterical insomnia recounted her sex experiences with her otherwise "admirable and high-principled father." For four years, when she was eight to twelve years old, her father would regularly take her into bed and "practice external ejaculation" with her, she told Freud. A sister confided the same thing had happened to her when she was six.

Encouraged by such lurid tales, Freud expanded his seduction theory. He broke up childhood sexuality into three periods. From birth to age four, sexual experience led to *conversion* symptoms, such as *hysterical paralysis.* If the child was seduced between the ages of four and eight, however, the experience was repressed in the unconscious, then revived in adolescence or maturity as *obsessional symptoms.* If the child was between eight and fourteen at the time of seduction, then *paranoia* was the unfortunate result. "You can see that I am in the full swing of discovery," Freud exuberantly told Dr. Fliess.

It proved to be another of Freud's false sex theories. After a year of promoting his "Neurotica," Freud abandoned his theory. He confessed that the seductions had never taken place. Either his patients had lied to him, or he had implanted the seduction idea into their impressionable minds. "I was at last obliged to recognize that the scenes of seduction had never taken place, and that they were only fantasies which my patients had made up or which I myself had perhaps forced upon them . . . ," he said.

But Freud adroitly turned the mistake to power. He simply reversed the fallacy into an abstraction, fashioning much of the present theory of psychoanalysis. *Even if the patient had not been seduced, he reasoned, they thought they had been.* It was the fantasy of this early sex that was at the core of neurosis. If the reality was false, then the fantasy was real. "If hysterics trace back their symptoms to fictitious traumas, this new fact signifies that they create such scenes in fantasy, and psychical reality requires to be taken into account alongside actual reality," he theorized.

The result is the theory of *infantile sexuality,* still the cornerstone of the psychoanalytic process. It is a tale of unconscious lust and frustration that supposedly shape our psyches near the dawn of life. It is an unlikely concept that some patients at first refuse to accept, then eventually learn to believe. The theory centers about the childhood *id* and its unrelenting, unconscious demands, what Dr. Otto Fenichel has called "a dynamic driving chaos of forces which strives for discharge and nothing else."

To traditional analysts, and most modern psychiatrists, childhood is the crucible of life. It is a time when the infantile *Trieb,* the drive or instinct, voraciously seeks its sensual pleasure. The adult neurosis is always built around this childhood foundation, or *Anlage,* analysts say. "The first six years of life are the most important," a Seattle analyst assures us. "These experiences are the precursors of virtually all that follows."

The adult patient may be suffering in his hectic here-and-now. But to the analyst his present life crisis is only a symptom of his underlying childhood conflict. "Many patients in various disguised, or not so disguised, ways relive or continue their infantile neuroses in their everyday lives before they ever came to analysis. But they don't know it," states Dr. Hans W. Loewald, a New Haven analyst.

The patient's adulthood becomes an enlarged projection of the child. The person reacts to his boss as he did to his father—actions related to how well his childhood Oedipus complex was resolved. His unsatisfactory adult sex life is a reflection of his infantile sexual *fixations* at various childhood stages. His attitude toward his mother, his first love object, colors his later *object relations* in many life situations.

(Analyst Erik Erikson has tried to extend analytic theory beyond childhood, particularly through his adolescent *identity crisis.* His work is well received philosophically, but it has had little effect on actual psychoanalysis.)

As adults, we unconsciously relive our infantile neurosis, then mistakenly react in the present the way we felt was appropriate in our childhood, analysts say. One analyst illustrates this with the case history of a married patient who complained that he suffered from premature ejaculation. In analysis, the patient revealed that he considered vaginas "dirty" and "sewer-like." The analyst concluded that the patient saw all vaginas in the light of infant "oral-sadistic and anal-sadistic fantasies." He was regressing sexually and therefore treating all women as if they were his mother.

This unraveling of the childhood unconscious is the zenith of the analyst's performance. It is the chance to exercise his most creative function: *the interpretation.* It is a cunning, almost literary insight which gives panache to psychoanalysis and to the psychological books and films on which a generation was raised. It is the artful key which makes the patient's unconscious become conscious, the first step toward analytic cure.

In this intriguing detective game, the analyst finds the clues in memories, word associations, dreams, fantasies, Freudian slips, free associations, traumas, the patient's *transference* to the analyst, and even in his *resistance* to the analytic process. As drama, it can surpass any of the literary arts. In its sexual content, it competes with the best of Henry Miller and D.H. Lawrence. In and out of the treatment room, finding the *hidden connection* between conscious appearance and unconscious reality is one of the outstanding conundrums of the twentieth century.

Psychoanalysis is heavily involved in the play of words and language, an indebtedness that has made it popular with the intellectually minded. Words are seen as tools of the unconscious, and the analyst adroitly uses word associations to make many of his most creative interpretations.

One case history in hidden connections utilized clever Freudian word play. It involved an obsession which challenged the analyst's skill of interpretation. The patient constantly needed to find the answers to difficult questions. If the answers did not satisfy him, he would suffer severe anxiety attacks. He had a reasonably normal sex life, but was so bashful that he would not undress in front of his wife.

His first attack struck when he was a young man on the way home from high school. He had asked himself "precisely" when the Renaissance period began and ended, a question that defies historical scholarship. He also recalled that at the age of eleven he had seen his sister place a wrapped package in the ash can. He unwrapped it and found it contained a blood-soaked menstrual cloth. He was upset but did not dare to ask what it was.

The analyst deduced that the connection was the word *period.* In one case, it was a *historic period,* the Renaissance. In the other, it was a *female period* involving menstruation. "Obviously what he had wanted to know at the onset of his illness was not the meaning of the historical period but that of the menstrual period," the analyst interpreted. The patient also revealed that at age fifteen he had seen a couple in intercourse through a window. According to the analyst, he supposedly asked himself, unconsciously: Does my father do that to my mother?

The patient then reported a dream in which he was making love to his wife. He was not sure if his son in the crib next to him was asleep. He remembered that as a boy, he would hear noises coming from his parents' bed and would pretend to be asleep. The patient was not aware of it, the analyst interpreted, but as a child he had observed the *primal scene,* his parents in the act of intercourse. (Analysts insist that this early scene is either witnessed or unconsciously fantasized by virtually all children. It is supposedly one of the worst traumatic shocks of our psychic lives.)

The analyst was now completing his finely woven plot. The primal scene had set up an infantile sexual conflict which unconsciously connected *questioning* (what were his parents doing?) to his later shyness and anxiety. The conflict was reinforced by the menstrual-period incident, then seeing still another primal scene at age fifteen. The analyst concluded that finally, at age sixteen, the patient's *period* questions set off the anxiety neurosis. No Agatha Christie plot could rival the daring, if not the logic, of such an interpretation.

The interpretation is the virtuoso performance of the analytic art. It is the single act which historically unites the analyst and Freud. The analyst listens, observes, connects. He then delivers what he believes is the meaning which makes the unseen visible, the unknown obvious. It is the metaphysician at the pinnacle of his power.

*Childhood memories* are the raw material of the interpretation, and the superior patient has a rich early recall. In one analytic case, a male patient suddenly developed headaches. He told his analyst that he felt there was a band around his head. When the pain became severe, he experienced sensual pleasure. His analyst believed that the precipitating, if not underlying, cause was that he missed his former business partner, with whom he had a sublimated homosexual relationship.

The patient seemingly had an excellent recall of childhood memories. He remembered that as a boy he would pull the blankets over his head whenever he suffered failure. He even claimed to remember that when he refused to stop sucking at his mother's breast, she smeared her nipples with a foul-tasting liquid. He sometimes bit her nipple causing it to bleed. He remembered that his father, who was a teacher, sometimes hit him over the head when he could not recall information.

The analyst listened, then finally made his interpretation. Under the blanket the patient has experienced fantasies which pictured him "floating in his mother's womb and sucking his father's penis." He suffered a sense of inferiority, but thought he could become a "big and strong man" through the fellatio. He also fantasized biting his father's penis as he did his mother's breast, an act of vengeance for the father's harshness. The repression of these and other sexual impulses had resulted in his neurosis, the analyst concluded.

But why pains in the head? First, the "symbol of the head as a penis," the analyst interpreted. Secondly, a *displacement* from penis to head, which referred to his once noticing that the head of his father's organ was free. As a boy he tried to pull back his foreskin to imitate it, but it became badly swollen and required a physician to place it back in position. The pain was like "a band" around the penis-head, the same pain he now felt in his actual head. The circuitous route had led from a sublimated homosexual relationship to fellatio with father to a penis-head which had caused the psychosomatic headache which brought him to the doctor in the first place.

But what if, like many of us, the patient has little or no recall before age five? Is the analyst hopelessly stymied in making his interpretation? Hardly. When necessary, an adroit analyst can reconstruct a memory that "probably" took place. It is called *reconstruction,* a touch of analytic creativity. The APsaA *Glossary* compares it to the work of an archeologist, "who extrapolates a description of aspects of past civilizations from fragments and traces."

One analyst describes a case of a reconstructed memory. A young heterosexual man unhappy in his sex life thought of his father as a "huge, fat, big-bellied, disgusting man." During the analysis, the patient recalled two homosexual incidents. One took place during adolescence. The other was at age nine when at camp he fondled a boy's penis as an "impulsive act." The analyst put the traces together and reconstructed a "plausible" analytic script.

When he was five and full of Oedipal desire, his mother left him alone at home with his father, the analyst reconstructed. His father walked around nude, sexually stimulating the child. These homosexual feelings for his father were latent but powerful within him. He then did with the younger boy at camp as he wanted his father to do with him. His negative feelings for his father, he was told, were a *defense screen* against homosexual impulses. The patient could remember no such incident. Nor could he recall feeling sexually attracted to his father. However, since he did have the homosexual experiences, he finally acquiesced to the analyst's probable story.

The art of interpretation is a labyrinth which can never be fully catalogued or explained. Each patient's story follows the same general script of repressed infantile urges, but the literary permutations are infinite. Typically, the analyst will wait weeks, or months, before making his first interpretation. To make *interventions* too early could upset the patient. (Critics claim the waiting time is really needed for Freudian indoctrination. Otherwise the patient would flee the analyst's office in premature disbelief.)

What if the analyst's fanciful interpretations are incorrect? Isn't that as dangerous to the patient as an incorrect medical diagnosis? A training analyst of the Downstate Medical Center in New York offers the profession's standard defense. "Incorrect interpretations do no harm, unless they are given incorrectly concerning the transference," he says. Otherwise, they become mere "suggestions," like those regularly made by nonanalytic therapists.

The interpretation is not only seen as the key to the cure of neurosis. It is also the versatile tool which permits the modern psychiatrist and Freudian-oriented psychologist to divine the meanings behind man's behavior and thoughts. Psychoanalysis is a near-complete system of psychology which has made many of us look at life through a Freudian prism.

With theological arrogance, analysts claim that all our actions are meaningful, and that only analysis can decipher the meanings. Life, they insist, is a play of *psychic determinism* in which there are virtually no accidents or random thoughts. What appears to be haphazard is really part of the scheme of our Great Unconscious.

In the Psychological Society, the unconscious mind is a brilliant instrument which can perform intellectual gymnastics even in people with the dullest conscious minds. The idea that an unknown part of our minds can effortlessly manipulate complex thoughts and symbols is one of the glamorous concepts of our time.

Freud offers an example of how this inventive unconscious is supposed to work. His patient had invented a magic word to help ward off evil. It was made up of the initials of his girl friend's name, to which he added the Christian "Amen." Freud describes the verbal detective work that went into deciphering it. "Her name contained an 's' and this he had put last, that is, immediately before 'amen' at the end. We may say, therefore, that by this process he had brought

his 'Samen' (semen) into contact with the woman he loved: in imagination, that is to say, he has masturbated with her."

Modern analysts strain to rival Freud, the master of metaphor. A
Michigan analyst describes a female patient who took an amphetamine
pill from her purse, then confessed that it was a "clutch." She
meant to say "crutch," but then suggested that perhaps the drug was
something she could "clutch" onto. The analyst noted that as she
was speaking the patient had *unconsciously* made a fist and "was
clenching an imaginary gear-shift lever directly over her pubic area."
He pointed it out to her, and asked, "What are you clutching now?"
The analyst interpreted that the pill symbolized "an illusory
penis" which she could grasp in order to relieve oncoming panic.
"The whole symptomatic act," he concludes poetically in the analytic journal, *JAPA,* "could be expressed through the various meanings of the one key word: *'she clutches her clutch when she feels
clutched-up in the clutch.'* "

The profession implies that without analysis to decipher it, life is
a psychic illusion. At an American Psychoanalytic Association meeting, a Philadelphia analyst claimed that cigarette addiction is caused
by several unconscious factors: (1) the exhaled smoke is experienced
as an embodiment of one's spirit, and proof of immortality; (2) the
smoke serves as a screen on which we project unconscious fantasies;
(3) heavy smokers need smoking in order to breathe—it relieves their
unconscious fear of suffocation.

A University of Rochester analyst even uses psychoanalysis to
explain the origins of the phrase "to lick a problem." It stems from
the child's solution to the problem of finding food, he says. The child
seeks "to find the nipple, to grab it, lick it . . ." The phrase "You can
lick my ass," seems aggressive, but, says the Rochester analyst, the
real meaning is hidden in its opposite: "to get close, to love each
other." He feels that if opposing members of the United Nations
Security Council would first "lick each other's ass," they would also
"lick their problems."

Such creative word associations and symbols all reinforce the ideas
of Freudian psychic determination. But *parapraxes*—Freudian slips
of the tongue, forgetting of names, dates, slips of the pen, bungled
actions—are among the most awesome of analytic theorems. In
every one of our minuscule actions, we are told, we are the puppets
of a controlling Unconscious with its own eccentric will. "Seemingly
unintentional performances prove, if psychoanalytic methods of investigation are applied to them, to have valid motives and to be

determined by motives unknown to the consciousness," Freud reminds us.

Even our mistakes supposedly harbor secret meaning. Freud himself recounts an extraordinary example in his classic work *The Psychopathology of Everyday Life*. It seems that while in conversation with a traveler on the way to Bosnia and Herzegovina in the old Austro-Hungarian empire, Freud mistakenly identified the painter of a fresco, *Four Last Things*, as either *Botticelli* or *Boltraffio* instead of the correct artist, *Signorelli*.

Freud was determined to prove that his error was not due to chance, but that it was dictated by a secret motivation. He noted that he and the traveler had also talked about a strange custom of local Turks in the area. Being fatalistic toward death, they answered physicians' dire warnings with the comment: "Herr, what is there to do?" These same Turks believed that sexual abnormality was worse than death. A few weeks before, Freud had been in the Tyrol village of Trafoi when he heard that a patient who suffered from a sexual abnormality had committed suicide.

He started reconstructing the motive behind his error. Because the tales of death and sex were painful to him, he had repressed them. Along with them he had repressed certain syllables representing the German translation of "Signor," from Signorelli: the *Her* in Herzegovina, and the *Herr* in the Turkish answer to the doctor. The correct answer, Signorelli, was stopped by the unconscious because of its connection with the unpleasant facts of death and sexual abnormality, Freud deduced.

The source of the incorrect answers, Botticelli and Boltraffio, were equally obvious, says Freud. The "bo" was a substitute syllable from "Bosnia." The "elli" in "Botticelli" came from the unrepressed segment of "Signorelli." "Boltraffio" was equally simple: "Bo" of "Bosnia" and the "traffio" from the little village, "Trafoi," where he first heard of the sex-caused suicide. The meandering path through provinces, sex, death, Turks, doctors, Italian and German translations had opened the door to his unconscious forgetting of the name Signorelli.

Analytic theory sees the unconscious as a fourth-generation computer. It even calculates numbers which supposedly just "pop" into one's head. One of Freud's virtuoso performances involved the number *2467*. While reading the proofs of *The Interpretation of Dreams*, he commented to his friend Fliess that he would make no further changes "even if it contains 2467 mistakes."

Connecting "2467" to its source rivals the plots of *Sleuth*. Immediately before concocting the number, Freud had read of the retirement of General E.M., an officer he remembered from his army medical duty. Freud was annoyed at not getting very far in his career since his army days, but was also pleased that while the general was now retiring, much of his own career lay ahead of him. The numbers were thus related to the two periods of Freud's life. The army incident had taken place when Freud was twenty-four years old, and he was now *forty-three.* The 24 made up the first two cardinals of the number: 24 plus 43 or *67,* the last two. Thus 2467 possible mistakes in his book.

The psychoanalytic idea obviously requires an altered thought process, a restatement of what is and what is not real. Psychoanalysts are trained to think in a system in which fantasy and reality fuse. The closest parallel might be the communion wine and wafer *as* the blood and body of Jesus; the Jewish Jehovah *as* the anthropomorphic, bearded patriarch.

A key analytic concept that the logical mind finds difficult to contemplate is the *unconscious fantasy.* It might best be described as a daydream that an unconscious drive would have if it has a consciousness to monitor it. Fantasies are several stages removed from reality, but analysts are convinced that they exist. The APsaA believes that they have a "psychic reality of their own," but they do admit that we should not expect a "logical evaluation on the basis of external reality."

The typical unconscious fantasy, like the snake-bug-penis vision of our St. Louis housewife, is sexual. A woman patient who had a frustrating marital sex life ostensibly had a fantasy involving her analyst. She noticed that a button on the analyst's coat was coming off. At the end of the session she said, "I wish you'd let me sew your button *off.*" The analyst interpreted that she fantasized cutting off his penis as part of her unresolved penis-envy wish.

Fantasies from analytic literature reveal an unbounded creativity. A patient developed nausea during his transference love to his analyst. It was interpreted that the analyst was forcing him to accept (swallow) interpretations he did not agree with. Behind this was an unconscious fellatio fantasy in which the patient was sucking the analyst's penis, the ultimate cause of his nausea.

The *womb fantasy* in men is said to reveal a homosexual attachment to the father. Analysts speak of the patient wishing to be inside the mother's womb in order, as Freud says, "to replace her during coitus—in order to take her place in regard to the father."

If fantasies are real, we might ask, Why don't we know we have them? Because, we are told, fantasies can only reach consciousness if their forbidden meanings are disguised. The erotic womb fantasy, for example, is known to us only in its disguise—the daydream of living alone on a deserted island or being alone in a church. The common fantasy of rebirth is actually a cover for the true fantasy of sexual intercourse with mother.

Several common fantasies are supposedly ensconced in our unconscious. In the oral period, it is the fear of being eaten. In the anal stage it is the fear of being robbed of body contents. During the phallic period it is the fear of being forcibly castrated. Analysts believe these fantasies are universal, a belief tied to the profession's view of itself as a supra-discipline which combines the anthropological, mythological, biological and psychological vectors of man.

Do analysts really think that such metaphysical abstractions exist? The question is simplistic, for the *fantasy* is elementary dogma when compared to its cousin, the *symbol.* Both are early catechism for the analytic mind, which juggles such ideas with the facility of a Puritan discussing *the elect.*

Analytic symbolism is defined by the APsaA as a "secret language," one Freud thought was related to a long-lost tongue. In that language, one thing means the other in the all-knowing unconscious. The symbol then becomes an acceptable disguise for unacceptable ideas or emotions, such as the symbol of *window* for the real, unspeakable *vagina.*

Symbolism may also take the form of numbers. Dr. Rene Spitz, who shared Freud's obsession with number symbols, wrote of the unconscious symbolism of "5." Dr. Moisy Shopper of St. Louis has explored the idea that "3" unconsciously symbolizes the female orifices: the urethra, vagina and rectum. The three-sided triangle, apex down, is a female symbol, as in the YWCA trademark, he says. When the triangle has its apex up, it is a male symbol, representing the penis and testicles.

Physical objects such as houses and cars also have symbolic importance. In the *Psychoanalytic Quarterly,* one analyst suggests that stone is the symbol for teeth in the repressed oral-sadistic phase of childhood. The famed *phallic symbol* occurs with great frequency in psychoanalysis. The *Psychiatric Dictionary* lists nineteen symbols for the ubiquitous male organ, including a knife, gun (or other weapon), automobile, airplane, bird, key, screw, hammer, tree, pillar, skyscraper, cigarette, pen, and of course, Freud's ever-present cigar.

In fact, if psychoanalysis had a professional symbol, it would undoubtedly be a penis. Freud was an amateur anthropologist who was enamored of the symbol Phallos, the Greek name for the organ. He collected penis symbols from around the world, including its use in such lucky charms as the clover leaf, mushroom and the pig.

Analytic metaphysics have had a profound effect on contemporary thought. This is particularly true in the modern tendency to think in terms of opposites and paradoxes. Millions of psychological devotees have been convinced that *things are often the opposite of what they appear to be.* The origin in psychoanalysis of this belief is unmistakable. "For example," Dr. Charles Brenner says, "a person may develop an attitude of great tenderness and affection toward people or animals in order to check and to keep unconscious very cruel or even sadistic impulses toward them."

The process is called *reaction formation,* the origin of the modern cliché of labeling people as being *really* the reverse of what they seem to be. It is also used to reverse what people say in order to arrive at the truth. Analytically, it is a defense mechanism which theoretically wards off a feared, opposite impulse within oneself. In lay reality, it has created a confusion of personal observation which threatens simple logic. As a guide to analytic topsy-turvy land, analysts have provided us with this backwards glossary: ·

- Many people who behave arrogantly are fighting deep-seated inferiority feelings.
- Others who seem to despise themselves as insignificant are covering up deep-seated arrogance.
- A convinced vegetarian in the forefront of the movement showed his true unconscious colors by later becoming a butcher.
- Eccentrics who fight particular evils, from pornography to pollution, are actually fighting against forces "which unconsciously represent their own instinctual desires."
- An individual may exhibit heterosexual activity only to cover homosexual desires.
- Courage may be merely a defense against the anxiety and guilt created by fear.
- Loving, kind behavior may be a defense against feelings of hatred. An hysterical mother who shows "extreme affection for the child" may unconsciously hate him.

This opposite business can degenerate into professional one-upmanship. The late Dr. Otto Fenichel had warned his colleagues against "assuming that the patient means the opposite of what she says or does." It requires, he said, clinical knowledge to determine "whether the opposite is meant" or not.

The analytic concept of *sublimation* has permeated our culture as deeply as the game of opposites. It supposes that what we do in our lives is not done for itself, for its social value or personal pleasure, but as a substitute gratification for some less acceptable unconscious drive. In analytic terms, the oral and anal infantile sex drives are desexualized and put to work doing anything from being a doctor to building a bridge.

It gives birth to such arcane modes of thinking as the analytic shibboleth that one wins the Nobel Prize for science because of the sublimated desire to see one's parents in intercourse. As Freud said, we "owe our highest cultural successes to the sublimation of our infantile instincts."

The classic example is the infant who loves to smear feces. When his parents object, he turns to mud pies, then later receives unconscious gratification by becoming a sculptor. One analytic theoretician tells us that a person might sublimate the same instinct by becoming a doctor specializing in internal parasites.

Examples of the sexual to the sublime abound:

- Interest in reading can be a substitute for unsatisfied infant hunger.
- Scientific curiosity may stem from an intense sexual curiosity in early childhood.
- Conversely, stupidity may be caused by repression of sexual curiosity.
- Friendship and social feeling may be sublimated homosexuality.
- The prayers and penances of religion may be the sublimation of obsessional neurotic impulses (i.e., washing of hands, etc.)
- Interest in collecting (stamps, etc.) may be a sublimation of the desire to hold back feces.
- An artist or writer may have unconsciously chosen his profession in order to sublimate his excessive instinctual needs for power, wealth, fame, love of a woman. The sublimation takes the form of converting his rich infantile fantasy life into art.
- The surgeon may be manifesting sublimation of analsadistic desires.

Every successful philosophical system has a dirty secret which propagates the idea throughout the culture. In psychoanalysis, the sexualized unconscious has undoubtedly titillated the public. But the true secret which gives analysis and all psychodynamic psychology its impetus is that every one of us, from birth to death, is still the *blameless child.*

Man once found solace in primitive worship, then later in the Church's forgiveness. But before Freud, no educated adult could find a plausible reason to avoid responsibility for his actions. It was left to psychoanalysis and psychodynamic psychology to create a blameless environment for the scientific, educated man. It is not done by covering up his faults, but by tracing them back to his childhood, when he was morally innocent. The parent is the eternal culprit, acting as the agent of civilization against the childhood impulses.

Freud once explained this blamelessness to a patient ashamed of his cowardliness. "I pointed out to him that he ought logically to consider himself as in no way responsible for any of these traits in his character," Freud said. "For all of these reprehensible impulses originated from his infancy and were only derivatives of his infantile character surviving in his unconscious; and he must know that moral responsibility could not be applied to children."

It is the *perpetual-child theory.* Not only neurosis, but unhappiness or inability to find love or friendship have been lifted from our adult shoulders and thrust back onto the sagging breast of mother. "My mother (or father) did such and such . . ." is the litany of the Psychological Society. Unhappily married forty-five-year-olds may not seek the answer in their own selfishness or immaturity, but in such blameless psychodynamic interpretations as "an unresolved Oedipus complex."

The system pits one age group against another. But despite the generational tension it has created, it has a near-perfect rhythm. While adults are uncovering the flaws induced in them by their aging parents, their own children have begun to analytically do the same. At its ultimate cycle, three generations of a family have already learned, through therapy or psychological self-education, that each of them, as perpetual children, are blameless. (Some therapists tell patients that they, too, are responsible because they misinterpreted the parental cues. But who can feel guilty about mishandling toilet training at the age of two?)

The analytic theory of childhood is obviously a sexual one, although the word is used in its broadest sense. As patients quickly learn, the infantile-sex stages number four: (1) the oral stage; (2) the anal stage; (3) the phallic stage; (4) the genital stage. In the world of psychoanalysis, the once innocent babe of Raphael has been replaced by a highly sexualized child. The analyst sees it as potentially crippled by infantile *fixations,* an arrested psychosexual development that takes place early in life.

In psychoanalysis, the infant's body is viewed almost as a giant phallus. The mouth, lips, tongue, anus, mucous linings of the rectum, the urethral lining of the penis, the thumb, the toes, the skin itself are all believed capable of delivering "sexual" gratification. As the official APsaA *Glossary* says, the mother's satisfying of the child's pleasure needs "introduces an erotic quality," which stimulates the child's erogenous zones. It is the centerpiece of classical analysis which no contemporary Freudian analyst would dare contest. "Psychoanalysis stands or falls by the recognition of the sexual component—impulses of the erotogenic zones," Freud said.

Each of the child's psychosexual stages contribute to the formation of neurosis and mental illness. But the nuclear core is the famed Oedipal conflict which evolves during the phallic phase, ages three to six. This Oedipus complex is the linchpin of the analyst's most evocative interpretations.

Analysts believe that every child experiences the Oedipal wish for incest. In the healthy person, the desire is resolved by age six. But if, as a child, the person did not renounce the unconscious wish for sex with the parent, the repressed memories are still dangerously rattling about in his adult unconscious. "We have, of course, learned from him [Freud] that the kernel of any neurosis is the Oedipus complex," disciple Ernest Jones reminded us.

How serious is this psychoanalytic claim of incest desire in a five-year-old? Is it merely an allegory taken from Sophocles' tale of *Oedipus Rex,* or is reality implied?

Its reality is more than implied. According to the American Psychoanalytic Association, the Oedipus complex plays a key unconscious role in the development of virtually all of human behavior. Their official *Glossary* explains that *"the child strives in a limited way for sexual union with the parent of the same sex, and the death or disappearance of the parent of the opposite sex."*

Just before his death, Freud wrote in *An Outline of Psycho-Analysis* that the Oedipal child in heat blends early masturbation with a desire to become his mother's lover. "He wishes to possess her physically in such ways as he had divined from his observations and intuitions about sexual life, and he tries to seduce her by showing her the male organ which he is proud to own," Freud explained.

During his self-analysis, Freud learned of his Oedipal love toward his mother, attractive Amalie Freud. It was first aroused as a boy when he took an overnight train trip with her from Leipzig to Vienna. "I must have had the opportunity of seeing her *nudam,*" he guessed.

What resolves this passion at age six? It is the *fear of castration,* one of analysis' most imaginative complexes. Analysts believe that all male children unconsciously fear that father will cut off their penis in retaliation for the desire to bed their mother. Freud called it "the severest trauma of his [the child's] young life."

Analysts are convinced of its reality. Dr. Charles Brenner, former APsaA president, claims the lurid theory is verified from "evidence from anthropology, religion and folk myths, artistic creations and various other sources." Some analysts even feel that circumcision is a primitive relic of castration, which Freud said was once "actually carried out by a jealous and cruel father on growing boys."

Why would a modern boy believe that such bloody mutilation is a real threat? Analysts say the answer is obvious. Once the boy sees the female genitals—sans penis—he becomes convinced "that his own castration is a genuine possibility," says Dr. Brenner. He then aborts his grandiose Oedipal scheme and renounces his mother as a lover.

The little girl is also Oedipally driven, but in a unique way. In a rage over rivalry for her husband's penis, the mother threatens the female child with internal castration, or as the APsaA *Glossary* euphemistically puts it, "injury to the genital and procreative organs."

The female castration anxiety is best known by its offshoot, *penis envy.* Penis envy has become a psychodynamic red flag to female liberationists, to whom Freud is the quintessential male chauvinist. Unlike the male child, the female discovers that she is already castrated and supposedly feels wronged. Freud believed that penis envy was responsible for what he called women's "jealous" and "envious" nature, the product of an unhappy genital comparison with the male young.

*Penis envy* is a common interpretation in the analytic chamber. In *JAPA,* an analyst describes a woman who, as a child, had been rubbed on the leg by the erect penis of a dog. Later, she saw her father's more substantial penis, and developed a fervent wish for the organ.

Some girls emerge from their Oedipal period psychosexually damaged. Frustrated in seeking Daddy's love, they return to their earlier attachment, to Mother, and live with the wish to have a penis and be a man. The late Karl Abraham theorized that intense or repressed penis envy would result in one of two female neuroses: (1) the type who prefers the male role and, all her life, holds the fantasy of acquiring a penis; (2) the vindictive type who seeks revenge on the "luckier" male by castrating him. Some women, he claimed, combined both neuroses in one person.

But with proper resolution of the Oedipus complex, the boy or girl child uses the parent of the same sex as a model. They develop the more mature *superego,* incorporating parental values into themselves. In the inverted Oedipus complex, the child identifies with the opposite-sex parent—the analytic explanation for homosexuality.

If the Oedipus complex is true, why can't we remember this first sexual desire? "The answer is simple," a new York analyst points out. "We prefer to forget this forbidden love. The memory of the incest wish is repressed and becomes unconscious. It is part of our *infantile amnesia,* the most common forgetting of all."

The forgotten and the repressed are what drives us, analysts say. It is what must be dredged out into the open through psychoanalysis if neurosis is to be cured. But what actually causes neurosis, according to analytic theory? In the beginning there is only the *id,* which represents the *pleasure principle.* The newborn infant is a mass of drives seeking pleasure, and has no ego, no superego, no sense of its own reality. Gradually the child develops an executive controller, the *ego,* in order to handle the increasingly important *reality principle.*

Although no one has ever observed the id, ego or superego, Freud visualized the structure as if it were a physical organ. He even constructed diagrams, claiming that the ego came out of the id, like Eve from Adam. The ego was "a portion of the id which has undergone a special development," he said. This ego stores memories, avoids excessive stimuli, and is the vehicle of adaptation and self-preservation.

The *id* is a term Freud borrowed in 1923 from Berlin physician Georg Groddeck. It was originally called by the mundane German name, *Das Es,* or *The It.* In fact, direct translation of the original terms, *Das Ich, Das Es* and *Das Über-Ich* are the prosaic *The I, The It, The Super-I.* Psychoanalysis may owe its glory to the ingenuity of Freud's English translator, Dr. Abraham Brill, who used the fanciful Latin translations of *id, ego* and *superego.* These three make up the *structural* features of the analytic psyche. There is also an unseen *topography* of the mind: the *conscious,* the *preconscious* and the *unconscious,* all working in unison with the structural functions. The conscious mind is the one we easily recognize. The dynamic unconscious mind, with its *unbound psychic energy,* is the home of our id drives, fantasies, infantile wishes, hidden motivations, repressed ideas and forgotten traumas, all living comfortably together somewhere in the human mind. Being furthest from consciousness, the unconscious is considered the deepest layer, an image that gave birth to the phrase *depth psychology.*

Freud's original theory had a conscious ego and unconscious drives, a metapsychology everyone could understand. In 1923 he changed the theory, elevating the id, ego and superego. The id is still totally unconscious, but the new ego lives in both the conscious and unconscious worlds. In the unconscious it operates the *defense mechanisms* (rationalization, repression, projection), which protect the self against the raging instincts. The superego is mainly unconscious, triggering guilt and shame automatically.

What interplay of these Freudian facets drives the patient into a $50-an-hour therapy? Basically, it is the childhood battle between id and ego. The ego fights to keep the unacceptable sexual and aggressive drives from entering our consciousness and, as Freud explains, pushes them "back into the unconscious state." These unacceptable early ideas which we do not know about are supposedly the causes of our mental turmoil.

Paradoxically, most children seem to avoid developing neuroses. But the seeds of early conflict bear neurotic fruit in adulthood. As Freud explained: "The child embarks on his attempts at defense-repressions—which are effective for the moment but nevertheless turn out to be psychologically inadequate when the later re-animation of sexual life brings a reinforcement to the instinctual demands which have been repudiated in the past." In other words, the sexual life of adulthood stirs up the id ghosts we thought we had buried in our nurseries.

A stimulus in the environment can trigger the repressed conflicts and overwhelm the beleaguered ego. The result is a neurotic symptom, whether *claustrophobia, excessive anxiety, homosexuality, nervous tic, inability to work or to have an orgasm,* say analytic theorists.

We are all vulnerable. Not even the modern educated mother can protect her child against the scourge. "We used to think parents could help prevent neurosis by proper handling of the child," says an official of the American Psychoanalytic Association. "We no longer think so. The neurotic conflict is inevitable."

The first stage is the *oral,* which runs from birth to eighteen months. The child's drives center around his oral cavity. Pleasure stems from sucking the mother's nipple, the bottle, his thumb and toes, even the modern pacifier. Later, the relaxed child is transformed into an aggressive beastie. It uses its new teeth to bite everything, particularly Mother's teats. Although Mother is the first love object, this oral-sadistic phase produces an ambivalence toward Mom, a duality in which there is unconscious hatred of the mother.

Freud compared sucking at the breast to sexual intercourse. "When children fall asleep after being sated at the breast, they show an expression of blissful satisfaction which will be repeated later in life after the experience of a sexual orgasm," he wrote. Nipple sucking is followed by autoeroticism—the sucking of thumbs, even toes —and then by what analysts call childhood masturbation.

Neurosis is the now immortalized product of parents' handling of these instinctual drives. The late theoretician Otto Fenichel has outlined how parents injure Johnny's tender psyche: (1) by giving the child excessive gratification; (2) excessively frustrating the child; (3) changing from one to the other.

In the oral stage the result is a potentially disastrous *oral fixation.* The oral cavity will, said Dr. Herman Nunberg, "acquire meaning of a 'sexual organ' unconsciously in the neuroses, consciously in the perversions." Though the child seems to progress satisfactorily to the next level, the child unconsciously retains what the *Glossary* calls "strong 'charges' of psychic energy or libido" fixed to the earlier stage. "In his unconscious functioning, at least," says the *Glossary,* "the neurotic is 'pinned' to the past."

Fixations can be the architect of our character, analysts believe. The orally fixated person develops as a special type, whose traits can read like a $5 Zodiac chart. The healthy sucking infant who had "pronounced oral satisfaction," as one analyst says, generally lives with self-assurance and optimism. The deprived infant, on the other hand, is doomed to pessimism and sadism, with a depressive, demanding attitude toward life. "Because I was not given what I wanted," their unconscious mutters, "I shall not give other people what they want." (Analysts like to make the unconscious talk.)

In the oral-sadistic character, the demanding nature can be "vampire-like." On the other hand, the oral type may be a nursing mother person, who, under favorable conditions, will be extremely altruistic and helping. Under harsher conditions, they can be annoying interventionists.

Analysts believe that *orality* may be the route to addiction, perversions, drinking, smoking and kissing. Its by-products ostensibly include the manic-depressive cycle of mental illness. It is responsible for the fantasy of cannibalism, the eating and incorporating of a coveted object. Analysts point to the slang expression: "I could eat you up!" *Animal Crackers* loved by children, says one prominent analyst, are "significant remnants of early childhood cannibalistic fantasies."

The stage which rivals the oral in analytic affection is the *anal-sadistic,* that period from eighteen months to three years when a child's "sexuality" revolves around his defecation. Before Freud, feces occupied the privy of philosophical thought. Through psychoanalysis, it has become an elevated salon subject.

Defecating becomes sexual through the pleasurable sensation of excretion, and conversely, in the stimulation of the rectal mucosa when holding back feces, analysts say. By mastering his sphincter muscles, the child gains social power over his parents for the first time. He moves his bowels as a symbol of love and compliance and holds back as a sign of self-assertion. Analysts speak of adult *sphincter morality,* the manipulation of people the way one used his anal muscles in childhood.

A child's personality problems may be born on the potty in toilet training, we are informed. In his essay "Character and Anal Eroticism," Freud set down the establishment view on infant defecation and the danger that faces those who deviate. "As infants they seem to have been among those who refuse to empty the bowel when placed on the chamber, because they derive an incidental pleasure from the act of defecation," he wrote. Even later in life, this type of person "found a pleasure in holding back their stools," Freud was convinced.

The resulting *anal character* has become the celebrated syndrome of psychoanalysis. It is the contemporary "uptight" man: orderly, parsimonious, obstinate. It is the *obsessive-compulsive neurotic,* the by-product of fixated anal eroticism.

Psychoanalysis also makes titillating connections between feces and money. Freud even claimed that chronic constipation could be cured by solving the patient's *money complex.* The equation is: Gold or money = feces. "Money, like feces, is irrationally retained or irrationally thrown away," Dr. Fenichel has explained.

Feces is also equated with the male penis, the birth of children, even the female vagina. A modern analyst recounts the case of a male patient who insisted on anal play with his wife. "Yes, I somehow wanted to poke my finger into her anus, her asshole, I guess I mean, and I'll be damned if I understand that since she seemed to dislike it, but I persisted," he told his analyst. The analyst interpreted that the woman he really was hurting in his fantasy was his mother. He wanted to tear into her "cloaca," from where he had once imagined his baby brother—his sibling rival—had been born.

Contemporary analysts are as infatuated with bowel movements as was Freud. A researcher at the Infant Development Research Project of the Lenox Hill Hospital in New York describes the case of Tommy, a cheerful boy who became afraid to move his bowels.

Tommy was almost three, but had not yet been trained. His mother, described as "psychiatrically well-informed" in the *Journal of Child Psychiatry* report, did not train him because "she was pregnant and did not want to give him any additional cause for resentment." When Tommy walked around the house with his diapers full, his mother persuaded others to pretend they smelled nothing.

Tommy's grandmother, who actively disapproved of the procedure, suddenly died. The analyst interpreted Tommy's bowel problem as stemming from the grandmother's death. The child had linked her death with her rejection of his foul-smelling diaper. He had, it was interpreted, "become afraid to release stool at all and to make a bad smell, because that would make people leave him and die."

The anal-fixated, obsessive-compulsive neurotic is a common psychoanalytic patient. His obsessions run from the need to continually wash his hands to the drive to become wealthy, analysts believe. At first glance, the obsessional character seems admirable: conscientious, clean, orderly, self-critical, meticulous, ascetic, frugal, moral, compassionate. But this upright character is actually in flight from genital impulses, we are told. He has regressed back to his anal-sadistic period and suffers from a punishing superego which fears that such infantile impulses, as the desire to "soil," will break through.

Freudian infantile pleasure is taken where it can, even in urinating. It is called *urethral eroticism,* and supposedly breeds ambition and power. This idea partially stems from urinary competition, the male child's drive to make his urine spurt as far as possible. In fact, female ambition is supposedly weakened by woman's biological inability to produce a high-pressure, long-distance stream.

Those who suffered from enuresis, or bed-wetting, have an "intense" and "burning" ambition, Freud said. Alexander the Great was reputed to have been born on the night Herostratus set fire to the temple of Artemis in the hope of achieving fame. Fire and urination are therefore symbolically connected, particularly among boys for whom the urinating penis is a fire-fighting tool.

Urinary pleasure overlaps several stages. But chronologically, the child proceeds from the anal to the next important stage, the phallic, which covers the years three to five (or six). It is named for the phallus, or penis, which is said to assume great significance to the three-year-old. This is a normal reaction, but if it becomes exaggerated, the fixation can later produce the phallic man. He is a reckless, openly aggressive individual, what someone might call "a big prick."

Having interpreted the infantile base of neurosis, the analyst must move on. How does he effect a cure? How does he make the permanent *structural change* that creates the New Person?

Today's cure is considerably more complex than the early catharsis. "Psychoanalysis seeks a reintegration of the person—what is usually called a 'structural change'—by helping him to recognize his unconscious feelings and fantasies, and the source of these feelings," explains Dr. Burness Moore, past president of the American Psychoanalytic Association. "It helps him to come to terms with what he is like, without too severe a condemnation. The person gains acceptance of his unconscious wishes, but he now seeks to attain them in acceptable fashions. He also learns to recognize his defenses against these wishes and the consequences of those defenses in his everyday life."

The dictum is simple: Make the unconscious become conscious in order to give the person *insight* into himself. As Freud said, "Psychoanalysis is an instrument to enable the ego to achieve a progressive conquest of the id." He has stated it even more succinctly: "Where id was, there ego shall be." The goal is the mature genital personality, the analytic *mensch.*

After his "cure," the person uses insight instead of repression, analysts say. The New Person will better handle his infantile impulses and the pathogenic defenses against them. He will now use *ego functioning* instead of the "symptomatic and defense activities" which characterize the neurotic.

As we have seen, analyzing the *transference,* in which the analyst takes on the image of the patient's parents, is vital to the cure. But analytic success also requires analysis of the *resistance,* the patient's opposition to the process. The patient fights the analysis, and thus reveals himself. He talks trivia, ridicules the interpretations, falls asleep on the couch, comes late. Each is a clue to the eternal question: *"What is the patient trying to hide?"*

"As used in its broadest sense," state Drs. Mark Kanzer and Harold P. Blum, "resistance includes any motivated departure from commitment to therapy." Some patients may resist by blaspheming with fake associations or fighting the improbable interpretations. "They are mocking the analyst as they feel mocked by their parents," interprets one analyst.

Even the patient's couch posture can reveal volumes of resistances, we are told. The late Dr. Felix Deutsch, author of *Analytic Posturology,* offered body-language clues to the unconscious:

- Excessive movement is a hint that the patient is discharging his unconscious through his body, not his mouth.
- A patient who tells his tale flatly, but squirms, is telling only part of the story. The squirm tells the other part.
- The patient who is sitting on the couch or lying down with one foot on the floor is looking to escape.
- If the patient enters and leaves the room without looking at the doctor, he is hiding a great deal.

One contemporary aspect of psychoanalysis continues to gain theoretical power. It is the *defense mechanism,* a much discussed analytic technology. In *The Id and the Ego,* published in 1923, Freud reintroduced the once fully conscious ego—the great compromiser —as being partly unconscious, elevating it in analytic theory. Anna Freud continued this tendency in her 1936 work *The Ego and the Mechanisms of Defense.* From 1939 on, Dr. Heinz Hartmann expanded the new power of the ego in analysis and became the co-father of ego psychology.

Ego psychology and its *defense mechanisms* are now in high vogue. The APsaA *Glossary* defines the defense as part of the ego's struggle "to protect itself against danger," such as anxiety, fear, guilt, shame and disgust. Many of the defense mechanisms such as *repression, rationalization, intellectualization, reaction formation* and *regression* have already become modern clichés. Still others are quite obscure. Here is a short glossary for the defensively inclined.

*Projection:* An idea or feeling that cannot be tolerated in oneself is projected onto the outside world. A classic example is the paranoid theory of suspicion and hate which Freud believed was based on unconscious homosexuality.

*Isolation:* To avoid guilt, the person splits his motive away from objectionable actions. A man plunges a knife into someone without thinking of the act. Another use is the splitting off of emotion from logical thought.

*Displacement:* The unconscious transference of emotions from a painful idea to one about which the person is indifferent. A young man who constantly feared that a gas jet was open had displaced a repressed death wish against his father, one psychiatrist reports.

*Undoing:* A ritualized, seemingly magical act common in compulsions, the second part of which undoes the first. Since the child connects defecation with "narcissistic loss," counteracting actions are *undoing*. Example: the reading of magazines and newspapers on the toilet by adults.

*Denial:* The denying of painful sensations. A patient tells his analyst: "I had a dream about an angry man, and I cannot figure out who it represents. It is surely not my father." Actually, it is his father, but through denial he has consciously eliminated the idea.

In modern psychoanalysis, analyzing the patient's *resistances, transferences* and *defense mechanisms* has replaced dreams as Freud's "royal road to the unconscious." But some dream interpretation is still vital to the analytic ritual. The dream has always challenged man. Is it sheer nonsense, or does it contain meaning, even prophecy, within its seeming chaos? The seer, the shaman, the ancient astrologer traditionally interpreted our night stories. That magical function has now been assumed by the psychoanalyst.

The Old Testament equated knowledge of dreams with wisdom, and promised power to those who could master them. In *Genesis,* Joseph dreamed continually about power, envisioning that "eleven stars" had bowed down to him. His jealous brothers sold him into slavery in Egypt, but by interpreting the Pharaoh's dreams, he earned the governorship of all Egypt. Daniel, chief of seers to the king of Chaldea, also converted his skill at dreams and cryptic symbols into power. When Darius, king of Persia, conquered the Chaldeans, Daniel was named governor of Babylonia, a land his forefathers had come to as slaves.

The precedent was not lost on young Sigmund Freud. He was an apt student of the Bible and harbored similar dreams of glory, including someday, as he said, "ruling the nation." Freud thought the name Joseph played a magical part in his life. "Above all," says biographer Ernest Jones, "the biblical Joseph as the famous interpreter of dreams was the figure behind which Freud often disguised himself in his own dreams."

Freud was a good dreamer, who carefully recorded his night tales. During his engagement to Martha Bernays, he compiled a private dream notebook in which he remarked that dreams of traveling seemed prophetic. Each was followed by a journey. As a young doctor, Freud enhanced his dreams through the use of drugs, particularly cocaine. When he tried another drug, ecgonine, to compare its effect, the result was a "sharp" dream in which he walked among "the most beautiful" and "vivid" scenery.

*The Interpretation of Dreams,* published in November 1899, was Freud's favorite work. "Insight such as this falls to one's lot but once in a lifetime," he wrote. Scientists in Freud's day felt that dreams were not significant. They believed that they were mainly nonsense fortified with segments of pseudo-reality. No, Freud insisted, dreams are all meaningful. He saw them as *via regia,* the royal road, to the unconscious. His key was that every dream, whether pleasant or a nightmare, was actually a *wish fulfillment.* "Dreams contain the psychology of the neurosis in a nutshell," he wrote.

Freud explained that people could not interpret their dreams because what they recall is a disguise. "For the remembered dream is not the genuine article but a distorted substitute for it," he said. The *dream censor,* the nocturnal blue nose, disguises the repressed wish. What we think we dream is the *manifest content.* If we could look behind this subterfuge, we would find the true tale, the *latent dream.* The real dream, he assured the world, is "full of sense." Only what we think we have dreamed is "senseless."

The ordinary *day residues* make up much of the disguised dream. But the real-dream *constructors* are the same repressed infantile impulses that underlie our neuroses. The dream censor softens the dream to make its forbidden meaning unrecognizable, a process called *dream distortion.* Like most of analysis, the dream is therefore childhood played out once again, what Freud called "an infantile scene modified by being transferred to a recent experience."

In the intricate analytic mechanism, the *dream work* converts the real dream, first by condensing the material, then by *displacing* the meaning. The result is a translation of the latent material into dramatized visual form, including symbols of a "predominantly sexual kind," as Freud says.

How does the analyst reconvert the disguise to the real dream? Freud explained by giving us a personal example. At age seven he dreamt that he saw his mother, with a peculiar peaceful expression on her face, being carried to her bed by bird-beaked people. Young

Freud awoke in tears, screaming. The interpretation was obvious: the vulgar German word for fornication is *vögeln,* from *Vogel,* bird. Freud's anxiety was not set off by the fear that his mother was dead, as he had thought. It was caused by his repressed incestuous desire to make love to her.

Even our nightmares are often secretly sexual, we are told. Although Freud later admitted that not all dreams are sexual (there are childhood wishes against hunger, cold, etc.), he did believe that anxiety dreams were disguised passion plays.

If dreams are wish fulfillment, why do we have painful dreams? We misunderstand, say psychoanalysts. Human emotions are ambivalent and contain elements of what moralists call *evil.* Therefore, the hidden wish in an unpleasant dream is one we prefer to hide. "Analysis is able to demonstrate that these unpleasurable dreams are wish fulfillments no less than the rest," states Freud, who again provides a vivid personal case history.

Freud dreamt that he saw his son at the front in World War I, with his head bandaged, his hair flecked with gray and wearing false teeth. It seemed an obvious expression of fear that his son had been wounded or killed. But where is the wish in such horror? Deep analysis showed, said Freud, that within him there was "a concealed impulse" which harbored envy of the young by one who had grown old. The dream was a disguised, secret wish for his son's death, he interpreted.

The dream is ostensibly a play with literary symbols which analysts insist they can translate. Like Joseph or Freud, the reader who would read his own dreams or impress his therapist might enjoy this short glossary:

- *Emperors, empresses, kings and queens* are the dream symbols for parents.
- Brothers and sisters are symbolized by small *animals and insects.*
- The human figure is represented by a *house.* Men are houses with smooth walls. Females are houses with balconies (breasts, etc.) or projections.
- *Water* is the symbol for birth.
- Dying is symbolized as a journey or departure, by *plane, train,* etc.
- *Clothes and uniforms* in one's dream symbolize the opposite: nakedness.
- The penis is symbolized by scores of items. Penile erection adds such symbols as *flying machines,* including the *zeppelin.*

- Dreams of *flying* are erection dreams. Women, too, have such dreams. In their case it involves the clitoris.
- *Boxes, trunks, bottles, pockets*—many things which are hollow—are symbols for the female genitals.
- The breasts are represented by most fruits: *apples, peaches,* etc.
- Pubic-hair symbols are *woods and bushes.*
- *Machinery* is a symbol for the male genitals.
- *Piano playing, sliding, gliding, pulling off a branch* are symbols for masturbation.
- Symbols for sexual intercourse include *being run over,* and rhythmic activities such as *dancing, riding* and *climbing.*
- *Neckties which hang down* are a male symbol.
- *Underclothing and linen* are female symbols.
- *Blossoms and flowers* are symbols for virginity ("Do not forget," says Freud, "that blossoms are actually the genitals of plants.")

Still another dream symbol was recently suggested in the *Psychoanalytic Forum* by a San Francisco analyst: the *courageous lion for the psychoanalyst.*

How these dream symbols can be used to reveal the core of a neurosis was illustrated by a New York analyst. His patient had dreamt that she was riding on a green-and-blue-striped bird, which landed in a magnificent landscape. The interpretation was obvious. *Bird* is a symbol for the male organ; *riding* stands for intercourse. "The dream must mean that the dreamer practices or wishes to practice sexual intercourse like a man, that is, from above," her analyst deduced. The dreamer's husband was being treated for impotence, and although somewhat improved, could only have intercourse from the female position. The wife played the male role, as in the dream of riding the bird.

Interpretations such as these provide the *insight.* But insight is not enough to cure the patient, analysts stress. The patient must convert that knowledge into character change. This second part of the cure is called *working through.* The professional *Glossary* defines it as a continuation of analytic work after interpretation to overcome resistances that remain.

The working through takes several months, during which time the analyst repeats the analysis of the defenses trying to block the cure. Theorists have compared it to the "work of mourning." It seeks to lead "the modes and aims of the instinctual drives" into new paths after decades of living astray.

In most therapies once a patient is showing improvement it is time to let up. Not in psychoanalysis. Improvement sets up the last obstacle to cure: the notice of *termination.* It can send a dependent patient into a frightening childlike tantrum, reviving his worst neurotic symptoms. "We may see our patients reduced to making inarticulate noises, beating the couch, crimping their toes and making uncoordinated movements," one analyst says.

Pleased that a patient's ten-year-old phobia was finally broken, one analyst gave notice that the terminal phase of three months would begin. The phobia immediately came back "in full force," and took six months more to abate.

This trying terminal period is needed if patients are to break the childlike state of dependence created by psychoanalysis, analysts explain. "Unless we are ready to discharge our patients in a state of regression," Dr. Glover has declared, "we must provide a 'terminal period' during which the mind can regain its earlier level of adaptation, minus, of course, those symptomatic defenses which in the first instance brought them to treatment." He offers the following weaning formula: (1) three months for anxiety cases; (2) six to nine months for obsessional cases; (3) a full year for the truculent, narcissistic patient.

Does virtually everyone get off the analytic couch cured? The profession tries not to discuss it, but there are many other ways to leave the analytic room. Some leave abruptly when they obtain symptomatic relief, what analysts call the *flight into health.* Others may quit because they are not being helped, because they dislike their analyst, or for such private reasons as lack of money, a change in jobs or a new, satisfactory marriage. The analysis might enter a state of stagnation, the patient may seek out another analyst for a second chance, or move on to less costly psychotherapies. Some patients even try *reanalysis:* a second cycle of three to seven more years.

How has classic psychoanalysis stood up? There is shoptalk that the mother of therapies is dying. Is it an exaggeration?

"Fundamentally, psychoanalysis is a very healthy profession," Dr. Burness Moore, past president of the American Psychoanalytic Association said when interviewed. "Psychiatry in America is for the most part psychoanalytically oriented. But even those psychiatrists who are supposedly non-analytically oriented regularly use a good deal of analytic theory in their practices. In fact, psychoanalysts still constitute the strongest and most vigorous groups within American psychiatry.

"In terms of new psychoanalysts," Dr. Moore continued, "there had been a slight dip in the 1960s nationwide, and more recently in the New York area. But now there is a corresponding rise in other parts of the country. Part of the original decline was, I presume, a reaction to excessive expectations. Patients anticipated that they would be remade as the idealized figures they wanted to be. But analysis cannot cure everything.

"Now I think the pendulum is swinging back toward analysis. There has been a multitude of new therapeutic approaches, including group therapy, milieu therapy, behavioral therapy, the use of psychotropic drugs, and even community psychiatry, with tremendous help from federal funds. There has been increased interest in the newest and latest things. But here, too, disillusionment has set in. I think people are finding group therapy too superficial.They are learning that drugs cannot cure everything. There are limitations to all these new techniques. None of them can provide the satisfactions of the intense one-to-one relationship that exists in psychoanalysis.

"There is nothing as flattering as imitation," Dr. Moore continued. "In New York City alone, there are some fifteen different organizations professing to give psychoanalytic training. Only three of them are accredited by our organization, for we consider that the others are not 'up to scratch.' The public, unfortunately, doesn't know the difference, but it illustrates the tremendous interest in psychoanalysis as a therapy."

To the troubled citizen in the Psychological Society, pondering his emotional balance and wondering where to turn for help, these words are reassuring. But so are scores of opposing claims made every day by other therapies, from the human potential movement to alpha brain wave training.

As the mother of therapies, psychoanalysis—whether Freudian or neo-Freudian—underlies much of the Society. As the fountainhead of the Unconscious, it needs to undergo the test of validity. We must gauge whether it truly cures, and whether as a philosophical foundation stone of modern psychiatry it is best described as a science or a cult, reality or mythology, methodology or superstition.

# VI

## *Psychoanalysis: Science or Delusion?*

"THERE IS A GREAT NEED for critical evaluation of psychoanalytic therapy. Studies up to the present time cast doubt on its efficacy. There are a number of assumptions in psychoanalytic theory that have never been adequately tested. The consequences of childhood experience, including the Oedipus complex, may not be of the order we think.

"I personally believe that we have to develop new models of both normal and abnormal behavior other than the psychoanalytic models. Instead, we require models that synthesize modern-day concepts, including neurophysiology, life experience, interpersonal relations, and heredity."

This comment is in the tradition of the radical outside the fraternity. But it was made during an interview with Dr. Alfred M. Freedman, past president of the American Psychiatric Association and head of psychiatry at New York Medical College. Dr. Freedman is in the position of having been titular head of his profession, yet skeptical of much dogma within psychoanalysis, an art which he feels may one day be proven no more scientific than astrology or phrenology.

Dr. Freedman is one of the growing number of dissenters in a psychiatric world once cowed by Sigmund Freud. The medieval tower of psychoanalysis still dominates much of American psychiatry and psychotherapy worldwide. But the minions within and out-side are chafing to test the analytic mystique which has simultane-ously formed and overwhelmed their profession.

The dissent involves every facet of the Freudian art. Psychoanal-ysis is accused of harboring an anti-science attitude which resists investigation of its methods and results. Its theory is challenged as being imaginative Victorian speculation posing as science. Its cure has been descibed as an overly complex disguise for simple sugges-tion. Its orthodoxy is seen as a form of cultism blocking open inquiry into the mind.

One critic of what he calls the "three connotations" of psychoanal-ysis—as a research tool, as a theory and as a therapy—is a leader of American psychiatry. He is Dr. Jules H. Masserman, a member of the orthodox American Psychoanalytic Association, a founder of the rival neo-Freudian American Academy of Psychoanalysis and the 1978 president of the American Psychiatric Association.

In a statement to the author, Dr. Masserman criticizes analysis as a research tool, pointing out that "psychoanalytic reports are too often based on uncontrolled theoretical and clinical preconceptions." The classical Freudian theory, he believes, was "germinal at the time" but now appears to be "operationally simplistic in modern thought" and in need of extensive modifications.

Most patients come into contact with psychoanalysis in its third form, as a therapy. Here Dr. Masserman is equally critical. He states: "Whereas this intensive, protracted and expensive therapy may be required as part of the training of 'orthodox' analysts, and may be useful in exceptionally difficult cases, more broadly based, reality-oriented and economical procedures are preferable for most patients, and are also practiced by most psychoanalysts."

The public has long been regaled by often-told tales of successful analyses. The merchant prince, the actor or writer has endlessly recounted how he found his inner self on the couch. It is a theme consistently played out at fashionable cocktail parties, and in the psychiatric literature. But less noticed are accounts of the failed analyses, especially those of knowledgeable professionals.

A young psychiatrist on Manhattan's West Side described his failure to find Freudian salvation on the couch. "I spent three and a half years in classical analysis and found that I didn't like the timeless quality of lying on the couch and listening to my own voice drone on day after day," he relates. "The analysis seemed only to increase my sense of boredom and depression. I felt, What's the use of all this—what's the use. I never regressed sufficiently, and I never developed a full-blown transference neurosis. In a sense, I never felt I had been in analysis."

Another young psychiatrist, who spent four years on the couch of a classical New York analyst, feels it was a waste of time and money. "I was too stupid to know any better," he confided when interviewed. "He was the doctor and the authority, and I was not secure enough to act contrary. I was married at the time and having problems with my wife. I couldn't understand her point of view, so I naïvely asked my analyst if he could help by seeing her. He not only refused, but he wanted me to understand that I had been experiencing latent homosexuality in making the request. I was supposedly trying to get closer to him through my marriage problem."

Some disillusioned professionals even found their analysis to be emotionally destructive. Dr. Edwin G. Boring, late chairman of the Department of Psychology at Harvard University, underwent a mental crisis at age forty. He felt depressed, was convinced that he was achieving little in life, and decided to try psychoanalysis. "The first analyst I saw repelled me. He seemed too mercenary," Boring recounted in the *Journal of Abnormal and Social Psychology.* Boring later met an analytic celebrity, a former pupil of Freud's, with whom he underwent classical analysis for 168 sessions at the rate of five times a week.

When it was over, Boring's professional assessment was negative. He had hoped for a personality change which never materialized. "The aftereffects were somewhat worse than the analysis. I was distraught," he wrote. He finished his analysis on June 21, but when he asked when to expect results, he was told to wait a month. "I waited anxiously hoping for a new personality by July 21. None came," he recalled. His analytically oriented friends advised him to wait six months, which he did with disastrous results. In those months he could not read or write effectively, and one of his four lifetime sabbaticals had been wasted, he said.

Another psychologist, the late Dr. Carney Landis, of the Psychiatric Institute at Columbia University, underwent analysis with a close adherent of Freud, with similar disappointing results. Landis found that his questions were typically parried. "When your analysis is complete, you will understand that without further explanation," he was told. Dr. Landis comments, "I never achieved such complete understanding."

Landis found psychoanalysis emotionally enervating. After only ten hours, "I was possessed by a thoroughgoing anxiety which pervaded all my thinking and interpersonal relations," he complained. At various times he experienced "prolonged periods of irritation and a general bellicose attitude." The transference, that essential love-hate relationship to the analyst, he found "vastly overrated."

Landis and his analyst viewed childhood differently, a common culture gap in therapy. "This disagreement usually grew out of the fact that the analyst had an urban European background, while mine was that of a small Middle Western village," Landis explained. Landis also questioned the analyst's dream interpretations as arbitrary, rejecting the interpretation of train dreams as Freudian death symbols, for example. No, said Landis, they were freedom symbols. Living in a small town, trains had come to mean the chance to escape to the city.

He became convinced that Freudian dream interpretation was an elaborate guessing game in which the analyst could not lose. "Since the dreams were made up of a potpourri of elements, there were many possible lines of departure," Dr. Landis said. "The analyst could select any of the elements and say 'Does this mean that?' If I accepted, fine; if not, nothing lost."

When the analyst commented on Landis's neurotic problems, Landis replied: "What is normality?" The analyst countered by saying that he did not know because he never dealt with normal people. Landis queried back: "But suppose a really normal person came to you?" The analyst candidly replied, that "even though he was normal at the beginning of the analysis, the analytic procedure would create a neurosis."

Dr. Landis was an early skeptic of the Freudian art. Isn't it possible, he asked, that the complex analytic artifacts—the childhood fantasies, memories, the feelings of unreality, the love transference —are actually *produced by analysis rather than revealed by it?* If the cues were different, would not the script change?

"Personally, I believe that the phenomena are as much a result of method and procedure as of any basic personality structure revealed by the method," Dr. Landis argued. "Suppose all the stress were placed on adolescence and the struggle of the child to become independent of the family. The dynamics would be entirely different." The same change would take place, he theorized, if "the analyst would soft-pedal all sex reports and emphasize fear or anger."

Dr. Joseph Wortis, professor of psychiatry at State University of New York at Stony Brook, had his analytic discouragement at the feet of Freud himself. As a young physician at Bellevue Psychiatric Hospital in 1933, Dr. Wortis received a psychiatric fellowship from English psychologist and writer Havelock Ellis. He decided to use part of the grant to undergo a training analysis with Freud.

The Freud he found was an aging man, somewhat irritable and easily angered by criticism. When the young doctor offered comment, Freud attributed it to his *Widerstand,* his resistance. He blamed it on Wortis's "normality" and lack of introspection. Freud confessed that a normal person could become neurotic in analysis, but only because "the germ of neurosis" was carried by the person. Being normal, Freud believed, merely meant that one's complexities were stored away, out of reach. "There is no reason to feel proud of it," he told Wortis.

Freud interpreted a dream in which Wortis saw two adults outside a house and a line of servants entering the door. The house, Freud thought, represented a mother's womb, with Wortis's brothers and sisters issuing from it. The adults were Wortis's friends, Havelock and Françoise Ellis, who represented father and mother symbols. Wortis had refused to kiss Françoise in the dream, but the refusal actually meant the opposite, Freud explained. She was an Oedipal figure.

The theme of magical opposites permeates all psychoanalysis, including dreams. Freud told Wortis that dreams often mean the opposite of what they seem. If told backwards, they may reveal their secrets. Eventually, says Wortis, he found that he could sometimes get Freud to say something by proposing the *opposite.* "I thought there was more than a streak of pessimism in him, and I began to believe this personal quality had found expression in psychoanalytic theory," Wortis concluded.

Thirty-five years after Freud's death, arguments over psychoanalysis rage more passionately than ever. Is it the breakthrough which has created a true psychology of man? Or is it a nineteenth-century philosophical stab which is still unconfirmed, or perhaps been disproved, by modern research? What are the actual figures of success and failure on the couch?

The first statistical claims for psychoanalysis emanated from the Berlin Psychoanalytic Clinic for the years 1920–1930. They reported on 472 ideal Freudian patients: psychoneurotics and those with sexual and character disorders. By the end of six months, 161 patients had left. Of those who remained, three out of five reportedly had a successful outcome. If the dropouts are considered failures, however, the figure drops to a lackluster 40 percent. Among non-neurotics, including alcoholics and psychotics, the results were particularly poor.

Subsequent reports were released by the London Clinic, the clinic of the Chicago Institute for Psychoanalysis, two private practitioners and the Menninger Clinic. They were all collated by psychoanalyst Robert P. Knight. Of the 692 ideal patients, 193 dropped out before six months. Among those who stayed, 61 percent of the analyses were reported successful. But again, counting dropouts, the success claim falls precipitously to 44 percent.

These unsubstantiated claims, in which analysts graded their own work, are hardly dramatic. In his study on analytic cases, Dr. Hans J. Eysenck, of the University of London, reported a 44 percent success rate, a figure which rises to 66 percent if only those who complete treatment are counted. The late British research analyst Edward Glover believed this is unwarranted generosity. "It is probable that this correction is too wide, and that, as far as clinic treatment is concerned, a figure of fifty percent is fairly representative," Glover stated.

Do analysts exaggerate their results? Dr. Glover believed they do. The error is mainly in the false counting of those who only *improved*. "We may be pretty certain that unless the case is marked 'much improved,' the therapeutic result is not satisfactory," he warned. Using Glover's rule of psyche, we can estimate that in psychoanalytic cases collated by both Knight (an analyst) and Eysenck (a skeptic) a patient has approximately a 50–50 chance of getting off the couch in somewhat better mental condition than when he first lay down on it.

Does the American Psychoanalytic Association, the rock of Freudian tradition, concur with this 50–50, heads-or-tails chance of therapeutic balm?

The APsaA has made two statistical attempts at validation. The Central Fact-Gathering Committee of the APsaA, chaired by Dr. Harry Weinstock, made the first try. But it was an abortive attempt which ended in official obfuscation, cover-up, and eventual censorship. The committee received responses from analysts who reported on 1269 psychoanalytic cases. Again, analysts judged their own cases, and there was no scientific control group.

It was revealing, however, for some comment was made on every patient, whether analysis was completed or not. The therapeutic community eagerly awaited the report. But in December 1957 the

APsaA decided against publishing it, noting that the "controversial publicity on such material cannot be of benefit in any way."

Mimeographed copies became scarce, bootleg items. Gossip about the results was furtively bandied about. When the figures were finally released a decade later, it showed predictably good results for the patients in eleven diagnostic categories covering most of those who had completed their long analyses: 186 "cures," 375 "improved cases" and 16 "unimproved."

But the reason behind the report's underground status was hidden in its evaluation of *all the cases* in the same categories. The same 186 were "cured," *but 128 others were now graded unimproved or untreatable; 62 had been transferred to other analysts; nine had been hospitalized; 168 had left analysis for "external reasons."* More than half the cases were judged simply as "improved," the vague category which Drs. Glover and Knight had rejected. In all, the report claimed a cure rate of only some 1 in 6 of those originally accepted for treatment. Even in the ideal "neurotic reaction" patients, the Weinstock report claims only a 19.7 percent cure rate of those in analysis. It was a reason, not an excuse, for psychoanalytic organizational anxiety.

The quashed Weinstock study had also posed the unthinkable. Did analysts believe that psychoanalysis was an effective therapy? Dr. Weinstock specifically asked: "Given a young person, whom one could analyze four years or more, with all conditions favorable, what would be your expectancy of result, in percentage of cure, improvement and failure?" The replies were upsetting to the faithful. Forty-five percent of responding analysts expected "no cure in any of the conditions." Only a sanguine one-third (35 percent) expected a 50 to 100 percent cure in the neuroses, but less in other disorders.

The APsaA published a new report in October 1967 to correct the "methodological difficulties" of the Weinstock study. Using virtually the same cases, it finally produced the anticipated claim of potency. Improvement in total functioning was now the success criterion, and expectedly, 97 percent of patients who completed treatment were judged improved.

"The official report published in *The Journal of the American Psychoanalytic Association (JAPA)* can in no way be considered a serious scientific document," Dr. Arthur Shapiro, research psychiatrist and clinical professor at Mount Sinai School of Medicine, commented when interviewed. "There were no controls, no independent evaluation of the patients. The report is subjective and biased. It reminds me of the unsubstantiated claims published in journals before 1950, including one uncontrolled study which reported a ninety percent improvement using watermelon seeds as a therapy for hypertension. The analytic association sample represents only about twenty percent of the potential patients in treatment, and forty-three percent of the sample did not complete analytic treatment. I understand that seventy percent of the initial reports were lost, which is inexplicable.

"A 'fudge factor' is implied in the official report of ninety-seven percent improvement," Dr. Shapiro continued. "The data presented in the appendix indicated that in neurotic conditions with good prognosis, less than twenty percent of the follow-up cases should be considered cured—that is, completed treatment without residual symptoms. This is strikingly low for a therapy which purports to be superior to other therapies in its ability to cure rather than merely relieve symptoms."

Psychoanalysis is charged not only with failing to prove its effectiveness but with maintaining a strict sense of anti-science. Dr. Edward Glover believed that analysts do not sufficiently "apply to the data or observations or to the methods of interpretation such scientific controls as are available." As a result, he feared, "a great deal of what passes as attested theory is little more than speculation, varying widely in plausibility."

From Freud to the newest psychiatric candidate, analysts boast of the "science of psychoanalysis." Freud first used this effective ploy in a society in which science is God and the distinctions between true science and *scientism* are cloudy to an uninstructed public and impressionable professionals.

The Social Science Research Council, under Dr. R. R. Sears, has issued a detailed study of psychoanalysis. The report deflates many of the profession's scientific pretensions. It frankly calls psychoanalysis "a bad science." The Council then adds: "Psychoanalysis relies upon techniques that do not admit to the repetition of observation, that have no self-evident or denotative validity, and that are tinctured to an unknown degree with the observer's own suggestions."

Critics are convinced that an anti-research bias pervades the psychoanalytic profession. Analyst Dr. George L. Engel of Rochester, New York, has placed the blame. He says it falls "at the doors of those who fail to recognize the obligation to develop research psychoanalyst scientists as well as practitioners."

A psychiatric research team at Brookdale Hospital in Brooklyn, Drs. Merton Gill and Justin Simon, found this bias strong enough to cripple their attempts. They hoped to quantify psychoanalysis by tape-recording actual sessions. Their aim was to see how independent judges, other than the treating analyst, would evaluate the process. But they found the treatment room protected by an impenetrable Freudian curtain.

Their intrepid study came to naught. "We learned that analysts don't like to have their sessions tape-recorded," Dr. Simon summed up when interviewed. Reporting in *JAPA,* the analytic researchers warned their colleagues: "We can no longer afford to ignore the fact that, in addition to dissension within their own ranks, analysts are faced with widespread disbelief and distrust of their findings."

A suspicious analyst might interpret his profession's fear of scientific controls as *paranoic.* In 1952, an American Psychoanalytic Association committee named to examine the validity of the analytic treatment reported back empty-handed. "This four-year study has shown that a very strong resistance exists among the members of the American Psychoanalytic Association to the problem of evaluating results, even on the basis of their own definition," the committee concluded.

Dr. Hans Strupp, a research psychologist at Vanderbilt University, blames the pervasive anti-science bias on Freud himself. "Freud saw little need for statistical studies of treatment outcomes. As far as he was concerned, no numbers were needed to demonstrate what to him was self-evident," says Strupp.

The anti-statistical, anti-research tendency of psychoanalysis is nourished by the analysts' faith in the Freudian system. Analysts typically deride other psychotherapies as purveyors of "mere symptom relief." In contrast, psychoanalysis is hailed as the surgery of the soul.

The late Dr. Herman Nunberg, who practiced in New York and Berlin, was praised by Freud as having written the "most complete and accurate presentation" of analysis. In it Dr. Nunberg stated that in psychoanalysis "the workings of the psychic apparatus are laid open," and permanently repaired. The completely analyzed person is ostensibly cured and as close to Freud's "ideal fiction of normality" as therapy can make someone.

Critics are skeptical of such grandiose claims. Dr. Edward Glover was annoyed at the abuse of such words as "thorough analysis" and particularly of "exaggerated expectations and sometimes even exaggerated claims of overenthusiastic practitioners." This tendency has tainted the profession with "a psychoanalytic mystique which not only baffles investigation but blankets all healthy discussions," he added.

Doubts about analysis have been increasing dramatically among helping professionals. "Psychoanalysis, for which many have sacrificed so much, has not become the therapeutic answer; it seems to be mired in a theoretical rut vigilantly guarded by the orthodox," charges prominent analyst and psychiatrist, Dr. Roy R. Grinker, Sr., an active member of the American Psychoanalytic Association.

O. Hobart Mowrer, Ph.D., former president of the American Psychological Association, believes that "there is not a shred of evidence that psychoanalyzed individuals benefit from the experience." Dr. Hans J. Eysenck is equally doubtful. "Few patients are warned before undergoing analysis that not only is there no evidence that it will improve their status, but there is evidence that it may actually make them worse," he says.

Psychoanalysis has insisted on blind affirmation from its practitioners. This rigidity has strengthened its orthodoxy, but has also stimulated rebellion within the profession. Dr. Melitta Schmideberg is one of the angered psychoanalytic fraternity. Her credentials are impeccable. She is the daughter of Melanie Klein, British analytic prophetress, and had practiced psychoanalysis in New York and London for decades before finally resigning from the international organization a few years ago. In London, she had been a member of the analytic priesthood as a *training analyst,* and boasted of early friendship with Freud, Ferenczi, Karl Abraham, Ernest Jones and others of the inner circle.

Her complaints against psychoanalysis are encyclopedic. She charges: (1) lack of personal concern for the analytic patient; (2) faulty method; (3) excessively long treatment; (4) childlike dependence of the patient; (5) emotional immaturity of the analyst; (6) failure of scientific investigation of validity; (7) contradictory theory. Dr. Schmideberg reports in the *International Journal of Psychiatry* that a leading analyst once told her that the analyst "who puts concern for the patient before the method ceases to be an analyst."

Dr. Schmideberg doubts the validity of analytic results. She believes they are "assumed almost as an article of faith," but are seldom objectively measured. She attacks the failure to help patients who have been in analysis for long periods without improvement.

Dr. Schmideberg is particularly concerned about patients who have been severely damaged by analytic treatment. She recalls several patients who came to her from other analysts in a harmed condition. A fifty-four-year-old accountant, who began his analysis thirty years ago, had been in treatment "almost all the intervening years," a near record on the couch. He originally entered psychoanalysis because he suffered from anxiety and a feeling of inferiority. Since his lengthy treatment, says Dr. Schmideberg, "his sense of inferiority had increased because he had been unable to practice his profession and had had to spend most of his money on treatment."

She also recounts the case of a woman patient who had been in treatment with a New York analyst for ten years because of anxiety. When she eventually came to Dr. Schmideberg, she was in a "deteriorated schizophrenia-like condition."

The profession carefully avoids open discussion of such taboo topics as *psychonoxious,* or *psychiatrogenic,* damage to the patient. Freud admitted there were emotional side effects from analysis, but minimized them. "Serious and lasting aggravation of a neurotic illness is not to be feared from incompetent employment of analysis. The disagreeable reactions will soon die down," he wrote confidently.

Critical practitioners refute the Master on this point. Dr. Gert Heilbrunn, a Seattle member of the American Psychoanalytic Association, fears that analysis produces an excessive dependency in patients with a weak ego. "There is a type of patient who becomes too dependent on his analyst," he explained when interviewed. "His transference may not be dissolvable, and the analysis in effect becomes interminable. He is constantly thinking of the analyst. Later he becomes tied to other people in the same dependent way." Dr. Heilbrunn tries to screen out these patients and treat them with brief sit-up psychotherapy instead.

An excessive couch-produced regression to childhood is another psychiatrogenic problem. This is particularly true in borderline analytic cases who may be nudged over into psychotic episodes. A former medical director of the New York Psychoanalytic Institute estimates that only one in ten patients is ideally suited for psychoanalysis. Many patients do not have the *ego strength* to take the childlike flight from reality brought on by analysis.

Dr. Norman B. Atkins spells out the danger for those who are mentally disturbed. "The psychoanalysis of exceptionally troubled people such as psychotics, borderline patients, addicts and those with severe psychosomatic disorders is frequently complicated by their tendency to serious, prolonged and psychotic regressions," he warns in *JAPA*.

Dr. Atkins describes a thirty-two-year-old male who regressed dramatically during psychoanalysis. He stopped shaving and bathing, lost his urinary and fecal continence, had spontaneous ejaculations without erection. He described the odor from his own anus as the "smell of a rotting animal." In the third year of analysis, the patient was convinced he was going insane and should have shock treatments instead.

Silence as used by the analyst is one of the techniques that can be calamitous for some patients. Dr. John Frosch believes that silence (known to go on for as long as six consecutive weeks) may trigger a fearful psychosis. "Silence tends to accentuate the sense of unreality and to mobilize frightening unconscious fantasies," he states in *JAPA*. "I should like to remind you of what Wallerstein said regarding one of his patients. 'She demanded that I say something—anything. She had lost herself, everything had become unreal, just words. She asked, "Do I exist?" ' She demanded that I say something to prove she existed."

Dr. Albert Ellis, a prominent New York psychologist, is angered that insufficient attention has been given to dangerous analytic side effects. Analysis provides a good excuse not to work at self-improvement, Ellis says. The patient is encouraged instead to concentrate on "irrelevant events and ideas" such as the Oedipus complex and the supposedly "pernicious influences of unloving parents."

Analysis can also foster a weakened sense of independence, Ellis fears. "While many forms of therapy abet the patient's being dependent on the therapist, classical analysis is surely the worst," he complains. He is convinced that analysis usually "does more harm than good and is contraindicated in the majority of instances in which it is actually used."

One of the most vulnerable aspects of analysis is the *interpretation,* the nucleus of all insight psychotherapy. Critics believe that the interpretation may be a pseudo-technology, a flexible, almost literary device in the hands of an imaginative therapist.

A young male patient exhibited a strange compulsive symptom. He insisted on disconnecting all the lamps in his house every time he went out. His conscious fear was that a short circuit would start a fire. But the analyst interpreted that the patient harbored an unconscious fantasy in which he wished the house would burn down. As a result, his father would become distraught, take to drink and be unable to work. The boy would then symbolically replace him as head of the household and fulfill his repressed Oedipal desire to mate with his mother. Disconnecting lamps had become a symbolic desire for incest.

Critics have charged analytic interpretations with being "extremely variable." Even the late establishment analyst, Dr. Lawrence S. Kubie, admitted that proving that an analytic interpretation is "adequate, unique and necessary" is quite difficult. "Analysis has rarely been able to present data that meet this ultimate criterion of validity," he has pointed out. The obvious problem is what scientists call *reliability,* the consistency of interpretation from one analyst to another. Would several analysts hearing the same case material make the same interpretations?

Dr. Allen Wheelis, a prominent San Francisco psychoanalyst, thinks not. "A dozen psychoanalysts listening to the same material are likely to formulate a dozen different estimations of its unconscious meaning," he has stated. When interviewed, Dr. Wheelis candidly admitted, "I think we should be more modest about how much we can know. There is a great deal of conjecture in interpretation. I prefer to tell my patients, 'I think that this might be the case,' that they might consider it."

Even contradictory interpretations seem to be possible in analysis. One training analyst recounted a dream brought in by a candidate analyst. The patient's friend, Mr. M., was crossing the street. He had his hat on and was smiling. In his dream associations, the patient described M. as a voyeur, an exhibitionist and impotent. The analyst interpreted that the patient wishes to expose his penis without shame. M. is behaving like a happy child and the patient identifies with him.

Later, the same candidate presented the dream to another training analyst. "This colleague," stated the analyst, "emphasized the homosexual component. According to his interpretation, the dream expressed the patient's homosexuality. M. is a woman with a penis, and crossing the street means he is a prostitute."

A discipline that can interpret the same dream as being *either a happy child exhibiting his penis* or *a prostitute crossing the street* troubles logicians. Philosopher Ernest Nagel, University Professor Emeritus at Columbia University, sees psychoanalysis as riddled with logical fallacies. "I have little doubt myself that for every ingenious interpretation of a case, another one no less superficially plausible can be invented," he states.

This subjectivity is the Achilles' weakness of psychodynamic psychology. In the official organ, *JAPA,* Dr. W.W. Meissner confesses: "Thus the analyst becomes an intrinsic and integral part of the data he reports, and psychoanalysis is faced with the dilemma of becoming a science, at least in part, of subjectivity." The result is a confusing mixture of two unconscious minds—the patient's and the analyst's. It becomes a therapeutic *folie à deux*.

The patient may accept or reject the analyst's interpretation. But to the suspicious analyst, rejection may mean the patient is offering *resistance* to the revealed truth. To break it, the analyst may bring up the same interpretation again and again in other contexts until it is finally accepted, then "worked through."

This psychic hammering is a form of brainwashing, says one critical psychiatrist. "The interpretation sounds bizarre and without merit to the patient, so he refuses to accept it at first," he points out. "But the analyst keeps coming back with so much triangulation of the idea that the patient finally accepts the interpretation, even if it is patently false. It is a form of brainwashing."

Analysts claim that other psychotherapies use mere suggestion to persuade the patient to get well. Critics thrust the same charge back to analysis. Dr. Hans Strupp thinks analysts are fooling themselves about the healing power of their colorful interpretations. "The psychoanalytic position that psychotherapeutic change is due to unconscious rearrangements brought out solely or predominantly by 'correct interpretations,' " he says, is both "untenable" and "factually incorrect."

As we have seen, Hans Strupp and other investigators are convinced that the mainspring in all therapies, including psychoanalysis, is *suggestion.* The best patient in all therapies is the most suggestible one. Cues, ideas, life support, criticism are dispatched from a dominant therapist to a dependent, usually gullible patient. "All forms of psychotherapy employ suggestion," says Strupp, "and the patient's suitability for psychotherapy is based on his potential openness to suggestion."

The result in psychoanalysis is what we might call *psyche-think.* The patient is subtly indoctrinated to produce information for his analyst in a special Freudian form. Critics believe that free association, for example, is really not so free. Dr. Hiram K. Johnson, writing in *Psychiatric Quarterly,* claims that the patient learns to deliver material which conforms not only to analytic theory but to the "personality, ideology and 'school' of the person conducting the analysis."

Even our dreams show the influence of analytic psyche-think. Wilhelm Stekel, at first a friend and later an antagonist of Freud, put it simply: "Patients dream in the dialect of whatever physician happens to be treating them . . . Sadger's patients will dream about urinary eroticism; mine perhaps of the symbolism of death and religion; Adler's of 'top dogs' and 'underdogs' and of the masculine protest."

The conscious mind can also be seeded with suggestive ideas. Then, like a rare archeological find, they will be unearthed during the same psychoanalysis. Freud once admitted this seeding, but made it sound intellectually harmless. "We give the patient the unconscious idea of what he may expect to find and the similarity of this with the repressed unconscious one leads him to come upon the latter himself," he said.

The classic case involving the first child analysand, Little Hans, is an exquisite model of psychoanalytic suggestion. (Ernest Jones believed the case inaugurated the later "brilliant success of child analysis.") Hans was actually treated by his father under Freud's supervision.

At several points, the zealous father-analyst pummeled Hans with leading questions:

Father: When the horse fell down, did you think of your daddy?
Hans:   Perhaps. Yes. It's possible.

*   *   *

Father: When you were watching Mummy give Hanna [his sister] her bath perhaps you wished she would let go so that Hanna should fall in?
Hans:   Yes.

*   *   *

Father: It seems to me that, all the same, you do wish Mummy would have a baby.
Hans:   But I don't want it to happen.
Father: But you wish for it?
Hans:   Oh, yes wish.

In an unguarded moment, Freud admitted that suggestion guided the child through the Freudian forest. "It is true that during the analysis Hans had to be told many things which he could not say himself, that he had to be presented with thoughts which he had so far shown no signs of possessing and that his attention had to be turned in the direction from which his father was expecting something to come," Freud confessed.

This obvious prompting of the child patient raises serious questions about the intellectual integrity of all child psychoanalysis. Dr. Paul Chodoff, clinical professor of psychiatry at George Washington University, is among those who are dubious.

The first problem is language, Chodoff says. The child has an "incomplete mastery" of language and makes "idiosyncratic use of it." The analyst must rely heavily on play therapy, then translate the play data back into language before making his interpretation. It is virtually impossible to know, says Chodoff, "whether the child is in fact really accepting his interpretations in a meaningful way." He suggests the ultimate criticism: "One might wonder whether the analytic experience was simply not very comprehensible to the child."

The critical Dr. Schmideberg also is convinced that the suggestion which guided little Hans also takes place in adult psychoanalyses, if in a more sophisticated form. "For intellectual types, it [suggestion] is more likely to be attached to a high-sounding analytic interpretation," she says.

Dr. Schmideberg describes secret methods of analytic suggestion including subtle cues that tell the patient how to feel. "If the patient is told that in order to be successfully analyzed he has to pass through a phase of depression, he may feel that the analyst expects him to produce states of depression." Since direct criticism of the patient is not permitted, the analyst attributes the criticism to the patient himself, she explains. The analyst does this by suggesting to the patient: "You unconsciously think . . ."

With all its liabilities, is psychoanalysis at least better than the many psychotherapies it has spawned?

Dr. Lester Luborsky, professor of psychology at the University of Pennsylvania, examined over a hundred validity studies and concluded that he could find no special benefit in analysis or any other method. Rather than method, success seems tied to the patient's mental health at the time of treatment. "They [the studies] indicate that the healthier a patient is to begin with, the better the outcome," Dr. Luborsky concluded.

Comparison between psychoanalysis and shorter psychotherapy was performed by analyst Dr. Gert Heilbrunn. His raw material was 241 of his own cases, drawn from over a fifteen-year period. He treated some patients by full-term classical psychoanalysis, while other patients received either "brief psychotherapy" of less than one hundred hours, or "extended psychotherapy" of over one hundred hours.

The result was no testimonial to analysis. The briefest of therapy proved the best for psychoneurotics. The psychoneurotics showed almost all their gains in the *first twenty hours* of brief therapy. "This indicated clearly," reports Dr. Heilbrunn, "that more than two-thirds of the psychoneurotic patients got well quickly and did not have to present themselves for further treatment."

Not only analytic validity but Freudian theory itself is under strong academic challenge. "As a result of a succession of personal and professional experiences," states psychologist O. Hobart Mowrer, "I have become increasingly convinced, during the last ten or fifteen years, of the basic unsoundness of Freud's major premises."

Freud was generally farsighted in anticipating such criticism. He made most of his theories indistinct enough to escape targeting. How can anyone disprove the existence of the id, the ego, the superego? The appeal of this abstract trinity has been its childish simplicity at a time of biological ignorance. It is not unlike the power of mythology among the ancients.

Arguing against historic Freudian metaphysics is not easy. But new research is fortifying those who see the Freudian concepts as basically superstitious. Specific physical areas of the brain, not Freud's imaginative divisions, may be the operating centers of certain emotions and thought.

Work in electrical brain stimulation, pioneered by Dr. Jose M.R. Delgado of Yale and others, shows that target areas in the brain can be stimulated to produce anger, affection, even laughter. A painful response has been produced as close as one-fiftieth of an inch from a pleasurable one in the same brain. EBS has stimulated rage in an experimental animal, which displayed affection when the probe was moved only slightly. Dr. Delgado found that by stimulating the anti-appetite center in the hypothalamus, he could alternately persuade the animal to starve or to gorge itself with food.

During treatment of epileptics by EBS, neurosurgeon Dr. Wilder Penfield accidentally found that long-forgotten memories were suddenly discharged from the brain. The memory poured out as long as the current was applied. Analytic *structure* and *topography* of the mind, concepts which so overwhelmed psychology, now seems archaic in the light of such experiments. Perhaps we ought to ask the psychodynamic professional: Is the unconscious seat of a repressed id impulse one-fiftieth of an inch from the storage center for dream symbols?

Logician Ernest Nagel is convinced that the Freudian mind structure does not meet proper scientific criteria. When interviewed, he explained that the analytic functions of id, ego and superego were *psychic,* yet analytic theoreticians speak of them as *somatic* realities. To Dr. Nagel this analytic idea is "a ghost in the machine" of the human body. "I will not venture to say that such locutions are inherently nonsense, since a great many people claim to make good sense out of them. But in all candor I must admit that such locutions are just nonsense to me," he states.

Dr. Charles R. Shaw, director of research at Hawthorn Center, Michigan, agrees. He calls the "vivid, graphic representation" of the id, superego and ego as "vastly oversimplified." If taken literally, he says, "it presents a point of view and presumed knowledge which are quite spurious."

Psychoanalysis obviously suffers from an irremediable scientific deficiency. Scores of Freudian errors are buried in current psychological and psychiatric theory, ennobled as truth by professional orthodoxy. After three-quarters of a century, some are only now being revealed as false. One is the analytic concept of *bisexuality,* or, as Freud stated, that all humans have an "innately bisexual constitution."

According to psychoanalytic theory, sex drives are not differentiated by gender during the oral and anal stages, but are *polymorphous perverse.* The child receives its true psychosexual orientation only at the Oedipal stage when it decides on its love object. In adults, *bisexuality* is the rationale for what Dr. Max Schur called the "ubiquitous latent homosexuality," an idea which turns up in numerous analytic and psychotherapy cases, and increasingly in current novels and films. This unconscious homosexuality is ostensibly at the core of an entire class of mental illness, *paranoia,* the classic persecution disease.

Conceived by Dr. Wilhelm Fliess, Freud's intimate Berlin colleague, bisexuality was so eagerly adopted by Freud that he claimed credit for it before apologizing to Fliess. The idea of bisexuality has stirred up rampant sex confusion in our culture. It is responsible for the contemporary Freudian cliché of the woman hidden in the unconscious of every man, and vice versa. "You are certainly right about bisexuality. I am getting used to regarding every sexual act as one between four individuals," Freud wrote Fliess enthusiastically.

New scientific evidence indicates that the bisexual theory is not true. Dr. John Money, Johns Hopkins University School of Medicine medical psychologist who specializes in sexual identity, reminds us that analytic theory predated new knowledge in genetics, chromosome counting, behavior genetics and hormonal action on human sex characteristics.

"Basically, Freud believed there was a little bisexuality in all of us at all times, I suppose until we die. That is not true," Dr. Money stated when interviewed. "Sex identity is fixed early in life, and once differentiation takes place, it is fixed and there is no backtracking."

There are several sexual possibilities. Bisexuality is one for only a certain group of people, he says. In those males where psychosexual differentiation is heterosexually complete, no feminine vestige of bisexuality remains. A considerable number of males fail to differentiate psychosexually as heterosexuals, and feminine traits, not bisexuality, become obvious. The third group is ambiguous, and remain bisexual and ambivalent. These are the only ones who fit Freud's fanciful theory. Dr. Money points out that bisexuality, when it exists, does not necessarily occur in 50–50 proportions, as many would believe. It can appear in varying ratios, even one as unbalanced as 90–10.

"The general rule here is not that all members of the species grow up bisexual," Dr. Money outlined in the *International Journal of Psychiatry,* "but they are bipotential at the outset and differentiate to become, as a general rule, unipotential. Whatever the outcome, masculine, feminine or ambivalent, it becomes fixed."

The Freudian idea that the Oedipal confrontation determines sexual choice is also challenged by Dr. Money: "I wouldn't take that as true," he says. In the inverted Oedipus complex, the child supposedly turns to homosexuality, while in the properly resolved Oedipus complex, the child develops an attraction toward members of the opposite sex.

No, says Dr. Money. Psychosexual identity of children is determined much earlier in life than age five. It starts in the embryo and becomes firmly fixed sometime between eighteen months and two and a half years of age, long before the child enters the supposed Oedipal conflict. By that time, it is generally too late to change psychosexual identity. He speaks of boys born without a penis who can assume female identity if raised as girls beginning prior to two and a half years of age. But in those unfortunate cases where parents have sought sex change for a child for similar reasons at age four and a half, it is too late for real adjustment.

The Johns Hopkins researcher is convinced that *psychosexual status,* the gender identity the child feels, is the result of many factors.

It includes its chromosome make-up, its social environment in the first two years and a predisposition based on hormonal action within the uterus. These prenatal hormones may come from within the fetus itself, from the mother through the placenta or even from drugs.

The hormones leave permanent traces within the brain pathways which affect the child's later behavior. He gives the example of a group of 25 girls who suffered from an "androgenital syndrome." Each of them had received an overdose of androgen, male hormones, while in the womb as a result of an adrenal malfunction. At birth the girls exhibited an enlarged clitoris. Later in life they showed the classic tomboy behavior.

The effect of prenatal hormones on the little child can be dramatic. Androgen administered to pregnant women has produced females with a penis and an empty scrotum, while cyproterone, an anti-androgen, has, in animals, produced males with female external genitals. Dr. Money points out that there is a clinical analogue in which this happens spontaneously in human beings. The Freudian concepts of bisexuality and the Oedipal theory do not, stresses Dr. Money, meet the test of such new psychosexual information.

The dream is another ancient unknown on which modern analysis and psychiatry have capitalized. Research on dreaming is less advanced than work on sexual development, but information from more than twenty sleep laboratories fails to support, or at least makes irrelevant, the hallowed psychoanalytic theory of the meaningful dream.

By monitoring thousands of dreamers, researchers have learned that we dream in regular patterns during the night. They are loosely defined in four stages. In the deepest, Stage 4 (delta sleep), man is immobile and difficult to wake. But every 90 minutes, on the average, we enter a lighter stage labeled Stage 1—REM, or Rapid Eye Movement Sleep.

In this extraordinary condition, muscles go limp and eyes move from side to side at high speed. Oxygen consumption increases, the heartbeat becomes irregular, and the face may grimace and look agitated. It is in this stage that man does most of his dreaming, creating often bizarre vision-stories.

The REM stage reoccurs regularly throughout the night. With its onset, we start the strange dream mentation in segments averaging 20 minutes. The human animal dreams four or five times every night, some 20 percent of the time that we are asleep. As the night goes on, the dreams become progressively more vivid. The last dream, usually the only one remembered, is the most emotional product of REM sleep. We can also dream in non-REM sleep, but these dreams are generally more rational, like the mind drifting in waking thought.

All mammals engage in REM sleep. Monkeys, at least, dream as man does. At the University of Pittsburgh, Dr. Charles Vaughan taught monkeys to press a bar when they saw an image. During the REM-sleep stage, the monkeys pressed the bar at a frantic pace and would grimace, even bark, as if "seeing things" in their sleep.

What is the purpose of REM sleep and its dream state? Animal research indicates it may help process long-term memory. Researcher W. Fishbein deprived mice of REM sleep and found they performed only half as well in learning a task as did other mice.

Why do the eyes move so rapidly during the dream? Researchers first thought the eyes were "watching" the internal dream vision as if looking at a movie. A more advanced opinion is expressed by Dr. Merrill Mitler, of Stanford University, a colleague of prominent sleep researcher Dr. William C. Dement. He believes the eye movement and the dream itself may be a product of neural energy discharged from a portion of the brain.

Dr. Mitler explained when interviewed that insertion of electrodes deep into the brains of cats indicates that rapid eye movement is triggered by intense neural activity emanating from the brainstem, the most primitive part of the brain located above the spinal column. It is an electrical phenomenon called PGO spikes, which discharge in bursts. They somehow are related to ocular motor activity, including the rapid eye movement in REM sleep. The firing normally takes place off and on, but in experiments with cats the PGO spikes were almost totally confined to REM sleep.

Is this the long-sought source of our dreams? Dr. Mitler, and others, believe it is. They feel that the ancient riddle of the dream may be near a solution. Our night stories may merely be an accidental offshoot of these neural bursts without any particular meaning. "It is my opinion," says Dr. Mitler, "that the dream is a by-product of the REM stage, created by the processing by the mind of endogenous—from within—neural activity. What we call a dream is the result of the mind trying to make sense out of these bursts."

Then why is the dream so bizarre and disconnected? "Probably," says Dr. Mitler, "because the neural energy is coming into the mind in a pattern that it is not normally used to in regular thought. I believe that dreams have less meaning than we used to think they had."

Other researchers point to the physical changes going on in the REM state. These may include a "hot" brain temperature and hypothalamus-directed increase in adrenal secretions which trigger the anxiety and stress felt in many dreams. This new information indicates that the dream is probably more physiological than psychological. It may merely be a desperate attempt by the brain to keep up with the physical changes taking place during REM sleep.

One reasonable non-Freudian explanation is that during the dream the mind insists on converting all neural charges into thoughts and images. In REM sleep, each rapidly fired PGO spike triggers a random image from the brain memory bank. The mind then frantically tries to connect these disconnected, almost random images into a story. Because it is overwhelmed by the electrical storm from the pons, apparently the best the mind can do is to put together a poorly organized, surrealistic tale called a dream, one with considerably less meaning than waking thought and action.

Dr. Svi Giora, of Tel-Aviv University, has outlined several other discrepancies between Freudian dream theory and current research. Writing in the *American Journal of Psychiatry,* he points out that although Freudian theory sees *day residues* as the raw material of the dream, everyday thought is more typically found in the non-REM sleep-thinking. Similarly, enuresis (bed-wetting), and sleepwalking, which are supposedly evidence of unconscious conflict, do not take place in the REM-dream stage, as Freudian theory suggests. They are seen in the usually non-dreaming, non-REM stage.

Sleep researcher Dr. Allen Rechtshaffen, of the University of Chicago, believes dream research refutes another popular Freudian belief—that we forget our dreams because we repress them. No, he says, the dream seems to be an ephemeral mentation which vanishes by itself. "When we awake someone in the REM state, we get a dream report about eighty to ninety percent of the time," he explained during an interview. "But if we wait five minutes there is a lot of forgetting. There seems to be a failure of the mind to consolidate our dreams. If it were repression, as theory suggests, we would not get the good response immediately on awakening."

If psychoanalysis is not a science, if it is not the most effective of therapies, if it is covertly subjective and suggestive, why should it stand so imperiously in the world of psychology and psychiatry?

The reasons are many. One obvious answer is that it is a highly candid sexual and mystical view of man. It is a vision that rivals prior perceptions as "the greatest story ever told." It has the ingredients of sex, mystery, love, martyrdom and conflict that have made the Bible tales such seductive inspiration for millions.

Psychoanalysis is complex. But basically it is a theory of personality being shaped in early childhood by fierce conflicts between urges we never suspected we had, and the disapproving adult world which would strangle them. Although non-orgasmic, these childhood urges are supposedly sexual, and no less passionate than the lust of male adolescence.

The rich tale is obviously that of infantile sexuality. The theory is a cornerstone of psychoanalysis. However, new information in biological psychiatry, primate research, dream studies and direct observation of child behavior casts it in the image of aging metaphysics, even sophomoric invention.

Child psychologist Robert I. Watson, author of *Psychology of the Child,* charges analysis with relying on "adultomorphic" bias, the reading of adult feelings into infant behavior. "One of the problems with psychoanalytic theory, appears to be that much of it is derived from introspective ruminations of adults about their own childhood with very little direct observation of the behavior of infants and young children," he states. "Psychoanalytically oriented individuals have also been singularly reluctant to test hypotheses with controlled studies, like that of Sewell."

In that study, Dr. William H. Sewell observed 162 farm children of "old American stock," and compared the parents' child-rearing practices with the children's personalities. Sewell concluded "that psychoanalytically derived concepts were of little or no value in predicting either emotional problems or lack of them," says Watson.

Infantile sexuality is denied by Dr. Paul Chodoff, a George Washington University psychoanalyst, who considers it relatively rare, and more pathological than normal. "I do not believe, as many analysts do, that infantile sexuality is an innate universal drive which must find outlet or be distorted into neurosis," he stated when interviewed. "There is a definitive lack of objective proof for the existence of infantile sexuality as used in this sense. I believe that strongly sexualized behavior as seen in some children tends to be pathological rather than a normal phenomenon, the result of unusual constitutional drives or, more often, a serious disturbance within the family.

"Personally, I did not observe much behavior that could be interpreted as sexual in my own children when they were little," Dr. Chodoff continued. "Some analysts do talk about how sexual their children are, but usually they are referring to behavior which can be interpreted in a number of ways. I believe that Freud introduced the concept of an innate infantile sexuality partly out of a need to save his general theory when his childhood seduction idea turned out to be false."

Child psychiatrist Dr. Peter H. Wolff, of the Harvard Medical School, is also critical of the infantile sex theory. He believes that by connecting the child's bodily curiosity with sexuality, psychoanalysis is in error. The relationship is "in no sense evidence for the psychosexual life of infants" imagined by analysts, but only "analogies of form," Dr. Wolff states in the *International Journal of Psychiatry.*

The Freudian theory of *infantile amnesia*—that we have forgotten our childhood conflicts—is a convenient way of avoiding proof. It has satisfied millions, especially the educated, for two generations. Not surprisingly, this key concept now appears to be false. Modern research indicates that most adults have not forgotten their early childhood. Instead, *most of it was never originally remembered.* Studies show a striking failure of human memory in the early years of life.

"The fact is that no matter how the process of memorizing during infancy is measured, there is clear proof that it is far below the efficiency of that of the older child or adult," states the Social Science Research Council. Tests of recognition, memory pictures, rote memory regularly show that human memory "has proved to be poor at the earliest level and to increase by a fairly constant rate to a later period," they point out.

Several studies, including those by psychologist David Wechsler and R.S. Woodworth, support this conclusion. Dr. George Miller explains that the ability to remember is linked to the ability to reason and the previous amount of information stored away. The young child is limited in his skill to mentally record what is happening because of the absence of prior record. If there is a physical failure of childhood memory, then the Freudian theory of repressed memories also fails. We can hardly repress what we never remembered.

Dr. Robert Sears summarizes the case: "There is no good evidence, then, (1) that there is a sharply delimited infantile amnesia; (2) that the generally poor recall of childhood experiences requires other explanation than that of poor learning . . ." Infantile amnesia is apparently a biological trick of an undeveloped memory system, not a Freudian twist of unconscious repression.

Analysands themselves have found that the brilliant flash of childhood recollection is more often a legend taken from Hollywood films or early Freudiana. Whether repressed or never recorded, many patients have learned the expensive lesson that their early childhood is usually undredgeable.

Undaunted analysts have substituted the *reconstruction.* Dr. Wolff of Harvard is one critic who is skeptical about such rebuilt memories. "The clinical reconstruction of early childhood experience deals with the subject's present view *about* his past, and not with the discovery or archeological artifacts that have been buried," he states.

Even the existence of infant psychosexual stages, from oral to phallic, is being refuted. Dr. Roy R. Grinker, Sr., argues that these "so-called libidinal stages of development" are "in need of revision." Grinker believes the oral stage is "not the only or major condition of satisfaction and frustration" in young babies. He offers the research of Dr. Harry Harlow, who demonstrated that monkeys preferred a surrogate terry-cloth mother they could "feel" to a plain wire-frame one which "gave" milk to satisfy both hunger and orality.

Oral and anal clichés have become sharply etched caricatures in the Psychological Society. Modern man speaks of people, even nations, as having an oral character of generosity or greediness. We are familiar with the anal stereotype of orderliness, miserliness and stubbornness, aspects of the contemporary "uptight" man. Although these clichés are already in our language, they are being reexamined.

The idea of orality, the reverence given to infant sucking, produced an early psychological worship of breast-feeding. Speaking of Freud, Jones says, "It is worth mentioning that, as one would expect, he was fed at the breast."

This Freudian breast bias collapses under examination. Dr. H. Orlansky reviewed the studies and found them highly contradictory. Children breast-fed ideally for six to ten months had fewer behavior problems than other children. But another study contradicted this result: college students judged emotionally secure were found to have been breast-fed little or none at all, or for periods of over one year. William Sewell compared the behavior of five-year-olds with their feeding patterns as infants. He found no relationship between the child's later adjustment and how he was fed as an infant.

Many psychiatrists emphasize the emotion with which the mother gratifies the child's oral needs. But comparative anthropology has a way of undoing prepackaged ideas. The late anthropologist Ralph Linton cited women of the Marquesan Islands who seldom nurse babies because of the importance of shapely breasts in their culture.

The Marquesan child is fed indifferently on a flat stone while a handful of mixed coconut milk and breadfruit trickles down its throat. "The child would sputter and gasp and swallow as much of the mixture as it could," Linton described. "The mother then wiped off the child's face with the edge of her hand, took another handful and poured it on." This failure to gratify the child's oral needs is apparently not harmful to Marquesan children, Linton stated.

The penile erection in infants is trumpeted by analysts as *prima facie* evidence of infantile sexuality. But once again, studies deflate analytic hypothesis. Researcher H.M. Halverson observed nine infants for ten days, and found that seven of them had an erection at least once a day. Rather than being a sign of pleasure, the erections tended to show that the child was uncomfortable. In 85 percent of the cases, the erection was accompanied by crying, restlessness or the stiff stretching of legs. Only when the erection subsided did the children become relaxed. Halverson concluded that the penile erection was the result of abdominal pressure on the bladder, serving a simple bodily, rather than a Freudian erotic, need.

The zenith of Freudian infant autoeroticism is genital manipulation. It supposedly begins early in life and reaches its climax at the Oedipal stage in a childhood orgy, in which the young masturbator has visions of his mother, instead of nude centerfolds, floating in his young fantasy.

Freud claimed that childhood masturbation was a universal practice which reached its peak at the "flourishing period of sexual activity at about the fourth year." Freud was not speaking of touching the genitals sporadically, but of purposeful masturbation in *all* boys of four. "The boy enters the Oedipus phase; he begins to manipulate his penis and simultaneously has fantasies of carrying out some sort of activity with it in relation to his mother," Freud said in *An Outline of Psycho-Analysis.*

Freud never observed childhood masturbation or infant sex habits. He relied solely on adult reconstructions. "Why do I not go into the nursery and experiment?" Freud asked rhetorically in a letter to Fliess. "Because with 12 1/2 hours' work and no time and because the womenfolk do not back me in my investigations," he wrote. Like Freud, many analysts are convinced that the penis is the child's lovemaking instrument. Dr. Jacob Arlow, a leading New York theoretician, speaks of the child in heat, with "a wish to exhibit his penis to his mother, to press his penis against her, to have her admire his penis."

Most mothers and pediatricians see little evidence of this. Genital manipulation in most children appears to be a casual, sporadic examination of the body. Only in a few hypersexual children do nonanalytic observers see the supposed eroticism.

H.L. Koch studied preschool boys and girls during four hundred half-minute observations. The incidence of genital manipulation in boys was low—less than two and a half times for the entire eight months' period, and less than one time for girls.

The true situation is probably as our pre-Freudian grandmothers believed: *the human child is generally a nonsexual being.* "The manipulation of genitals in young children probably is to be regarded merely as an undesirable habit similar to bad table manners or nose picking," says Merry and Merry, authors of the child development text, *The First Two Decades of Life.* Even so-called "sex play" evidenced by young children, they report, is generally misunderstood by adults. "Like masturbation [in children], most of this sex play is the result of curiosity and exploratory activity, and probably has little, if any, sexual significance."

Analysis' most creative tale is the Oedipal theory of the boy's incest wish for his mother. Nonanalytic professionals are baffled by the complex, which is supposed to be universal in five-year-olds, but is rarely seen in nonanalytic psychiatric work. As Drs. O. Hobart Mowrer, Paul Chodoff and others suggest, the Oedipal wish is probably a rare pathology of distorted mother-child relationship—perhaps a reflection of young Freud's own illness.

The primate laboratory offers proof of the natural, desexualized relationship between sons and mothers. Jane Van Lawick-Goodall, Ph.D., the renowned chimpanzee researcher, recently published her behavior studies of chimpanzees from Tanzania in the *American Journal of Psychiatry.* She reports that chimpanzees are promiscuous. Females mate with several males, although they may pair-bind for several mating periods. Up to the age of five or six years, the male youth lives in the tree "nest" with his mother. He starts to move about with others during his seventh year, and by the ninth or tenth year the adolescent chimp leaves home. After that, he returns frequently to his mother's home.

Though the mothers and sons were affectionate, as in human groups, *they scrupulously avoided sexual play or incest.* Dr. Goodall never observed a son trying to mate with his mother, although the mother would mate with every other male available. "In one instance the mother, during four days of oestrus, was mated by every other mature male in her group with the exception of her two adult sons, who were also in the group," she reports. The absence of mother-son incest has also been observed in Japanese and rhesus monkey groups.

The Sears study concludes that the Oedipus complex is "a sharply etched grotesquerie." The sample on which Freud constructed his infantile theory, they say, was "far from characteristic of contemporary American children."

With its obvious scientific inadequacies, how did psychoanalysis become so potent in American psychiatry? In some ways it was the chance result of an event wedded to an American tradition of gullibility, particularly for movements boasting a jargon of science.

It began with Freud's appearance at Clark University in 1909 at the invitation of psychologist G. Stanley Hall. At the meeting the Freudian system found a warm reception among a number of influential Americans. Psychologist William James, who attended the lecture, reportedly told Ernest Jones: "The future belongs to your work."

Freud credited the visit with being a turning point: "Psychoanalysis was then no longer a delusional fancy; it had become a valuable portion of reality. It was like the realization of a fantastic daydream," he wrote. (Freud's enthusiasm did not extend to America itself. For years he claimed that its bad cooking had injured his stomach. He was put off by its "aggressive" women, and concluded that the American experiment was a "giant mistake.")

In addition to Hall and James, there was Adolf Meyer, the lion of American psychiatry, and Harvard neurologist James J. Putnam, whose conversion to analysis was invaluable to the movement. In 1910 Putnam delivered a laudatory paper on analysis before the American Neurological Association, of which he had been president.

Meyer, although not a total convert, introduced Freudian dynamic psychology into Bloomingdale (the Westchester Division of New York Hospital) and Manhattan State Hospital, where scores of young psychiatrists learned the new faith. A similar conversion of William Alanson White, then superintendent of St. Elizabeth's federal asylum, inched analysis closer to, first, respectability, and then to its dominant position in American psychiatry.

Freud had little or no honor in Vienna, where Professor Julius von Wagner-Jauregg, head of the university's Department of Psychiatry and discoverer of the cure for the brain disease caused by syphilis, was contemptuous of Freud's metaphysical sex ideas. But in Switzerland, in 1904, Eugen Bleuler at the University of Zurich began to use Freud's methods on patients with the help of assistants Carl Gustav Jung and Karl Abraham.

In 1907, an influential convert to analysis, Dr. Frederick Peterson, clinical professor of psychiatry at Columbia, advised a bright young resident, Dr. A.A. Brill, to study with Bleuler at his clinic in Switzerland. Brill was later to meet Freud and to translate his works into English, thus accelerating the American acceptance of the Freudian art.

From 1908 to 1913 the Manhattan State Hospital on Ward's Island was the unofficial center for analytic training. Brill, who was on the staff, was viewed as Freud's emissary. On February 11, 1911, he formed the New York Psychoanalytic Society. Of the twenty-seven members, fourteen were from Manhattan State Hospital. The American Psychoanalytic Association was formed three months later, in May 1911.

By 1913 the training analysis had come into fashion: one should be analyzed before he analyzed others. But it was then considered a brief and informal affair. (Wilhelm Stekel claimed that Freud had analyzed him in eight hours!) Analysis was then often practiced in America as a sit-up affair. Dr. Clarence Oberndorf, an American analytic pioneer, did not move his patients to the "recumbent" position on the couch until after he met Freud in 1921.

Freudian theory had become respectable in psychiatry by 1940. But after World War II it became *the* dominant power. The prophet of conversion was Dr. Karl Menninger. As head of the wartime psychiatric program, he brought Freudian theory into the service in both treatment of patients and training of young psychiatrists. The impetus was carried over into postwar Veterans Administration programs and from there to psychiatric residences in general. The wartime-bred Freudian became the psychiatry instructor of the 1950s, the department chairman of the 1960s and 70s and the mainspring of Freud's conquest of American psychiatry.

Was there much criticism of Freud during this early period? Paradoxically, some of the most vitriolic criticism of Freudian theory came from analysts spawned by this revolution, the neo-Freudians who even today accept much, but not all, of the Master's teachings. Freud paid too little attention to cultural factors and was too bedded down in sexuality, they believe. Although neo-Freudians consider themselves proper psychoanalysts, orthodox Freudians disparage both their theory and training. "I do not consider any of these schools of thought to be psychoanalysis," classical analyst Dr. Burness Moore comments.

None of the neo-Freudian theories can individually compete with

Freud, but collectively they boggle the unconscious. Like classical analysis, it, too, is organized, as the American Academy of Psychoanalysis. It is the psychic housing for medical psychiatrist-analysts who agree with, but don't necessarily agree with, Sigmund Freud.

The neo-Freudian movement has its ancestry in the Psychological Wednesday Society, which began meeting in Freud's waiting room in 1903. One of the group, Alfred Adler, was to become the first heretic of the Freudian church. He and the other Viennese analysts had organized a court revolt against the foreigner Jung, who had been "anointed" as "Crown Prince," the terms Freud used to described the expected succession.

Adler had come to disbelieve Freud's sexual theories, including infantile sexuality. He placed his emphasis on the ego, on the dominant drive to overcome feelings of inferiority. Dr. Kurt Adler, son of the disciple, explained during an interview that his father stressed "man's striving for superiority" not as a power drive but as an attempt to overcome natural feelings of inferiority.

Adler's phrases have psychological popularity. They include "masculine protest," the drive toward mastery; "inferiority complex"; and the concept of "life style." (For female liberationists, Dr. Adler explains that "masculine protest" means that *the culture demands male supremacy.*) Individual psychology, as Adlerian theory is known, is not potent in psychoanalysis, but it is a force in psychotherapy. Adlerians maintain fifteen institutes worldwide, including the Alfred Adler Institute in New York.

Adler broke away in 1912. Freud spoke of it sadly: "I had quite got over the Fliess affair. Adler is a little Fliess come to life again." The apostasy of Carl Gustav Jung was even more traumatic for Freud. The first theoretical tiff came in 1908, when Jung postulated that *dementia praecox* (schizophrenia) had an organic cause, a "toxin" that attacked the brain.

The heresy that finally tore them apart was Jung's reluctance to accept the sexual base of neurosis, an idea that outraged his native Switzerland. As Jung said, "Both with students and with patients I get on further by not making the theme of sexuality prominent." In 1913 the two formally parted, and Jung resigned the presidency of the International Psycho-Analytic Association.

Jungian psychology is a mystical art based on *archetypal images,* mythological models which include the range of Greek gods. Each of us supposedly is connected to a *collective unconscious,* which links the past and the present and is passed on from generation to generation. Even emotional problems of a grandfather may magically be passed on to the grandson. "As we see it, we have penetrated a dimension of the psyche that is a mystery and is best expressed in those terms," explains a Jungian analyst. "The use of rational terms gives the mistaken impression that something is grasped completely when it cannot be."

Jungian analysis has been dormant in America. But it appears to be stirring, perhaps in response to the rising popularity of the occult. "We used to get one or two applicants a year for our training institute," says Dr. Edward Edinger of the C.G. Jung Foundation for Analytical Psychology in New York. "We now receive ten or twelve."

The criticism of three other early Freudian disciples helped shape neo-Freudianism. Wilhelm Stekel, one of the original four in the Wednesday group, became Freud's hated enemy. His theorems stimulated interest in the "here and now." Stekel was an early believer in *active therapy* and in shorter treatment. He felt that the therapist's personality, not the method, was primary in the cure.

Otto Rank, a member of the early inner circle, conceived an idea so unusual that it, too, led to a break with Freud. The Rank theory was that the very trauma of birth, not the infant experience, created human anxiety. Vestiges of Rank's idea are still heard in the desire to "return to the womb," a neurotic dependency that blocks the exercise of positive will.

An extraordinary twist in the Freudian revolt is the quasi-heresy of Melanie Klein, a British laywoman born in Vienna. She practiced child analysis in Berlin and Budapest before being invited to England by Ernest Jones. Despite its partial apostasy, her movement is a vital part of organized British psychoanalysis.

She converted Freud's childhood causation into a baby theory. In Kleinian analysis, the Oedipus complex, the superego and the sense of guilt all begin as early as five months of age through close mother-child contact during the oral stage. This, not the Oedipal wish of the five-year-old, is the scene of the crucial neurotic conflict, they believe. The Kleinians, who make up perhaps half of the British Psycho-Analytical Society, have popularized the concepts of *oral envy*, the greed of the child in breast-feeding which ostensibly dominates much of the person's life thereafter.

Even among official American Freudians, there is an intra-Freudian schism. The late Sandor Rado, a student of Freud, split with the New York Psychoanalytic Institute over the libido theory.

He taught *adaptational psychodynamics,* which refuted infantile sex as an instinctual drive. Neurotic conflicts, said Rado, were miscarriages of the child's attempt to adapt, generally to the family environment. Rado established the "Columbia School" of analysis at the Columbia University Psychoanalytic Clinic for Training and Research. But his somewhat tamer revolt has been contained—if uneasily—within the motherly fold of the American Psychoanalytic Association.

None of these early Freudian heretics was able to mount a formal school of medical psychoanalysis to contest the classical, or "kosher," Freudians. That was left to two later *dynamic culturists,* who developed new orthodoxies replete with their own training academies.

Karen Horney, a Berlin-trained analyst, came to America in the early 1930s and taught at two classical institutes. By 1941 she had become an apostate and had set up the rival Karen Horney Clinic in New York.

The Horney ideas have a touch of native pragmatism missing in Freud. Horneyites believe man acts in three ways: moving toward people, moving away from people and moving against people. The first is socialization, the feeling of being wanted and dependence; the second, a detachment and independence; the third, a sign of hostility and aggressiveness. In Horneyan theory the significant aspect is not the category, but the question as to whether the person is choosing in a "spontaneous" way rather than as a "compulsion."

The Horney movement developed the now popular split-screen idea of man as both a self-image and a reality, generally with an unfortunate gulf between the two. The *idealized self* is neurotic and prideful. The *actual self* is the personality as it exists at a point in time. The *real self* represents the potentially constructive forces within the person that need to be freed to make the *actual self* better.

Harry Stack Sullivan, whose theories sustain the prestigious (for a neo-Freudian) analytic academy—the William Alanson White Institute in New York—notched the heresy one step further. Sullivan has evolved as the first significant American-born psychoanalytic theorist. In fact, his phrase *interpersonal relations* now means virtually anything that takes place in the Psychological Society.

Sullivan was critical of much of Freud. Man's search for security, Sullivan believed, was perhaps more important than Freud's pleasure principle. Sullivan did not deny infantile sexuality, but downgraded it. Freud's four stages (oral, anal, phallic and genital) have become six in Sullivania: infancy, childhood, juvenile, preadolescence, early adolescence, late adolescence.

Children in the latency period, whom Freud dismissed as nonsexual, have been resurrected by Sullivan as Stage 4 preadolescents. "It is during this period, about eight to ten years of age, that they get chums, that for the first time someone else becomes important. We think this time of childhood is very significant psychologically," states a spokesman at the White Institute. (No school has yet resurrected the psychological significance of middle age.)

Sullivan also called on a trinity to explain "self." His threesome is described not in Latin but in catchy Americanisms: *good-me, bad-me* and *not-me.* The good-me is the non-neurotic self-image which develops secure feelings from warm beginnings. The bad-me is the unfortunate self-appraisal produced by a hostile or anxious environment. The not-me is the disassociated repugnant feelings created by traumas which may later reappear during emotional crises.

As a group, the neo-Freudians use the couch somewhat less and insist on shorter treatment. They see patients fewer sessions per week and show more concern for the here and now. But in the final accounting they, too, seek the hidden meaning in the unconscious dynamics of the child which made the man.

The neo-Freudians have even made overtures of friendship, but the traditional analytic establishment is unyielding. This dogmatism of classical analysis has helped to cast it in the image of a stern organized religion, even a cult. In it, *training analysts* are its priests and disciples.

The religious nature of analysis has been noted by several observers. "It is impossible to overemphasize the fact that the direct implications of the concepts and methods of psychoanalysis inevitably lead the researcher into the area of theology," stated Dr. Hiram K. Johnson. Dr. Roy R. Grinker, Sr., concurs: "There is much to say about the religious quality of the psychoanalytic 'movement,' the dogmas for which belief is expected from each new student. There is much to compare with religion in Freud's form of leadership and the use of psychoanalysis as a closed system, practiced as a way of life."

Some psychiatrists say, usually in whispers, that the way of life is maintained by a system of internal indoctrination and external intimidation that rivals that of the strictest church.

"There is considerable intimidation in both hospitals and medical colleges where analysts and analytically oriented psychiatrists are in control," a professor of psychiatry in New York explains. "You have to toe the line if you want to get along. In one analytically controlled institution, I proposed trying the new idea of rapid emergency psychotherapy along with a controlled study to compare the results with psychoanalysis. I was then a third-year resident. After that, I wasn't invited into the inner sanctum and could get no promotion."

Dr. Percival Bailey, professor emeritus of psychiatry of the University of Illinois, recalls that in one institution, analysts blocked the appointment of a biologically oriented psychiatrist as chairman by threatening to resign en masse.

Promotion within the analytic hierarchy is granted only to the most pious and compliant. Dr. Harold Voth, winner of the Karl Menninger Award, has been passed over for training analyst at the Topeka Institute for Psychoanalysis. Dr. Voth is convinced that his independent views are involved. A colleague, Dr. Robert Cancro, advised him not to publish his controversial article on Freud's personality "until after he had been made a training analyst." Says Dr. Cancro, "Unfortunately, many contemporary psychoanalysts confuse theory with truth. They not only reify theory, but treat it as revealed dogma."

One analyst, who has attended both the Freudian New York Psychoanalytic Institute and the rival neo-Freudian William Alanson White Institute, believes this dogma is perpetuated through the classical training analysis for would-be psychoanalysts. He calls it a "purifying procedure" which brainwashes the candidates first to supinely accept, then to promulgate the Freudian dogma.

"The training analyst rules at the New York Psychoanalytic," he explained. "Some graduates have told me that they played the game during their training analysis, then took their real analysis afterwards." He recounts his own training analysis as highly unsatisfactory. He did not like his Germanic analyst, and the analyst did not like him. "My analyst sat in judgment on my analysis and my career. I was told rather harshly: 'You must be a mensch. You are not a mensch. I will make you a mensch.'

"Once I dreamt that my analyst was playing with a globe, as Charles Chaplin did in *The Great Dictator*," he continued. "When I candidly told the analyst about the dream, it triggered a furious outburst: 'You are mocking me. You need to mock me.' I learned that the training in a Freudian institute is not an education but an attempt at purification."

Another psychiatrist, who dropped out of the institute and back into general psychiatry, considers analytic training an "intimidating and coercive" procedure. "People who are very adaptive and compliant get through easily," he explained. "However, if you argue, you are assumed to be putting up *resistance,* which is an indication of some internal conflict. Since they consider Freudian theory as complete truth, only compliant candidates are considered healthy."

A prominent American psychoanalyst, Dr. Fredrick C. Redlich, former dean of the Yale University School of Medicine, believes this method of training excludes many independent minds from the profession. Speaking before the New York Medical College, he lamented that his fellow analysts "have created a tightly controlled shop through a careful system of educational supervision-control." He added, "One could almost speak of censorship. The boundaries are tight. There is little room for the doubter, the critic, the maverick."

The psychiatric gadfly, Dr. Thomas S. Szasz, is convinced that training analysis is a surreptitious method of maintaining power over the analyst-to-be. The training analyst learns the candidate's innermost secrets. He then reports them, he says, to the all-powerful Education Committee, thus violating the traditional confidential doctor-patient relationship. "Spying may be a strong word with offensive connotation, but its use is justified here because it fits the facts," Dr. Szasz suggests.

If psychoanalysis answers all the criteria of a dogmatic faith—including a sense of infallibility—is its revealed truth the reality of man's mind?

Hardly. Contemporary research and logical examination have shown it to be an anti-science and an illogical set of theories developed mainly out of the eccentric mind of Sigmund Freud. It bears no relationship to the objective knowledge of the mind, as meager as that information is. As a religion, it does not even ennoble the best instincts of man. It might be viewed as a highly respectable mass delusion born from the typical human tendency to invent, then worship, what we do not yet know.

Dr. Arthur Shapiro calls psychoanalysis a "concoction of the mind." When interviewed, he elaborated on his criticism. "Many patients today are more educated, cultured, intelligent, informed, accomplished and successful than their treating psychoanalyst. This presents a problem, for such patients would not pay sixty dollars an hour for simple reassurance and support. Nor would they pay such a fee perhaps four times a week for a magical ritual based on primitive shamanism. The only appropriate possibility would be an esoteric system not easily understood by even an educated patient. It would also require an unapproachable and prestigious physician whose very presence would enhance the procedure. Such a technique has been created, and it is called psychoanalysis.

"It is obvious that psychoanalysis is a seemingly complex, intellectually convoluted system. But in actuality, it is a disguise for its true method, which is the simple placebo effect. Just as bloodletting was perhaps the massive placebo technique of the past, so psychoanalysis —and its dozens of psychotherapy offshoots—is the most used placebo of our time. It is an expensive placebo, ranking with the unicorn, which was an ancient placebo reserved for the wealthy, the nobility, and even the Pope. But psychoanalysis probably does no worse than any historic placebo—some patients improve, some patients do not, and still others deteriorate."

One of psychoanalysis' strongest defenses against the charge of being a religion, or a cult, is that it has been so closely allied with medicine, and thus science. Particularly in America, the professional equation has been: *a psychoanalyst is a doctor is a psychiatrist is a scientist.* The medical connection in America has granted analysis the prestige it lacked in Europe, and contributed greatly to its acceptance by patients and the general culture.

But it is now obvious that the medical aspects of analysis are a façade, since it is not necessary to be a medical doctor to be a classical, accredited psychoanalyst. There are even those within the profession who believe that medical training, through its very selection of doctors, may be detrimental to the analytic calling.

Psychologist Stanley Appelbaum, Ph.D., of the Menninger Clinic, a practicing Freudian analyst and a member of the American Psychoanalytic Association, is skeptical of his profession's medical connection. "I do not think medical training has any value in psychoanalysis," he stated when interviewed. "If it had any value, we would have to assume that those prominent analysts worldwide who practice without a medical degree are somehow sub-par in comparison to their colleagues. This is not true. Anna Freud, for example, is not a doctor.

"Psychoanalysis is a language science and a behavioral science," he continued. "It has very few values and styles of thinking in common with hard sciences. Our only stock-in-trade is words. We need people who are capable of evocative use of the language. I think that historians, English professors and writers would do at least as well as psychoanalysts as people interested in biology, chemistry and physics—those who are now coming into the profession through medical school."

Psychoanalysis is confused about its own role in society. That confusion has helped to make analysis and its allied helping professions as much a cultural and emotional problem as they are a solution. Psychoanalysis represents a danger in the Psychological Society it helped to shape. It is not only that it has many of the manifestations of a religion, even if a distorted and unloving one, but that it has so long posed as a science. In that pose, it has for a half-century helped to block much true research in psychiatry by diverting the curious and the talented into the pursuit of Freudian ritual and dogma.

Both within and outside the profession, observers have begun to wrestle against the hypnotic hold of psychoanalysis and its psychodynamic mythology, seeking free inquiry into the most precious of all human functions, the mind.

# VII

## The Shadow
## of Dr. Freud

"I THINK THAT SIGMUND FREUD had sexual conflicts within himself which he did not resolve. His belief in constitutional bisexuality, for example, was an excuse for certain personal traits. I believe many analysts are brilliant and dedicated people, but analysis tends to attract those with a personality similar to Freud's—passive men and aggressive women."

This daringly aired suspicion about the prophet would normally be relegated to men's room gossip at neo-Freudian conferences. But it was made during an interview with Dr. Harold M. Voth, teaching psychiatrist at the Menninger Foundation and a member of the American Psychoanalytic Association. Dr. Voth is convinced that Freud displayed "a considerable degree of femininity" in his personality, a trait that has colored the entire profession by making what he calls the "neurotically troubled" Dr. Freud a model.

The personality of Sigmund Freud, who died almost forty years ago, lives on in the disciplines of psychotherapy, psychoanalysis and much of modern psychiatry. Freud's personal needs and conflicts have become almost inseparable from the entire framework of the Psychological Society which he created.

Those driving needs have infiltrated the psyche of millions of individuals as well, remaking much of our personalities in his image. By offering his catalog of foibles as the symbols of *normality,* Freud achieved immortality. He has successfully projected his personality and his style of thought onto much of humanity, especially the impressionable American psyche. We have all—some unwittingly, others unwillingly—become the children of Sigmund.

There is no need for another formal biography of Sigmund Freud, for Dr. Ernest Jones's three-volume work is classic. Nor need we create a dubious psychobiography of Freud's unconscious. His *conscious* thoughts are readily available to us in biographies, his own autobiography, his other voluminous writings, his letters to Wilhelm Fliess, to his fiancée, Martha Bernays, and to many others, and even the memoir of his personal physician, Dr. Max Schur.

But there is a need to draw from these varied sources to construct a portrait of the personality of Dr. Freud, one which will illuminate how much, and in what way, his neuroses and character have shaped so much that is intangible yet so pervasive in our Society today.

Although the impact of Freud's personality has been broad, it has not generally been beneficent. The portrait that emerges is one of a man driven by the furies of hostility and envy, weighed down by depression, death wishes, phobias and severe, debilitating neuroses. He was professionally distorted by his extreme superstitiousness and gullibility—the antithesis of a man of science. Freud the man is more the unhappy philosopher than the intrepid researcher who society thought would unlock the key to our confused behavior.

The failure of psychotherapy is now obvious. What is less apparent is how closely that failure is tied to the personal shortcomings of the prophet himself. As a theoretician and scientist, Sigmund Freud was impulsive. His work was tainted by an unmistakable style of excessive enthusiasm which often led to inaccuracy. He was an adroit, even brilliant, theory maker, but his wish to have something true overrode all objections.

Freud was a self-confessed impetuous thinker, a "conquistador" of the mind, he called himself. The result was that both his career and the disciplines of psychotherapy and psychoanalysis which he spawned are lavishly strewn with errors which Freud presented to the world with absolute confidence, even arrogance.

Freud's first monstrous error was his seduction theory. In 1896 he was convinced that all his hysteria patients had been seduced in childhood by adults. It has the verisimilitude of all Freudian concepts: a veneer of detailed argument which makes the untruth ring with reality. It was his challenge to the French, who believed hysteria was a hereditary disease. For a while he basked in this theory as his "momentous revelation," the "caput Nili [source of the Nile] of neuropathology."

But as we have seen, he recanted a year later. On September 21, 1897, in a letter to Dr. Wilhelm Fliess, his Berlin confidant, he privately announced that he no longer believed that hysteria was caused by the parental or adult seduction of the patient as early as one year of age. The patients had either lied to him, or he had put the idea in their impressionable minds, he confessed. Without the theory, he bemoaned, he had lost his "hope of eternal fame" and "certain wealth, complete independence, travel."

Freud's personality consistently deterred him from being objective. He was a proficient self-hypnotist and a man of passionate, unrestrained beliefs. He believed thoroughly and evangelically in a theory right up until the moment he dropped it. Then, just as fervently, he would transfer his faith to the one replacing it.

From the discarded seduction theory, which Dr. Ernest Jones called "this far-reaching blunder," Freud's new concept of psychoneurosis rose phoenix-like. It was infantile sexuality, the ingenious conversion of the false seduction theory from reality into a fantasy and then back into reality.

The seduction theory was a short-lived blunder. Freud typically held on to his scientific errors longer, then replaced them with other theories without a word of explanation. In the unfortunate cocaine episode, for example, Freud not only exercised poor judgment but stubbornly defended his mistake against overwhelming scientific evidence.

In 1884 he obtained an experimental dose of the relatively new alkaloid, cocaine, a derivative of the South American cocoa plant. He took one-twentieth of a gram internally and found it turned his bad mood into cheerfulness. Acting as a stomach anesthetic, it gave him the feeling of having dined well. Following the suggestion of an army doctor who noticed its effect on Bavarian soldiers, Freud used cocaine as a work-prodder. He found that it banished his fatigue.

He became an instant enthusiast, labeling the alkaloid his *magical drug.* "I take very small doses of it regularly against depression and against indigestion, and with the most brilliant success," he wrote. At age twenty-eight, Freud felt in great need of a psychological and physical panacea. He was described as suffering from "periodic depressions and fatigue or apathy, neurotic symptoms which took the form of anxiety attacks."

Freud had the literary, unscientific tendency to consider himself the perfect, universal sample of one. He made the same assumption with cocaine. Because he did not suffer a physiological craving for the drug, he assumed it was nonaddictive and began a campaign to spread its use all about him.

He gave it to his sisters, pressed it on his friends. He gave it to fellow doctors, suggesting they use it on their patients. He treated patients with it himself, including one for whom he ordered a large dose and who subsequently succumbed. He even sent cocaine to his fiancée, Martha Bernays, "to make her strong and give her cheeks a red color," as he said. The drug, Freud told her, had converted him, a young doctor who had suffered severe depressions, into "a big wild man who has cocaine in his body."

He prescribed cocaine for his friend and fellow physician, Dr. Ernst von Fleischl-Marxow, whose unbearable pain from amputated fingers had addicted him to morphine. Freud placed him on cocaine as a "harmless" substitute, but Fleischl eventually died of cocaine toxicity. As Dr. Max Schur, later to become Freud's personal physician, explains, cocaine "could be addictive with even more dangerous consequences than morphine addiction." Dr. Ernest Jones disconsolately summed up the cocaine incident: "In short, looked at from the vantage point of our present knowledge, he [Freud] was rapidly becoming a public menace."

Freud was the perfect propagandist. In 1885 he published an essay on the glories of cocaine in which he reverently referred to it as an "offering" instead of a "dose." He falsely stated that "absolutely no craving appears after the first or even over repeated taking of the drug." For cases of morphine addiction, Freud "unhesitatingly" prescribed subcutaneous injections of cocaine "without minding an accumulation of the drug."

By 1886 came word that cocaine could lead not only to delirium tremens but to addiction, toxicity and death. There was a general alarm in Germany, and Freud was accused of having unleashed "the third scourge of humanity." Freud was obstinate in defending himself. In 1887 he penned a defense claiming that only morphine addicts would fall victim to the drug. He insisted that cocaine was harmless when taken by mouth, and that the hypodermic needle was the villain.

Not only was he wrong on all counts, but in the article's references he omitted mention of his 1885 paper in which he suggested treatment by the subcutaneous method. When he applied for a professorship, Freud excluded his original cocaine article from his bibliography.

(By 1914 Freud had more realistic notions about cocaine. He wrote that cocaine, "if taken to excess" could produce paranoid symptoms. Withdrawal of the drug produced the same effect, he admitted.)

His misadventure did have a touch of serendipity. Dr. Karl Koller, a young ophthalmologist friend, found that cocaine was an excellent topical anesthetic for the eye. Freud was miffed for being remembered as the menace of the cocaine period, not as the benefactor of eye surgery.

The Koller discovery took place at the university hospital while Freud was away visiting his fiancée. Relating the cocaine anecdote, Freud avoids mention of his naïveté. But he shows an early sign of both his hostility and his driving lust for fame. He says that he must "explain how it was the fault of my fiancée that I was not already famous at that early age."

Freud took cocaine off and on for almost fifteen years. Initially he took it for emotional reasons, but later the cocaine served as a topical nose treatment for his sinusitis, a therapy prescribed by Dr. Fliess, who was a rhinologist. (Nasal inhalation is a common method of getting "high" on cocaine.) During the 1890s, Dr. Max Schur informs us, Freud took "frequent local applications of cocaine." No one has yet evaluated the hallucinatory effect of cocaine on Freud's mind during the formative years of psychoanalysis. Without cocaine, could Freud have created such improbable flights of human fancy?

The cocaine episode was one of the many unscientific expeditions of the Vienna neurologist-turned-philosopher. Freud's sexual toxicological theory—that the body could be poisoned by sexual frustration—was another scientific error that found its way into popular superstition. The failure to use the sexual system sufficiently dammed up the libido and triggered chemical substances which did damage to the mind, he theorized.

Freud explained that the somatic effect of this process produced the "actual neurosis" (the German word was *aktuell,* or current) while its mental expression was a psychoneurosis. He divided the patients into two groups, those suffering either from *anxiety neurosis* or from *neurasthenia.* Anxiety neurosis was caused by the frustration of "coitus interruptus, undischarged excitement and sexual abstinence." In neurasthenia it was sexual abuse: "excessive masturbation and too numerous nocturnal emissions."

The cure was simple: more genital sex. "If it was possible to put an end to the abuse and allow its place to be taken by normal sexual activity, a striking improvement in the condition was the reward,"

Freud assures us. The theory has now been discarded, but Freud's sophomoric idea of a body poisoned by sexual frustration lives on in common psychological superstition.

The Oedipal love triangle is a prime example of how Freud's personality has distorted psychology and psychiatry. During his self-analysis, Freud learned that he felt passion for his mother and jealousy against his father. As an adult, he had a recurring thought in which he visualized his "beautiful and slim" mother, Amalie. Judging from his belief in the trauma of the *primal scene* (seeing one's parents during intercourse), Freud as a boy must have watched his attractive mother having sex. What might have been overlooked by a less driven child seemed to dominate Freud.

Freud obviously experienced Oedipal lust, a disturbance which non-Freudians, such as child psychiatrist Dr. Stella Chess of New York University, believe affects only a small number of children. He then suffered the delusion that his abnormality was normal and universal. "With boys the wish to beget a child from their mother is never absent," he wrote. Ernest Jones has called this *single-idea obsession,* which led Freud to extrapolate his own feelings onto all humanity, as not only Freud's great strength but his debilitating weakness. In the case of the Oedipal theory, Freud has impressed his own pathological childhood onto modern society as a typical situation, thus creating psychic chaos in the Psychological Society.

Freud's relationship with his mother was a long and satisfying one, the quintessence of the heralded Jewish mother-son love. She lived to be ninety-five, dying when Freud was seventy-four. Freud hinted repeatedly of the power of her love, stating more than once that "if a man has been his mother's undisputed darling he retains throughout his life the triumphant feeling, the confidence in success, which not seldom brings actual success with it."

Freud was Amalie's favorite, *"Mein goldener Sigi,"* as she called him. "The only thing that brings a mother undiluted satisfaction is her relation to her son; it is quite the most complete relationship between human beings," he wrote. Freud added a metaphysical sex idea: for the mother, he said, "the little boy brings the longed-for penis with him."

Freud was afflicted with a host of neuroses, many of which were revealed during his intimate twenty-year relationship with Dr. Wilhelm Fliess. The intimate friendship also helped to introduce several strange ideas into modern psychology. Freud and Fliess agreed that their letters were to be destroyed, but Fliess later reneged. The letters fell into the hands of Marie Bonaparte, a close friend of Freud, and were eventually published in part as *The Origins of Psychoanalysis.*

The published letters began in 1887. Freud's advisers omitted the first four years and withheld other sensitive letters. Freud's physician, Dr. Max Schur, later printed some of the unpublished letters in his own work, *Living and Dying.*

The letters from Freud to Fliess reveal a tender, lovelike companionship which lasted fifteen years before it was eventually crushed by mutual hostility. It was this intimate relationship that prompted Freud's concern with latent homosexuality. Freud himself termed his need for Fliess and for the frequent meetings (Congresses) in Berlin, Vienna, Munich as "feminine."

In one letter to Fliess he wrote: "But there can be no substitute for the close contact with a friend which a particular—almost feminine—side of me demands." Years later Freud told Sandor Ferenczi of the "homosexual cathexis" involved in the Fliess relationship. When Ernest Jones first met Freud in 1908, he observed, "I dimly sensed some slight feminine aspect in his manner and movements."

Freud exhibited this feminine side in several ways, Dr. Harold Voth contends. "Throughout his life, Freud had a liking for masculine women of high intelligence," he states. "He referred to Martha's nose and mouth as almost masculine and unmaidenly in their decisiveness. Hers was a firm character that was not easily influenced. When differences existed between then, she regularly stood up to him, and in all major issues, Jones says, she proved to be the stronger."

Dr. Voth is concerned that Freud's feminine, passive feelings have influenced modern analysts and, through them, their patients and society. "One of the difficulties with this type of analyst is that they view masculine assertiveness and aggression as a neurotic manifestation. They tend to project their own conflicts and values about this onto their patients. As a result, much harm may be done to the patient and others in the patient's life," he says.

Little is known about Freud's heterosexuality, but it is suspected that it was not essential to his life. "Freud once claimed that civilized man could not reach full sexual satisfaction," says Dr. Voth. "I think he felt this way because he could not realize it in himself."

This suspicion is confirmed by an initially unpublished letter from Freud, who once touchingly wrote Fliess: "As you well know, in my life a woman has never been a substitute for a comrade, a friend." He wrote Fliess of his "love" for "one's friend and only correspondent" during his period of isolation in 1896. When both correspondents underwent similar surgery within weeks of each other (removal of a furuncle on the scrotum), Freud viewed it as "a secret biological sympathy" between them.

The bond between them moved Freud to near poetry. "Here I live in bad temper and darkness until you come," he wrote his Berlin companion. "I get rid of all my grumbles, kindle my flickering light at your steady flame, feel well again, and after your departure I again have eyes to see and what I see is beautiful and good."

Freud once told Ernest Jones of the lingering power of Fliess in his life, even after the two had split. Following an emotional episode in which he fainted in the Park Hotel in Munich, Freud explained, "I saw Munich first when I visited Fliess during his illness and this town seems to have acquired a strong connection with my relation to that man. There is some piece of unruly homosexual feeling at the root of the matter."

Rather than being his own private concern, Freud's needs have become part of our modern mythology. His concept of *latent homosexuality*, for example, has converted his own concern with homosexuality into a needless anxiety for millions of normal heterosexual men and women. As a result, thousands of therapists have since obediently searched the psyches of patients to find a distorted sexual drive similar to Freud's. As Dr. Max Schur has said, "One of the most difficult accomplishments of a regular analysis is to show the analysand both the existence of latent homosexuality and its adaptive possibilities."

Freud and Fliess were highly compatible, not only in their emotions but in their idiosyncrasies, many of which have been passed on to us. They were both intrigued with the metaphysical, the magical, the mystical. It was during this long relationship that Freud revealed his superstitious and gullible nature. These two traits of Freud's have inundated much of modern psychology and psychiatry with the unproven and the unlikely.

Dr. Fliess, a nose specialist, had developed a sexual-nasal reflex theory. He believed there was a connection between the mucous membranes of the nose and the female genitals. It was part of his broader concept of *periodicity*, an astrology-like theory that related events to periods. Fliess considered 28 days to be the female period and 23 days the male. Combinations of the numbers could predict, like the zodiac, the *critical periods* and *critical days* of one's existence. It could forecast spans of happiness or despair. Even one's death could be divined through the permutations of these mysterious figures.

Freud was an enthusiastic believer in Fliess's magic numbers. To him his Berlin colleague was the "Kepler of Biology." On May 25, 1889, Freud wrote that his migraine, one of several ailments the friends shared, fit into the period of 28 plus 28/2. In October, Freud wrote: "My mood is holding up bravely. I shall let you know the date of my next breakdown for your calculations."

Freud converted Fliess's theory into complex mathematical equations. "Martin [Freud's son] took to bed with an acute onset of illness on January 14 ($5 \times 28^2 - 10 \times 23^3$) between 2 and 3 o'clock in the afternoon," he announced to Fliess on February 1, 1900. In anger at the Viennese medical community, which denied Fliess's mystique, Freud, says Schur, asked, in effect: "How many years would it take the medical world to recognize the importance of the series 28 and 23?"

As with other aborted ideas, Freud dropped his interest in periodicity slowly and reluctantly. Dr. Schur says that Freud did not overcome his faith for decades, "if indeed he ever did." Fliess's influence on Freud was potent. In fact, Freud eventually credited Fliess with having conceived the terms *sublimation, latency* and *bisexuality.*

Although he considered the trait in himself to be unscientific, Freud's superstitions were deeply set. In the *Psychopathology of Everyday Life,* in which his "number juggling" as he called it, soared to circuslike virtuosity, he made a minor admission. "Moreover, in these unconscious thought operations with numbers, I find I have a tendency toward superstition whose origin for long remained unknown to me," he said. He also revealed his superstitious nature in a number of asides. "Certain things should not be mentioned in jest, otherwise they come true," he once wrote. On another occasion he spoke of the "heavenly influences" on human events.

Freud's view of his own death was dominated by a magic number obsession. He was convinced that he would die when he was fifty-one, the sum of the male and female period of 23 and 28. At the age of forty he wrote Fliess that it "did not seem probable that he would make his appointment." He had contracted a serious infection on his "last critical date."

Later, his death obsession revolved about the numbers 61 and 62. He informed Jung (who had replaced Fliess as his confidant) that the numbers came up in an "uncanny" way during a trip to Greece. His hotel room number was 31, approximately half of 61–62. By 1936, at the age of eighty, he had become preoccupied with the number 81 1/2. He eventually died in his sleep at age eighty-three, having outlived all his magic numbers.

As a physician and neurologist, Freud occasionally sought to logically explain his superstitions. In a letter to Jung in 1909 he stated why he believed he would die at sixty-one or sixty-two. In the year 1899, when he was first struck by the thought, he was assigned a new phone number, 14362. In that same year, he published *The Interpretation of Dreams*. The link between the two was obvious, Freud said. The 43 in the phone number was the same as his age in 1899. Freud then asks almost incredulously, "What, then, was more natural than that the other numbers should signify the end of my life, namely 61 or 62?"

Superstition, mysticism and an inexplicable naïveté, were only pieces of his convoluted neurotic personality. It is fashionable today for analysts to say that Freud was too neurotic to be admitted to a modern psychoanalytic institute. This may be true, but Freud has stormed their portals through a projection of his personality onto that of modern psychoanalysis, all analytic candidates, many psychiatrists and, ultimately, patients and the public as well. The negative character of psychodynamic theory, with its emphasis on abnormalities in functioning individuals, is a magnificent legacy of Freud's own neuroses.

As a youth, young Sigmund exhibited unusual behavior. At the age of seven he walked into his parents' bedroom and intentionally urinated on the floor. He describes himself as a victim of *neurasthenia,* a phrase that incorporated modern neuroticism and a form of hypochondriasis. Freud claimed to have suffered as a young man from "a mild case of typhoid," and "a light case of smallpox." Dr. Schur has pointed out that many simple gastrointestinal diseases were then described as "mild typhoid." Once, after a spell in bed for "sciatica," he decided "not to have sciatica anymore" and simply got out of bed.

On his father's side, Freud inherited what he called a possible "neuropathological taint." Of four first cousins of one uncle, two were insane. Another cousin died of epilepsy. The only evidence of the "taint" in his immediate family, Freud believed, was his own and his sister Rosa's "pronounced tendency toward neurasthenia."

This tendency showed itself in lifelong indigestion, often with constipation, in an irritable spastic colon, a train phobia and a severe moodiness which tended more toward depression than elation. His neurotic moods left him tired and often in bad temper. "I have a great talent for complaining," Freud wrote. In 1884, at the age of twenty-eight, he commented that during the past fourteen months, he had experienced only three or four happy days. His moods changed rapidly and drastically. On March 12, 1885, he wrote his fiancée, Martha Bernays, "I never felt so fresh in my life." On March 21 his mood reversed completely: "I can't stand it much longer."

In his adult life, during the 1890s when Freud was between thirty-five and forty-five, he suffered from what Ernest Jones called "a very considerable psychoneurosis." It was so severe that, as Jones relates, there were "only occasional intervals when life seemed much worth living." Jones defines Freud's general emotional state: "And so the years went on with a constant struggle against the spells of depression, the anxiety with recurrent attacks of *Todesangst* [fear of death], and all other troubles, internal as well as external."

His physical pain from migraines, frequent sinus infections, operations on his sinus bones and what was presumably a heart condition in 1896 also drained him. (Jones considered the heart condition psychoneurotic. Dr. Schur was convinced it was organic.) In 1896 Freud wrote Fliess: "Good mood and zest for living are wholly absent. Instead I am diligently noting down the occasion when I must occupy myself with the state of affairs after my death."

In addition to health problems, he suffered from money worries and a gnawing fear of death. "My state of mind also depends on my earnings," he revealed. "I once knew helpless poverty and have a constant fear of it." His death obsession tortured him for years. In an initially unpublished letter to Fliess he wrote that he would "perish nicely and suddenly from a rupture of the heart" between forty and fifty.

In 1900, three years after his self-analysis began, he was still generally disconsolate. "No one can help me in the least with what oppresses me; it is my cross, I must bear it; and heaven knows in the process of adaptation my back has been noticeably bent," he wrote. Freud's self-analysis kept dredging up unhappy early memories and reconstructions. At one point, so much anal material emerged that Freud coined a word for it: "Drekkology," a play on the German-Yiddish word for feces.

Cocaine at first and cigars throughout most of his life were his emotional crutches. Resuming cigar smoking after a temporary abstinence, he remarked, "I was able to work and was master of my mood; before that it was unbearable." (Despite his complaints,

Freud, was, of course, a prodigious producer.)

One unusual neurotic symptom was his tendency to faint. He was known to have fainted at least four or five times. Once it was over the sight of hemorrhaging blood. Usually it was because of some slight to his extravagant ego. In 1909, just prior to their leaving for America, Freud and Jung were in Bremen. Freud informed his disciple that he, Jung, harbored unconscious death wishes against him. Jung protested strongly. During the argument Freud suddenly fainted.

In 1912 Freud and Jung quarreled again over an article in which Jung had omitted mentioning Freud. Jung was apologetic, but Freud continued the criticism, then suddenly fell to the floor in a dead faint. Jung carried him to a couch. Freud's first words on awakening were: "How sweet it must be to die."

In a letter to Ludwig Binswanger shortly after, Freud revealed that he had two similar attacks before. "Repressed feelings," Freud said, played the main part in his fainting neurosis. He attributed those repressions to guilt over the death of his younger brother when Freud was one year and seven months old.

This historic neurotic personality has had a profound impact on our culture. It has thrust Freud's worst indispositions into our language, our mental habits and our psychology. Just as the psychic make-up of Jesus became the projected ideal, if not the practice, of Christianity, so several of Freud's neurotic foibles have been adopted as dogma within psychoanalysis. Eventually they became the inheritance of the entire Psychological Society.

One trait was his bad-tempered insistence that secret hostility was paramount in the human psyche. This idea has permeated not only modern psychodynamics but our common style of thought.

Freud was tormented by hatreds and by the guilt created by these thoughts. In 1897, during his famous self-analysis, he reconstructed memories of the death of his younger brother Julius. He discovered that he had felt murderous wishes against the child. As Freud says, "I welcomed my one-year younger brother with ill wishes and real infantile jealousy." The child died not long after.

After Julius' death, his younger sister Anna (not the daughter of the same name) was born. Once again, the Freudian hostility was aroused. He uncovered the same death wish against this new usurper of his mother's affection. Dr. Schur relates the force of Freud's sibling hate: "He indicated specifically that a little child, whose younger sibling had died, might after the birth of the next sibling harbor the wish that the same fate should meet this new competitor."

Freud thought the worst of human impulses. And his single-idea obsession made him confident that his weaknesses were those of all mankind. He diligently searched for unconscious hatreds, even where they did not exist. When his fiancée's parents, the Bernays, objected to him as a suitor, Freud was outraged that Martha—whom he could not afford to marry for years—did not fight them and drop their habits, including the use of kosher food.

He could not understand her lack of hostility. He considered her a noble character, but, as Jones relates, "there was a certain incompatibility between his desire to acquire goodness from Martha and his almost equally strong desire to get her to share his feelings of hatred and hostility."

Hostility was penned up inside this almost shy, somewhat feminine man, like a caged feline. His was an angry soul which hated even when it loved, a trait he has passed down to us as *ambivalence*. "We know that with Freud intense love and hate were specially apt to go hand in hand," comments Jones. His distorted love-hate emotions first made a victim of Breuer, then Fliess, then Jung, Adler, Stekel and anyone else who initially advanced, then stood in the way of, his grand design for immortality.

Freud's confusion between hate and love has become ours. He was so consumed by the idea of unconscious hate that like a distorted reversal of the *Sonnets from the Portuguese,* it became to him synonymous with love. "It might be said that we owe the fairest flowers of our love life to the reaction against hostile impulses (i.e., unconscious death wishes in regard to loved ones) which we divine in our breasts," the unhappy philosopher wrote.

People mistook his mask of shyness for weakness, Freud once explained. He boasted that he was actually "bold and fearless." Freud's ego was massive, and filled with dreams of immortality which he painfully converted into reality.

Freud has retold an anecdote which is an early revelation of this driving ambition. At the age of fifty, he was given a medallion by his Viennese adherents. On one side was his own portrait. On the reverse was a Greek illustration of Oedipus answering the Sphinx's riddle. The inscription was from Sophocles' play *Oedipus Rex:* "Who divined the famed riddle and was man most mighty." Freud turned pale. In an agitated voice he asked who had thought of it. He then revealed the reasons for his concern. As a young man he had often walked around the university courtyard inspecting busts of learned professors. He daydreamed that one day his would be there. In his daydream he had envisioned this exact inscription.

Competition and envy were the triggers for his hostility against brothers and sisters, colleagues, friends and eventually his father. The unraveling of Freud's self-analysis, Schur reminds us, had a consistent theme: "the ubiquitous existence of murderous wishes against one's parents and siblings."

He perpetually read unconscious hostility into his cases, including that of Dora, the Wolf Man and the Rat Man. He did this even over the reasonable objections of his patients, who said they felt no such hostilities. The Rat Man compalined that he could not have wanted his father's death, for he loved him and feared losing him. Freud countered with one of the convoluted semantic twists that once made his ideas invincible. The fear of death was actually a wish, he said. Every one of man's fears corresponds to a former unconscious wish, he told his now guilty patient.

Only Freud's superstition rivaled his hostility in intensity. Even his theory of the origin of superstition was self-incriminating. "Superstition derives from suppressed hostile and cruel impulses," he commented. He believed that obsessional neurotics of high intelligence harbored frequent evil wishes against others, but repressed the idea because of conscience. But unconsciously they expected severe punishment, even death, for their wickedness.

Max Schur traced Freud's superstitious fear of death to his harboring of such death wishes, first against others, then against himself. It was *aggression turned inward,* as analysts say. "In terms of wishes, his superstition meant that because he wanted Fliess, Fleischl, his father, his brother Julius, his sister Anna and anyone else he hated to die, he would die," his physician suggested. Freud's death-wish neurosis was so strong that he falsely believed that man had a death instinct, Thanatos, that was normal and universal. Even most psychoanalysts now deny this reverse view of existence.

Freud was obviously driven by furies. He also had a need to think good and to expiate his guilt. But he knew that constitutionally his depressed, competitive personality made him feel otherwise. What better expiation for his hate-drives than to make them the universal traits of man? What more glorious immortality than to see his neuroses and hostilities become the apparent normality of the society that was to follow?

Modern psychoanalysis, much of modern psychiatry and most of psychotherapy are the perfect mirrors of those neuroses. They are the nurturing home for Freud's murderous death wishes, calamitous sibling rivalries, unconscious enmity against parents, bisexuality, incest drives, latent homosexuality, inverted love-hate relationships, dogmatized superstition and unseen hatreds of every description.

It is a singular victory. It is the transfusion of one man's bile into an entire culture. Children do not necessarily or even regularly hate new children in the family. Nor are most people latent homosexuals or unconscious bisexuals. Nor do most boys unconsciously wish their fathers dead as Freud did. Nor is the infantile sex experience the determinant of our character. Nor is ambivalent love-hate the rule for most emotions.

Of course, it *can* be true, particularly for the psychic duplicates of Sigmund Freud who may be multiplying each day. As his ultimate conquest, Freud may see his clones thrive as the inevitable product of an impressionable, anti-intellectual Psychological Society.

We should pose one thought. What if Freud had not suffered from a spastic colon, near-continuous depressive moods, neurasthenia, homosexual tendencies, bad temper, migraines, constipation, travel phobias, death fears, heart irregularity, money phobias, infected sinuses, fainting spells and hostile drives of hate and murder? Would the modern theory of the mind have been more sanguine? Would it have instead stressed the empathy and concern that people feel for their siblings, their parents, even for all humanity?

What if Freud had not been a victim of superstition, magical numbers and childish gullibility? Would psychiatry and psychotherapy today reflect the influence of a more scientific and reasoned approach to the human mind?

The Freudian neurosis has infiltrated our psyches and our culture more deeply than we yet understand. If we recognize that much of it is a reflection of Freud himself, and we know the dimensions of that personality distortion, it may help us to free ourselves from its pervasive influence. We might no longer have to live in the shadow of Dr. Freud.

# VIII

## Our
## Psychologized
## Young

"I AM AFRAID THAT THE WHOLE environmental school which has dominated child care in America in the last twenty-five years has made parents too anxious, too insecure and too guilty," says Dr. Louise Bates Ames, co-director of the famed Gesell Institute of Child Development.

"They created the attitude that the child's psyche is fragile, which it is not. Most of the damage we have seen in child rearing is the fault of the Freudian and neo-Freudians who have dominated the field. They have frightened parents and kept the truth from them. In child care I would say that Freudianism has been the psychological crime of the century."

This heretical comment by a leading psychologist, made during a recent interview, refutes the very basis of child care theories of the last several decades. This generation of youth under twenty-five is the first to be born into the Psychological Society. They have been raised as laboratory subjects in a massive experiment in which parents have served as surrogates for the professional psychologist and psychiatrist.

Parents have been told repeatedly that parenthood is a creative opportunity to use the principles being discovered by modern psychology. Not only would they be able to mold their child's personality, but they could *scientifically* ward off the crippling effects of neurosis and psychosis by using their expertise. As a result of this promise, parenthood has become a near craft called *parenting,* a how-to-ism spewed out by child psychiatrists, child psychologists, parent educators, social workers, guidance counselors and even by the friends and family of the educated parent.

The tone was set some three decades ago: *parents will receive the credit for producing emotionally healthy children. Conversely, they will be dishonored for the failed psyches of their young.*

Child psychiatrist Dr. Peter B. Neubauer has shaped that challenge. "Environmental factors can foster health and achievement or bring retardation and pathology," he warned anxious parents. "This realization has placed new and complex responsibilities on parents, teachers and community services."

Dr. Neubauer also praised parents for feeding the psychological enthusiasm. "It is certainly encouraging to see how eager are millions of parents to learn how they can contribute to the development of their children; the upsurge in this field is nothing less than extraordinary," he said.

This upsurge has been with us since World War II, and shows no sign of abating despite annoyed critics such as Dr. Ames. It is maintained by constant reminders of the vulnerability of the young psyche and warnings that parents have the responsibility to protect that fragile device.

The result was foreordained. Parental guilt has reached a stage of suffocation in contempory America. It has consumed the parents of nervous, anxious, slow-learning, overactive, poorly behaved, drug-addicted and, of course, mentally ill children. Through therapist after therapist, they search out the reason for their child's condition and the hope of a cure.

Too often they view themselves as the cause of the problem and therefore as the source of the cure. Aided by unsubtle propaganda of the Psychological Society, parents come away convinced that they have committed the *modern crime of inexpert parenthood,* one of the most heinous sins of our era.

Despite some newly developed doubts, the psychological establishment still insists that Mom and Pop are the villains. Dr. H. Neil Carp tells us that "black sheep" children may be the product of parents whose sin is that they did not want these offspring. The children were born too early, too late, or at an inopportune time, or in a period of financial stress in the family's history, he says.

Parents have been castigated at every turn. A study of four hundred male drug addicts in New York concluded that a damaging Portnoy relationship between mother and son was behind the addiction. The $99,000 survey, supported by federal funds, claimed that mothers fed their sons' addiction through a combination of "ingratiating, sabotaging and seductive behavior."

Parents have also been warned to keep carefully attuned to the current fashions in child rearing lest their child's psyche be injured by their indifference. But as parents have learned to their dismay, these fashions are as mercurial as the length of hemlines.

"Attitudes toward child raising changed from decade to decade in this period, reflecting whatever knowledge or insights we thought we had arrived at," parent educator and child care writer Eda J. LeShan states candidly. "This has undoubtedly been true throughout history, but during the last fifty years, these attitudes have had the prestige of 'Science' behind them."

Unfortunately, science has not been able to make up its mind about the raising of children. This has left worshipers of the child-rearing cult in the unsettling position of following an undulating dogmatism. What is "known" today is often debunked within a decade. New concepts, new authorities and new practices are then set up, all of which leave parents in the wake of discarded psychological ideas.

Eda LeShan explained when interviewed that the most recent shift in expert opinion is to one of *doubt.* "My generation of parents— those with grown children—was the first to be sensitive to the fact that environment greatly affected our children. Before that, it was assumed that the biology of the child, his genetic make-up, created his personality. When the pendulum swung to environment, mainly after World War Two, we went through a period of excessive optimism during which we felt we could change everything. That lasted from 1935 through the 1960s. We thought we had the tools and the information, and we felt we could create the perfect child-raising environment with our new knowledge. We found this was overly optimistic."

Is it possible that modern psychology has instead had a negative effect on the ancient art of child raising? Dr. Louise Bates Ames's estimate that Freud has been the major influence in American child care is accurate. Prior to Freud, the onus of proof was on the matured child. Each child was acknowledged as a human being in his or her own right, with an individual personality and natural temperament. The child was neither a mirror nor an imitation of the parent, who was not held responsible for all the child's later transgressions.

Sigmund Freud and the environmentalists who succeeded him have changed that. In their psychological child care system, which has infiltrated millions of psyches worldwide, the child is a tender, vulnerable reed very susceptible to parents' influence. In this system, *it is the parents, not the child, who are tested.* If they have done a good job, it will be seen in the actions and stability of the child. In one graceful psychological move, responsibility has shifted from emerging person to parent, from *self to others.*

This environmental system is based on the psychodynamic theory in which the unknowing or uncaring parent forces the child to repress its unconscious drives. In the process, fixations are created which later emerge as neurotic behavior in the adolescent or adult. What do parents do wrong? What kind of expert child handling can avert these neuroses?

Theory states that too much gratification for the child is as bad as too little. But in practice, child care experts have focused on the dangers of *too little.* From this came the bias called *permissiveness.* It was designed as an antidote to traditional rearing which supposedly frustrated the child's psychological needs and distorted its personality.

In reality, American parents have always been relatively permissive. When the French intellectual, Alexis de Tocqueville, visited America in 1835, he observed that American children were less obedient to their parents than were European children and that American parents were more permissive.

This tendency became exaggerated after World War II when experts converted Freud's theories into hard-core permissiveness. Dr. Benjamin Spock, author of the paperback *Baby and Child Care,* which has sold more than twenty-five million copies since 1946, was not the most permissive of the new authorities. But his book has illustrated the changing fashions in child management. Each edition has incorporated less permissive doctrine. In the most recent one, Spock even laments the way parents have permitted children to rule the psychological roost, what he calls "today's child-centered viewpoint." Spock illustrates his new firmness with ideas that would gladden a Victorian parent: "A baby of 9 months shouldn't get the impression that it's all right to pull his mother's hair but that he owes her respect."

These new antidotes are belated, for permissiveness is still dominant among most parents conditioned by a generation of propaganda. The result is a frightened mother and father who often patronize the child, suffocate him with pseudo-attention, condescension and mock love. Not unlike the parent who once feared a summertime polio attack, the contemporary parent is constantly anxious about the child's precarious emotional state.

The strongest skeptics of the great child care scare have been uneducated parents who raised their children by instinct. It is the college-educated, many of whom have been in therapy themselves, who have been entranced by the environmental, psychodynamic theory. They have gullibly bought the textbook idea that parental fine-tuning of a youngster's unconscious determines whether the child will become neurotic or worse.

*Modern research indicates that the skeptics have been right all along: that environmental or Freudian theory is false.* Its long acceptance has been a continuing damaging influence on child-parent relationships. In its place is a new professional awareness of the importance of the child's biology and natural temperament.

Dr. Stella Chess, professor of child psychiatry at New York University Medical Center, is a leading dissenter against excessive environmentalism. She and her husband, Dr. Alexander Thomas, have been conducting a twenty-one-year study, watching a group of children grow up from birth. They have been doing what Freud failed to do, and what his followers have ignored in favor of speculative theory. The goal? To identify natural biological temperament and *to see how the child's own nature reacts with the environment to produce personality.*

The Chess-Thomas study involves 136 children, all of whom are now young adults. Their behavior was recorded from birth onward every three months until the child was eighteen months old. The children were then followed up every six months until they were five, then every year thereafter. The researchers questioned parents, then personally observed the children in nursery or at school. As a check on parent reporting of infants' behavior, the researchers went into the home and observed twenty-three of the children.

The parents were middle- and upper-middle-class, mainly Protestant and Jewish. They were college-educated and psychologically oriented. Their typical bias was toward the modern environmental theory that parents molded children's personality. Half of the mothers breast-fed their children. Most were permissive in toilet training. Almost all of them sent their toddlers to private nursery schools.

The Chess-Thomas study has stayed with the 136 children. Forty-two, or 31 percent, of the children, have been diagnosed by the researchers as having "behavior disorders," while 69 percent are considered generally normal.

The study has abruptly turned around many shibboleths of the Psychological Society. Much of the onus has been shifted *from parent to nature:* from supposedly poor parenting to the vagaries, whims and accidents of nature.

The main revelation of the work is that the child's own constitution—the biology it was born with—is the major factor in the shaping of the child's personality. *Temperament, nature, constitution, inborn traits,* all the words that were discarded in the Fredudian-environmental revolution, are now used to describe what makes a child.

"We have found that a child's natural temperament plays a major role in determining his behavior," Dr. Chess commented when interviewed. "We do not see the Freudian theories at work in child raising. Instead of psychodynamic factors, we find that the child's own temperament, and how the parents view that temperament, are the important factors. Freudian theory gives lip service to 'constitutional factors' as they call them, but once mentioned they are not handled at all in practice. When they speak of strict toilet training, for example, they talk as if it had a similar effect on all children, which it does not."

In the study, Dr. Chess found that the child's basic nature—seen from birth onward—often dictates its behavior. If the child's temperament is not taken into account, the teacher, the psychologist and even the parent can make mistakes in handling him or her.

She gives several examples of such failure. The child in nursery school who stands at the periphery of the group instead of participating, is apt to be called "anxious and insecure" by professionals. This may be true, says Dr. Chess. But it is equally likely that the child has a normal-temperament tendency to warm up slowly. We may be dealing, she says, with a child who is naturally, constitutionally *shy.*

If an infant has irregular sleep habits and cries out loudly at night, modern psychologists and child care counselors often feel the child is "responding to a hostile, rejecting mother," Dr. Chess points out. But it is also quite possible that the infant is expressing temperamental *irregularity,* an inborn characteristic.

The confused mother often develops guilt and anxiety because she cannot handle her child. Many psychologists would view this mishandling as a sign of deep-seated neuroses in the mother. The reality might be quite the opposite, says Dr. Chess. The neurosis may be built into the child, and the mother's confusion could be caused by the fact that her infant has a "temperamental pattern that characterizes a very difficult child," she points out.

Infants judged to be temperamentally difficult immediately after birth—before the parents could affect them—were later slated to become emotionally unstable in 70 percent of the cases. These "difficult children," as they were termed, made up only 1 in 25 of the original group, but they accounted for almost 1 in 4 (23 percent) of all behavioral disorders.

The difficult children earned the label "mother killers." They slept poorly, awoke two or three times a night crying. They felt hunger irregularly. As they got older they could not conform to the family's eating habits. Their elimination patterns were equally unpredictable. A negative mood permeated their young lives, especially in their reactions to new situations.

Says Dr. Chess about this type of child: "He cries when immersed in the bath for the first time; he cries and spits with each new food; he cries at each new visitor to the home; and almost every excursion brings an initial response of withdrawal, clinging, loud protest or crying."

What kind of monsters did they have as parents, the psychologically prone might ask? They were the same as the parents of the normal children, reports Dr. Chess. Most important, they generally had other normal children themselves. Other psychological superstitions also failed to account for the children's unusual behavior. The difficult children were not the oldest, the youngest, or in any other specific birth order. They were not unwanted, nor did the parents have any special theories about child raising.

Ironically, most parents of the "mother killers" believed that warm and accepting parents invariably produced happy and stable offspring. As a result, when their children proved to be unstable, they suffered an outbreak of guilt for having failed. Many believed that their *unconscious rejection* of the child had produced such disaster. Because of this belief in psychological theory, says Dr. Chess, "it was not unusual for the mother of a difficult infant who screamed frequently and made all routine a crisis to develop self-doubts and feelings of guilt, anxiety and helplessness." *The child's failure had falsely become the parent's sin.*

Another researcher, Dr. William B. Carey, a Pennsylvania pediatrician, has confirmed Dr. Chess's results. He studied 200 babies and found that there are strong temperamental differences among children. He described this variance by labeling the babies either "easy," "intermediate" or "difficult." Most of the children were in the first two groups while twenty-eight were difficult. How can parents live with a difficult child? To help themselves and the child, Dr. Carey advises firmness and consistency, on the one hand, and patience and tolerance, on the other.

The Psychological Society has been eloquent in its outrage against unknowing or uncaring parents. But Harvard psychiatrist Dr. Robert Coles defends the modern parent as being unfairly maligned. "Parents are often enough resented and never forgiven for all their failures of omission or commission," he complains. "In this century, the love they give us, the good and decent intentions they possess and offer to us as something to imitate and make our own, the cultural heritage they hand down . . . all of that somehow is either taken for granted or overlooked in favor of 'complexes' of various kinds."

A potent pro-parent conclusion evolves from Dr. Chess's work. It is that *the present psychiatric theory that the first six years of life are the exclusive molders of personality is patently false.* If biological temperament is a key factor in shaping personality, these first years are not the period in which personality is formed. It may simply be the time in which constitutional temperament begins to reveal itself regardless of parental behavior.

Personality probably evolves throughout life as the biological nature of the person comes in contact with his unfolding environment. Rather than a parent-molded product, personality now appears to be a nature-given tendency which is revealed as it reacts with environment up until death itself.

The vital role of adolescence, for example, has been ignored by most professionals. During puberty the child undergoes hormonal change, intense peer-group pressure, intellectualization, true sexualization and the growth of spiritual needs. These surely affect personality as potently as early childhood, perhaps even more so.

The study of neurosis and behavior obviously requires more direct observation at all stages of life. As Dr. Chess says, Freudian dynamics "rush in to fill the vacuum created when the fact of temperamental individuality is unappreciated and ignored."

Instead of being the all-powerful influence, parents now seem to be only one factor in the shaping of the child's psyche. Judging from evidence, *parents are probably much less important in the making of their child's personality than we have ever suspected.*

Surprisingly, the new biological information is more easily accepted by parents than by professionals. Many parents who have more than one child have long noticed that each of their offspring is temperamentally different from the moment of birth. Because of fear of ridicule, they have kept these observations to themselves. But they are now in a position to confront conventional wisdom.

How could so many psychiatric and psychological professionals have been so wrong? Eda LeShan sees the error as a case of "new learning" contradicting the old. "We had too little awareness of the innate differences among children," she states. "We now know that some children have a regular constitutional system that works beautifully. Others, the arrhythmic children, do not. They need a structured routine and more discipline. Poor Dr. Spock—and most of us —got a reputation for permissiveness because we did not take into account the enormous differences in children's heredity which Dr. Chess has found.

"We tried to be very gentle with children, and generally failed to discipline them," Mrs. LeShan continued. "Critics said we were crazily permissive, but it wasn't that. It was because we didn't understand the physiological aspects of the problem. We do now. For a full generation, we tried to understand the child's needs from the child's point of view. The error was that we did not distinguish among the children we were dealing with. Some children can handle freedom. Others are high-strung and nervous and need structure rather than free choice. At first, theories of child care were biological. Then, after the Freudian revolution it became environmental. Now, ideally, it is fifty-fifty."

Fear of damaging the child's psyche still dominates many parents' attitude toward child raising. Mrs. LeShan offers the example of one father who says, "Every time I yell at my kids I have a feeling that I'm being reported to some secret psychiatric police force!"

This fear is even imparted to professionals who try to defy the psychological establishment. Dr. Chess describes the fierce opposition to her research which she initially faced. "It was our repeated experience in the early and mid 1950s to find most of our colleagues reproaching us for returning to an outdated and discredited constitutional position," she recalls.

The Gesell Institute of Child Development has had similar professional pressure applied to stop their unfashionable child care research. Up until 1950, the institute was called the Yale Clinic of Child

Development and was headed by Dr. Arnold Gesell, the famed child psychologist and pediatrician. Gesell was the predecessor of Dr. Benjamin Spock as the nation's baby doctor. His book *Infant and Child* was the bible of its day.

Gesell believed that behavior is mainly a function of physical structure and that the child's highly individual "constitutional factors" ultimately determined the way the child reacted to his environment, a theory now corroborated by Dr. Chess's work. Personality, even attitudes toward the opposite sex, develops at different stages of the child's growth through his own biologic individuality, he believed.

"I am convinced that we had to leave Yale in 1950 because of the pressure of environmentalists and Freudians at the university," charges Dr. Louise B. Ames, co-director of the now independent clinic. Dr. Ames, a Yale Ph.D. in experimental psychology, frankly believes that the influence of child care environmentalists for the last thirty-five years has hurt the emotional stability of children, including millions who have now grown to adulthood.

"Our way back," says Dr. Ames, "is to pay more attention to heredity and the child's individual personality as he expresses it through his behavior. We've been in the Dark Ages. The Freudians have been the supra-environmentalists in child care and I think they have been proven wrong.

"Because of their power in American psychiatry, the new mental health clinics supported by the government started out treating disturbed children by assigning one person to help the child, and another person to help the husband and wife to find out what they were doing wrong. If the child had no parents, then they helped the grandmother. It proved to be too expensive a technique. People didn't like it, and I don't think it worked. People were bringing in a mixed-up child for help, and finding that a psychological professional was using it to look into their marriage and their sex life."

What about physical punishment, which has been a strict taboo in the modern permissive school? "Dr. Gesell believed that an occasional spanking is not usually harmful, but he did consider it the weakest form of discipline," Dr. Ames explained. "The best form of discipline is to set up the life situation so that the child doesn't get into trouble. If the child gets a tantrum in a supermarket because he wants everything he sees, there is no sense in trying to punish him. It is best to go to the supermarket without him until he outgrows that stage, which he will."

Dr. Ames is annoyed at the child care professional who tends to blame the parents of disturbed children. "Parents of disturbed children shouldn't blame themselves," she says. "If the child is made of good material, it will be hard to do it serious damage emotionally, even if the parent did a poor job.

"For example, if the parent criticizes the child all the time, is cold, cruel and unloving, he or she could create a shy and scared child. Such a poor parent could make the child unhappy, but not mentally ill. If the child's constitutional material is poor, however, the best handling in the world probably won't save the child. The parent who gives the child love and concern can still have a mentally ill child. That is the tragedy of being a parent."

What does it mean to be a good parent? Are there any formulas which cut across the sanctimonious psychological dogmas? Dr. Salvatore Ambrosino, executive director of the Family Service Association of Nassau County, New York, believes that in the final analysis, child raising is a question of personal judgment.

"The good parent has to rely on his gut feeling a lot," Dr. Ambrosino suggested when interviewed. "That's why books on how to raise children are so limited. It basically comes down to the parents' judgment." Dr. Ambrosino is not against parents learning about child care, but he is afraid that some parents "have been made too self-conscious, and too insecure about their roles."

He is concerned that the educated parent has been the greatest offender. "Rather than helping the parent build on natural feelings and understanding, the educational process can make him artificial," he says. "When people become 'educated,' they try to gain control over life and its relationships through knowledge and words. Knowledge is a piece of reality. But another, perhaps more important piece of reality is where you are with your feelings. I know a parent who is brilliant, but when she is with her kid she allows the child to interrupt her ten times in a row. She gets really angry at the child, but she is afraid of her feelings because of what she has been taught about child raising. Intellectually she believes that she must always be loving to her child and never be angry.

"A number of people react like that, which is wrong. Parents who are permissive with children are not aware that control of the child is a form of love—and just as important as the 'giving love.' A number of educators and people in the helping professions have learned from Freud and Dewey that the child is like a flower. The adult must help it unfold, by nourishing and feeding it emotionally, without throwing impediments in its path. The mistake is that in order for the child to develop fully, it does need impediments put in its path—in the form of intelligent discipline, hard work and restraints."

How much can the parent mold the child? How much does the child's constitution count in the molding? Dr. Ambrosino has a favorite analogy which he uses in lectures. "I tell parents that some children are like soft clay, others like wood, and some like pure steel. Those that are like clay are easily formed by us. Those that are like wood are shaped somewhat, but they leave splinters. Those of steel resist everything that parents stand for. It may sound discouraging, but I think raising children is like throwing dice. If we are lucky, we get children who fit our own dispositional bent, and things work out well for us as parents. If not . . .

"I think many of the psychological shibboleths about child care are wrong. Nice, successful people who have a good marriage often have great trouble raising children. And unfortunately, people who are shits often have no trouble with their kids at all. We used to think that healthy parents with a healthy marriage raised healthy kids. I'm afraid its much more complicated than that."

Dr. Ambrosino believes that in the late 1970s we are beginning to make progress. "I don't think that we're making parents in the 1970s as self-conscious as we did in the forties, fifties and sixties," he says. "We are helping them to realize that while they play an important part, they are *only one* influence in the child's life. We used to feel that if there was a divorce and the child took to drugs, that the parents were always at fault. We realize now that there are constitutional differences in children. Some will take to drugs and others won't. Parents who have more than one child know this instinctively. They could see the difference in their children's personality in the crib, from three to six weeks after birth. Experts pooh-poohed this idea, but they were wrong. The skeptical parents were right."

If the environmental theories are weak, if educated parents have become self-conscious and often too permissive, what can be done?

Some believe there is hope in the theory of the late Dr. Haim G. Ginott. He tried to make parents less afraid to discipline their children, but better able to control their own anger at the child. The technique gravitates around a special language to be used in speaking to children.

It is based on the old aphorism: Direct your anger at the behavior, not the child. In their book, *Liberated Parents, Liberated Children,* two of Ginott's pupils, Adele Faber and Elaine Mazlish, describe the method. "For example, if a child's messy room bothers a parent, the parent should feel free to express his genuine feelings—but not with insults and accusations. Not with, 'Why are you such a slob?' The question is, how could a parent express these same angry feelings helpfully? Again, he could describe. He could say 'The sight of this room does not give me pleasure!' or 'I see something that makes me angry!' "

The Ginott concept is a halfway measure between the Freudian-based permissiveness, which critics believe has produced millions of "brats," and traditional discipline, which included parental firmness and anger. Its problem is that it involves a *special language* between parent and child, and like the patronizing Freudian tone, it is blatantly artificial.

Dr. Ambrosino believes that the Ginott method can be helpful, if only as a bridge to natural, uninhibited child rearing. "All formulas are artificial," he says. "But if the parent could use this form to handle the situation, then become more spontaneous and natural with the child, that would be beautiful."

What is behind the cloying, overprotective aspect of child care that has so tarnished modern parent-child relations? One source of damage was obviously Freudianism, which saw the child as a piece of fragile glass. Life in such homes was dominated by an unseen sign on the child which read HANDLE WITH CARE! It is not unlike living with a live bomb, a tension which still dominates millions of households.

This concern for the young is related to several facets of the American culture. The first is the development of an independent young working class, able to exist without parental guidance. The second is the traditional power of American egalitarianism and our fervent belief in the perfectibility of democratic man.

The child care movement has been part of that American drive, a concern which is becoming worldwide. If the child was indeed a blank slate, as environmentalists believed, then perfectibility was possible in the form of love, indulgence and education: every child a musician (piano and guitar lessons), an artist (drawing lessons and art appreciation), a physically sound human (good food, exercise, proper home environment). And through schooling, reading and persistence, many educated parents hoped to produce the ultimate in the new American mode—a genius.

Its social good in the creation of an ever-expanding, commercially fruitful middle class is obvious. But so is the heartache of parents whose children could not reach anywhere near this perfectibility despite parental love and attention.

What did parents do wrong? Nothing in particular, everything in general. They assumed too much, tried too much, hoped too much. The seeds of their frustration were there all the time: in their relative impotence; in the general untruthfulness of psychological theorems and platitudes; in their false anxieties; in the overwhelming power of biology and the idiosyncrasies of the human animal.

Even the simplest child-raising functions have become personal traumas for some parents. "Did I do anything wrong in toilet-training my child?" worried mothers often ask. "My child has colic. I must have done something wrong to upset him emotionally," is another parent wail.

Research generally absolves the parent. Childhood colic has been blamed on the unhappy mother who creates tension in the home. Nonsense, say researchers. Dr. Benjamin A. Shaver told the American Orthopsychiatric Association that colic appears in some children for no obvious reason when the child is about three weeks old. It disappears, for no equally apparent reason, when the child is about three months old.

Dr. Shaver and a team composed of a psychiatrist, psychologist, social worker, obstetrician, pediatrician and an infant observer studied 57 mothers during the last six months of pregnancy and the first six months after their babies was born. They checked to see if there was any difference in the mothers of children with colic and those without. The colicky babies were self-determined. There was no disparity in the amount or quality of caring in the two groups.

Pediatrician Dr. Jack L. Paradise studied 146 infants and came away with the same conclusion. Psychological ideas on the parental cause of colic have led to "self-blame, frustration and heightened anxiety" among mothers of colicky babies, he says. The anxiety these mothers felt *was the result, not the cause,* of the baby's colic.

Toilet training is another parent phobia. Long after the child is trained, there is a lingering belief that emotional problems were born on the potty, caused by faulty toilet training. Dr. Stella Chess helps explode this myth. Fewer than 5 percent of the children in her study have problems focused on toilet training. Typically, these children have other difficulties as well.

Bed-wetting is a first cousin to faulty toilet training in the fears of overpsychologized parents. The bed-wetter generally needs to urinate more often during the day as well, but the problem is aggravated at night. The combination of a small bladder and the habit of sound sleeping generally produces the problem called *enuresis.*

Modern psychology claims that bed-wetting is an emotional difficulty aggravated by bad parenting. In a study of 824 children Dr. F. Tabia showed that the "well-adjusted" and "clinically disturbed" ones had the same rate of enuresis, approximately one in ten cases. The late Dr. Harry Bakwin believed that bed-wetting probably is genetically based. Dr. Bakwin showed that parents who were bed-wetters when they were young produced children who were bed-wetters 40 percent of the time.

The power of human heredity was understood in Freud's time by many psychiatrists, including his mentor, Dr. Theodore Meynert, a professor at the University of Vienna. But in the years since Freud's ascendancy, its potency in psychology was purposefully shelved as faulty dogma. Only today is heredity reappearing as a vital factor in understanding the development of personality and behavior.

As we have seen, one method of showing the power of heredity on personality is to conduct studies on *monozygotic,* or identical, twins, two children born from the same egg. In almost all respects these twins are biologically the same human being. Fraternal twins, born from two separate eggs, are different. They have the separate biology of normal siblings.

One of the best laboratories of nature vs. nurture is in the study of identical twins separated after birth and raised in different homes. Since we are dealing with virtually the same biology, we can isolate out the effect of environment. Researcher H.A. Newman traced twenty pairs of identical twins who had been reared apart for various reasons, mainly because of adoption. Most did not even know they were twins, identical or otherwise.

One of the case histories illustrates the profound power of genetic make-up. Two identical twins, Edwin and Fred, were brought together by chance at the age of twenty-two. They had been adopted as infants by two families of the same social class in the same New England town, and for a short time went to the same school, not suspecting that they were twins. Then their respective families moved to the Midwest, but a thousand miles apart.

When they finally got together, the similarities in their lives proved to be startling, almost eerie. They were both interested in electricity and both had become expert telephone repairmen in different

262 / The Psychological Society

branches of the same company. They married in the same year to women of the same age and type. The most amazing similarity was that each had a fox terrier dog named Trixie.

The long-denied importance of *constitutional factors* in psychiatry and child raising is finally becoming evident to certain professionals. "In daily practice, we psychiatrists are continuously aware that the differences between children are in part differences which were present from birth," says Dr. Charles R. Shaw, director of research of the Hawthorn Center in Michigan.

What do Freudians, who so influenced American child care, say to all this? Freud personally paid lip service to constitutional factors. "In the pathogenesis of the major neuroses, heredity plays the part of a condition potent in all cases and even indispensable in the majority of them. It cannot without the assistance of specific causes; but the importance of hereditary predisposition is demonstrated by the fact that the same specific causes operating on a sound person would produce no manifest pathologic effect . . ."

Freudians often quote Freud on heredity to escape criticism. But the Freudian emphasis has always been on the parent's personality as the source of the child's trouble. One of the centers of Freudian influence in child care and child psychiatry is Yale University, whose Child Study Center is psychoanalytically oriented. A psychoanalyst who is also a pediatrician is director of Yale's Child Development Unit, a subgroup which cares for children from birth to age five, the all-important Freudian years.

About half the children they treat have mental health problems, a large minority of whom are victims of childhood autism, the mysterious behavior disturbance which this analyst assumes is mainly biological in origin. It is "only somewhat alleviated by or made worse by life influences," she stated when interviewed.

The majority of children seen at Yale suffer from less severe, but still debilitating, emotional problems. The cause? This time it is the familiar modern psychodynamic litany: a disturbed relationship between parent and child.

The parent is seen as the focus of the problem. "Some parents are immature in their own personality development," the director of this Yale unit explains. "There may be stresses in marriage or parenthood. Some adults are ill-equipped for parenthood on the basis of what has happened in their own lives. It is reflected in the way they take care of their children. Some parents can't cope with the child's needs, or react negatively to them. Or conversely, they may overreact and become overly upset over normal developmental behavior in the child. For some immature parents, the child's needs are seen as a personal assault on them."

The Freudian impact on child care has been enormous. It is seen in detail in agencies such as Yale's, but it permeates the entire child care world, including the biases of educated housewives from Connecticut to Kansas City. Its theorem is basically that the parent brings a baggage of unconscious needs and frustrations to married life and unceremoniously dumps them onto their children without their knowing the origin of what they are doing or even that they are doing it. It is a *historical* theory. What happened to the parent in the past is now bottled up unconsciously. It will show itself in the present in the care of the child in a disguised, mysterious form.

"Sometimes a parent may have predominantly negative and hostile unconscious feelings toward the child that they consciously want to take care of," the Yale analyst explains. "The parents' attitude toward the child comes out of their own feelings from the past. Sometimes the child may remind the parents of someone out of the past whom they hated. Unconsciously, they transfer that hatred to the child."

Since Yale (and many other child care clinics) consider many parents of disturbed children to be somewhat disturbed themselves, they insist on treating both the parent and the child. Psychotherapy at Yale is done by one of four "helping" specialists: a psychiatrist, a psychologist, social worker or early-childhood educator (teacher) with training in child therapy. Two different therapists generally handle the parent and child, then later confer.

What happens in the joint child-parent therapy? "We start with the behavior that the child presents," she says. "Then we look at the dynamic interaction between the child and the parent, using some psychoanalytic propositions to understand them. For example, we might have a two-year-old who is unusually negativistic. He says 'No' to everything—picking up toys, toilet training, etc. Every transaction becomes a fight. We try to learn what it is about the parent-child relationship which creates this special problem. Why do both sides have to fight? What is it about the parent's own experience that makes him or her behave as childishly as the child?

"We may find, for example, that this parent had a fighting relationship with important figures in the past," she continues. "This did not come to the fore initially but was revived when the child became more active and more negative. The old fighting relationship which was ostensibly forgotten by the parent triggers the new pattern of fighting with the child."

The Freudian Oedipal theory is not lost in Yale's child care world, where it is believed that it can create emotional disturbance in children. "In the normally developing child between three and a half and five, there is certain overt behavior and fantasy which involves the Oedipal theory," the Yale analyst states. "For example, a four-year-old may be clinging excessively to one of the parents. We would tell the parents that one of them is being seductive to the child, or else being excessively punitive. Some parents can handle the use of such words as 'seductive.' With others, we might say that they are inviting this type of behavior by taking the child into bed with them more than they should. Or that most children cannot handle the sight of parents who are nude."

Has Freudian theory hurt the art of parenting? The director of Yale's Child Development Unit thinks it has been both negative and positive. "Before the advent of ego psychology in analytic thought, there was too much emphasis placed on gratifying the child, and too much concern about traumas. It was not balanced by limits on behavior. Since the early 1940s, leaders in the field have espoused a much broader view. But as in any field, there is a problem in that what gets translated into handbooks on child care lags behind theory. The fear of children's fragile psyche that some parents now have came out of early Freudianism. They are afraid they would be responsible for a long-lasting trauma in the child. It is true that conscientious young parents who have read a lot about child care do get paralyzed at times. I sometimes advise parents to stop reading and to use their natural instincts. We say in the field, 'Some parents read because they worry. Others worry because they read.' "

Child care has always been somewhat of an obsession in America. Many parents see in their children expectations for a future denied to them, either by birth or luck. In many ways, Americans live through their children, hoping to gain immortality through future generations.

It is not a bad morality. In fact, it may be the most beneficent philosophy in the disordered history of man. But it has a negative corollary, one in which Americans take an equal pride. It is the belief that through research and expertise, rather than philosophy, we can find the ideal way to prepare our children for this Nirvana of tomorrow.

This combination of hope and expertise has wedded the American parent to parenting as a technology. Unlike one born from true science, it is an ever-frustrating one which has probably disturbed more child-parent relationships and injured more psyches than it has benefited.

The changing fads in child care have been documented in a study done by the University of Illinois College of Education. In the 1890s mother was glorified as an ideal. The good parent of that day was one who had "good character," and who then set herself up as a model for the child. "A joyful mother will make baby happy," one Victorian expert wrote, "while a sad one usually has a sober child. Be happy."

The happy mother begetting a happy child did not prove to be a reliable equation. Many contented parents produced malcontents and vice versa. But experts volunteered to fill the gap, and by 1910 a new *schema* was developed for the anxious parent. It was discipline, firmness and exercise of authority.

Nail biting in 1910, for example, was treated with this expert advice: "Get some white cotton gloves and make her wear them all the time—even in school. They will not only serve as a reminder but also make her ashamed when people ask about them." Shame and ridicule were prime child-raising tools. Parents were warned not to fondle the child too much. It might make the baby precocious.

The next two decades, the twenties and thirties, were destined to become the era of *scheduled child care.* The infant was raised within a strict discipline of feeding, weaning and toilet training. If he was hungry, he cried until he either stopped or, happily, reached the feeding time. Love was considered important, but not so much love that it interfered with the child's all-important schedule.

The tendency toward strictness which carried over from the decade 1910–1920 was reinforced in the twenties and thirties by a new psychological prophet, Dr. John B. Watson, author of *behaviorism.* Watson argued that children could be conditioned for either genius and success or doltishness and failure. It was the parent's responsibility to ensure the proper upbringing.

Like Freudianism, it was an environmental theory. But while Freudians tended toward cuddling and permissiveness, Watson's concepts aped those underlying Marine boot-camp training. "There is a sensible way of treating children. Treat them as though they were young adults . . . ," Watson stated. "Never hug or kiss them, never let them sit on your lap. If you must, kiss them once on the forehead when they say good-night. Shake hands with them in the morning

. . . Let it learn to overcome difficulties from the moment of birth."

Watson's effect on impressionable mothers of the 1920s and 1930s created child raising by the clock. But by the time World War II was over, the system had changed once more. Demand feeding, and new Freudian concern for Johnny's unconscious needs, overwhelmed the Watsonians.

As we know, the forties, fifties, sixties, even the seventies, have been the heyday of permissiveness, an attitude based on the theory that the child instinctively knows best. This new attitude began in force at the end of the 1940s, when returning war veterans and their wives became intrigued by child care concepts which matched their wartime idealism. They wanted to do better for their children than had been done for them. They had material to work with: the largest baby boom in American history.

Many of the self-help articles of the 1940s era were blatantly permissive. One frankly titled "Spoil That Baby" was typical of the new evangelism. The author, a psychiatric social worker, made bold pseudo-scientific statements of the type that has since influenced impressionable parents. "Psychiatrists and pediatricians have scientifically established the fact in recent years that a baby needs affectionate attention just as much as he needs food," she wrote. "Actual cases are on record of infants who have become seriously ill and have even died for want of mother's love. Far more frequently, however, babies apparently adjust to lack of affection and give evidence of their deep frustration only in later life, through psychosis, neurosis or general maladjustment."

One Beverly Hills psychologist even advised readers to "Let Them Get It Out of Their Systems." When children act mean and angry, advised the expert, they should not be disciplined. "If we follow this course [discipline], we are headed for trouble," wrote the 1940s child expert. "Sooner or later . . . instead of getting the meanness out, we stamp it in. It goes down deeper and deeper and becomes more fixed in our child's personality and character."

The permissive conformity born of such glib advice is a testimonial to our national gullibility for fads and for *scientism,* and to our loss of confidence in our own values. As we have seen, Dr. Donald J. Holmes, a former University of Michigan psychiatrist, believes that psychiatry and psychology have been oversold to the American parent. He advises parents to depend more on their own common sense and less on amateur psychoanalysis in solving the problems of their children.

Child-raising trends are now in the process of transition. Many parents are still frightened that discipline will injure their child's psyche, but the return to tradition has begun. It is not a return to the strictness of 1910, but to the 1890s concept that the best mother and father are those who act as models for the child.

Dr. Ambrosino, of the Family Service Association, refers to it as Maslovian, a concept of self-fulfillment. "If the modern parent is able to self-actualize and become a good adult living up to his potential as a person, he will be a good parent by serving as a model for the child," he says. Dr. Ambrosino and others take it for granted that the fulfilled person will also be the fulfilled parent. Right or wrong, we have now come full circle from the 1890s.

It is obvious that child care fashions are thin and transient. The creation and dissemination of knowledge on how to raise children now appears to be one of the great academic hoaxes of our times. Judging from the accumulated evidence, it appears probable that the *intelligent, intuitive parent knows as much, or more, about child care as the child educator, the parent-child expert, the psychologist, the social worker or the psychiatrist.*

A Milwaukee study on child adjustment shattered all the psychological shibboleths of child raising and exonerated parents who choose their own way. In a study reported in the *Journal of Educational Sociology,* Irving W. Stout and Grace Langdon, a school principal and a teacher, picked 159 boys and girls, most of whom were ten to fourteen years old, as "well-adjusted."

They were selected not merely for being good students or "goody-goodies," but because they had reasonable control of their emotions, were able to think for themselves, had the ability to play with other children, gave the appearance of being happy and were liked and respected by their peers.

The researchers then tried to learn what kind of upbringing created these well-adjusted children. The answers were disappointing to psychological fans, for none of the theories held up. The children were products of a diverse set of child-raising ideas, with no agreement by their parents as to what was correct in child rearing.

Some came from poor homes, others from wealthy backgrounds. There were children who had one dead parent. Some of the parents had only been to grade school; others had college degrees. There was no special birth order, nor did only children predominate. Some had been breast-fed, others raised on the bottle. In some homes the parents spanked the children or even sent them to bed with only bread and milk for supper when they were "bad." In other homes, they used the modern "Let's talk it over" technique.

The one unifying fact was that the children and the parents did things together as a family. This concept of family unity has existed outside the world of psychology for generations. It is the hallmark of intelligent parents who intuitively know that a well-cemented, active family is a practical way to raise children.

Many modern child care notions are now being revealed as exaggerations, even as blatantly false. One theory is that *mothering* must be continuously applied to the child in broad, warm strokes. Its absence at any stage of development, we have been taught, will produce an emotionally malformed child.

Some warmth and nurturing is obviously good for the growing child. But anthropologist Harold Orlansky, reporting in the *Psychological Bulletin,* found a cultural exception which refutes the universal mothering theory. Albanian mothers are just as idolized as any in the world. But Orlansky describes a very detached child-raising technique in some portions of that culture. "Until they are one year old, the Albanian children are bound securely to a wooden cradle customarily placed in the darkest corner of the room, often with a cloth thrown over their heads so that no light is visible," he states.

Does this seemingly barbaric method hurt the child? Apparently not, says Orlansky. Evidence shows that their "social behavior, as measured by responses to . . . standardized tests was equal or superior to the norms for Viennese children of the same age."

To many, the symbol of the spoiled children of the postwar era is the dean of pediatricians and child-care experts, Dr. Benjamin Spock, whose manual *Baby and Child Care* is the mother's Koran. Spock has been accused of fathering permissive attitudes, a charge he has consistently denied. In 1974, in a historic article, Dr. Spock did seem to rebel against attitudes long held by his profession. In his now controversial "How Not to Bring Up a Bratty Child," Spock urged parental firmness. A newspaper headlined "Spock Recants!"

Dr. Spock denies that he recanted or that he was ever a permissivist. But he does admit that parents had been misled all these years by experts, including himself. "Inability to be firm is, to my mind, the commonest problem of parents in America today," he said.

The dean of child care blames this common shortcoming on psychology, calling it the "fear of alienating a child, the guiltiness about arousing hostility." Dr. Spock singles out the professional experts as the perpetrators of this generation-long error. "In the twentieth century parents have been persuaded that the only people who know for sure how children should be managed are the child psychiatrists, psychologists, teachers, social workers and pediatricians—like myself," he admits.

In this morass of contradiction and psychological propaganda, what is the parent to do? Not very much. As Dr. Gesell has demonstrated, children go through a series of developmental phases. Most problems are eliminated by normal growth rather than through psychological intervention. Secondly, the child's highly individual inborn factors determine much of its behavior. No matter what parents would like to do about it, there is little they can do, except to use their best instincts to provide a reasonable home environment.

The truly disturbed child will require professional assistance. But the number of supposedly disturbed children, which has been falsely estimated as high as one in four by some professionals, is not as large as anxious parents and over-eager experts believe.

In the raising of children the parent is generally the most knowledgeable guide. This reassuring philosophy is repeated by no less an expert than Dr. Spock himself. "The more people have studied different methods of bringing up children the more they have come to the conclusion that what good mothers and fathers instinctively feel like doing for their babies is usually best after all."

The modern sin of parenting has not been one of psychological ignorance. It has been quite the opposite. By absorbing the half-truths, shibboleths and outright fallacies of the Psychological Society, the parents of the last thirty-five years have unfortunately put into massive practice an idea whose time should not have come.

FREUD IN THE CLASSROOM

Although parents have reveled in the role of amateur psychologist, psychologizing of the young has not stopped at the threshold of the home. The American school system is equally immersed in the probing and molding of children's psyches.

Surprisingly, most Americans are unaware of the role of psychology in the classroom. But young people regularly come in contact with it in the form of personality testing (including the Rorschach inkblot test), psychological evaluation and counseling, and even more complex psychotherapy.

The psychological program is in force from kindergarten to college. In fact, more than one school system begins I.Q. testing the summer before kindergarten. In all its manifestations, school psychology has become one of the most active segments of the Psychological Society as it insists that our children's psyches be probed by a team composed of schoolteachers, guidance counselors, social workers, school psychologists and even consulting psychiatrists.

Their stated goal is the mental health of the young. But this prying into youngsters' minds and emotions is equally satisfying to the bureaucratic mentality which feeds on the amassing of often irrelevant information on schoolchildren. The effort is euphemistically called *a search for mental health,* a distorted modern concept which parents and teachers confuse with social adjustment and happiness.

The schoolteacher, ostensibly a nonpsychologist, is actually the prime bastion in this work. The teacher-as-psychologist is a popular contemporary model which begins early in training, when the would-be pedagogue is introduced to a highly psychologized curriculum called "professional education."

Critics such as Dr. James B. Conant, former president of Harvard and author of *The Education of American Teachers,* and James D. Koerner, author of *The Miseducation of American Teachers,* have shown that the training of American teachers is often as much a *psychological* as a *knowledge* experience. Through "educational psychology" and other "method" courses, more emphasis is often placed on the whys of learning and the personality of the child than on the actual curriculum. Several critics, including Koerner, are convinced that this psychological emphasis has been greatly responsible for the recent lowering of academic school performance.

The result of all this is a modern teacher who is proud to be part of a professional team which hopes to mold the child's personality and life attitudes. In such an environment, social adjustment and personal insight are emphasized at the expense of learning.

American education, particularly at the grade-school level, is becoming a form of preventive mental hygiene. This attitude is obvious in such journals as *Today's Education,* a trade bible of the National Education Association. In a typical article, "The Quiet Ones, the Noisy Ones," a psychiatrist advises teachers how to interpret why some children are quiet in class, while others are noisy. "The noisy child may suffer from a profound sense of being bad and needing punishment," he suggests.

Some teachers are bashful about this role as stand-in psychologist, but they are professionally prodded. Guidance counselor Irving Doress tells teachers to confidently accept themselves as teacher-therapists. "Don't sell yourself short because 'I'm not a therapist' or 'I had only three psych courses' or 'I might destroy the child's psychological balance,' " he states. "Take a chance, follow your instincts. You'll probably do no more harm and much good."

Many schoolteachers do take that chance. Faculty gossip, particularly among younger teachers, often centers more on Johnny's psychological problems than on his grades. If his psychic woes are solved, many teachers believe, Johnny's academic problems will miraculously clear up. In this psychologized environment, learning deficiency is not the result of student ineptitude or poor instruction but of a *psychological failure.*

This view of the classroom as a psychological laboratory is candidly expressed by psychiatrist Dr. Stonewall B. Stickney, former director of school mental health services of Pittsburgh. "Schools are our community mental health centers," he writes in the *American Journal of Psychiatry.* Of the 390,000 children in the Pittsburgh system, Dr. Stickney believes 39,000 are "emotionally disturbed."

Dr. Stickney sees the school as the natural place for the identification and treatment of the disturbed. He reveals that Pittsburgh hopes to psychologically diagnose all children before they enter the first grade. Although cloaked in beneficence, Stickney's idea is a perilous one. Not only does it misplace school emphasis, but such programs have historically been failures.

Our schools are taking on the aura of a psychiatric clinic. Without informed taxpayer consent, the modern school has become involved far beyond its competence in both the "intellectual and personality development of children." This phrase was coined by Dr. Raquel Cohen, a Harvard medical school psychiatrist, who asks for closer collaboration between the teacher and therapist.

What some parents might see as an intrusion, schools now see as an opportunity. There have always been extra school personnel, but their traditional roles were quite different from today's "mental health team in the schools," as Dr. Margaret M. Lawrence calls it in her school-counseling text.

In pre-psychological days, the teacher taught; the guidance counselor advised children on college and vocations; the social worker was concerned with the child's socioeconomic problems. The handful of school psychologists were mandated to test children's intelligence, to locate and help those unable to learn in the normal classroom.

These job descriptions are now archaic. The guidance counselor, the social worker and the school psychologist have all become *psychological professionals* treating children in the school environment. The world *therapy* is almost never uttered. *Counseling* is the softer, preferable term. "Therapy" would infringe on the prerogatives of private psychologists and psychiatrists, but the young school patient would be hard pressed to describe the difference.

Aided by the National Defense Education Act of 1958, the nation's sixty thousand school guidance counselors have in recent years been transformed from simple pragmatists into substitute "psychologists," even if only on the third rung of the helping-professions ladder.

In the *Personnel and Guidance Journal,* Lawrence M. Brammer, professor of educational psychology at the University of Washington, says defiantly, "The Counselor is a Psychologist." He warns that the "social workers and psychologists look with mild contempt on school counselors who identify only with the guidance model." The answer, he says, is to join the other two school professions and take up the "counseling psychologist model."

Many guidance counselors have taken his advice. As a result, the schoolchild is immersed in a psychological environment in which he is cajoled, invited, seduced, even bludgeoned into seeking counseling.

In a typical elementary school, children with day-to-day problems are often referred to the counselor: a child who has been skipping school; a child who is a petty thief; or a child who is unhappy in class. At the high school level, the problems of puberty are typical. "Many of these young teenagers talk to us, because we're neither teachers nor parents. They don't feel we have an ax to grind and they discuss things with us they wouldn't talk about at home," says one counselor.

To the schoolchild, they are all "shrinks." But in the hierarchy of counseling the school psychologist is generally a rung above the others. The presence of over seven thousand school psychologists is now taken for granted, but their legal and ethical right to treat our children is not firmly staked out.

A school psychologist in an affluent Westchester, New York, suburb, candidly points out that their psychological work with children is actually extralegal. "By employing school psychologists, this school system has made a commitment to mental health," he stated when interviewed in his small senior high school office. "Actually, school psychology did not begin because of any commitment to mental health. We are here because the law of New York State says that in order to label a youngster as mentally retarded he must be diagnosed as such by a school psychologist. In doing our counseling work with youngsters we have been responsive to the community."

The gap between diagnosing mental retardation and the actual job of the modern school psychologist is enormous. "Our job is to look after the best interests of the youngster, from the point of view of mental health," says the Westchester school psychologist. "I don't do psychotherapy—I counsel. It's different in that counseling is more pragmatic and short-term. It is the application of psychological skills to helping people manage, to deal with stresses, to be all right."

The student comes to the school psychologist's office for therapy or counseling once a week for the traditional fifty-minute hour. What do the youngsters talk about? "The problems are generally in three areas—boy friends or girl friends, the pressure of schools, and the feeling that they are being put upon by parents,"the Westchester school psychologist responds. "I tend to be sympathetic to the youngster's point of view. The child is my client. My responsibility is to him. If I work with integrity, that's who I service."

The question of the school psychologist's integrity may not be as obvious to the taxpayer who is paying his salary. The child may even be in counseling without his parents' permission or even their knowledge. "We are not required to notify the parents if the child comes in for counseling," states this psychologist. "In the elementary school, the parents are always notified. But as the child gets older, it is left to our discretion."

The school psychologist deals both with students who are referred by the teacher and with those who drop in on their own. In either case the regimen is much the same. The youngster is given a battery of psychological tests which often include deep projective tests such as the Rorschach inkblots and the Thematic Apperception Test. He is then put into counseling, generally once a week for months or even for a year or two.

The work of school psychology raises many ethical questions. If the parent and a teenager differ strongly, and the child is being secretly advised by the taxpayer-supported school psychologist, is the psychologist operating with integrity? Who authorized the school to delve into the psyche of our children? The label of "mental health," with its frightening implications of "mental illness," has apparently intimidated most parents into obedient silence.

One large Connecticut school system employs fifteen school psychologists, each with a master's degree and further graduate credits.

Surprisingly, in this state and most others (including New York) *school psychologists need not be licensed psychologists.* They may test and counsel schoolchildren, but few are sufficiently trained to practice in the community. Of the fifteen school psychologists in the Connecticut city, only one is a licensed psychologist.

In this system the children's first contact with the school psychologist is through "class meetings," a primitive group-therapy session. The children are not psychologically knowledgeable, but they are not totally naïve. They know they are being encouraged to talk out their problems in front of other children. "The kids know it involves feelings, behavior, emotions and getting along," a school psychologist revealed during an interview.

Large numbers of students come in contact with the school "shrink." During a year approximately one in ten, or one thousand of this Connecticut district's schoolchildren are given a full psychological evaluation by the psychologists. (This system does seek the consent of the parent.) The evaluation is usually triggered by the teacher's feeling that the child has difficulty in learning or has a problem in personal social adjustment, one of the educational goals.

The evaluation begins with the psychologist observing the child in the classroom. The student is put through a battery of educational and psychological tests, followed by psychological interviews with the child, then with the parents. The social worker and language pathologist may also be called in. If further referral is necessary, the child may be sent to a private psychiatrist, at the cost of $60 an hour. "If we prescribe, we pay for it," a school spokesman states.

"The child may be too shy or withdrawn, or exhibit any behavior which the teacher feels is beyond expected behavior: inattentiveness, extreme physical activity, pugnaciousness, or unhappy or depressed behavior," the Connecticut school psychologist explains. "The philosophy behind what we do is that modern education is more than just the three Rs. Getting along with other people is part of the democratic sociological goal."

Not all parents see this goal as sharply as does the psychological establishment. "Some parents take affront at the idea," the school psychologist admits. "They argue with us: 'You can't say that my child is crazy!' But we present it as a constructive idea which will help the child. Most then go along with us."

This lower-level psychologizing has its own bureaucratic momentum. The results, including the scores on psychological tests, reports on counseling sessions, psychological evaluations and recommendations, are entered on the child's record. The psychological report stays with the child from kindergarten through the completion of high school. Does it follow him to college? No, we are assured, the university does not see the detailed information. But it does see the notation that the youngster was interviewed by the school psychologist, which itself may be meaningful to a college admissions officer.

The very presence of psychology in our school is controversial. Firstly, as we have seen, almost all the personnel involved are actually laymen. Secondly, the entire practice of school psychology may be seen as an intrusion of bureaucracy into the family structure. Further, school counseling may not be legal. In most states, school personnel may not practice psychotherapy on children. By labeling it as *counseling* instead of *psychotherapy,* they may have invented a semantic subterfuge to circumvent the law.

Some skeptical professionals do question the school-psychology operation. Dr. Henry Winthrop, professor at the University of South Florida, raises several points, which he groups under "bad faith."

The problem of *confidentiality* is a key. "Let us imagine a school psychologist in a high school, college or university to whom students come voluntarily with their problems or to whom they are referred," Dr. Winthrop writes in *Mental Hygiene.* "What are we to say to such a psychologist who promises the students to keep the information confidential and then passes it on to others?"

This "pass along" information is crucial if the student is being labeled emotionally disturbed. "What shall we say of the school therapist who, in dealing with a student who comes for counseling in good faith, assigns that student a psychiatric label, which he then inserts in the counselee's folder so that this diagnosis can follow the counselee for years and impair the transfer from one school to another?" asks an annoyed Dr. Winthrop.

Winthrop is particularly severe with school personnel who read the results of often inaccurate psychological tests as if they were scientific gospel. He asks his colleagues: "Consider the terrible situation in which a silly and overserious psychologist decides that a student is mentally deranged and bases that decision only upon the results of a few, routine psychological tests. Is it any wonder that many students despise 'head-shrinkers'?"

It has now become apparent that psychology has been oversold in the schools. Enlightened parents may be aware of this, but many are overwhelmed by the school system's supposed good intentions. But as we have seen with parents' generation-long flirtation with child psychology, such intentions are often perilous when mixed with modern psychological theories.

There is no real evidence that the anxieties, neuroses or eventual psychosis rate of children is in any way reduced by school intervention. There is the equal possibility that the effort is actually a *neurotic stimulus*. With our taxes, we are helping poorly trained helping specialists to tamper with the psyches of an already overpsychologized generation.

This generation of the young has been enmeshed in psychology from the time of their birth. We have been continually promised that psychological intervention, in the home and in school, would strengthen their psyches and ward off emotional instability. Thus far, the promise has been considerably more impressive than the reward.

# IX

## The New Therapies,
## the New Messiahs

A WOMAN IN HER FORTIES, dressed in a long peasant skirt, sat crouched on the floor as her "primal-type" therapist spoke to her reassuringly. After fifteen minutes of dramatization of her father's death, the therapist asked the distraught subject to lie down on a mattress in the center of the darkened room.

The woman was told to increase her breathing depth. The therapist placed his elbow in the region of her solar plexus and pressed until she emitted short bursts of painful sounds. He offered her a baby bottle to suck on, but she refused. He worked closely with her, cajoling, then pressing to elicit deeper and deeper breathing. His frustration increased as she failed to achieve the hoped-for *primal,* the dramatic, sometimes violent return to screaming infancy hailed by some therapists as the most startling innovation since Freud's miracle cure of Viennese hysterics.

The therapist was on the verge of giving up when his assistant suddenly produced a white bed sheet. He placed it over the patient's face and body. Within seconds she started to thrash about in strong, fitful kicking motions while emitting a wail punctuated by infantile jabberings.

When her thrashing threatened to throw her off the mattress, group members rushed to hold down the sheet, trapping the "infant" within the crib of her fantasy. The pitiful wailing and thrashing kept up for five minutes, when the cry finally wound down. When the sheet was removed, an exhausted middle-aged woman returned from her hysterical voyage back in time.

The incident, witnessed at a Philadelphia growth center, was one of the fashionable new manifestations of the Psychological Society. It is an offshoot of Primal Scream therapy, developed by Arthur Janov (Ph.D.), a Beverly Hills psychologist who operates the Primal Institute in Los Angeles.

"Primal therapy is *the* movement in psychiatry today," Dr. Janov commented when interviewed. "We are perhaps the busiest clinic in the world. We receive three thousand applications each month from people all over the world who want to be treated. We accept only ten. Primal therapy has become a phenomenon. The reason for its success is that it is true.

"It is a highly precise therapy, which is why I insist on training all therapists at my institute," he continued. "In the hands of an untrained person, it is a highly dangerous technique. There are some two hundred and fifty phony therapists claiming to do Primal practicing right now. We are suing two or three of them for unauthorized use of the name."

Janov has popularized primal therapy through a promotional technique borrowed from Freud himself. Like Freud's claims of miraculous cure made in *Studies on Hysteria* (1896), Janov believes in the magic of Primal as the only cure for man's troubled psyche, what he calls *psycho-physical illness.* "By implication, this renders all other psychological theories obsolete and invalid," Janov says.

Janov is one of the Psychological Society's new messiahs, a successor to those who have followed the first messiah, Freud. It is part of an apparently endless chain of philosopher-healers who offer the masses psychic bliss in exchange for personal immortality. Each messiah is ennobled as the head of a new psychological school. Each is encouraged to pen popular books on how to achieve health, happiness, even wealth, through their mental technology. In the theological vernacular, it is a perpetual second coming of Freud, a contemporary reincarnation of the Viennese miracle worker.

The popularity of the new messiahs is enormous, for they offer the public something that psychoanalysis with its customary five or six years on the couch, or even $50-an-hour conventional psychotherapy of a year or two's duration, cannot. The new therapies are brief, less intellectual in an age of hurried ideas, more emotional, and they offer the promise of an *immediate, even if transient, feeling of well-being.*

In conventional therapy the patient ponders and talks. In the new "quickie" therapies, which can take anywhere from only days to months, the patient participates with his feelings, his screams, his games, his obscenities, even his body. In addition to costing less, taking less time and promising as much as traditional methods, the new therapies seem to many distraught patients to even be more *fun.*

The message of each pretender to Freud's throne generally contradicts those of the competitors. But this does not dim the interest of the hopeful, gullible consumers of the Psychological Society.

Janov's claims are obviously scientific hyperbole. But his impact on therapy users, who feed on newness, is real. In addition to Janov's patients, thousands have been screaming, crying and kicking out their repressions in the offices of the two hundred and fifty "unauthorized" primal therapists.

"I practiced traditional psychoanalysis for years, but I have now moved almost completely into primal," says Herman Weiner, Ph.D., a training analyst at the National Psychological Association for Psychoanalysis. "Like many of my colleagues I was initially skeptical. I even refused to read Janov's book. Now I believe primal will replace traditional therapy to an enormous extent—it is a real revolution." Dr. Weiner glanced down at the mattresses on his office floor, one for the patient, the other for the therapist. "Freud brought us halfway down, to the couch. Janov, all the way down," he observed.

As a theorist, Janov is deified by his followers. But as a movement leader, he has gained their hostility. "Most innovators are proud if other people practice their method, but not Janov," says one primal practitioner. "He's really out-of-sight—on a personal ego trip. He utilizes the Freudian idea of abreaction, and the bioenergetic idea that neurosis and tension are also in the body. There are also Gestalt techniques in primal, but Janov gives credit to no one except for some mention of Freud."

Why the interest in primal therapy? Many believe it is because Janov rediscovered the earlier, more exciting Freud. Through *catharsis* and *abreaction*—the talking out and unloading of emotions —Freud supposedly released repressed traumatic memories in his patients. Freud claimed that hysteria patients "suffered from reminiscences." Once freed of these agonizing memories, they would be cured.

The painful-trauma theory has been mainly discarded by formal psychoanalysis. But it has been vigorously reconstructed by Janov. Janov calls it the Primal Pool, a dammed-up pool of anguish which must be flooded out. As in early Freud, *Pain* is the essence of the Janovian theory. (He always capitalizes this sacred word.) "The severity of neurosis depends on the amount of accumulated Pain," Janov states.

Like Freud, Janov is not particularly interested in the hectic here and now. Since his cause of mental illness is early pain, Janov claims that nothing which deals with present symptoms can result in a cure. To move his patients back, Janov puts them into Primals, the bizarre reliving of infant and childhood experiences, sometimes accompanied by bloodcurdling screams.

Janov's description of a Primal Group seems like a Fellini interpretation of London's ancient Bedlam. The decibel level rises to "close to jet noise," he says. In the tableaux of the Primal Group room, one adult patient wails and sucks like an infant. Another patient is playing with a teddy bear; one man, hooked on pornography, stands surrounded by books and holding his penis; another waits in terror, as a whip held over him by a therapist reminds him of his punishing father. An exhibitionist shows his genitals, then falls screaming to the floor: "Mamma, show some feeling, please!"

Janov's startling experience is duplicated by therapists elsewhere. "When Otto Rank proposed that birth was a traumatic experience, he wasn't given much credence," says Dr. Weiner. "I would not have believed it, but I have seen the trauma of birth re-created in birth Primals. The patient's thumbs turn in to a fetal position. Then the feet turn in; the face becomes contorted. The person's voice changes and emits infant sounds. I have even seen long infantlike plugs of mucous come out of their throat.

"Most of the primals I have seen are early ones with mother, from birth up to one year," Dr. Weiner continued. "When the Primal Group is here I stand in the darkened room and listen to ten people on the floor all going at once. All I hear is 'Mommy, I'm afraid. Mommy, love me. Mommy, don't hate me.' There is a lot of crying, and writhing in pain. We seldom see joy. What we are seeing is the repressed pain of infancy. Even if the whole theory of primal therapy is false, which I doubt, it works like nothing since shamanism."

The Janov idea, simply stated, is that childhood trauma produces such pain that the young person seeks escape in neurosis. Janov's theory fits the key psychological supposition that the child's personality is environmentally produced in the first years of life. There is little attention given to genetics, or to the child's temperament or constitution. As Janov says: "Primal Therapy is based on the assumption that we are born nothing but ourselves. We are not born neurotic or psychotic. We're just born."

It is a replay of the Freudian theory of parents as arch villains. Throughout Primal Scream, Janov speaks of the misery of childhood, of brutal parents, especially fathers. He talks of Pain accumulated by the young which must be let out in primals if one is to recover.

Primal Therapy, as practiced by Janov, is itself a punishing technique. In the first twenty-four hours, the patient may be asked to stay up all night. They sob, even fear they are going crazy during the pretreatment period. As Janov says, "The patient arrives suffering . . . he may be kept waiting five to ten minutes beyond his appointed time in order to allow more tension to build."

As in psychoanalysis, the patient lies on a couch, but now his body is spread-eagled. The patient speaks of his early life, and is encouraged to call out for his parents. He is told to keep his mouth open so as not to "swallow" his feelings. He is asked to *feel* and to *breathe*. His throat and chest become tight, he begins "gagging" and "retching." He tries to speak, begins "thrashing and writhing about in pain," and finally a "scream" erupts in the form of a phrase—"I hate you!" or "Daddy, be nice"—along with "torrents of Pain." Says Janov, "This is the Primal Scream."

Is Janov accepted by the psychological community? He is a popular new messiah, but in the clawing inner world of therapy, where one man's holy cure is another's nonsense, Janov is receiving his share of criticism.

Basically his critics say (1) that *abreaction* is not truly curative, (2) that Primal Therapy is early disproven Freud all over again, (3) that the Primal regression to childhood is possibly dangerous, (4) that many Primals are *faked.*

Joseph Hart, Ph.D., a former Janov staff member who opened his own Center for Feeling Therapy in Los Angeles, is among the strongest of critics. "I disagreed with parts of Janov's theory and therapy, and suggested corrections which he would not accept," Hart recalled when interviewed. "He felt that if the patient has enough Primals, he would lose all his defenses, and be cured. I don't believe that is true.

"When we left Janov, forty percent of the patients came with us," Hart continued. "After working with them, we found that most had been *faking* their Primals. They were simulating regression, just as some of Charcot's patients had done in France in Freud's time. It's hard to say if they were consciously faking, but they had learned to do what their therapist wanted."

Fake or real, the Primal is a replay of the ancient phenomenon of self-hypnosis triggering a hysterical incident. The phenomenon was seen by the Greeks; by religious evangelists; by Antoine Mesmer, the father of hypnotism; by Charcot, Freud's mentor in France; and by Bernheim, the nineteenth-century master of suggestion who taught Freud. There is no possibility that the patient truly remembers his crib experiences. A more reasonable explanation is that Primal patients are modern hysterics who are undergoing an emotional *catharsis*—a technique which psychiatric history has shown not to be curative.

The interest in new messiahs is growing along with the Society's hunger for a psychological breakthrough. At a New York Hilton conference, a crowd of a thousand social workers, psychologists and psychiatrists overflowed into the aisles to listen raptly to both Dr. William Glasser, originator of Reality Therapy, and Dr. Laura Perls, a co-founder of Gestalt Therapy. Although their "truths" are intellectually contradictory, the audience applauded each with equal enthusiasm.

To the detached observer, the psychotherapies being peddled sound like a therapeutic babel, a mélange of inconsistencies and exaggerations. To the troubled citizen of the Psychological Society, however, they present a golden opportunity to choose one that best suits him, then to switch to another as psychological fashion moves on.

If we start our count with classical Freudian psychoanalysis, we estimate that there are over one hundred varieties of therapies, a cornucopia of hope expanding each year. Some are outdated, still others are at the pinnacle of their fashionability. Many are temporarily elevated by the Society, then relegated to the therapeutic freeze with Wilhelm Reich's orgone box.

From the smorgasbord of therapies, new messiahs blend several into one catchy new technology. One ingenious pastiche is the "scream therapy" of Dr. Daniel Casriel. Situated in a former town house off Park Avenue in New York, the Casriel Institute of Group Dynamics *sounds* different. To a visitor, the piercing scream of a patient seems incongruous in the impressive Manhattan setting.

Isn't this just another Janovian Primal? Not really. In shaping a therapeutic mix, Dr. Casriel, a former psychoanalyst, has merged four contemporary trends into one: Encounter, Primal Therapy, psychoanalytically derived insight therapy and group process.

Janovian therapy is reputed to cost $6000. Screaming the Casriel way is considerably cheaper. His technique, which he says was developed simultaneously with Janov's, is totally group-oriented. Casriel is a middle-aged, balding man with a New Yorkish psychiatric demeanor. He practiced traditional therapy until he saw Encounter-like interaction at work at Synanon, the drug-addiction halfway center he popularized in his book, *So Fair a House.* Today, says Casriel, ten thousand people a week are screaming for Casriel therapists in New York, Miami, Washington, Boston, Paris, Canada, Holland and even Caracas, where he trained several therapists.

At first glance, a Casriel group seems like any other group therapy session. Patients take the "hot seat," and pour out their anguish: divorces, separations, inability to find love, anger at a dull or unrewarding job. After a go-around to establish identities and complaints, Casriel asks the group to hold hands. This is followed by the command to let out a scream. The novices are hesitant at first. Then they join in a crescendo that fills the building.

From this point on, the technique fluctuates between typical group accusation and loving support, plus Casriel's own innovations. A common complaint in group therapy is the inability to assert one's rights in a harsh competitive world. Dr. Casriel formulates an appropriate message for such complaints—"I'm entitled!" He asks the patient to confront each member of the group in turn, eyeball to eyeball, and repeat that statement.

He insists that it must be preceded by *Fuck You!* ("In the English lanaguage, it is *the* visceral statement," confides Casriel.) No matter how shy or generationally removed from public use of such language, the patient starts out slowly, then builds up a volume that would rival the bellow of a longshoreman nicked by a loading hook. *"Fuck you! I'm entitled!" "Fuck you! I'm entitled"* (or *"Fuck you! I'm me"*) is angrily thrust at each member of the group.

At the conclusion the patient is flushed and agitated. Dr. Casriel moves in swiftly. He asks the patients to hold one angry note and convert it into a *scream,* louder and longer. Some scream for five or ten seconds, others hold it for a minute or two. Many end the scream with tears. As a reward, they receive a close embrace from Casriel, one of his staff or another moved patient. The general scene is one of talking, complaining, supporting, attacking, followed by screaming, crying, then hugging.

At the center of the room, imperiously awaiting the fall, are two mattresses. Once having screamed in place, a patient may elect to hit the mat. I witnessed a fearful young man on the mat thrash about like an infant, screaming out his claimed parental neglect until he became hoarse.

"I believe I've found what professionals are looking for, a quick way to get to feelings, the science of emotions," Dr. Casriel explained during an interview. "Emotions have a logic of their own. I have found that the classical treatment of emotional problems through introspection is inefficient. I think it is because most people are not neurotic, but are suffering from character disorders. They are withdrawn and isolated. Scream Therapy removes their encapsulation, and gets them in touch with their basic feelings. It removes their fear of emotions, and permits them to show anger while not fearing that they will go crazy; to show their need and not feel defeated."

Casriel is not contemptuous of his competitor, Arthur Janov, but like all psychological messiahs, he makes his own claims to the psychic throne. "Both Janov and I agree on the validity of getting at basic feelings, but he limits his feeling to Pain. I think there are four basics: fear, anger, pain and pleasure or love," says Casriel. "Scream therapy is a feeling therapy. Getting patients to feel anger, fear and pain is easy. The hard part is to get them to feel entitled to pleasure. We want the patients to recondition themselves through emotional experience, to gain new identity—one in which they see themselves as adequate, lovable human beings who can get their needs met if they put effort into it. But I now am convinced that this can happen only by learning to *feel.*"

Casriel, Janov and others have been called *ventilationists.* The term is used by Leonard Berkowitz, professor of psychology at the University of Wisconsin. The ventilationist theory is that the airing of one's feelings, particularly anger and hostility, is emotionally beneficial. It stems from a discarded Freudian concept that visualized emotion as a form of energy. If too tightly bottled up, it could explode. But if regularly ventilated, it would come out harmlessly, reducing one's tension.

The ventilationist theory is false, says Dr. Berkowitz. Rather than reducing hostility, letting it out actually *increases* it, he says. "The therapist or group members usually approve the patient's display of aggression. As a number of researchers have shown, these rewards heighten the likelihood of subsequent violence," reports Berkowitz. He quotes a study in which seven-year-olds were given a reward for punching a Bobo doll. When these boys later competed against other children, they proved to be more aggressive.

Among the popular contemporary messiahs we must single out Dr. Thomas A. Harris and his late mentor, Dr. Eric Berne. It was that improbable duo who popularized the burgeoning therapy of Transactional Analysis, one of the therapy rages of the Psychological Society. A sophisticated California psychoanalyst, Berne surprised the academic community when he translated esoteric Freud into the popularized *Games People Play,* then *What Do You Say After You Say Hello?,* foundation documents in what is commonly called T-A. It is a parlor game, a business, a religion that rivals Alcoholics Anonymous in the conviction it generates among converts.

Tom Harris, formerly head of the Harris Institute of Transactional Analysis, is an unsophisticated Californian known to many as "Dr. Tom." He is a robust, friendly psychiatrist who, at a New York Hilton T-A workshop, approached his charges in red-and-black-checked blazer, red slacks and a white sport shirt nattily embroidered at the breast pocket with his psychic emblem of cheer, *I'm OK! You're OK!*

As author of that super-best-selling book, Harris is the psychological Billy Graham, the prophet of a program that is growing with the geometric fervor of a pyramid sales scheme. Along with his wife, Amy, Dr. Harris has helped to make the game of Transactional Analysis a serious contender in the psychotherapy sweepstakes.

A T-A workshop is a continual selling performance, accomplished with the maximum of hoopla. The therapy is sold with jokes, sight gags, homilies, slogans such as trading stamps and "O.K. Corral," near burlesque and an uncommon amount of laughter for a socio-medical therapy. It is the first therapy that has made the complete transition from the Europeanized, intellectualized Freudianism to the church-supper optimism of Middle Western Americana. If Dale Carnegie's technique could be crossed with Sigmund Freud's, its offspring would be Transactional Analysis.

The sales pitch is catchy, even irresistible to many seeking an understandable, inexpensive cure. "Transactional Analysis is a new way to talk about behavior, a new way to sort yourself out, a new way to figure out what's really going on between you and your boss, your wife, your husband, your children, the teacher, the salesman, or your club president!" says a T-A sales brochure.

T-A's growth is phenomenal. There are T-A centers throughout America and teaching members in twenty-seven countries. Chaplains at Mather Field in California have learned the new therapy, as did corporate personnel, including a vice president at American Airlines. At the Central Presbyterian Church on urbane Park Avenue, a T-A analyst-minister advertised "I'm OK! You're O.K.!" on its announcement board as the New Salvation. When pressed as to why they like it, enthusiasts mouth the same praise: "It works!"

The secret of T-A is that it advertises itself as a people's psychology. Unlike other therapies, which insist on public ignorance of their magic, T-A invites, even seduces, its patients to learn its seemingly simplistic system. "Our material is written so that a junior high school student can understand it," a T-A official states.

Virtually anyone can play Transactional Analysis. To join the International Transactional Analysis Association, a person attends the basic T-A "101" course, generally a two-day $80 workshop.

It requires formal training to become a T-A therapist, but the route is theoretically open to everyone. Its clinical and teaching members are typically psychiatrists, clinical psychologists or social workers, plus a handful of nurses and ministers. But degrees are not an official requirement. One T-A therapist started as a prisoner in a maximum-security jail in Illinois.

The happy system is based on three simple circles generally scrawled on a blackboard: *The Parent, the Adult, the Child.* Each represents an *ego state.* Cumulatively they are supposed to depict our total personalities. The circles are often in disagreement, each looking at a life situation from different vantage points. The Parent in us thinks as our parents did, either helping or scolding us inside. The Adult is our everyday decision-maker. The Child, or the Kid, as T-A lovingly calls it, is that part of us which operates on feelings: wants, simple joy and disappointments. "Listen to the voices within you and you will 'hear' your Parent, Adult and Child," a T-A primer advises.

Each person's circles talk to the other person's circles. The Adult of the patient's mother might say, "What time is it?" The Adult of her son might answer, "It's twelve o'clock." But if the emotional Child of the son answered, it would more likely say, "Why are you always rushing me?" This is one of the *transactions,* as they are called, that take place as people interact. As your hurt Child talks to someone's critical Parent, the calculating Adult of the other person may be answering to your nurturing Parent ad infinitum, even ad nauseam.

Like Primal and many other modern therapies, Freud is at the unruly base of the business. In T-A the Freudian bias once more places blame on the parents. As T-A says, it is our *Parent Tapes* which affect us.

In T-A theory the multiple knocks of childhood, such as parent scolding, create a person with a loser syndrome. T-A calls the state "I'm *not* OK—you're OK!" Dr. Tom explains: "Right from birth, life is pretty rugged. The child almost immediately develops 'not OK' feelings. My own experience leads me to conclude that this 'not OK' position exists in the early portions of childhood in ninety-five to ninety-six percent of the population. Later in life the 'not OK'-ness is seen in feelings of inferiority and inadequacy, with a loss of self-esteem from disappointment."

Freud also saw the child as vulnerable and the parent as arch villian. But Freud's child was a selfish id-driven infant. T-A's Child is an innately kind, adventurous spirit who has been made not OK by the parental damper.

"The Child is the most creative and best part of one's self," says Mary Boulton, a social worker trained in T-A by Eric Berne and now co-director of the New York branch, the Gotham Institute of Transactional Analysis. "Our critical Parent Tapes tell us 'Don't do this and that,' that it is not permissible to enjoy things unless they have a worthwhile purpose. We in T-A believe that the Puritan ethic has a strong dampening effect on the Child in us, and has contributed to making us feel not OK."

In elevating the Child in us to noble proportions, T-A is achieving psychology's ultimate Americanization. A T-A primer eulogizes that marvelous little person stymied within. "You will probably not change your script until you decide to start seeing the Child in you as great, and as lovable, knowing that you deserve all the positive strokes you can get," it claims.

*Stroke* and *script* are parts of a colorful T-A vocabulary. "People live for strokes," says a Harris staff member. Theoretically, strokes are both positive and negative (compliments, caresses, or even a kick in the shins), but the term is usually used in the positive sense.

The T-A *script* is a mystical concept that rivals Freudian determinism, and borrows from it. It believes that virtually all that happens stems from a life decision made when we were five to seven years old. "Each person decides in early childhood how he will live and how he will die, and that plan, which he carries in his head wherever he goes, is called his script," Eric Berne once commented. "His trivial decisions may be decided by reasons, but his important decisions are already made: what kind of person he will marry, how many children he will have, what kind of bed he will die in, and who will be there when he does. It may not be what he wants, but it is what he wants it to be."

The life script appeals to optimistic Americans because T-A dangles the lure that their lives can easily be changed—through T-A therapy. "You can decide not to lead a dull life, not to head for an unhappy ending. You can change your script line by line," says a T-A primer. "This means that you can stop playing at life, and start living it."

All humanity is diagnosed by T-A. But instead of gradations from neurotic to schizophrenic, T-A has four mental positions, most of which are "sick." The first is the negative "I'm not OK—you're OK," which Dr. Harris feels 96 percent of us suffer in. Two percent have drifted into the less inviting No. 2 position, "I'm not OK—you're not OK," which compares with schizophrenia, says Harris. According to T-A theory, it is the result of parental "discounting," compounded by being initially "not OK." The No. 3 position, which also involves 2 percent of society, is "I'm OK—you're not OK," made up mainly of the criminals who have had a brutal and violent upbringing.

The No. 4 position, "I'm OK—you're OK," is the goal of the Transactional movement. To reach No. 4, one must gain insight into oneself.

The best seller *Games People Play,* by Eric Berne, first popularized the therapy. According to disciple Harris, the games we play are "crooked," usually destructive transactions which occupy 90 percent of our waking time.

T-A is perhaps the first therapy to make pain funny. T-A games, as updated by Harris, include "Mine Is Better than Yours," "Now I've Got You, You S.O.B.," "Schlemiel" and other esoteric maneuvers. In the game of Schlemiel (a Yiddishism for *fool*) the player continually makes a mess of things, then apologizes. His payoff is the forgiveness. "Because the titles are colloquial, they frequently bring a laugh," complains Dr. Harris. "They are actually defenses to protect individuals from greater or lesser degrees of pain growing from the 'not OK' position."

T-A is in many ways a "pop" version of psychoanalysis, a debt Harris frankly admits. "The question has always been how to get Freud off the couch and on to the masses," he declares. Although T-Aers usually deny it, even their circles seem reminiscent of the Freudian trinity. The irrepressible Freudian id is the T-A Child; the Adult is Freud's much admired ego; the superego is almost identical with the Parent.

There are also obvious differences between psychoanalysis and

Transactional Analysis, one of which is T-A's sexual deemphasis. Eric Berne nudged T-A somewhat toward sex, but Harris-oriented T-A is as clean as a Bible Belt church supper. At a recent workshop, mention of "burning a bra" was greeted with a 1940 finishing-school titter.

Others besides Freud have shaped T-A. Dr. Tom was a student of American psychiatrist Harry Stack Sullivan, who brought *interpersonal relations,* and eventually *transactions,* to modern psychotherapy. Alfred Adler devised the concept of *life style,* which antedates the T-A script. The Adlerian *inferiority complex* shaped the crucial T-A idea of "not OK"-ness.

Does Transactional Analysis work? T-A hope draws the multitudes, but it obviously delivers less than it claims. Psychotherapies all follow a pattern of initial giant promise, then reduced acceptance and, finally, disillusionment. T-A is on its first leg up, a force which may itself be temporarily curative.

To its credit, it does have an upbeat view. But as a description of human behavior, T-A is thin and misleading. The concept of a life script being written in childhood, for example, is a twist of the old Freudian saw of *repetition compulsion.* Secondly, the idea that most young people (96 percent, says Harris) feel "not OK" is an exageration at best.

Its effectiveness has never been seriously validated. Like most therapies, T-A is best suited for those who are not really sick. At a recent T-A session, a middle-aged woman upset the group by her talk of suicide. When fellow members told her that depression was part of her "Poor Me" game, the woman angrily answered that she was playing no game. She was depressed, period. She appeared in need of serious psychiatric treatment, not the game of Transactional Analysis.

Thinking-insight therapies such as T-A are still in demand, but after several generations of rejection the *body* is being resurrected as a tool of therapy. Touching, massaging, hugging, palpating, vibrating the body to elicit feelings is the basis of several new psychological schools.

In the insight therapies wedded to the word, the admonishment "Do not touch" is a conspicuous warning. But paradoxically, it was the theoretical work of an early psychoanalyst, Wilhelm Reich, which provides the authority for the body movement. A member of the Viennese Psychoanalytic Association, Reich was well acquainted with Freud. He began as a traditional analyst, then developed the theory that *character resistance,* or *characterological armor,* as he called it, was the key to the patient's hidden past. This armor was invested not just in memory and emotion but in the *body* as well.

Freud had theorized an entity called psychic energy, which obeyed the law of constancy developed by a German physicist and philosopher, Hermann von Helmholtz. Reich believed this psychic energy existed not only in Freud's trinity of the ego, id and superego but in the muscles as well. Muscular tension and emotional repression were one and the same. He believed that by freeing the blocked muscle, he could unlock the neurosis.

Reich was checking a patient's musculature for tension when he suddenly touched the man's neck. To his surprise, the patient "immediately assumed the attitude of a hanged man," with his head down and tongue protruding, Reich said. In this *unblocked* posture, the patient poured out his infantile fear of death, specifically that he would be hanged for his sin of masturbating. The hanged-man posture only appeared when the patient's breathing was shallow. When Reich taught him to breathe deeply, the patient shed the strange posture, and supposedly his emotional problems as well.

Reich died in an American federal penitentiary, where he had been sent for fraud involving his *orgone box.* Patients sat inside it and were supposed to be healed by accumulated psychic energy. A member of his Orgone Institute (part of the American College of Organomy) was Dr. Alexander Lowen, a psychiatrist-psychoanalyst who split from the group in 1954 to form his own related school, Bio-Energetic Analysis.

If Reich was the originator of body analysis , Lowen is the creator of the *Bioenergetics,* as it is usually called. The father of this now voguish therapy is a small, lithe, energetic man, perhaps in his early sixties, who maintains the bouncy pace of someone a decade younger. This psychiatric Charles Atlas is convinced that a trained bioenergetic therapist can make a "character analysis" of a patient by looking at his body. Dressed in athletic shorts or a leotard, the patient presents himself to the therapist, who finds the diagnosis in the patient's eyes, expression and mouth lines.

"The person's outside condition belies his internal condition," Dr. Lowen commented when interviewed at the headquarters of the Institute for Bio-Energetic Analysis, the coordinating center for over a hundred psychiatrists, clinical psychologists and social workers trained in the art. "In classical analysis, the doctor only listens to the patient. We listen but we also *look*—a technique that is unique to bioenergetics. The blocked emotional feelings of the person are demonstrated by his muscular pattern. In general terms, the muscular system and the stance of the individual are a good key to his inner psyche."

Lowen reminds us that *body language* is an ancient concept which unites the mind and the body. We say, "Shoulder your burden," "nose in the air," "stiff-necked," "no backbone," "tight ass," "chesty," "hard-hearted," and, of course, the ultimate metaphor, "He's a prick."

Lowen has merged Freud and Apollo by giving imaginative anatomical meaning to psychological phenomena, and vice versa. In psychodynamic theory, repressed memories are closeted in the unconscious id. In bioenergetics they are also hidden in the body. As an institute booklet describes it: "The specific physical mechanism which underlies all psychological disturbances is chronic muscle tension." It adds the caveat that bioenergetics is not just a psychic massage parlor. "Clinical experience has shown that pathological muscle tension cannot be released without an understanding of the emotional factors which created the condition . . ."

Psychic affliction can even be spotted in the bearer's body style, Lowen claims. Lowen speaks of the *schizoid* character, which he describes as a tendency to withdraw from reality. "We can see the schizoid character in the dull, vacant eyes, and the seeming inability of the person to make eyeball-to-eyeball contact," says Dr. Lowen. "The expression of the face is masklike. The person seems to be holding his body together, for fear that it will fall apart."

One "Schizzy" (as Lowen sometimes calls it) trait is a lack of alignment between the head and the rest of the body. The head supposedly inclines to one side, a sign of *dissociation.* Lowen describes a subject under stress who suffered blurred vision when he held his head up straight. When he tilted it back, his vision immediately cleared up.

Each of these body traits has its origin in early life experiences, Lowen believes. The claimed inability of the schizoid type to "snarl and bite" (curl the upper lip and bare the teeth) is based, says Lowen, on a reluctance to reach out with the mouth and suck. It is the result of an infantile conflict in which mother did not fulfill the child's oral needs.

What is the bioenergetic cure for neurosis or the schizoid character? The therapy is an almost gymnastic regimen. First, correct breathing is taught, for Lowen believes that inability to breathe fully and deeply is responsible for such diverse ailments as anxiety, failure of orgasm, even claustrophobia. The reason so many people breathe badly is that *we are afraid to feel emotions,* Lowen says.

In the disturbed schizoid, says Lowen, breathing is mainly limited to the thorax. The neurotic breathes mainly in the diaphragmatic area. The truly healthy person breathes with "his whole body," the man breathing, as Lowen says, "into his balls." What analysts call *repression* cannot be lifted until the patient learns full respiration.

The bioenergetic exercise utilizes a "breathing stool" about two feet high. A rolled-up blanket is placed on the stool. The patient puts his feet on the ground, then arches backward over the stool. The mouth is kept open. As the body adapts to the stress, the breathing will become deeper and fuller.

Lowen warns that the beginner should not hold the position for more than two minutes. It can produce lower-back pain and some anxiety as feelings erupt. It can create dizziness, even tingling sensations, which are intense and can result in numbness or paralysis. But as the patient's tolerance increases, these symptoms diminish and disappear, he assures us.

Ventilation, or getting out tension and aggressiveness, is vital in bioenergetics. As Lowen says, "To kick is to protest, and every person has something to kick about." Men punch a bed with their fists, while women use tennis rackets for the same purpose. Both sexes use a towel, vigorously twisting it while shouting or screaming "No!" or "Leave me alone." One New York bioenergetic analyst explains that while hitting the bed a psychoanalytic *transference* can take place. The bed becomes a parent, and the patient touches, talks back to or hits his mother or father.

As the body assumes new importance in the Psychological Society, it has converted several verbal therapists. But it has also aroused animosity in others, who view it as an anti-intellectual activity. New York psychologist Bruce Maliver believes that bioenergetics, and other body movements such as Rolfing, are "anti-rational" techniques selling "over simplified cures." (Rolfing is a body technique devised by a physiologist-turned-psychotherapist, Dr. Ida Rolf, and her chiropractor son, Dr. Richard Demmerle. Now used in several Encounter groups, it unites chiropractic and psychotherapy.)

There is no scientific evidence for the validity of body therapies. Lowen and others have taken the reasonable idea that a psychologically tense person might also have a tense body, and elaborated it into a surrealistic theory. Its speculation that the body "remembers" the past is blatant anti-science. The bioenergetic concept that psychological types have specific phsyical shapes is, to be charitable, an exaggeration. Despite the Greeks, there is not even solid evidence that a healthy body contributes to a healthy mind, or vice versa.

Virtually all these new therapies are ingenious amalgams of their competitors. This is perhaps best illustrated by California psychologist Paul Bindrim, the father of Nude Marathon. He has combined at least three contemporary therapies, including Bioenergetics, Encounter and Primal-like therapy, *in the buff.* Bindrim decided to heighten Encounter by undressing the participants. Eighty-degree temperature, nude bodies, splashing water and the pursuit of Abraham Maslow's *peak experience* are obvious competitors to the dreary offices of conventional therapists.

"When I began nude marathons in 1967, the ethics committee of the American Psychological Association got after me on the charge that nude therapy violated Principal Number Three, the customs of the community," Bindrim explained when interviewed. "But fortunately, Abraham Maslow was then president of the American Psychological Association, and he defended me on a television show. The charges were dropped, and psychologists won the right to treat patients in the nude.

"In addition to the weekends at a pool, I also do individual therapy with patients in the nude," Bindrim continued. "I remain clothed, however. Opening up nudity for psychotherapy has been a great advance. Previously, if a man complained that he was anxious about his small penis, we would only discuss it in the abstract. Now he can take his clothes off, and we can look at it without violating APA ethics."

Bindrim recognizes his debt to other messiahs. "I met Lowen and trained in bioenergetics, which I now use in my work. I go directly to the musculature that is being held tense," he says. His Nude Marathon Regression Therapy draws on the Primal return to infancy in which a warm California pool recapitulates the mother's womb. The nude patient is held horizontally by fellow patients and his body is rocked to and fro as in a crib. To help revive early feelings, the patient is given a baby bottle to suck on. "We preceded Janov's Primal work," says psychologist Bindrim, "and we do it in a better way. We accomplish our goal in one weekend marathon a month, and only one to two hours a week of nude therapy."

Bindrim is incensed at the criticism of Nude Therapy as an excuse for licentious behavior. While admitting that some unscrupulous therapists may permit such action, he stresses that participants at his sessions "can't do anything they couldn't do at a good party in someone's home." They can "kiss and hug," he explains, but everyone signs a contract not to engage in sex during the marathons. Behavior is a matter of good taste. "If a man has an erection, he observes the same social custom he would if dancing closely with a girl. He moves back a few inches," says Bindrim.

In this babel of modern therapies, one name, *Gestalt,* resounds with more power, even with more respectability, than the others. Its Germanic meaning of *configuration* (often incorrectly translated as *whole*) has become synonymous with feeling therapies. If bioenergetics brought the body to Freud, then the Gestalt Therapy of Fritz Perls (and his wife, Laura, and friend, the late Paul Goodman) has sought to replace past-oriented Freudianism with a glorification of the existential, experiental here and now.

Gestalt is not just "in," it *is.* The 1960s counterculture derived much of its impetus from Perls, both as the creator of Gestalt and as a philosophical guru. Perls had contempt for the verbalism of conventional psychotherapy, which he dismissed as "mind fucking." Although not known to most of the public, Perls was a subculture giant whose posthumous charisma burns bright.

He eschewed the Freudian search for the *why.* "Any time you use the words *now* and *how,* and become aware of this, you grow," Perls, who died in 1970, wrote in his last book, *Gestalt Therapy Verbatim.* "Each time you ask the question *why,* you diminish in stature. You bother yourself with false, unnecessary information. You only feed the computer, the intellect. And the intellect is the whore of intelligence. It's a drag on your life."

Gestalt has become the symbol word for *feeling* versus *thinking.* The phrase "Do your own thing" was a Perls creation, a touch of existential poetry which many have turned into anti-intellectual conformity. Perls first used it in a poem, "The Gestalt Prayer," which begins with the now familiar phrase "I do my thing, and you do your thing."

Perls has been called the Prophet of NOW, offering us the present as superior to the delayed pleasures of the Puritan ethic. Perls, who held both M.D. and Ph.D. degrees from his native Germany, was originally a traditional psychoanalyst. He took his first personal analysis with Karen Horney at the Berlin Psychoanalytic Institute, prior to her split with Freudian orthodoxy. Later he worked with Wilhelm Reich, an association that ended with the rise of Hitler.

Perls spent the war years in South Africa, then came to America, where he established Gestalt Therapy in the early 1950s.

His movement escalated into prominence during the six years Perls spent at the Esalen Institute in the late 1960s. There he introduced Gestalt to the human-potential addicts seeking Happiness through Encounter. In his final years the one-time Berlin Freudian was a sandal-wearing, white-bearded California guru, flashing an open smile, love beads and even a sports car.

Gestalt is at the core of the burgeoning *personal growth* movement which is a rival of the psychodynamic *insight* movement for the affection and pocketbook of Americans. There have been Gestalt marathons, Gestalt Encounter sessions, Gestalt group sessions, a Primal-Gestalt Center. The method has even been taught to school guidance people at the Bank Street College of Education in New York. Gestalt Therapy institutes have been opened across the nation.

"Gestalt Therapy is at its peak in this country," Dr. Laura Perls (Doctor of Science), widow of Fritz Perls and surviving head of the movement, explained in her New York apartment. "Some people mistakenly believe Gestalt is another therapeutic technology. It is actually a methodologic concept which can absorb and use other techniques. Gestalt works with the obvious, what is immediately available in the treatment context, not the abstract. In psychoanalysis the transference to the therapist is considered a repetition of infantile relationships. We believe it exists in the here and now in the actual relationship between the two people. What is transferred is the behavior patterns of the patient, which have become automatic."

Gestalt lives on its sense of the present, a feeling Laura Perls attributes partially to Oriental influence. The East has only recently become potent in America, but Oriental concepts were circulating in Germany in the 1920s, when Hermann Hesse was writing his novels and Fritz Perls was an analyst in pre-Hitler Germany.

In therapy, the Gestaltist uses everything available in the present —the patient's words, voice, posture, eyeball contact. The concept of *awareness,* now a therapy cliché, stems from Gestalt. "The therapy involves each person in the situation at the moment, whatever the patient presents at the time. We are not as tied to verbalizations as the Freudians," says Daniel Rosenblatt, Ph.D., of the New York Institute for Gestalt Therapy.

As an active therapy, Gestaltists use what they call *experiments* to exploit the here and now. They use everything, even the patient's walk. One therapist describes a patient who walked strangely forward on the balls of his feet. The therapist directed him to walk backwards and observe what he was doing. According to the Gestaltist, the experience revealed that the patient thought his original walk was feminine. He was defending against it with what he thought was a masculine walk.

The prime virtue in Gestalt is *awareness,* and the cardinal sin is *blocking.* Gestaltists believe that people expend a lot of energy in chasing fantasies—what we call *thinking*—not directly related to our behavior. Our minds are usually fixed in a pointless, dreamlike state, creating internal noise which is not personally gratifying, they say. True awareness is consistent with behavior and thus increases pleasure, the god of Gestalt.

One Gestaltist gives eating as an example. It involves *kinesthetics,* the physical acts of chewing, swallowing, tasting, all of which an aware person will be cued into as they happen. The blocked person, however, will eat absent-mindedly, thinking about anything except the act. The same can be true of sex, working or talking.

We cannot expect to gain emotional insight through intellectualization, Gestaltists warn. We must expand our awareness. Gestalt has elevated awareness to the same magical level as Freudian insight and interpretation. "Awareness *per se*—by and of itself—can be curative," said Perls.

The *physical* is implicit in Gestalt, one reason for its modern marriage with Encounter. Laura Perls says she will do virtually anything physical with patients, male or female, if she feels it will increase awareness. "I will light a cigarette, feed someone with a spoon, fix a girl's hair, hold hands or hold a patient on my lap," she says. "I also touch patients or let them touch me." When a female group member at Esalen asked Fritz Perls, "Could you explain the difference between words and experience?" Perls kissed her, then proudly exclaimed, "O.K. That'll do it!"

Perls was a critic of Freudian abstractions, which he tended to dismiss as "elephant shit." Yet his last technique, the *dreamwork seminar,* was derivative of Freud's royal road to the unconscious. The supposed difference is that Freud analyzed the dreams, while Perls used them as experiences in themselves. The patient first told his dream in the third person, then shifted to psychodrama and acted it out in the present, playing all the parts. The dream meaning becomes obvious, Gestaltists believe, as long as the despised "thinker" is not clued in.

Perls is said to have claimed that his impact was greater than

Freud's. If we excuse this hyperbole, we must admit that Perls's concepts of "Do your own thing," awareness and self-actualization have had a massive cultural effect. His concentration on feeling instead of thinking and his intent search for pleasure have been potent in shaping the counterculture, the new quest for hedonism and the sometimes frightening move toward anti-intellectualism.

But what of Gestalt itself? Is it a true therapy?

Perls once spoke of there being three existential psychotherapies: the *Logotherapy* of Viktor E. Frankl; the *Daseinsanalyse* of Ludwig Binswanger; and *Gestalt Therapy*. The other two, he said, had tried to do away with concepts and rely on phenomenology, what *is*. But, he crowed, other existential philosophies had borrowed concepts from elsewhere: Buber from Judaism, Sartre from socialism, Binswanger from psychoanalysis. Only Gestalt, says Perls, "has its support in its own formation."

This is patent nonsense. Like all therapies, Gestalt borrows from many philosophical schools, including the Oriental, the psychoanalytic, even the Reichian. The greatest Gestalt hyperbole is its insult of other therapies as "intellectual." Actually, Gestalt concepts are so complex and numerous that they rival the jargon of the psychoanalytic word jungle. Rather than simplifying Freud, Gestalt has rejargonized him. Its *impasse* and *retroflection* are somebody's else's "mind fucking." Perhaps most important, Gestalt has established an obvious value system that the patient must strictly conform to if he hopes to be cured.

Perls's influence has flowed over into the broader *human potential movement.* It is sometimes called *human growth* or—the ultimate— *humanistic psychology.* It houses other giants besides Perls: Carl Rogers, the originator of client-centered therapy; Mike Murphy, the layman who inherited the land at Big Sur which became the Esalen Institute; the late Alan Watts, the East-West philosopher who popularized the expanded-consciousness movement; Paul Bindrim, of Nude Encounter; Bill Schutz, the Messiah of Joy; Fred Stoller, the father of Marathons; and the inspirational giant of Humanistic Psychology, Abraham Maslow.

The *humanistic movement,* as it is self-servingly called, is a broad umbrella which covers a variety of here-and-now therapies, including Encounter, the feelies and nudies, Sensitivity Training, Gestalt, various marathons, Bioenergetics, Primal, assorted groups for single, married, divorced, gay patients, Biofeedback, Rolfing, even the new meditational groups.

The human growth movement is blatantly romantic. It insists that each of us has within us the potential for emotional stability and happiness. By calling on humanistic techniques, we not only will grow emotionally but will find our authenticity. If the individual can be *self-actualized,* he will, in a new theological sense, be Saved.

Fritz Perls outlined this psychological rainbow with the marketing audacity of Madison Avenue. "The average person of our time, believe it or not, lives only five percent to fifteen percent of his potential at the highest," Perls said. "So eighty-five percent to ninety-five percent of our potential is lost, is unused, is not at our disposal. Sounds tragic, doesn't it? And the reason for this is very simple: we live in clichés."

This offer of unlimited potential has made the movement a success dream. It is the ultimate Americanism: rather than a person suffering his way to personal growth through time, he is offered the lure of *instant maturity* through a dozen weekends of growth experience.

Its seductive call is the *peak experience,* a psychological orgasm designed to "turn on" the person as vividly as LSD. Abraham Maslow, the father of humanistic psychology, defined peak experience as the fireworks of life. "The peak experience is felt as the self-validating, self-justifying moment which carries its own intrinsic value with it," Maslow, who died in 1970, wrote in *Toward a Psychology of Being.*

Maslow, a Brooklyn College psychologist, entranced his impressionable public by reverently speaking of the peak as a "pure delight," as "only good and desirable," never "evil or undesirable," one that occurs outside of "time and space" in the same way that makes the creative artist become oblivious of his surroundings.

The weakness of traditional religion has accelerated the quest for the peak experience. Simultaneously, the group appeal of humanist psychology is strengthened by the breakdown in the normal community. As one educator observes, Encounter provides "warmth and ready-made temporary family." Carl Rogers, Ph. D., an intellectual mentor of the Encounter movement, explains it: "I believe that individuals nowadays are probably more aware of their inner loneliness than has ever been true in history."

As friendship and love are vitiated by modern pressures, many turn to group psychology as a substitute. The result has been a massive system designed to provide instant affection in groups by the hour. Carl Rogers estimates that some 750,000 people a year take part in intensive group experience. Rogers tells of asking a Western audience how many had been to an Encounter group or to something similar. Three-quarters of the audience raised their hands.

*Encounter* is a broad label which can cover almost any "personal growth" experience. A Stanford University team came up with seventeen types, including such standbys as the T-Group (Sensitivity), Gestalt, Psychodrama, Esalen Eclectic, Rogerian Marathon, Eclectic Marathon, Synanon or Attack Therapy, Personal Growth, even a leaderless group "led" by a tape recorder. Rogers adds other categories: sensory awareness groups, body awareness groups, relativity workshops, couples groups, family groups, and, of course, the basic encounter group.

The physical site of humanistic psychology is the *growth center*, a unique product of the Psychological Society. Esalen in Big Sur, with its mountain-sea splendor, sets a picturesque but false tone for the industry. Some growth centers are nestled in the countryside, but many are decorated in poverty-baroque and located in urban cheap-rental districts.

Their magic is enhanced by fanciful names, a style initiated by Maslow in 1962, when he compiled the *Eupsychian Network*. The Association of Humanistic Psychology has published a list of 177 growth centers, including eleven overseas, six of which are in London and one (the Tivon Growth Center) in Israel.

Their titles are awesome, even mystical: Aureon Institute (New York), Anthos (New York), Kairos (San Diego), Adanta (Atlanta), Genesis (New York), Dynacom (Montreal), Quaesitor (London), Heliotrope (Fort Lauderdale), Integro (North Wales, Pennsylvania), Interface (Washington, D.C.), G.R.O.W. (New York City), Outreach (Ann Arbor, Michigan).

Esalen once provided a forum for such diverse humanistic voices as Maslow, Perls, Rogers, Schutz. Today the growth centers have become the department stores of self-actualization. One institution, the Center for the Whole Person, in Philadelphia and New Jersey, has offered Transpersonal Encounter, Gestalt Marathon, Bio-psychosynthesis Workshop; Primal Encounter, Meditation Encounter, Intimacy in Relationships, Marriage Marathon, Basic Encounter, Happy Marathon, Hypodrama, Voyages into Gestalt and Fantasy, and even a *Resurrection Weekend.*

Newness is vital to the humanistic movement. Two of the most popular techniques are *meditation* and *psychosynthesis.* Meditation Encounter combines group Encounter with Eastern tranquillity, promising an "altered state of consciousness through seven levels of meditation." Bio-Psychosynthesis Workshop offers a new imported fantasy technology developed by Roberto Assagioli in Italy.

The same skills used to market deodorizers have been pressed into service by some in the humanistic movement. Aureon, a Woodstock, New York, center, has advertised "The Quest for Zest" as part of its "Psychomat" of Encounters.

Most growth centers eschew the therapy label even though there is an implied therapeutic promise. They often refer to themselves as "educational" outlets. One center, G.R.O.W. in New York City, once sponsored a suspect Ph.D. program through affiliation with Indiana Northern University. Together with the prestigious Union Theological Seminary, it recently offered a certificate in "human relations education."

The principles of Encounter are closeness, trust, authenticity and confrontation. In the humanistic jargon, it is an opportunity to "let it all hang out." The participant is placed in a ready-made family where he can reveal all without fear, and receive both acceptance and feedback on how he "comes on" to others. Through confrontation, a key Encounter idea, he also receives negative feedback which may alter his illusions about himself.

In theory it is a therapy of the healthy as well as the sick, *an everyman's healing*. The emotional possibilities of Encounter are infinite. A man tearfully tells of the loss of his wife, and receives the warm embraces of several women in the group. An intense teenage girl screams out, "I hate you; you're a ball buster," to another young woman who has just criticized several of the men. A woman in her thirties exposes her breasts, then is warmly assured that they are not as small as she had feared. A forty-five-year-old mother, bitterly complaining about the demands of her teenage daughter, is alternately attacked and defended by the group.

In most Encounter groups, language is uninhibited. Even maiden aunts soon learn to accept "fuck," "shit," "ball," even "hard on," "cunt" and "cock," with the same aplomb once reserved for "Pass the sugar." Some groupies openly express the desire to "screw" someone in the room of the opposite, or even the same, sex.

For an activity designed to cut down hypocritical life games, Encounter is paradoxically built on games. One group member stares into another's eyes for two minutes; two men or two women minutely examine each other's hands; partners touch another person's face, body, even rear end, to increase social facility; they confess which person in the room they like best or least and why; they arm-wrestle;

join hands and scream in unison; play "Tug," a game in which one person falls backward while another "catches"; lift someone off the ground and rock him like a child; sit in quiet contemplation and "peel" oneself down layer by layer, like an onion. These games are in addition to spontaneous confrontations that erupt as individuals on the "hot seat" open their minds and hearts and receive either warmth or cruel feedback in return.

If several hours of Encounter are valuable, why not a continuous day or two? The result is the popular *Marathon,* a time-extended Encounter which offers a new psyche and a suntan for $135, including meals. The originators of the Marathon were George Bach and Frederick Stoller. Bach theorized that the main changing agent in Encounter is group pressure, and that time is essential for the "pressure cooker" to boil away the phony emotions and start people interacting "authentically."

Enthusiasts even claim that Marathon duplicates years of Freudian psychosexual development in one frenetic weekend. Members often meet nonstop for twenty-four hours without sleeping, a technique which supposedly produces regression, in which normal defenses are broken down.

Therapist Elizabeth Mintz believes that Marathon subjects start the weekend on the adult ego level, but then regress to Freud's anal-sadistic phase in which anger is freely expressed. They revert further back to the oral-dependency stage (birth to eighteen months), then eventually to the height of maturity, the Freudian genital stage with "enhanced self-acceptance and acceptance of others."

Is Encounter truly therapeutic, or is it another healing myth of the Society?

It is true that the comradeship of marathons and encounters can stimulate temporary love and warmth in a group just as does a cruise or a summer at camp. But critics are doubtful that any permanent change is accomplished. Dr. Michael Beldoch (Ph.D.), a Freudian analyst, agrees that the most dramatic Marathon results come in the regression of sleepless predawn hours. But he does not feel that the process reveals the truth. The same child-feeling can take place when a person is drunk or very tired, or even when emerging from anesthesia, he says.

Some traditional therapists not only see Encounter as competition for the therapy dollar but believe they are anti-Freudian, even antitherapeutic. Dr. Bruce L. Maliver of New York is an outspoken Encounter critic. "A case in point is the encounterists' view that the expression of emotion is in itself curative," he says. "The fact is that emotional expression alone—catharsis if it's big enough—was long ago shown to have no lasting effects on the personality."

Even Encounter advocates are concerned about its short-lived benefits. Carl R. Rogers, whose client-centered therapy preceded Maslow, calls Encounter "the most rapidly spreading social invention of the century, and probably the most potent." Despite his enthusiasm, Rogers is concerned about the *relapse,* the tendency to slip back into old behavior patterns. He quotes a participant who says, "I experienced a lot of acceptance, warmth and love at the workshop. I find it hard to carry the ability to share this in the same way with people outside the workshop." Rogers also sees danger to people who reveal themselves, then are "left with problems which are not worked through," and will require conventional therapy.

Dr. Michael Beldoch is skeptical of the abundant love exhibited in sessions which he believes is too easily faked. "Members tell each other that they love each other with an amazing frequency and an even more startling ease," he says. Beldoch also opposes the philosophers of Encounter who place "the blame for our painful human condition on our very capacity for reason. It is on this rallying cry of anti-reason, that "the cherished half-truth of the encounter group is built and upon which it will fall," he predicts.

The most complete study of whether or not Encounter works was conducted at Stanford University with 170 student subjects who completed one of eighteen Encounter groups. Sixty-nine students not in any group served as the control. Known professionals named the two best leaders in each type of therapy to conduct the sessions, which were taped. Participants rated what they thought of the experience and outside observers did the same. Six months later the entire group and the controls were followed up.

Did Encounter prove valuable? Yes and no, with more weight to the negative side. As in all therapies, most of the participants *thought* the experience was positive, if not overwhelmingly so: 57 percent voted positive, 29 percent neutral and 14 percent negative. At the end of six months, however, the *relapse* factor has begun to show. The consensus was now 46 percent positive, 32 percent neutral and 21 percent negative.

At the six-month follow-up, all participants and controls were asked to describe changes in their behavior. Most of the participants judged themselves changed (56 percent). *But so did most of the controls (52 percent), who had not participated in any group.*

In a "social network" report from parents, friends and relatives the Encounter groupies did even less well. They judged 80 percent of the participants as having made some positive change. But even more of the controls (83 percent) were judged improved. "The unique effect of the Encounter experience in the view of participants in the social network is questionable," the study author concluded.

Encounter can sometimes be a hostile, even dangerous, experience. The American Psychiatric Association's *Task Force Report on Encounter* charges that the technique is potentially dangerous. Stimulating emotion and spontaneity in "impulse-ridden individuals" who need control can be quite harmful, warns the APA.

The Stanford study showed Encounter to be a psychonoxious hazard for some, even in the hands of the well-trained leaders. There were a sizable number of casualties, from broken bones to psychotic breakdown among the students. Nearly 10 percent were judged to have been hurt by the process—an alarming risk, according to the researchers.

One student, "D.A.," committed suicide. He was not considered a casualty because of his long history of psychiatric disturbance. The majority of casualties resulted from *attack.* "One leader told me I was a dumb shit," said one casualty. Another explains, "The leader dismissed me and my whole life." One lamented, "The leader said I was on the verge of schizophrenia." Three students had psychotic episodes and were still "highly disturbed" at follow-up time.

Critics are also concerned about the growing exploitation of all humanistic psychologies. For some, Encounter is a psychologically approved cover behind which sex can be obtained, even sanctified, as therapeutic. In *Hot Springs,* Stuart Miller details the successful pursuit of sex at Esalen. Elsewhere two psychologists were shocked by blatant sexuality at a rural Encounter weekend. One of them walked into a barn and saw on the hay "a naked man and woman, apparently just parting from having sexual relations." It was a group leader and a female member, both of whom looked up "but did not seem either shocked or surprised," he says.

The possible exploitation of Encounter troubles Dr. Rogers. "In the first place," he states, "I must acknowledge that it may all too easily fall more and more into the hands of exploiters, those who have come onto the group scene primarily for their own personal benefit, financial or psychological. The faddists, cultists, the nudists, the manipulators, those whose needs are for power or recognition, may come to dominate the encounter group horizon. In this case, I feel it is headed for disaster."

Both Fritz and Laura Perls have expressed the belief that disaster may have already overtaken much of the humanistic therapies. "I think Encounter the way it is done by Carl Rogers and Sensitivity Training is good," Laura Perls explained at her apartment treatment center. "But I believe that many other Encounter techniques are aggressive, bullying and manipulative in applying prescribed confrontation techniques. Confrontation may be good for some people, but not for others."

Before his death, Fritz Perls was worried that much of the movement had already turned to faddist dust. "I want to talk about the present development of humanistic psychology," he stated. "It took us a long time to debunk the whole Freudian crap, and now we are entering a new and more dangerous phase. We are entering the phase of the turner-on-ers: turn on to instant cure, instant joy, instant sensory awareness. We are entering the phase of the quacks and the con men, who think if you get some breakthrough, you are cured . . . If this is becoming a faddism, it is as dangerous to psychology as the year-decade-century-long lying on the couch."

Perls and Maslow are the acknowledged prophets of humanistic psychology, but even they had predecessors in the movement: aging psychiatrist, J.L. Moreno, and the late psychologist Kurt Lewin. Like Perls, both were refugees from Hitler's Europe. Moreno is the father of *psychodrama,* a technique which dates from the Vienna of World War I. Lewin, also originally an Austrian, initiated the first *sensitivity training* courses in 1946.

Moreno, who now lives in Beacon, New York, where he runs his Psychodrama Institute, is credited with the term "Encounter." In 1914 Moreno published *Einladung zu einer Begegnung,* or *Invitation to an Encounter.* Moreno wrote about his existential idea: "A meeting of two: eye to eye, face to face. And when you are near I will tear your eyes out and place them instead of mine, and you will tear my eyes out and place them instead of yours, then I will look at you with your eyes and you will look at me with mine." No modern growth master could improve on this sentiment.

Psychodrama grew, but the direct line to Encounter was drawn by Lewin. In 1946 he conducted a seminar workshop in "human relations" in New Britain, Connecticut, where he taught at a local college. Lewin started the T-Group (Training Group) virtually by accident. It was the offshoot of the casual discussion among members and leaders. Before long, arguments over workshop views, even personal matters, developed. What started out as a conference about a workshop changed into a group of people confronting each other in the here and now. One movement historian defines it as "an unstructured group centered on the study of its own dynamics."

A formal T-Group program was set up in Bethel, Maine, which eventually became the National Training Laboratories. It is now the NTL Institute for Applied Behavioral Science, affiliated with the National Education Association. It is the father of the much discussed *Sensitivity Training*. NTL now sponsors "training labs" around the country in which businessmen, executives, teachers, school principals, government employees retreat to encounter their fellowmen and their own emotions in such luxury settings as Lake Arrowhead, California—generally with all expenses paid by their employers.

T-Group and Sensitivity Training are the *establishment wing* of the human potential movement. Rather than a sporter of beads, the typical T-Group participant is middle-aged, often upper-middle-class, and seeking (or being pressured to seek) a better "human-relations insight."

The corporate goal is to convert the last generation's déclassé Organization Man into this era's Humanistic Man. Establishment sponsors of Sensitivity have included ITT, General Electric, Monsanto, Pillsbury, Union Carbide, Bankers Trust, American Airlines, Westinghouse and others. One NTL session was limited to top executives making over $25,000 a year, who were told they would find "self-awareness" while living "in a quietly elegant Colonial mansion with yawning fireplaces."

Business supports the T-Group in the hope of eradicating the image of the uptight, insensitive businessman which has injured corporate prestige. T-Group propaganda also casts itself as a pragmatic tool which can increase both personal initiative and corporate profits.

Sensitivity has also been a darling of the education profession, which has trained thousands of teachers at NTL. The Bureau of Child Guidance in New York has put staff psychologists and social workers through the Sensitivity hoop. Sensitivity has also expanded into a do-it-yourself movement in which physicians and nurses at hospitals, PTA groups, and corporations (one thousand executives at Standard Oil of New Jersey) have set up their own T-Groups.

The United States government has invested millions in a near-coercive Sensitivity Training program for federal employees in the Department of Agriculture, State Department, General Services Administration, Peace Corps, HEW and other agencies. From 1968 to

1970 the Department of Labor paid $1,443,000 to the Human Development Institute, a Bell and Howell subsidiary, to teach sensitivity to supervisors.

The government agencies deny that they have given "Sensitivity Training," preferring to call them "touch-and-tell" sessions. According to a subcommittee headed by Senator Sam Ervin, the General Services Administration ordered its employees to submit to T-Group training. Paired-off couples were asked to hold hands, look at each other and complete such sentences as "I am most ashamed of . . ." One Department of Agriculture female worker, one of two thousand given Sensitivity Training, walked out indignantly. As she said, "It just got down to sex life and just downright uncalled-for vulgar language."

Sensitivity is unique because it *appears* to be virtually leaderless. The trainer works unobtrusively, asking members to consider him one of them. By creating a leadership void, the trainer hopes group members will fill it with their own personality.

The ploy is a transparent one for the sophisticated groupie. Spencer Klaw, a *Fortune* writer, participated in a two-week NTL session at Arden House, a 96-room mansion willed to Columbia University. He reported continual stage direction by two trainers, including an NTL executive and a Harvard-trained psychologist. When group members claimed they weren't nervous, they were challenged by a trainer who thought "maybe people were more worried than they were willing to admit."

Has Sensitivity Training been the miracle it sought to be? There are few reliable statistics, but there are now almost as many skeptics as enthusiasts. Several American companies, including TRW, Inc., Champion Paper, Honeywell and Aerojet General have reportedly dropped NTL training.

Some business critics see Sensitivity as a danger to both corporate effectiveness and executive psyches. Byron Calame of the *Wall Street Journal* described the case of a division manager in a competitive industry who was "ferocious" but effective. After training, says one source, "he stopped being a beast," and lost both his effectiveness and his job. In another case, a Midwest company stopped Sensitivity after a V.P. suffered a "total breakdown" during a session and had to be hospitalized.

NTL denies that Sensitivity is dangerous. "NTL Institute records suggest that fewer than 1 percent of participants have had significant problems during training under NTL Institute auspices," they state. "In almost all cases they have been persons with a history of prior serious disturbances."

Others dispute this NTL claim. Dr. Louis Gottschalk studied thirty-two T-Group participants at NTL headquarters in Bethel, Maine, and reported a 19 percent casualty rate, including two cases of psychotic reactions.

One critic, George Odiorne, of the University of Massachusetts School of Business, feels Sensitivity is an "emotional binge" which goes far beyond management needs into an area of "personal therapy." Sensitivity has also been criticized on a particularly American basis: *that it doesn't work.* Two University of Minnesota psychologists, Marvin Dunnette and John P. Campbell, report that there is little evidence that Sensitivity actually changes work behavior for most people. "It cannot be said with any certainty whether T-Groups lead to greater or lesser changes in self-perceptions than other types of group experience, simple passage of time, or the mere act of filling out a self-descriptive questionnaire," they report in the *Psychological Bulletin.*

Sensitivity is only one of the new humanistic psychologies that face a brutal modern paradox. They seek to create self-actualization and a greater range of personal freedom. But almost all use a psychological technology based on strict conformity to group ideals.

Groups insist on obedience to their collective will and value systems. "During a workshop the member identifies not only with individual members of the group but with the group itself," state Encounter enthusiasts Gilbert A. Schloss and Robert Siroka. "The values expressed in the group become its tribal values, norms to which members respond or against which they react."

Anyone who has been in a group can testify to the pressure on the dissenter: the virgin in a sexually liberated group or the shy person in an openly aggressive group. He or she must conform to the "tribal" values or suffer ostracism. "Free choice can only be exercised when the individual is not threatened by humiliation, reprisal, rejection or ridicule," explains Dr. Morris Parloff.

The anti-intellectual nature of the so-called humanist revolution is also under attack. In an open letter to the Association of Humanistic Psychology, analyst Rollo May criticized the movement's tendency to omit "thinking, reflecting historical man" in favor of "feeling, touching man in the 'now.'" It is, he said both "anti-intellectual" and "anti-humanistic." It can also be dangerous, "as we learned in Germany in the great romantic, anti-intellectual surge on which Hitler came to power," he warned.

Dr. May and others have also criticized the search for immediate love and friendship in groups as a poor substitute for long-term relationships. Humanistic psychology groups may do some good, says May, but they "are simplistic and they destroy Buber's and my sense of intimacy."

The filling of one's life with groups paid for by the hour or day has a plaintive tone in our fragmented society. None is more pathetic than the flood of people surging to *est* (Erhard Seminars Training), the most popular of the new group activities. Now in its sixth year of life, *est* has trained almost one hundred thousand Americans in a $300 60-hour two-weekend *experience* which many of its adherents believe has remade their lives. *Est* was founded in 1971 in San Francisco by Werner Hans Erhard (born Jack Rosenberg) and now has branch offices throughout the country.

The training ostensibly operates without theory, but it actually combines many techniques from the traditional and humanistic therapies. Its gimmick is a perverse twist, which first shocks, then pleases its participants. The twist is that *est* provides an authoritative, almost combative environment in the typically permissive Psychological Society. The *est* trainee is more likely to be called "an asshole" in front of hundreds of people than to be lavished with approval. The goal of *est,* like many of the group psychologies, is to increase human awareness. In *est* it is called "Getting It."

To reach this Maslovian peak experience, trainees go through what seems like psychological basic training, replete with trainers who often ridicule them. The training is usually carried on in hotel rooms, where a trainer sits on a raised stage with a blackboard. Participants are encouraged to be recognized and speak up, but when they do, they are generally met with intimidation. Rules are established on a no-nonsense basis: no watches, no talking unless recognized by the leader, no leaving one's seat, no smoking, no going to the bathroom except at breaks. Individuals who violate the rules are escorted from the room. The training begins in the morning and continues for about fifteen hours with breaks only every four hours. Food is permitted only during the second break.

The formal material presented by the trainer is a pastiche of many ideas ranging from Freud to Eastern philosophy. The *sharing,* or telling others about oneself, is the typical catharsis that one finds in all therapies. The *processes* are large group exercises, techniques borrowed from Gestalt and psychodrama.

Part of *est*'s appeal seems to be its very harshness. Trainer Ted Long brought that gruff manner to London when working with trainees there for the first time. Ten minutes after the meeting began, he spoke to a stocky middle-aged trainee in the back row who was taking notes. "He's talking to you, asshole! Not to the walls! When the man says no note-taking, he means *no note-taking!* Put your goddam notebook away, keep it away, or get the fuck out of the training! This goes for everyone in the training!" Rather than leaving in annoyance, the now conditioned audience just sat and waited for more. "What a marvelous way to kick off the show!" commented one *est* trainee.

After several days of insult, discomfort, hunger, swollen bladders and boredom, what does the *est* trainee finally "get"? A smiling indoctrinator at a guest seminar summed it up this way: "The trainee learns to accept that he is an all-capable and all-loving individual." People are in that magnificent state before they come to *est,* she explained, but they are blocked by their belief systems. As an *est* board member says, "What you 'get' finally is that there is nothing to get aside from the fact that you are making yourself miserable by your own misperceptions and faulty identifications."

*Est* stresses that self-appreciation is not gained by learning anything. *"Getting it"* takes place by *experiencing it* in the sixty hours of training. "Understanding is the booby prize," *est* people are fond of saying.

"Getting it" also means that you are "alright," one of their favorite phrases. Trainees get to know themselves better and to love themselves with all their faults. One satisfied trainee confided that she had once been guilty about being "tight" with money, and tried to compensate for it by giving gifts she could not afford. Now she knows she is cheap and it doesn't bother her.

Does it work? For some, the *est* peak experience creates an enthusiasm reminiscent of evangelism, with the same assurance that their lives have been transformed. This response is typical of all new movements, from T-A to Encounter to TM (Transcendental Meditation). Unfortunately, the transformation generally diminishes with time.

As movements age, the conversion has decreased efficiency as excitement about the technique wanes both in the media and in word-of-mouth endorsements. With this reduced reinforcement, the movement's power of suggestion is weakened. This, plus the realities of societal pressure, brings the person back to his less *OK* or less *Alright* self. There is no reason to suspect that *est* is any different from other movements in this inexorable failing.

The power of suggestion in therapy is now understood. What is less understood is its potential danger. *Est* is no exception. Three psychiatrists from the Neuropsychiatric Institute at the University of California claim that *est* can be a dangerous, psychosis-producing experience in some trainees. Reporting in the *American Journal of Psychiatry,* they describe five patients who developed psychotic symptoms, including delusions of grandeur, paranoia, uncontrollable mood swings and delusions, following their *est* training. Only one had a history of psychiatric disturbance.

One case involved a thirty-nine-year-old married executive, Mr. A. He had no history of mental illness. His one "traumatic" experience was his mother's death when he was twenty-three, but he had long considered the issue resolved.

Mr. A. took *est* training at the urging of several close friends. He hoped to better his marital relationship and improve his working skills. By the second day he felt an increase in energy and self-esteem. In the vernacular, he had "gotten it." Suddenly, powerful feelings of remorse over his mother's death struck him. At home, he jumped into the swimming pool nude. He felt godlike and was determined to see if he could survive underwater without air. For two days he carried on various manic activities trying to "validate his new grandiose self-image" by attempting a series of hazardous feats. Finally his wife called the police and had him hospitalized.

Neither *est* nor any other new movement is the last stage in the compulsive quest for peace of mind. Ten years ago Abraham Maslow predicted that the humanistic, or Third Force, psychology would only be a transition for a newer emerging form. He envisioned a "still higher Fourth Psychology which would be transpersonal, transhuman, centered on the cosmos rather than on human needs and interest." This new *transpersonal psychology* will be a "religious surrogate," which will fulfill the needs of the "frustrated idealism" of the many, he predicted.

Maslow was an accurate prophet. The Fourth Force has arrived as the *meditative revolution,* the application of Oriental concepts of mind and body control. Several guru-led systems, including TM (Transcendental Meditation) have placed millions of middle-class Americans in supposedly psychotherapeutic trances.

One of the popular new meditation movements is Arica, the brainchild of a Chilean layman, Oscar Ichazo. His guru stance has attracted millions of dollars in donations and scores of thousands of followers. Although not formally billed as a therapy, Arica attracts the apparently rotating clientele that has been analyzed by Freudians, screamed for Casriel, hit beds in bioenergetics, toyed with their Child in T-A and confronted one another in Encounter.

An Arica announcement boldly states: "Survival of the planet depends on humanity evolving to a new level of consciousness." Arica offers the lure of "Permanent 24," an ecstatic state derived from the teachings of George Gurdjieff. No one in Arica has reached that blissful state. In fact, most of us are slogging around in the lower depths of 6000.

The Arica route to higher consciousness is a wall-to-wall-carpeted one, complete with a fanciful escalator rising magically from the street up to its national headquarters on Manhattan's 57th Street. Set into its walls are abstract stained-glass motifs from its Oriental antecedents, and from Tarot cards for the more traditionally mystical. In its gilded poshness, it seems like the set for a TV commercial on "how to raise your consciousness."

Arica is itself a mélange that combines touches of Zen, the Sufi system (the mystical side of Moslemism), astrology, Reichian body theory, Yoga, dance, Buddhism, Transcendental Meditation, Gestalt, bioenergetics, a touch of Esalen Encounter and a healthy measure of pure American hokum.

It has several hundred exercises, three *instincts* (Conservation, Social Relations, Syntony), twelve mentations, each of which corresponds to a different body part. *Charisma* is in knees and elbows and asks "How am I presenting myself?" *Orientation* is in the genitals and asks "Am I moving toward life?" *Elimination* is in the colon and kidneys and asks "Is it essential?"

Arica is visualized in a series of *Enneagrams,* circles whose circumference is divided into nine points, a "diagram of the way energy is organized and flows." The enneagram was revealed to Ichazo in a Spanish desert in a hallucination in which he danced in the dissected circle. The enneagram, says Arica philosophy, helps one accomplish the *meditation of the day.* The subject goes through seven stages on the enneagram circle, each of which takes two minutes. Its purpose, says Arica, is to help us "to tune into our own internal rhythms and the way in which they correspond to the energies and rhythms in the cosmos."

Each day has its own zodiac-like signature. Sunday is Old Gold in color, representing Regeneration. Wednesday is Yellow, standing for Mercury, connoting Intelligence. In doing step No. 5 of the

Meditation on Tuesday, for example, one works with Red. The color is "expanded in gradual stages, until it fills the cosmos," which, says Arica, first encompasses the room, then the street out to the universe. (On Friday, one fills the street with his Green.)

The magnificent exercises of Arica, which include WOOSOO—washing with cold water under the covers on awakening in the morning—can be learned in the sixteen-hour intensive "Open Path" to a four-day intensive course. The jargon of Arica has a humorous, gibberishlike tone. Its words—Trialectics, Protoanalysis, Mudras, Social Mandala, the Doors of Compensation—have origins not even its staff claims to know. Arica spokesmen seem sincere, but their attempt to appear mystical is couched in a cosmic language that soars to the level of college lampoon.

Arica was born in the city of that name in the northwest of Chile, where in 1970 a group of fifty Americans (fifteen from Esalen) came to spend nine months to learn Arica from Oscar Ichazo. Ichazo is a former Bolivian who traveled about the world learning the Asian arts, including Japanese sword play. The students propagated the word back in America, where many became instructors in the first Arica centers, which have now expanded throughout the United States and Canada plus one in London's fashionable Belgravia.

The philosophy of Arica is a diffuse one born of Orientalism and Western whimsy. Arica is philosophically devoted to the *destruction of the ego,* to reduce man's concern with himself and increase his vision of the cosmos. As the ego develops, says Ichazo, *karma,* in the form of the evils of money and power, accumulates. Arica hopes to restore purity by destroying the ego, extinguishing the individual's intellect and personal desires so he may reach Permanent 24.

"In America, and most of the Western countries, people are heavily oriented in their head, their Path center," an Arica spokesman pointed out. "Arica training is designed to break down this tyranny of the head, and make us more body-oriented, to put more emphasis on the Kath, or body center."

John C. Lilly is credited with giving fashionability to Arica. An avowed mystic, Lilly is also a scientist who worked on dolphin intelligence. He journeyed to Chile and reported back in his book *The Center of the Cyclone* that at moments his Arica "trip" approximated the effects of LSD. For an instant he believed he had been in Satori 12, a stage of consciousness ostensibly granted to few mortals.

In an interview at Arica national headquarters, a New York City psychiatrist who worked with the movement confirmed that Arica is a logical extension of the Maslovian revolution, an attempt to reach the "peak experience" through higher consciousness. Arica even calls itself "In-trip to take," especially "among those who have been involved in the human potential movement."

Will Arica replace Encounter and the remainder of the humanist movement? There is little doubt that Maslow intended transpersonal, anti-intellectual experiences to bring his followers to the next step, the Fourth Force in modern psychological worship.

But Arica? The atmosphere at one of the introductory meetings —replete with young actorlike M.C.s with vacant smiles and manner, Oriental mantras shouted in a Western carpeted salon and a hovering officialdom not unlike caterers at a wedding—seems less focused on reducing your ego than on increasing theirs.

The search for peace of mind through meditation is based on the skill of certain Yoga, Zen and Oriental masters, who have ostensibly achieved unusual biologic states, including a decreased use of oxygen and an absence of pain. In search of this wisdom, one Occidental, Durand Kiefer, traveled and studied widely in the Orient, including nine months spent in a Japanese monastery practicing the Zen technique of *zazen*. He later stated that it was hard work. He achieved his hoped-for bliss only a few moments at a time.

Most Westerners would prefer their meditational Nirvana to be quicker and easier. To those who find Arica, Transcendental Meditation and other paths too mystical, a modern technology offers a popular alternative. It is *biofeedback,* the method which has popularized man's ubiquitous "alpha wave."

Biofeedback is a legitimate medical-research tool. Dr. Neal Miller, of the Rockefeller University, has demonstrated that the involuntary nervous system is actually quasi-voluntary. He showed that a rat could be taught to blush in one ear. Simultaneously psychologist Joe Kayima, at the University of California, proved that students could regulate the amount of alpha and beta waves emanating from their brain by using a "feedback" machine.

Beta, the wave which oscillates at fourteen cycles per second or more, is the basic tool of the human mind. It does the work called *thinking*. It adds, decides, solves problems by providing the electrical energy for the brain to be used as a computer. Alpha, which has a slower frequency of seven to twelve cycles, is a quieter brain wave which is strongest when man closes his eyes while awake or when his mind is pleasantly vacant. The theta wave, whose frequency is only two to six cycles per second, is more dominant when man is hallucinatory or drowsy. Delta, a slow oscillating wave, appears prominently when we are asleep.

The existence of these brain waves was discovered by Hans Berger in Jena, Germany, in the 1920s. The possibility of regulating them for therapeutic reasons has created a psychological industry—biofeedback. Its core idea is the glorification of alpha. Since alpha is often strongest when man is quietest, the biofeedback business has dangled before anxiety-prone Americans the promise of peace through technology. As one biofeedback firm advertises on its business card: "Tranquillity Through Self-Regulation."

Biofeedback enthusiasts claim the meditative state can be learned on a machine. One institute claims that in eighteen hours they can teach virtually anyone to make alpha dominant in the brain at will.

I visited such an institute, located in a town house on New York's fashionable East Side. It is a layman-owned company with cooperative M.D.s and Ph.D.s on its board. For twenty minutes I was hooked to a machine in a darkened room. I was left alone to listen to my alpha and beta blips while resting in a large, soft black armchair. I closed my eyes (following a hint dropped by my facilitator), thought about little or nothing. In a few minutes I had supposedly regulated my brain waves. I was rewarded by listening to the cognitive beta waves recede and the alphas surge forward. The feeling? Somewhat like falling off to sleep.

The glamorization of alpha as a safe "high," an altered state without drugs, has created a multimillion-dollar brain-wave industry in both feedback equipment and training centers. At the same New York institute a demonstrator delivered a pseudoscientific sales message on the blessings of alpha. The sum of his message is that we are wrong in believing that *thinking* is man's highest calling. This is the siren song against intellect which permeates both the humanistic Third and the meditative Fourth Psychology movements.

When the mind truly pays attention, the "brain cells get quieter," he proposed. The beta waves recede and the mind slows down to the alpha range. The mind then has less ability to think, but it has suddenly increased its awareness, a consciousness in which perceptivity is supposedly heightened.

The demonstrator also assured his audience that anxiety and fear —the energy bleeders—are reduced. "Most people are in an energy-starved condition, mainly as a result of their image-making being out of control," the alpha salesman explained. By increasing our attention by producing more alpha, we can decrease our fears and experience energy maximization.

The virtues of the alpha "high" have been extolled. Enthusiasts compare it to taking drugs without drugs, to the ultimate in relaxation, to a great peaceful inner trip. Researcher Eric Pieper, of New York University, says volunteers are anxious to participate in alpha research without pay. Dr. W. Grey Walter suggests that diplomats should have their alpha pattern endorsed on their passports so they can be matched for international negotiations.

But experience with biofeedback is already tarnishing these hopes. Its commercial use as a bliss machine is undoubtedly based on inflated, unsubstantiated claims. Many people do not find alpha pleasant. Some even find it increases their anxiety.

T. Mulholland, reporting to the Massachusetts Psychological Association, showed that alpha "highs" might be subjective, even imaginative. One subject who reported a euphoric alpha high, commented, "There's a rabbit in here so real I can almost touch it." Without telling him, the researcher then turned off the feedback tone. The subject kept up his alpha production, but thinking the study was over, his magnificent high stopped abruptly and his rabbits vanished.

Critics even suggest the unthinkable: that the alpha state may merely be a less alert one. One researcher believes that alpha may be the *stupid wave.* Reporting in the *Annual Review of Psychology,* he suggests that alpha waves may be related to under achievement. He found that a group of students with poor academic achievement also had unusually high alpha production.

There may be more medical than psychological value in alpha. Physicians working with biofeedback equipment have taught patients to "regulate" their heartbeats and even to increase their hand temperatures in order to relieve migraines. The work is still experimental, but workers at the Menninger Foundation studying migraine are optimistic.

Despite initial expectations inevitably followed by disappointment, new therapies continue to multiply with no apparent end. One NIMH researcher recommends "creative writing" as psychotherapy. Many new therapies are born in the warm sun of California, then wend their way eastward. One California theorist has developed a therapy called Thou Are That. The therapist suggests that "each person look around the room and pick an object that stands out vividly for him." One woman, he recalls, identified with a brightly colored section of the wall. She became quite depressed and cried when she realized that she, like the wall, was "unfinished at the top."

The permutations of therapies in the Psychological Society are infinite. Less varied are the patients. They are modern wanderers, seeking ancient meaning in each new technology. The same searching types, if not the very same faces, appear at each new group gathering. As anxious as freshmen at an orientation seminar, they are hopeful that this will be *the* great experience. They swap tales of their treatments, improvements and discouragements. To the eavesdropper, their talk about *est,* TM or Encounter seems a modern replacement for the trivial gossip of prior eras.

The equation of the Psychological Society is that psychological activity is *per se* therapeutic. It is an illogical contention, but it is firmly rooted in the Society. Increasingly, however, experienced practitioners who have seen dozens of therapies rise and fall are turning cynical.

One of the most experienced therapists is Albert Ellis, Ph.D. "The bases of psychodynamic and psychoanalytic therapy and most of the so-called humanistic theories are just nonsense," says Ellis, a psychologist who has traversed the spectrum from psychoanalysis through Encounter to his own latest modification, a theory called Rational Emotive Therapy, or RET.

RET was formally conceived in the 1950s, but in recent years Ellis has honed both it and his skepticism of other movements. He has brought RET closer to what might be called an *anti-therapy therapy.* "The psychoanalytic idea that if I see the origin of my disturbance I will get better is false. We are probably born with a constitutional, genetic tendency to be disturbed. In any case, it is usually impossible to find the origin of disturbances in our past history," Dr. Ellis commented when interviewed in the mid-Manhattan townhouse where he lives and works.

"In the Encounter techniques, I have found that they make you feel better rather than help you get better. There is a tendency in Encounter and in Gestalt therapy to overemphasize feelings at the expense of rational thinking and to encourage all feelings, even though they may be inappropriate. Training a person to be aggressive or angry, for example, may be harmful. In too many of the so-called humanistic psychologies, emotion is sacrosanct. Actually, letting out one's emotions is very rarely curative."

What is Dr. Ellis's alternative? In the Psychological Society such healthy skepticism is met with still another technology, including Ellis's RET, which he calls "the no cop-out therapy." It has an A-B-C-D rhythm based on the gap between a person's emotional reactions to a situation (what he calls "C") and a valid and reason-

able response to the action ("A"). The patient, says Ellis, has interv-
ened his own *belief system* ("B") between the two. It is often a set
of illogical, impractical or self-indulgent ideas.

"It is the patient's belief about his action, rather than the action
itself, which gets him in emotional difficulty," Ellis points out.
"When he fails, his belief system tells him it is horrible. Failure is
not good, it is even a pain in the ass, but it is not horrible. Being sad
or disappointed is a rational reaction to failure, but being depressed
is not. I find that increasingly in our society much of what we call
emotional disturbance is *whining*. People have low frustration tolerance and think that in the permissive society everything including
competence in work, love and sex should be easy. Instead of just
wanting things, people feel they need them, that they *must* have
them. When they don't get them, they become distraught. They are
searching for guarantees in life. This is deadly—the sure route to
anxiety.

"Their belief systems are so controlled that they feel they must be
noble, great and perfect," Ellis continued. "In love, they want a mate
who will love them totally and forever and fulfill all their needs. In
sex, they seek perfect potency, with perfect orgasm, whether male or
female. It is a destructive set of belief systems which makes the
person feel 'I am shit' because I fail in work or love, or both, instead
of his saying the rational truth: 'It is bad' and not 'I am bad.' We
try to teach the client to dispute [Ellis's "D"] his destructive beliefs.
Of every hundred people who come here for therapy, I find that
ninety-five feel inadequate because of their distorted belief system.
And when they can't live up to their beliefs, they whine."

Although cloaked in the special language of the Society, the Ellis
philosophy is reminiscent of pre-psychological thought: that Man is
responsible for his actions. That concept continues to fade as imaginative new therapies proliferate to solve psychic problems being
manufactured at an equal pace. As man's vulnerability to modern
culture rises, psychological technologies designed to help the citizen
cope with stress are created—opening up still greater possibilities for
vulnerability. It is a cycle of self-fulfilling neurosis which makes the
Psychological Society so destructive.

# The Individual and
# the Psychological Society:
# The End of Neurosis?

WE LIVE IN THE AGE OF NEUROSIS. It is an era in which man stands
self-accused of harboring a mass psychological disease. He views
himself as a *problem,* a set of emotions and drives at variance with
society's goal of continuous internal tranquillity.

Virtually everyone speaks of being *somewhat* neurotic. It is not
that we see ourselves as an isolated example. For in addition to
diagnosing ourselves as neurotic, we see those surrounding us as
suffering from this same gnawing, undefined ailment. Our mates,
friends, business associates, the thousands who touch our lives seem
to be living in a heroic, if fruitless, struggle for stability.

The extent of this condition has been documented. As we have
seen, an estimated seven million Americans are now in therapy, and
approximately ten million more have already been through that
psychological hoop. The involvement with neurosis seems to grow
with both affluence and education. Dr. George E. Vaillant, of the
Harvard Medical School, questioned 643 alumni of one private college twenty-five years after graduation: 31 percent of them had been
to a psychiatrist.

Neurosis has a specific psychiatric definition, but it has also assumed a catchall quality in the Psychological Society. It now encompasses nervousness, inability to cope, fear, failure in work or love,

inappropriate decision-making and simple unhappiness. Neurosis has become a semanticist's dream—or nightmare. Through an unparalleled linguistic trick, it has come to mean virtually anything negative in this era of psychological conformity.

The trick was in creating a standard—*normality*—from which one's deviation could be measured. Freud called normality an *ideal fiction,* but it might also be described as a fantasy in which the psyche effortlessly balances anxiety and stress on the shoulders of a stout ego. All mankind aspires to this ideal condition, but like Sisyphus rolling his stone endlessly uphill, few, if any, achieve it.

The marketing of normality is the sales device which sustains the new Society. Underlying its success is a well-merchandised axiom that *unhappiness is synonymous with sickness.* It is a popular but false premise which has taught millions to view their insecurity, even their failure in life, as an *abnormality,* thus shaping the neurotic profile of the second half of the twentieth century. By equating unhappiness and neurosis, the establishment of the Psychological Society has created a specious equation which ensures the continuation of a paying, believing clientele.

The common habit of confusing emotional health with happiness is confirmed by a Food and Drug Administration survey of the nation's health. "Many laymen see good health as a state beyond the mere absence of disorders, encompassing feelings of unlimited energy, freedom from anxiety and depression, and the presence of contentment and happiness," the FDA study states.

This professionally inspired view is disseminated daily, not only in the popular media and in an infinite number of personal conversations but in professional journals as well. A typical ad in a medical journal for a sedative-hypnotic "tranquilizer" dramatizes man's current view of himself. It depicts a troubled miniature face lost in a giant human profile, with the single telling headline: *The Inadequate Self.*

This inadequate self is the self-diagnosis of millions. It is very often the professional assessment as well. Since neurosis is supposedly a variation from a state of normality which probably does not exist, we have all become victims of a statistical fallacy. If we were to chart neurosis on a mathematical bell curve of distribution, then *normality* —instead of occupying most of the graph—would be a thin, lonely spike surrounded by massive curves of neuroses.

What exactly is *neurosis?* The official psychiatric classification is found in the latest edition (1968) of the American Psychiatric Association's *Diagnostic and Statistical Manual of Mental Disorders,* in which "Neuroses" are catalogued. The definition is heavily interlaced with Freudian analytic theorems. It states: "Anxiety is the chief characteristic of the neuroses. It may be felt and expressed directly, or it may be controlled unconsciously and automatically by conversion, displacement and various other psychological mechanisms. Generally, these mechanisms produce symptoms experienced as subjective distress from which the patient desires relief."

This official APA diagnosis has drawn a giant psychiatric net around all of humanity. *Who does not experience subjective distress from which one desires relief?* The manual lists eleven neuroses to which mankind is ostensibly prone: anxiety neurosis; hysterical neurosis; hysterical neurosis, conversion type; hysterical neurosis, dissociative type; phobic neurosis; obsessive-compulsive neurosis; depressive neurosis; neurasthenia neurosis; depersonalized neurosis; hypochondrical neurosis; other neurosis.

The modern concept of neurosis is, of course, mainly the invention of Sigmund Freud. He defined it as the result of an unseen intrapsychic conflict, the classic battle of the ego and the infantile id. As we have seen, this poetic psychodynamic theory is marred by contradiction and scientific failure, but it is a psychological tale which has changed the face of society.

One of the difficulties with the word "neurosis" is that it is as readily applied to the well as to the sick. *Some* psychoneurotics do exhibit some manifestations of mental illness. In Freud's day several such patients suffered from conversion hysteria—paralysis, blindness, deafness and other seemingly somatic illness supposedly triggered by a psychological cause. "For some reason, this type of neurosis is seen very rarely today," a Columbia Medical Center psychiatrist comments. Since conversion hysteria was generally the disease "cured" by psychoanalysis, the cure seems to have miraculously survived without the disease.

The obsessive-compulsive syndrome is another serious disturbance. This diagnosis should not lightly be applied to individuals whose *style* is compulsively oriented, what the analytically chic call "anal." The true obsessive-compulsives are tortured by *rituals,* which paralyze much of their lives. The same is true of highly phobic personalities, whose fears of heights, cars, closed spaces and any potential danger restrict their daily functioning. Others who are seriously neurotic might also be diagnosed as *borderline psychotics.* Fortunately, as Dr. Roy R. Grinker, Sr., reminds us, most borderline cases have a "stable instability" which generally prevents breakdown into full mental illness.

But most citizens of the Psychological Society do not suffer from these relatively serious ailments. The millions who are called or who call themselves *neurotic* are generally not sick in the clinical sense. They are *troubled* by their lives and their increasingly difficult search for dignity and love. Rather than attributing the problem to its almost infinite number of causes—from societal fashion to biological temperament to simple chance—we have grasped at the word *neurosis* in order to help define our inner turmoil.

Is there actually an ailment called neurosis, or is it another Freudian fantasy? This is a surprising question after thirty-five years of postwar psychological indoctrination about the debilitating effects of this curse of the unconscious. But paradoxically, the psychiatric profession has begun to question its very existence. *In fact, the American Psychiatric Association is currently planning to eliminate totally the classification of neurosis from the next edition of its official diagnostic manual.*

"We do not believe that neurosis is any longer a useful basis for classification of psychiatric disorders," Dr. Robert L. Spitzer, chairman of the APA's task force for revising the manual, stated when interviewed at the New York Psychiatric Institute. "Over a hundred years ago, 'neurosis' referred to a neurological disorder. Later it came to mean primarily a psychological disorder whose symptoms were manifestations of hysteria. In psychoanalytic theory, it is an illness whose primary symptom is a compromise between a defense and an impulse. More recently, psychoanalytic theory includes some character and personality disturbances as neurotic in nature.

"As the profession generally uses the term, neurosis is defined more by what it is not than what it is," Dr. Spitzer continued. "When a psychiatrist uses the term 'neurosis,' he generally means it is not a psychosis, it is not an organic mental disorder and it is not an acute reaction to overwhelming stress. Neurosis no longer has a precise meaning as a basis for psychiatric classification and therefore it will not be used in the new manual."

The task force headed by Dr. Spitzer was appointed three years ago by the APA. It has since become the centerpiece of an internecine debate between the two disparate segments of the profession: the scientifically oriented psychiatrists and the Freudian psychoanalytic wing. The argument centers on the psychodynamic theory of neurosis, which has been the cornerstone of Freudian control of psychiatry, and its potent influence in contemporary Western culture. Without this ubiquitous unconscious disarrangement of the universal psyche the mystical power of psychology and psychiatry would be diminished, perhaps even eliminated.

"The word *neurosis* has become a symbol to some—a kind of code word—of whether or not the psychiatrist is sympathetic to Freud," Dr. Spitzer states. "However, if the classification in the new manual is based on evidence rather than ideology, it seems to me that we are pursuing the correct course. It is time that psychiatry became more data-oriented and less wedded to unsubstantiated theory."

The debate between data-oriented psychiatrists and Freudian sympathizers over the new APA manual has been the subject of professional gossip for the past few years. The Freudians now sense that they have lost, and some are annoyed. "Many members of the American Psychoanalytic Association are disturbed that the task force has not agreed to accept psychodynamic formulations in the new manual," Dr. Spitzer explained. "They have complained that the composition of the group—which includes twelve members and about a hundred advisers—did not include a sufficient number of analysts. In making our selection, we did not seek balance but chose those psychiatrists who we felt were most qualified for the task."

The recommendation to drop neurosis as a classification for diagnosis has the task force's acceptance, but the new manual will not gain formal APA approval until 1979. If it is adopted (and most believe it will), what will replace neurosis in the lexicon of psychotherapists? A draft of the new manual now lists "Anxiety Disorders" in place of "Neuroses," with no mention of that classic word in the entire psychiatric guide.

If after two generations of being conditioned to thinking and feeling neurotic, how should the individual in the Psychological Society react to the professional conclusion that neurosis is not a definitive psychiatric diagnosis? How does one now shed the sense of neurosis? And what should replace it?

The two terms we are dealing with are *neurosis* and *anxiety*. How do they differ? Is it merely a matter of semantics, or is there a clear distinction between the two? One psychiatrist at Mount Sinai, New York, believes the distinction is so important that he considers the American Psychiatric Association task force's move as "the most significant step in psychiatry in the last twenty-five years."

The distinction between neurosis and anxiety is enormous. Neurosis is a product of the Freudian unconscious and serves as evidence that a *psychic abnormality* has been created within the mind. It is negative in both its make-up and its impact on our lives.

*Anxiety* is a simple and intelligent substitute for the term *neurosis.* It has meaning to both laymen and psychiatrists. Unlike neurosis, anxiety is an emotion that everyone feels and recognizes. In excess, it can be crippling. But in *moderate form, anxiety is the essence of normality.* In fact, anxiety is probably the most significant emotion that separates Homo sapiens from his animal cousins. All animals have a "fear" mechanism, but it requires a stimulus to set it off: the sensing of specific danger from something in the environment. The closest animals come to anxiety is what Howard Liddell calls "vigilance," the emotion that keeps it alert against danger.

Human anxiety, however, is a more complex and pervasive emotion, one which we feel during most of our lives. The infant is not yet anxious, but he has an innate primary emotion which expresses itself as a "startle reaction." His body moves rapidly into a defensive position against the threat of noise, for example. Two researchers, C. Landis and W.A. Hunt, point out that the younger the child, the less secondary behavior will follow the startle pattern.

But as we grow into childhood, and then mature, the basic emotion of anxiety attaches itself more to concepts. In the obsessive-compulsive personality, it may be an elaborate ritual, such as continually washing one's hands in an attempt to relieve that anxiety. This is *not* normal anxiety.

But there are numerous everyday threats which do mobilize our anxiety, and which are *normal* in every way. With our giant brain capacity, and our knowledge of the vagaries of fate, we can conceptualize future threats to our work, our love, our community, our children, our income, our traditions. These thoughts stimulate our anxieties. If the threat is immediate and specific, we might best label this emotion as *fear.* But if a less concrete or even collective sense of unease exists—as it increasingly does in this complex society—it can manifest itself as *generalized anxiety.* In many ways, man is the only animal who is almost perpetually anxious.

Neurosis is an arcane Freudian device which we can never see or even interpret without the aid of a therapist. But anxiety is real and personally measurable. We know just how anxious we are or are not. If, as we have said, this human sign of alertness is excessive, it can be debilitating. *But unlike neurosis, anxiety—if reasonable and controllable—is not only normal but generally healthy and constructive.*

"Anxiety is essential to the human condition," says Dr. Rollo May. "The confrontation with anxiety can (note the word *can* and not *will*) relieve us from boredom, sharpen the sensitivity and assure the presence of the tension that is necessary to preserve human existence. The presence of anxiety indicates vitality. Like fever, it testifies that a struggle is going on within the personality. So long as this struggle continues, a constructive solution is possible. When there is no longer any anxiety, the struggle is over and depression may ensue. This is why Kierkegaard held that anxiety is our 'best teacher.' "

Since anxiety is man's fate, what is its origin? How much of what has been called neurosis is learned and how much of it is biologically inborn?

This question is, of course, a conundrum of the age. Certain anxieties—like those involving money—appear to be learned. But there is an equally convincing argument that the *basic disposition toward anxiety* is a constitutional, inborn factor that merely expresses itself in learned ways. The work of Stella Chess, of New York University, who followed over a hundred youngsters from birth to age twenty-one, shows the importance of the person's *natural temperament* in the creation of personality.

Certain studies indicate a somewhat genetic base to anxiety. British researcher F.W. Brown investigated 63 cases of anxiety neurosis and found that their close relatives suffered considerably more neuroses than did a control group. In another survey, researcher Eliot Slater studied the records of two thousand World War II soldiers who had been diagnosed as psychoneurotic. He found that over 50 percent of their first-degree relatives—parents, children, or brothers and sisters—also suffered from some psychopathology.

Since twin studies are a good laboratory of inherited traits, researchers have checked both fraternal and identical twins to see if neurosis is inherited and possibly genetically based. In six twin surveys done between 1953 and 1966, 173 pairs of fraternal (dizygotic) twins, of whom at least one sibling in each pair had a so-called neurotic illness, were studied. In approximately one in four cases (23 percent) both siblings shared the condition. But in a study of 141 identical (monozygotic, or one egg) twins, the two twins shared the ailment in a majority of the cases (52 percent), a statistical indication of an inherited trait.

The biology of anxiety is complex. But there are other factors which can bring a troubled patient into the therapy room. One, which is often overlooked in the Psychological Society, is the vagaries of historical, or generational, style. Could part of what we have called neurosis be the phenomenon of *emotional fashion?*

What happens when a person's natural temperament, and particular level and type of anxiety, are in conflict with the culture's mores? This cultural view of neurosis might explain the excessive diagnosis, and self-diagnosis, of neuroses that pervade our society.

A woman raised in Victorian England who was sexually inhibited, for example, would be considered emotionally normal. The same type of woman, suffering from sexual anxiety in the late 1970s, would soon find herself in psychotherapy for her "neurosis."

The individual in the Psychological Society has been falsely taught that he lives in a continuum between normality and insanity, with the common aberration called "neurosis" in between. By calling on a professional psychologist or psychiatrist, he hopes to have his instability measured, then treated.

No such Freudian continuum exists. And it is now becoming clear that the concept of neurosis may have been a metaphysical one which covered up the very normality of our anxiety. Most of mankind is therefore left with two basic conditions to contemplate. One is insanity, which will strike a small percentage of us with its onslaught of tragedy relieved only partially by modern psychopharmacology. Or, faced with the dilemma of sanity, we must find a way to a better existence.

The human animal is a highly idiosyncratic one: each of us has a specific temperament and style. Even within the nuclear family, the enormous differences in individual personalities are obvious. Each person comes equipped with a personality which is uniquely his own, and which identifies him throughout life.

In the conformity demanded by the Psychological Society, that once precious emotional individuality is carried more with guilt than with pride. We face overwhelming pressure to conform to psychological expectations, to consider our every anxiety, every fear, every insecurity as a sign of psychopathology. We imagine—and are subtly told by the Society's professionals—that there is an ideal, virtually anxiety-free paradigm from which we somehow deviate.

In establishing such a model, which exists only in psychological fantasy or in emotional blandness, the society serves as its own neurotic-producing stimulus. It forces millions to perceive their individuality—the very essence of human normality—as a psychological disturbance.

The psychological revolution has damaged the psychic fiber of individual man and woman. It is time for comprehensive repair. It will not be done through the unstable criteria of modern psychodynamic psychology and its artificial standards of normality and neurosis. Nor will it be done through the uncertain first aid of psychotherapy. More likely, the precepts of philosophy and the strict regimen of true scientific investigation, both of which have too often been abandoned in the Psychological Society, will provide the touchstones to guide us toward a surer, more ennobling existence.

# Notes
# and
# References

The following references, arranged in order of appearance by chapter, are the more important sources used in researching this volume. In addition, there are numerous other references used as background and scores of personal interviews, several of which are indicated in the text.

CHAPTER I

Riesman, David, *The Lonely Crowd* (New Haven, Conn.: Yale University Press, 1950).

Robertson, Nan, "One Child in Ten Found to Need Mental Aid," *The New York Times,* October 19, 1966, p. 37.

Parry, Hugh J., "National Patterns of Psychotherapeutic Drug Use," *Archives of General Psychiatry,* Vol. 28, June 1973, pp. 769–83. (Georgetown study.)

Freud, Sigmund, *Collected Papers,* Vol. 5 (New York: Basic Books, 1959), p. 337 (comment on normality and psychosis).

Srole, Leo; Langner, Thomas S.; et al., *Mental Health in the Metropolis: The Midtown Manhattan Study* (New York: McGraw-Hill, 1962).

Carey, Frank, "Portrait of U.S. Families: Disturbed," *New York Post,* April 24, 1972. (Confirmed in interview with National Institute of Mental Health.)

Lyons, Richard D., "20 Million People or More Need Mental Care, U.S. Panel Asserts," *The New York Times,* September 16, 1977.

*The Present and Future Importance of Patterns of Private Psychiatric Practice in the Delivery of Mental Health Services, Task Force Report No. 6,* American Psychiatric Association, Washington, D.C., June 1973. (Statistics on patients.)

*Register Report No. 9,* Council for the National Register of Health Service Providers in Psychology, American Psychological Association, Washington, D.C., July 1977.

Bahn, Anita K., et al., "Survey of Private Psychiatric Practice," *Archives of General Psychiatry,* Vol. 12, March 1965, pp. 295–302.

Shabad, Theodore, "Soviet Ideologists Are Putting New Emphasis on Psychology," *The New York Times,* February 10, 1972, p. 2.

De Tocqueville, Alexis, *Democracy in America,* Vol. 1 (New York: Vintage Books, 1945).

Freud, Sigmund, "General Theory of the Neuroses," *The Complete Introductory Lectures on Psychoanalysis* (New York: Norton, 1966), p. 285 (comment on blows to man's confidence).

Roddy, Joseph, "Joyce," *Look,* April 18, 1967, p. 42 (quote from Joyce).

Norman, Russell P., in a review of *Psychoanalysis, Psychiatry and the Law, William and Mary Law Review,* Vol. 9, Summer 1968, No. 4, p. 1209.

Szasz, Thomas S., *Law, Liberty and Psychiatry* (New York: Macmillan 1963).

Freud, Sigmund, *The Future of an Illusion,* (Garden City, N. Y.: Anchor Books, 1964), p. 8 (comment on man's instinctual dispositions).

Freud, *The Psychopathology of Everyday Life* (New York: Norton 1965), p. 163 (comment on wrong key).

Hamburg, David A., et al., "Report on Ad Hoc Committee on Central Fact-Gathering Data of the American Psychoanalytic Association," *Journal of the American Psychoanalytic Association,* October 1967, pp. 841–61 (comment on number benefited by analysis).

Frank, Jerome D., *Persuasion and Healing: A Comparative Study of Psychotherapy,* rev. ed. (Baltimore, Md.:Johns Hopkins University Press, 1973), p. 8 (comment on psychotherapy).

CHAPTER II

Barron, Frank, and Leary, Timothy F., "Changes in Psychoneurotic Patients with or without Psychotherapy," *Journal of Consulting Psychology*, Vol. 19, No. 4, 1955, pp. 239–45.

Schmideberg, Melitta, "Iatrogenic Disturbance," *American Journal of Psychiatry*, Vol. 119, 1963, p. 899.

Henry, William E.; Sims, John H.; and Spray, S. Lee, *The Fifth Profession* (San Francisco: Jossey-Bass, 1971).

Rogow, Arnold A., *The Psychiatrists* (New York: Putnam, 1970).

*Task Force Report No. 6*, American Psychiatric Association, Washington, D.C., June 1973.

Eysenck, Hans J., "The Effects of Psychotherapy: An Evaluation," *Journal of Consulting Psychology*, Vol. 16, 1952, pp. 319–24.

Eysenck, Hans J., "The Effects of Psychotherapy," *International Journal of Psychiatry*, Vol. 1, 1965, pp. 97–168. Also published with comments by others as *Effects of Psychotherapy* (New York: International Science Press, 1966). (Eysenck's report and comments. Details on Cambridge-Somerville delinquency study taken by Eysenck from Teuber, N. L., and Powers, E., "Evaluating Therapy in a Delinquency Prevention Program," *Proc. Ass'n. Res. Nerv. Ment. Dis.*, Vol. 31, 138–47.)

Gottschalk, Louis A.; Fox, Ruth A; and Bates, Daniel E., "A Study of Prediction and Outcome in a Mental Health Crisis Clinic," *American Journal of Psychiatry*, Vol. 130, No. 10, October 1973, pp. 1107–11.

Frank, Jerome D., "The Role of Hope in Psychotherapy," *International Journal of Psychotherapy*, Vol. 5, No. 5, May 1968, p. 386 (comment on mathematics of spontaneous improvement).

Bergin, A. E., and Garfield, S. L., eds., *Handbook of Psychotherapy and Behavior Change: Empirical Analysis* (New York: Wiley, 1971).

Frank, Jerome D., *Persuasion and Healing: A Comparative Study of Psychotherapy*, rev. ed. (Baltimore, Md.: Johns Hopkins University Press, 1973). (Placebo study on pp. 141–43.)

Shapiro, Arthur K., "Placebo Effects in Medicine, Psychotherapy and Psychoanalysis," from Chapter 12 in Bergin, A. E., and Garfield, S. L., eds., *Handbook of Psychotherapy and Behavior Change: Empirical Evidence* (New York: Wiley, 1971), pp. 439–73.

Shapiro, Arthur K., "The Placebo Effect in the History of Medical Treatment, Implications for Psychiatry," *American Journal of Psychiatry*, Vol. 116, No. 4, October 1959, pp. 298–304.

Park, L. C., and Covi, L., "Nonblind Placebo Trial: An Exploration of Neurotic Patients' Responses to Placebo When Its Inert Content Is Disclosed," *Archives of General Psychiatry*, Vol. 12, 1965, pp. 336–45.

Brill, Norman Q., et al., "Controlled Study of Psychiatric Outpatient Treatment," *Archives of General Psychiatry*, Vol. 10, 1964, pp. 581–95.

Brill, Norman Q., "Results of Psychotherapy," *California Medicine*, Vol. 104, April 1966, pp. 249–53.

King, Wayne, "Child Psychotherapy Is Increasing Rapidly," *The New York Times*, July 30, 1973, pp. 1, 14.

Levitt, E. E. "Results of Psychotherapy with Children: An Evaluation," *Journal of Consulting Psychology*, Vol. 21, pp. 189–96.

Levitt, E. E., "Psychotherapy with Children: A Further Evaluation," *Behav. Res. Ther.*, 1963, Vol. 1, pp. 45–51.

Truax, C. B., and Carkhuff, R. R., *Toward Effective Counseling and Psychotherapy* (Chicago: Aldine, 1966). (Details on studies on psychotherapy with alcoholics, p. 9.)

Goodstein, L. D., and Crites, J. O., "Brief Counseling with Poor College Risks," *Journal of Counseling Psychology*, Vol. 8, 1961, pp. 318–21.

Barendregt, J. T., "A Psychological Investigation of the Effects of Psychoanalysis and Psychotherapy," in *Research in Psychodiagnostics* (Paris: Mouton, 1961). (Quoted by Eysenck, in *Effects of Psychotherapy*.)

Frank, Jerome D., *Persuasion and Healing: A Comparative Study of Psychotherapy*, rev. ed. (Baltimore, Md.: Johns Hopkins University Press, 1973). (Material on individual, group, minimal therapy on pp. 152–56.)

Lorr, M.; McNair, D. M.; et al., "Frequency of Treatment and Change in Psychotherapy," *Journal of Abnormal and Social Psychology*, Vol. 64, 1962, pp. 281–92.

Errera, Paul, et al., "Length of Psychotherapy," *Archives of General Psychiatry*, Vol. 17, October 1967, pp. 454–58.

Bergin, Allen E., "Some Implications of Psychotherapy Research for Therapeutic Practice," *International Journal of Psychiatry*, Vol. 3, No. 3, March 1967, pp. 136–60, including Critical Evaluations by Hans J. Eysenck, Jerome D. Frank, Joseph D. Matarazzo, and Charles B. Truax.

Luborsky, Lester; Singer, Barton; and Luborsky, Lise, "Comparative Studies of Psychotherapies," in *Evaluation of Psychological Therapies,* edited by Robert L. Spitzer and Donald F. Kline (Baltimore, Md.: Johns Hopkins University Press, 1976). (Compilation of various studies.)

Luborsky, Lester, et al., "Comparative Studies of Psychotherapies," *Archives of General Psychiatry,* Vol. 32, 1975, pp. 995–1008. (Larger version of prior reference.)

Pande, Shashi K., "The Mystique of 'Western' Psychotherapy: An Eastern Interpretation," *The Journal of Nervous and Mental Disease,* Vol. 146, No. 6, June 1968, pp. 425–32.

Frank, Jerome D., "The Influence of Patients' and Therapists' Expectations on the Outcome of Psychotherapy," *British Journal of Medical Psychology,* Vol. 41, 1968, pp. 349–56. (Study on placebo effects before pill is given.)

Calestro, Kenneth M., "Psychotherapy, Faith Healing and Suggestion," *International Journal of Psychiatry,* Vol. 10, 1972, pp. 83–113.

Strupp, Hans H., "Needed: A Reformulation of the Psychotherapeutic Influence," *International Journal of Psychiatry,* Vol. 10, 1972, pp. 114–20. (Comments on suggestion.)

Strupp, Hans H., "On the Technology of Psychotherapy," *Archives of General Psychiatry,* Vol. 26, March 1972, pp. 270–78.

Bernheim, H., *Hypnosis and Suggestion in Psychotherapy* (New Hyde Park, N.Y.: University Books, 1965).

Whitman, Roy M., "Which Dream Does the Patient Tell?" *Archives of General Psychiatry,* Vol. 8, March 1963, pp. 277–82.

Rosenthal, Robert, *Experimenter Effects in Behavioral Research,* enlarged ed. (New York: Irvington, 1976).

Torrey, E. Fuller, "What Western Psychotherapists Can Learn from Witchdoctors," *American Journal of Orthopsychiatry,* January 1972, Vol. 42, pp. 69–76.

Torrey, E. Fuller, *The Mind Game: Witchdoctors and Psychiatrists* (New York: Emerson, 1972).

Bergman, Robert L., "Navajo Medicine and Psychoanalysis," *Human Behavior,* July 1973, pp. 8–15.

"Witch Doctors' Effectiveness Admitted; African Use for Mental Disease Is Urged," *Medical Tribune,* March 22, 1963.

Truax, C. B., and Carkhuff, R. R., *Toward Effective Counseling and Psychotherapy:*

*Training and Practice* (Chicago: Aldine, 1966), p. 42 (comment on average effect of therapy).

Bergin, Allen E., and Garfield, S. L., eds., *Handbook of Psychotherapy and Behavior Change: Empirical Analysis* (New York: Wiley, 1971).

Chapman, A. H., "Iatrogenic Problems in Psychotherapy," *Psychiatry Digest,* September 1964, pp. 23–29. (Original article.)

Astrup, Christian, discussant in *Effects of Psychotherapy* by Eysenck. (Quote from p. 54.)

Werner, Harold D., "Conscious and Unconscious in Clinic Practice," *Psychiatry Digest,* April 1964, pp. 23–32. (Original article.)

Guttman, Herta A., "A Contraindication for Family Therapy," *Archives of General Psychiatry,* Vol. 29, September 1973, pp. 352–55.

Hadley, Suzanne, W., and Strupp, Hans H., "Contemporary View of Negative Effects in Psychotherapy," *Archives of General Psychiatry,* Vol. 33, November 1976, pp. 1291–1302.

Graziano, Anthony M., "In the Mental Health Industry, Illness Is Our Most Important Product," *Psychology Today,* January 1972, pp. 12–18.

Meehl, Paul E., discussant in *Effects of Psychotherapy* by Eysenck. (Material on statistical chances for success in psychotherapy, pp. 58–59.)

Sharaf, Myron R., and Levinson, Daniel, "The Quest for Omnipotence in Professional Training," *International Journal of Psychiatry,* Vol. 4, No. 5, November 1967, pp. 426–42.

Freeman, Walter, "Psychiatrists Who Kill Themselves: A Study in Suicide," *American Journal of Psychiatry,* Vol. 124, No. 6, December 1967, pp. 846–47.

Garfield, Sol L., and Bergin, Allen E., "Personal Therapy, Outcome and Some Therapist Variables," *Psychotherapy: Theory, Research and Practice,* Vol. 8, No. 3, Fall 1971, pp. 251–53. (Study on personal therapy for therapists.)

Shapiro, Arthur K.; Struening, Elmer; Shapiro, Elaine; and Barten, Harvey, "Prognostic Correlates of Psychotherapy in Psychiatric Outpatients," *American Journal of Psychiatry,* Vol. 133, No. 7, July 1976, pp. 802–8.

Mahrer, Alvin R., "Some Known Effects of Psychotherapy and a Reinterpretation," *Psychotherapy: Therapy, Research and Practice,* Vol. 7, No. 3, Fall 1970, pp. 186–91.

Lee, Stephen D., and Temerlin, Maurice K., "Social Class, Diagnosis, and Prognosis for Psychotherapy," *Psychotherapy: Theory, Research and Practice,* Vol. 7, No. 3,

Fall 1970, pp. 181–85. (Oklahoma experiment with psychiatrists varying the social class of the subject.)

Rosenthal, David, "Changes in Some Moral Values Following Psychotherapy," *Journal of Consulting Psychology,* Vol. 19, No. 6, 1955, pp. 431–36.

Mendel, W. M., "The Phenomenon of Interpretation," *American Journal of Psychoanalysis,* Vol. 24, No. 2, 1964, pp. 184–90.

Orne, Martin T., "On the Nature of Effective Hope," *International Journal of Psychiatry,* Vol. 5, No. 5, May 1968, pp. 403–9.

Lynch, Mary; Gardner, Elmer A.; and Flezer, Stanton B., "The Role of Indigenous Personnel as Clinical Therapists," *Archives of General Psychiatry,* Vol. 19, October 1968, pp. 428–34. (Report of the Temple University Community Mental Health Center.)

Torrey, E. Fuller, "The Case for the Indigenous Therapist," *Archives of General Psychiatry,* Vol. 20, March 1969, pp. 365–72. (Report on successful use of hospital aides as therapists and report of E. G. Poser's work with college students.)

Uhlenhuth, E. H., and Duncan, David B., "Subjective Change with Medical Student Therapists," *Archives of General Psychiatry,* Vol. 18, April 1968, pp. 428–38.

Strupp, Hans H., unpublished paper on Vanderbilt study, 1977. (Report on trained therapists versus college teachers as volunteer therapists.)

Luborsky, Lester, et al., "Factors Influencing the Outcome of Psychotherapy," *Psychological Bulletin,* Vol. 75, 1971, pp. 145–85.

Luborsky, Lester, "Research Cannot Yet Influence Clinical Practice," *International Journal of Psychiatry,* Vol. 7, 1969, pp. 135–40.

CHAPTER III

Gant, Herbert M, "Violence 'Remedies' Called Half-Answers," *Psychiatric News,* December 1968.

Farnsworth, Dana L., "The Psychiatrist as a Commentator on Acts of Violence," *American Journal of Psychiatry,* Vol. 123, No. 8, February 1967, pp. 1002–3.

"Psychologists Warned to Beware of Empiricism," *The New York Times,* September 7, 1965.

"Racing Car Drivers 'Skillful,' Said to Lack 'Death Wish,' " *Medical Tribune,* April 19, 1967.

"The Unconscious of a Conservative: A Special Issue on the Mind of Barry Goldwater," *Fact,* Vol. 1, No. 5, September–October, 1964.

Barton, Walter E., "Diagnosis by Mail," *American Journal of Psychiatry,* Vol. 124, No. 10, April 1968, pp. 1446–48.

Rome, Howard P., "Psychiatry and Foreign Affairs: The Expanding Competence of Psychiatry," *American Journal of Psychiatry,* Vol. 125, No. 6, December 1968, pp. 725–30.

Wedge, Bryant, "Training for a Psychiatry of International Relations," *American Journal of Psychiatry,* Vol. 125, No. 6, December 1968, pp. 731–36.

Wedge, Bryant, "Psychiatry and International Affairs," *Science,* July 1967, pp. 281–84.

Clark, Kenneth, "An Immense Proposal," *Intellectual Digest,* February 1972, pp. 50–52. (Text of his presidential address to the American Psychological Association dealing with psychotechnology. Reprinted from *American Psychologist.*)

Spitzer, Robert L., and Cohen, Jacob, "Common Errors in Quantitative Psychiatric Research," *International Journal of Psychiatry,* Vol. 6, No. 2, August 1968, pp. 109–31.

Altus, William D., "Birth Order and Its Sequelae," *Science,* January 7, 1966, Vol. 151, No. 3706, pp. 44–49.

Brody, Jane E., "It Can Be Tough to Be First-Born," *New York Times,* February 18, 1968.

Hare, E. H., "Associations: Important or Trivial," *International Journal of Psychiatry,* June 1967, Vol. 3, No. 6, pp. 537–38.

Atkins, Harry, "Freud Eggs," *The Sciences,* February 1970.

deMause, Lloyd, and Ebel, Henry, eds., *Jimmy Carter and American Fantasy: Psychohistorical Explorations* (New York: Two Continents/Psychohistory Press, 1977).

Alsop, Stewart, "Living with Two Nixons," *Newsweek,* August 19, 1968, p. 92.

Mazlish, Bruce, *In Search of Nixon, A Psychohistorical Inquiry* (New York: Basic Books, 1972).

Chesen, Eli S., *President Nixon's Psychiatric Profile* (New York: Wyden, 1973).

Barzun, Jacques, "History: The Muse and Her Doctors," *American Historical Review,* Vol. 77, 1972, pp. 36–64.

"Meeting Explores History from Psychologists' View," *New York Times,* April 26, 1971, pp. 37, 46.

Himmelfarb, Gertrude, "The New History," *Commentary,* January 1975, pp. 72–78.

Freud, Sigmund, *Leonardo da Vinci: A Study in Psychosexuality* (New York: Vintage Books, 1947).

Freud, Sigmund, and Bullitt, William C., *Thomas Woodrow Wilson: A Psychological Study* (Boston: Houghton Mifflin, 1967).

Stewart, Robert Sussman, "Posthumous Analysis," *The New York Times,* January 29, 1967, pp. 3, 42, 44. (A review of *Thomas Woodrow Wilson.*)

Coles, Robert, "Shrinking History," *New York Review of Books,* February 22, 1973, p. 15; March 8, 1973, p. 25.

Goldstein, Tom, "Use of Psychiatrists in Court Is Scored," *The New York Times,* November 17, 1974.

Radzinowicz, Leon, "Mental Illness and the Law," *Commentary,* May 1969, p. 100. (A review of *The Insanity Defense.*)

Bazelon, David L., "Psychiatrists and the Adversary Process," *Scientific American,* Vol. 230, No. 6, June 1974, p. 18.

"Insane Then Doesn't Mean Insane Now," *Time,* March 22, 1968, p. 53.

"Judges Change Attitudes after Attending Psychiatry Seminars," *Psychiatric News,* October 1968. (Dr. Seymour Pollack's comment on judges' attitude toward psychiatric testimony.)

Williams, Tennessee, *Memoirs* (Garden City, N.Y.: Doubleday, 1975).

Freedman, Alfred M., and Kaplan, Harold I., *Comprehensive Textbook of Psychiatry* (Baltimore, Md.: Williams & Wilkins Company, 1967), p. 968 (quote by Bieber on homosexuality).

Bieber, Irving, "Homosexual Dynamics in Psychiatric Crisis," *American Journal of Psychiatry,* Vol. 128, No. 10, April 1972, pp. 1268–72.

Krafft-Ebing, Richard von, *Psychopathia Sexualis* (New York: Putnam, 1969).

Ellis, Havelock, *Studies in the Psychology of Sex,* Vol. 1: Sexual Inversion (New York: Random House, 1936).

Kolodny, Robert C.; Masters, William H.; et al., "Plasma Testosterone and Semen

Analysis in Male Homosexuals," *New England Journal of Medicine,* Vol. 285, November 18, 1971, pp. 1170–74.

"Homosexual Chemistry," *Newsweek,* April 26, 1971, pp. 54–55. (Report on work of Margolese and Janiger.)

Kallman, F. J., "Comparative Twin Study on the Genetic Aspects of Male Homosexuality," *Journal of Nervous and Mental Disease,* Vol. 115, 1952, pp. 283–98.

Heston, L. L., and Shields, James, "Homosexuality in Twins," *Archives of General Psychiatry,* Vol. 18, February 1968, pp. 149–60.

Moore, Francis D., "Surgery in Search of a Rationale," *American Journal of Surgery,* March 1963, pp. 304–12.

Hirschowitz, Basil I., "Management of Peptic Ulcer," *GP,* March 1965, pp. 113–23.

Mordkoff, Arnold, and Parsons, Oscar A., "The Coronary Personality: A Critique," *International Journal of Psychiatry,* Vol. 5, No. 2, 1971, pp. 159–71.

Blakeslee, Sandra, "Freud in the Dental Chair," *The New York Times,* December 8, 1968, p. 10E. (Comment on tension and gum disease.)

Lewis, Howard R., and Martha E., *Psychosomatics* (New York: Viking, 1972). (Comment by Dr. Kubie on psychogenic diseases.)

Shapiro, Arthur K., and Shapiro, Elaine, "Clinical Dangers of Psychological Theorizing," *Psychiatric Quarterly,* Vol. 45, No. 2, 1971, pp. 159–71.

Shapiro, Arthur K., and Shapiro, Elaine, "Treatment of Gilles de la Tourette Syndrome with Haloperidol," *British Journal of Psychiatry,* Vol. 114, No. 508, March 1968, pp. 345–50.

Sheely, William F., guest editorial, *American Journal of Psychiatry,* December 1963, p. 604.

Rossman, Philip L., "Organic Diseases Simulating Functional Disorders," *GP,* August 1963, pp. 78–83.


CHAPTER IV

Kety, Seymour S., "Biochemical Theories of Schizophrenia," *International Journal of Psychiatry,* Vol. 1, No. 3, July 1965, pp. 409–46 (quote by J. W. L. Thudichum).

Wechsler, James A., *In a Darkness* (New York: Norton, 1972).

Wilson, Louise, *This Stranger, My Son: A Mother's Story* (New York: Putnam, 1968).

Arieti, Silvano, "New Views on the Psychodynamics of Schizophrenia," *American Journal of Psychiatry,* Vol. 124, No. 4, October 1967, pp. 453–57.

Alexander, Franz G., and Selesnick, Sheldon T., *The History of Psychiatry* (New York: Harper & Row, 1966).

Zilboorg, Gregory, *A History of Medical Psychology* (New York: Norton, 1941).

Redlich, Fredrick C., and Freedman, Daniel X., *The Theory and Practice of Psychiatry* (New York: Basic Books, 1966).

Stierlin, Helm, "Bleuler's Concept of Schizophrenia: A Confusing Heritage," *American Journal of Psychiatry,* February 8, 1967, pp. 996–1001.

Kahn, Eugen, and Pokorny, Alex D., "Concerning the Concept of Schizophrenia," *American Journal of Psychiatry,* March 1964, pp. 856–60.

May, Philip R. A., *Treatment of Schizophrenia* (New York: Science House, 1968).

Anthony, E. James, "A Clinical Evaluation of Children with Psychotic Parents," *American Journal of Psychiatry,* Vol. 126, No. 2, August 1969, pp. 177–84.

Pollack, Max; Woerner, Margaret G.; Goldberg, Philip; and Klein, Donald F., "Siblings of Schizophrenic and Nonschizophrenic Psychiatric Patients," *Archives of General Psychiatry,* Vol. 20, June 1969, pp. 652–58. (Hillside Hospital study on siblings.)

Heston, L. L., "The Genetics of Schizophrenia and Schizoid Disease," *Science,* January 1970, pp. 249–55.

Heston, L. L. "Psychiatric Disorders in Foster Home Reared Children of Schizophrenic Mothers," *British Journal of Psychiatry,* Vol. 112, 1966, pp. 819–25.

Fish, Barbara, "Research Today or Tragedy Tomorrow," *American Journal of Psychiatry,* Vol. 128, No. 11, May 1972, pp. 1439–40.

Guze, Samuel B., "Hereditary Transmission of Psychiatric Illness," *American Journal of Psychiatry,* Vol. 130, No. 12, December 1973, pp. 1377–78.

Rosenthal, David; Wender, Paul H.; Kety, Seymour S., Welner, Joseph; and Schulsinger, Fini, "The Adopted-Away Offspring of Schizophrenia," *American Journal of Psychiatry,* Vol. 128, No. 3, September 1971, pp. 307–16.

Kety, Seymour S.; Rosenthal, David; Wender, Paul H.; and Schulsinger, Fini, "Mental Illness in the Biological and Adoptive Families of Adopted Schizophrenics," *American Journal of Psychiatry,* Vol. 128, No. 3, September 1971, pp. 302–6. (Danish study.)

Kety, Seymour S., "Studies Designed to Disentangle Genetic and Environmental

Variables in Schizophrenia: Some Epistemological Questions and Answers," *American Journal of Psychiatry,* Vol. 133, No. 10, October 1976, pp. 1134–36.

Glick, Ira, et al., "Schizophrenia in Siblings Reared Apart: A Case Report," *American Journal of Psychiatry,* Vol. 124, No. 2, August 1967, pp. 236–39.

Essen-Meller, Erik, "Twin Research and Psychiatry," *International Journal of Psychiatry,* Vol. 1, No. 3, July 1965, pp. 466–75.

Stabenau, James R., "Heredity and Environment in Schizophrenia," *Archives of General Psychiatry,* Vol. 18, April 1968, pp. 458–63.

Cadonet, Remi J., et al., "Studies of Adoptees from Psychiatrically Disturbed Biological Parents, III," *British Journal of Psychiatry,* Vol. 126, 1975, pp. 534–49, and *Journal of Pediatrics,* Vol. 87, 1975, pp. 301–6.

Gottesman, Irving I., and Shields, James, *Schizophrenia and Genetics: A Twin Study Vantage Point* (New York: Academic Press, 1972). (Maudsley study, and material on H. Mitsuda, separated identical twins.)

Shields, James, and Gottesman, Irving I., "Cross-National Diagnosis of Schizophrenia in Twins," *Archives of General Psychiatry,* Vol. 27, December 1972, pp. 725–31.

Pollin, William, "The Pathogenesis of Schizophrenia," *Archives of General Psychiatry,* Vol. 27, July 1972, pp. 29–37.

Kallmann, F. J., "The Genetic Theory of Schizophrenia: An Analysis of 691 Schizophrenic Twin Index Families," *American Journal of Psychiatry,* Vol. 103, 1946, pp. 309–22.

Kallmann, J., and Goldfarb, Charles, "Heredity and Eugenics," *American Journal of Psychiatry,* January 1964, pp. 625–27.

Hoffer, Axel, and Pollin, William, "Schizophrenia in the NAS-NRC Panel of 15,909 Veteran Twin Pairs," *Archives of General Psychiatry,* Vol. 23, November 1970, pp. 469–77. (Initial veteran study on concordance for schizophrenia.)

Allen, Martin G.; Cohen, Stephen; and Pollin, William, "Schizophrenia in Veteran Twins: A Diagnostic Review," *American Journal of Psychiatry,* Vol. 128, No. 8, February 1972. (Revised figures on veteran twin concordance for schizophrenia.)

Pollin, William, et al., "Psychopathology in 15,909 Pairs of Veteran Twins," *American Journal of Psychiatry,* Vol. 126, No. 5, November 1969, pp. 597–610.

Mosher, Loren R.; Pollin, William; and Stabenau, James R., "Identical Twins Discordant for Schizophrenia," *Archives of General Psychiatry,* Vol. 24, May 1971, pp. 422–30. (Report from Center for Studies of Schizophrenia.)

Stabenau, James R., and Pollin, William, "Early Characteristics of Monozygotic Twins Discordant for Schizophrenia," *Archives of General Psychiatry,* Vol. 17, December 1967, pp. 723–34.

Pollin, William; Stabenau, James R.; et al., "Life History Differences in Identical Twins Discordant for Schizophrenia," *American Journal of Orthopsychiatry,* April 1966, pp. 492–509.

Pollin, William, "The Pathogenesis of Schizophrenia," *Archives of General Psychiatry,* Vol. 27, July 1972, pp. 29–37.

Allen, Martin G., et al., "Parental, Birth, and Infancy Factors in Infant Twin Development," *American Journal of Psychiatry,* Vol. 127, No. 12, June 1971, pp. 1597–1604.

Gottesman and Shields, *Schizophrenia and Genetics,* pp. 6–10. (Material on polygene inheritance of schizophrenia, and statistics by E. Zerbin-Rudin.)

Rosenbaum, C. Peter, "Metabolic, Physiological, Anatomic and Genetic Studies in the Schizophrenias: A Review and Analysis," *Journal of Nervous and Mental Disease,* Vol. 146, No. 2, pp. 103–26. (Material on risk in schizophrenia, plus various biochemical theories.)

Freud, Sigmund, "On Narcissism: An Introduction" (1914), *Collected Papers,* Vol. 4 (New York: Basic Books, 1959), pp. 30–59.

Freud, "Psycho-Analytic Notes upon an Autobiographical Account of a Case of Paranoia," (1911), *Collected Papers,* Vol. 3 (New York: Basic Books, 1959), pp. 397–470.

Schatzman, Morton, "Paranoia or Persecution: The Case of Schreber," *International Journal of Psychiatry,* Vol. 10, No. 3, September 1972, pp. 53–78, reprinted from *Family Process.*

Jones, Ernest, *The Life and Work of Sigmund Freud,* Vol. 2 (New York: Basic Books, 1955), p. 274 (comment on Wolf Man and rectal intercourse and defecation).

*The Wolf-Man,* edited by Muriel Gardiner (New York: Basic Books, 1971).

Will, Otto Allen, Jr., "Commentary," *International Journal of Psychiatry,* Vol. 10, No. 3, September 1972, pp. 85–88 (comment on Schreber case).

Bergman, Paul; Malasky, Charlotte; and Zahn, Theodore P., Oral Functions in Schizophrenia," *Journal of Nervous and Mental Disease,* Vol. 146, No. 5, May 1968, pp. 351–59 (sucking test for schizophrenia).

Mishler, Elliot G., and Waxler, Nancy E., "Family Interaction Processes and

Schizophrenia: A Review of Current Theories," *International Journal of Psychiatry,* Vol. 2, No. 4, July 1966, pp. 375–413 (double bind theory of schizophrenia).

Bender, Lauretta, "Childhood Schizophrenia: A Review," *International Journal of Psychiatry,* Vol. 5, No. 3, March 1968, pp. 311–19.

Bender, Lauretta, "The Life Course of Children with Schizophrenia," *American Journal of Psychiatry,* Vol. 130, No. 7, July 1973, pp. 783–85.

Treffert, Darold A., "Epidemiology of Infantile Autism," *Archives of General Psychiatry,* Vol. 22, May 1970, pp. 431–38 (extent of disease).

Ornitz, Edward M, and Ritvo, Edward R., "Perceptual Inconstancy in Early Infantile Autism," *Archives of General Psychiatry,* Vol. 18, January 1968, pp. 76–98 (comments on autism).

Wing, Lorna, "Treating Autistic Children," *New Scientist and Science Journal,* August 26, 1971, pp. 473–75.

Hanson, D. R., and Gottesman, I. I., "The Genetics, If Any, of Infantile Autism and Childhood Schizophrenia," *Journal of Autism and Childhood Schizophrenia,* Vol. 6, No. 3, 1976, pp. 209–34.

Pollack, Max; Levenstein, Sidney; and Klein, Donald F., "A Three Year Posthospital Follow-up of Adolescent and Adult Schizophrenics," *American Journal of Orthopsychiatry,* January 1968, pp. 94–109. (Hillside study on age and recovery.)

Barthell, Charles N., and Holmes, David S., "High School Yearbooks: A Nonreactive Measure of Social Isolation in Graduates Who Later Became Schizophrenic," *Journal of Abnormal Psychology,* 1968, Vol. 73.

Field, Harriet, "Early Symptoms and Behavior of Male Schizophrenics, Delinquent Character-Disordered Individuals and Socially Adequate Subjects," *Journal of Nervous and Mental Disease,* Vol. 148, No. 2, pp. 134–46.

Klein, Donald F., and Davis, John M., *Diagnosis and Drug Treatment of Psychiatric Disorders* (Baltimore, Md.: Williams & Wilkins, 1969). (Comment on treatment of schizo-affective disorders.)

Bleuler, Manfred, "Conceptions of Schizophrenia within the Last Fifty Years and Today," *International Journal of Psychiatry,* Vol. 1, No. 4, October 1965, pp. 501–13. Reprinted from *Proceedings of the Royal Society of Medicine,* Vol. 56, October 1963, pp. 945–52.

Straker, M., "Schizophrenia and Psychiatric Diagnosis," *American Journal of Psychiatry,* Vol. 131, No. 6, June 1974, pp. 693–94. (Comment on misdiagnosis of schizophrenia.)

Reid, Arnaud A., "Schizophrenia—Disease or Syndrome?" *Archives of General Psychiatry,* Vol. 28, June 1973, pp. 863–68. (Misdiagnosis of schizophrenia.)

Schorer, C. E., "Mistakes in the Diagnosis of Schizophrenia," *American Journal of Psychiatry,* Vol. 124, No. 8, February 1968, pp. 1057–62.

Heath, Robert G., and Krupp, Iris M., "Schizophrenia as a Specific Biologic Disease," *American Journal of Psychiatry,* Vol. 124, No. 8, February 1968, pp. 1019–24. (Taraxein theory of schizophrenia.)

Snyder, Solomon H., "The Dopamine Hypothesis of Schizophrenia: Focus on the Dopamine Receptor," *American Journal of Psychiatry,* Vol. 133, No. 2, February 1976, pp. 197–202.

Tourney, Garfield, "History of Biological Psychiatry in America," *American Journal of Psychiatry,* Vol. 126, No. 1, July 1969, pp. 29–42.

Grinker, Roy R., Sr., "An Essay on Schizophrenia and Science," *Archives of General Psychiatry,* Vol. 20, January 1969, pp. 1–24.

Shobe, Frank O., and Brion, Pacelli, "Long-term Prognosis in Manic-Depressive Illness," *Archives of General Psychiatry,* Vol. 24, April 1971, pp. 334–37.

Winokur, George, et al., "The Iowa 500: II. A Blind Family History Comparison of Mania, Depression and Schizophrenia," *Archives of General Psychiatry,* Vol. 27, October 1972, p. 462. (Statistics of risk among relatives of depressed patients' becoming depressed and committing suicide.)

Gershon, Elliot S.; Dunner, David L.; and Goodwin, Frederick K., "Toward a Biology of Affective Disorders," *Archives of General Psychiatry,* Vol. 25, July 1971, pp. 1–15. (Statistics on manic-depressive twin studies.)

Robins, E., et al., "Some Clinical Considerations in the Prevention of Suicide Based on a Study of 134 Successful Suicides," *American Journal of Public Health,* Vol. 49, 1959, pp. 888–99. (Incidence of suicide in affective disorders.)

Winokur, G., and Pitts, F. N., Jr., "Affective Disorders: VI. A Family History Study of Prevalence, Sex Differences, and Possible Genetic Factors," *Journal of Psychiatric Research,* Vol, 3, 1965, pp. 112–23 (estimate of 2 percent affective disorder in the population, as quoted in Gershon article, above).

Dorzab, Joe; Baker, Max; Cadoret, Remi J.; and Winokur, George, "Depressive Disease: Familial Psychiatric Illness," *American Journal of Psychiatry,* Vol. 127, No. 9, March 1971, pp. 1128–33. (Ten signs of depression: figures on Iceland; additional evidence of family risk in affective disease.)

Fieve, Ronald R.; Mendlewicz, Julien; and Fleiss, Joseph L., "Manic-Depressive

Illness: Linkage with the Xg Blood Group," *American Journal of Psychiatry*, Vol. 130, No. 12, pp. 1355–1935.

Baker, Max; Dorzab, Joe; Winokur, George; and Cadoret, Remi J., "Depressive Disease: Evidence Favoring Polygenic Inheritance Based on an Analysis of Ancestral Cases," *Archives of General Psychiatry*, Vol. 27, September 1972, pp. 320–26. (Polygenic inheritance of depression.)

Van Praag, Herman, et al., "Cerebral Monoamines and Depression," *Archives of General Psychiatry*, Vol. 28, June 1973, pp. 827–31.

Van der Velde, Christiaan D., and Gordon, Malcolm W., "Biochemical and Pharmacological Variations in Manic-Depressive Illness," *American Journal of Psychiatry*, Vol. 129, No. 3, September 1972, pp. 337–42. (Norwich Hospital study.)

Prange, Arthur J., Jr., et al., "Enhancement of Imipramine Antidepressant Activity by Thyroid Hormone," *American Journal of Psychiatry*, Vol. 126, No. 4, October 1969, pp. 457–67.

Malitz, Sidney, and Kanzler, Maureen, "Are Antidepressants Better than Placebo?" *American Journal of Psychiatry*, Vol. 127, No. 12, June 1971, pp. 1605–11 (ratio of depressed patients who are female).

Robinson, Donald S., et al., "Relation of Sex and Aging to Monoamine Oxidase Activity of Human Brain, Plasma and Platelets," *Archives of General Psychiatry*, Vol. 24, June 1971, pp. 536–39 (MAO in blood of patients).

Schildkraut, Joseph J., "Neurochemical Studies of the Affective Disorders: The Pharmacological Bridge," *American Journal of Psychiatry*, Vol. 127, No. 3, September 1970, pp. 134–36.

Covi, Lino, et al., "Drugs and Group Psychotherapy in Neurotic Depression," *American Journal of Psychiatry*, Vol. 131, No. 2, February 1974, pp. 191–98. (Johns Hopkins study using group therapy in depression.)

Text by Klein, D. F., and Davis, J. M., previously cited. (Material on effectiveness of antidepressant versus placebo.)

Cole, Jonathan O., "Depression" (editorial), *American Journal of Psychiatry*, Vol. 131, No. 2, February 1974, pp. 204–5.

Raskin, Allen, "A Guide for Drug Use in Depressive Disorders," *American Journal of Psychiatry*, Vol. 131, No. 2, February 1974, pp. 181–85.

Cade, J. F. J., "Lithium Salts in the Treatment of Psychotic Excitement," *Medical Journal of Australia*, 1949, pp. 349–52.

Bey, D. R.; Chapman, R. E.; and Tornquist, K. L., "A Lithium Clinic," *American Journal of Psychiatry*, Vol. 129, No. 4, October 1972, pp. 468–71.

Van der Velde, Christiaan D., "Effectiveness of Lithium Carbonate in Treatment of Manic-Depressive Illness," *American Journal of Psychiatry*, Vol. 127, No. 3, September 1971, pp. 345–51.

Stallone, Frank; Shelley, Edward; Mendlewicz, Julien; and Fieve, Ronald R., "The Use of Lithium in Affective Disorders, III: A Double-Blind Study of Prophylaxis in Bipolar Illness," *American Journal of Psychiatry*, Vol. 130, No. 9, September 1973, pp. 1006–10.

Prien, Robert F., et al., "Prophylactic Efficacy of Lithium Carbonate in Manic-Depressive Illness," *Archives of General Psychiatry*, Vol. 28, March 1973. (Veterans Administration study.)

CHAPTER V

Dewald, Paul A., *The Psychoanalytic Process: A Case Illustration* (New York: Basic Books, 1972). (Anecdote of housewife in analysis, p. 226.)

Shakow, David, and Rapaport, David, "The Influence of Freud on American Psychology," *Psychological Issues*, Vol. 4, No. 1, Monograph 13.

Sargant, William, "Psychiatric Treatment Here and in England," *Atlantic*, July 1964, pp. 88–95.

*Biographical-Professional Survey*, American Psychoanalytic Association, New York, 1972.

Aronson, H., and Weintraub, Walter, "Social Background of the Patient in Classical Psychoanalysis," *Journal of Nervous and Mental Disease*, Vol. 146, No. 2, 1968, pp. 91–97.

Weintraub, W., and Aronson, H., "A Survey of Patients in Classical Psychoanalysis," *Journal of Nervous and Mental Disease*, Vol. 146, No. 2, 1968, pp. 98–102.

Hamburg, David A., "Report of Ad Hoc Committee on Central Fact-Gathering Data of the American Psychoanalytic Association," *Journal of the American Psychoanalytic Association*, October 1967, pp. 841–61 (statistics on religious background of analytic patients).

Sigmund Freud, *Collected Papers*, Vol. 2 (New York: Basic Books, 1959), pp. 347, 354 (comments on being gazed at and on working six days a week).

*Roster*, American Psychoanalytic Association, New York. (Non-M.D. analysts.)

Greenson, Ralph, *The Technique and Practice of Psychoanalysis*, Vol. I (New York: International Universities Press, 1967).

Waelder, Robert, *Basic Theory of Psychoanalysis* (New York: International Universities Press, 1960).

Glover, Edward, *The Techniques of Psycho-Analysis* (New York: International Universities Press, 1958).

Glover, Edward, "Research Methods in Psycho-Analysis," *International Journal of Psychoanalysis,* Vol. 33, 1952, pp. 403–9.

Freud, Sigmund, "Turnings in the Ways of Psycho-Analytic Therapy," *Collected Works,* Vol. 2 (New York: Basic Books, 1959), p. 396.

Moore, Burness E., and Fine, Bernard D., eds., *A Glossary of Psychoanalytic Terms and Concepts,* The American Psychoanalytic Association, New York, 1967.

Blum, Harold P., "On the Conception and the Development of the Transference Neurosis," Journal of the American Psychoanalytic Association, January 1971, pp. 41–53.

Freud, Sigmund, "Observations on Transference Love," *Collected Papers,* Vol. 2, pp. 377–91 (material on patient love for analyst).

Freud, "Further Recommendations in the Technique of Psycho-Analysis," *Collected Papers,* Vol. 2, p. 346 (on "hire by the hour," etc.), pp. 351–53 (payment of analytic bills).

Halpert, Eugene, "The Effect of Insurance on Psychoanalytic Treatment," *Journal of the American Psychoanalytic Association,* January 1972, pp. 122–32.

Breuer, Josef, and Freud, Sigmund, *Studies on Hysteria* (New York: Avon, 1966).

Freud, Sigmund, *An Autobiographical Study* (New York: Norton, 1963).

Jones, Ernest, *The Life and Work of Sigmund Freud,* Vol. 1 (New York: Basic Books, 1953).

Freud, Sigmund, "Sexuality in the Aetiology of the Neurosis," *Collected Papers,* Vol. 1, p. 220.

Freud, *The Origins of Psychoanalysis: Letters, Drafts and Notes to Wilhelm Fliess (1887–1902)* (Garden City, N.Y.: Anchor Books, 1957), p. 67 (on free sexual intercourse).

Freud, "The Aetiology of Hysteria," Collected Papers, Vol. 1, pp. 183–219 (material on child seduction theory, including case of child stimulating adult woman's genitals).

Freud, *The Origins of Psychoanalysis,* p. 198 (anecdote about father practicing ejaculation with daughter).

Ibid, p. 218 (comment that he no longer believes in his *neurotica*).

Freud, *An Autobiographical Study*, p. 63 (quote that he may have forced patients into telling seduction tales).

Jones, Ernest, *The Life and Work of Sigmund Freud*, Vol. 1, p. 267 (quote from Freud on importance of "psychical reality").

Loewald, Hans W., "The Transference Neurosis: Comments on the Concept and the Phenomenon," *Journal of the American Psychoanalytic Association*, January 1971, pp. 54–66.

Freud, Sigmund, "Some General Characteristics of Obsessional Formations," *Collected Papers*, Vol. 3, p.361 (case of "Amen-Semen").

Berman, Leon E. A., "The Role of Amphetamine in a Case of Hysteria," *Journal of the American Psychoanalytic Association*, April 1972, pp.325–40 ("clutch" anecdote).

Feldman, Sandor S., "To 'Lick' a Problem," paper delivered at Fall 1967 meeting of the American Psychoanalytic Association.

Freud, Sigmund, *The Psychopathology of Everyday Life* (New York: Norton, 1965). (*Signorelli* case on pp. 2–6; "2467" mistakes on pp. 242–43.)

Shopper, Moisy, "*Three* as a Symbol of the Female Genital and the Role of Differentiation," *Psychoanalytic Quarterly*, July 1967, pp. 410–17.

Wilson, C. Philip, "Stone as a Symbol of Teeth," *Psychoanalytic Quarterly*, July 1967, pp. 418–24.

Hinsie, L. E., and Campbell, R. J., *Psychiatric Dictionary*, 3rd ed. (New York: Oxford University Press 1960), p. 712.

Brenner, Charles, *An Elementary Textbook of Psychoanalysis* (Garden City, N.Y.: Anchor Books, 1957). (Quote on reaction formation, p. 94.)

Fenichel, Otto, *The Psychoanalytic Theory of Neurosis* (New York, Norton, 1945).

Freud, Sigmund, "A Case of Obsessional Neurosis," *Collected Papers*, Vol. 3, p. 323. (Freud's comment on blamelessness.)

Freud, *The Origins of Psycho-Analysis*, p.222 (comment on seeing mother in the nude).

Freud, *The Ego and the Id* (New York, Norton, 1962).

Nunberg, Herman, *Principles of Psychoanalysis: Their Application to the Neuroses*, Foreword by Sigmund Freud (New York: International Universities Press, 1955).

Deutsch, Helene, *Neuroses and Character Type: Clinical Psychoanalytic Studies* (New York: International Universities Press, 1965).

Freud, Sigmund, "Anxiety and Instinctual Life," *The Complete Introductory Lectures on Psychoanalysis* (New York: Norton, 1966), p. 566 (material on Alexander the Great and urethral eroticism).

Freud, *The Id and the Ego* (New York: Norton, 1962). ("Psycho-analysis is an instrument. . . ." on p. 46.)

Freud, "Character and Anal Eroticism," *Collected Papers,* Vol. 2, p. 46.

Deutsch, Felix, "Analysis of Postural Behavior," *Psychoanalytic Quarterly,* Vol. 16, 1947.

Freud, Anna, *The Ego and the Mechanisms of Defense,* rev. ed., *Writings of Anna Freud,* Vol. 2 (New York: International Universities Press, 1967).

Hartmann, Heinz, *Essays on Ego Psychology* (New York: International Universities Press, 1964).

Freud, Sigmund, *Interpretation of Dreams* (New York: Basic Books, 1954).

Lehmann, Herbert, "The Lion in Freud's Dream," *The Psychoanalytic Forum,* Vol. 2, No. 3, Autumn 1967, pp. 229–43 (lion as dream symbol for the analyst).


CHAPTER VI

Boring, Edwin G., "Was This Analysis a Success?" *Journal of Abnormal and Social Psychology,* Vol 35, 1940, pp. 4–10.

Landis, Carney, "Psychoanalytic Phenomena," *Journal of Abnormal and Social Psychology,* Vol. 35, 1940, pp. 17–28.

Wortis, Joseph, *Fragments of an Analysis with Freud* (New York: Simon & Schuster, 1954).

Bergin, Allen E., "The Evaluation of Therapeutic Outcomes," in *Handbook of Psychotherapy and Behavior Change,* edited by Allen E. Bergin and Sol L. Garfield (New York: Wiley, 1971). (Material on Berlin Psychoanalytic Clinic and Knight's analysis of figures, pp. 220–25.)

Knight, R. P., "Evaluation of the Results of Psychoanalytic Therapy," *American Journal of Psychiatry,* Vol. 98, 141, pp. 434–46.

Glover, Edward, "Research Methods in Psycho-Analysis," *International Journal of Psychoanalysis,* Vol. 33, 1952, pp. 403–4.

Glover, E., *The Techniques of Psycho-Analysis* (New York: International Universities Press, 1958). (Comments on Eysenck and analytic improvement, p. 376.)

Hamburg, David A., et al., "Report of Ad Hoc Committee on Central Fact-Gathering Data of the American Psychoanalytic Association," *Journal of the American Psychoanalytic Association,* October 1967, pp. 841–61.

*Appendices A, B, and C to the American Psychoanalytic Association Summary and Final Report of the Central Fact-Gathering Committee,* American Psychoanalytic Association, New York, January 5, 1958.

Sears, R. R., *Survey of Objective Studies of Psychoanalytic Concepts,* Social Science Research Council, New York, Bulletin 51, 1943.

Engel, George L., "Research in Psychoanalysis," *Journal of the American Psychoanalytic Association,* Vol. 16, No. 2, April 1968, p. 203.

Gill, Merton M.; Simon, Justin; et al., "Studies in Audio-Recorded Psychoanalysis I: General Considerations," *Journal of the American Psychoanalytic Association,* April 1968, pp. 230–44.

Nunberg, Herman, *Principles of Psychoanalysis: Their Application to Neuroses,* Foreword by Sigmund Freud (New York: International Universities Press, 1955).

Grinker, Roy R., Sr., "Psychiatry Rides Madly in All Directions," *Archives of General Psychiatry,* Vol. 10, No. 3, March 1964, pp. 228–34.

Mowrer, O. Hobart, *Crisis in Psychiatry and Religion* (New York: Van Nostrand, 1961).

Eysenck, Hans J., *The Effects of Psychotherapy* (New York: International Science Press, 1966).

Schmideberg, Melitta, discussion on "Effects of Psychotherapy," *International Journal of Psychiatry,* Vol. 1, No. 4, October 1965, pp. 646–47.

Schmideberg, Melitta, "A Contribution to the History of the Psycho-Analytic Movement in Britain," *British Journal of Psychiatry,* Vol. 118, January 1971, pp. 61–68.

Atkins, Norman B., "Comments on Severe and Psychotic Regression in Analysis," *Journal of the American Psychoanalytic Association,* July 1967, pp. 584–605.

Frosch, John, "Severe Regression States during Analysis," *Journal of the American Psychoanalytic Assocation,* July 1967, pp. 491–507, 606–25.

Kubie, Lawrence S., "Psychoanalysis and Scientific Method," Chapter 3 in *Psychoa-*

*nalysis, Scientific Method and Philosophy,* edited by Sidney Hook (New York: New York University Press, 1959), pp. 57–77.

Kubie, Lawrence S., "Missing and Wanted: Heterodoxy in Psychiatry and Psychoanalysis," *Journal of Nervous and Mental Disease,* Vol. 137, No. 4, October 1963, p. 311.

Wheelis, Allen, *The Quest for Identity* (New York: Norton, 1958).

Wheelis, Allen, "The Vocational Hazards of Psychoanalysis," *International Journal of Psychoanalysis,* Vol. 37, 1956, pp. 171–84.

Wheelis, Allen, "To Be a God," *Commentary,* Vol. 36, No. 2, August 1963, pp. 125–34.

Salter, Andrew, *The Case Against Psychoanalysis,* rev. ed. (New York: Citadel Press, 1963).

Nagel, Ernest, "Methodological Issues in Psychoanalytic Theory," Chapter 2 in *Psychoanalysis, Scientific Method and Philosophy,* edited by Sidney Hook (New York: New York University Press, 1959), pp. 38–56.

Meissner, W. W., "Freud's Methodology," *Journal of the American Psychoanalytic Association,* April 1971, pp. 265–308.

Strupp, Hans H., "Needed: A Reformulation of the Psychotherapeutic Influence," *International Journal of Psychiatry,* Vol. 10, 1972, pp. 114–20.

Johnson, Hiram K., "Psychoanalysis: A Critique," *Psychiatric Quarterly,* Vol. 22, 1948, p. 321.

Stekel, Wilhelm, *The Interpretation of Dreams* (New York: Liveright, 1943).

Freud, Sigmund, "Analysis of a Phobia in a Five-Year-Old Boy" (1909), *Collected Papers,* Vol. 3, pp. 149–289.

Wolpe, Joseph, and Rachman, Stanley, "Psychoanalytic 'Evidence': A Critique Based on Freud's Case of Little Hans," *Journal of Nervous and Mental Disease,* Vol. 130, 1960, pp. 135–48.

Chodoff, Paul, "A Critique of Freud's Theory of Infantile Sexuality," *International Journal of Psychiatry,* Vol. 4, No. 1, July 1967, pp. 35–48. Reprinted from the *American Journal of Psychiatry,* Vol. 123, November 1966, pp. 507–18.

Schmideberg, Melitta, "The Role of Suggestion in Analytic Therapy," *Psychoanalytic Review,* Vol. 26, pp. 219–29.

Heilbrunn, Gert, "Results with Psychoanalytic Therapy," *American Journal of Psychotherapy,* Vol. 17, 1963, pp. 427–35.

Heilbrunn, Gert, "Results with Psychoanalytic Therapy and Professional Commitment," *American Journal of Psychotherapy,* Vol. 20, No. 1, January 1966, pp. 89–99.

Shaw, Charles R., *The Psychiatric Disorders of Childhood* (New York: Appleton-Century-Crofts, 1966).

Freud, Sigmund, *Origins of Psychoanalysis: Letters, Drafts and Notes to Wilhelm Fliess (1887–1902)* (Garden City, N.Y.: Anchor Books, 1957).

Money, John, "Progress of Knowledge and Revision of the Theory of Infantile Sexuality," *International Journal of Psychiatry,* Vol. 4, No. 1. July 1967, pp. 50–54.

Giora, Zvi, "The Function of the Dream: A Reappraisal," *American Journal of Psychiatry,* Vol. 128, No. 1, March 1972, pp. 1067–80.

Watson, R. I., *Psychology of the Child* (New York: Wiley, 1965). (Sewell studies.)

Wolff, Peter H., "Psychoanalytic Research and Infantile Sexuality," *International Journal of Psychiatry,* Vol. 4, No. 1, July 1967, pp. 61–64.

Harlow, Harry F., and Harlow, Margaret K., "The Effect of Rearing Conditions on Behavior," *International Journal of Psychiatry,* Vol. 1, No. 1, January 1965, pp. 43–49. Reprinted from *Bulletin of the Menninger Clinic,* 1962, Vol. 26, No. 5, pp. 213–24.

Orlansky, H., "Infant Care and Personality," *Psychological Bulletin,* Vol. 46, 1949, pp. 1–48.

Linton, Ralph, *Culture and Mental Disorders* (Springfield, Ill.: Charles C Thomas, 1956).

Halverson, H. M., "Genital and Sphincter Behavior of the Male Infant," *Journal of Genetic Psychology,* Vol. 56, pp. 95–136.

Freud, Sigmund, *An Outline of Psychoanalysis* (New York: Norton, 1949).

Merry, F. K., and Merry, R. V., *The First Decades of Life* (New York: Harper & Row, 1958).

Lawick-Goodall, Jane, "The Behavior of Chimpanzees in Their Natural Habitat," *American Journal of Psychiatry,* Vol. 130, No. 1, January 1973, pp. 1–12.

Oberndorf, C. P., *A History of Psychoanalysis in America* (New York: Harper Torchbooks, 1964).

Alexander, Franz G., et al., eds., *Psychoanalytic Pioneers* (New York: Basic Books, 1966).

Alexander, Franz G., and Selesnick, Sheldon, *The History of Psychiatry* (New York: Harper & Row, 1966).

Bailey, Percival, *Sigmund the Unserene* (Springfield, Ill.: Charles C Thomas, 1965). Foreword by Roy R. Grinker, Sr. (Dr. Grinker's comment on religious quality of analysis; Bailey report on threatened analytic rebellion.)

Cancro, Robert, "Orthodoxy and Psychoanalysis," *International Journal of Psychiatry*, December 1972, pp. 62–65.

CHAPTER VIi

Voth, Harold M., "Some Effects of Freud's Personality on Psychoanalytic Theory and Technique," *International Journal of Psychiatry*, Vol. 10, No. 4, December 1972, pp. 48–60.

Cancro, Robert, "Orthodoxy and Psychoanalysis," *International Journal of Psychiatry*, December 1972, pp. 62–65.

Freud, Sigmund, "The Aetiology of Hysteria," *Collected Papers*, Vol. 1, p. 198 ("Caput nili" quote).

Freud, *The Origins of Psychoanalysis*, p. 218 (letter of September 9, 1897, to Fliess).

Jones, Ernest, *The Life and Work of Sigmund Freud*, Vol. 1, pp. 78–97 (material on cocaine).

Schur, Max, *Freud: Living and Dying* (New York: International Universities Press, 1972), pp. 29, 69, 81, 83, 84, 95, 99, 156, 212 (material on cocaine).

Ibid., p. 257 (comment on "homosexual cathexis").

Freud, Sigmund, *The Origins of Psychoanalysis*, letter of May 5, 1900. (Comment on "feminine side" of Freud.)

Schur, Max, pp. 242 (previously unpublished letter ". . . a woman has never . . .").

Freud, Sigmund, *The Origins of Psychoanalysis*, letter of January 3, 1899 ("Here I live in bad temper. . . .").

Jones, Ernest, *The Life and Work of Sigmund Freud*, Vol. 1, p. 317 (fainting incident in Munich).

Schur, Max, *Freud: Living and Dying*, pp. 194, 198, 201, 212 (previously unpublished letters to Fliess on magic numbers); pp. 159, 184–87 (fear of death at various ages); pp. 231–32 (letter to Jones about dying at sixty-one or sixty-two); p. 59 (comment on psychoneuroses, from Jones); p. 110 (comment beginning with "Good mood . . . ," from letter to Fliess, November 22, 1896); p. 63 ("My state of mind . . . ," from letter to Fleiss, September 21, 1899); p. 53 ("rupture of heart . . . ," from letter to Fliess, June 22, 1894); p. 268 (letter to Binswanger, January 1, 1913, regarding fainting attacks).

Jones, Ernest, *The Life and Work of Sigmund Freud.* Vol 1, p. 317 (anecdote about "How sweet it must be to die"); Vol. 2, p. 146 (fainting incident in 1909).

Schur Max, *Freud: Living and Dying,* p. 235 (comment on Freud's wish for sibling's death).

Freud, Sigmund, "Notes Upon a Case of Obsessional Neurosis," *Collected Papers,* Vol. 3 (New York: Basic Books, 1959). (Reading hostility into Rat Man case.)

Freud, *The Psychopathology of Everyday Life,* p. 260 (quote on origin of superstition).

Schur, Max, *Freud: Living and Dying,* pp. 341–42 (death wishes of Freud).


CHAPTER VIII

" 'Black Sheep' Respond to Mother," *Medical Tribune,* March 27, 1967.

LeShan, Eda, J., "The 'Perfect' Child," *The New York Times Magazine,* August 27, 1967, p. 63.

Spock, Benjamin M., *Baby and Child Care* (New York: Pocket Books, 1968).

Fishman, Katherine Davis, "The Less Permissive Dr. Spock," *The New York Times Book Review,* February 16, 1969, p. 4.

Thomas, Alexander; Chess, Stella; and Birch, Herbert G., *Temperament and Behavior Disorders in Children* (New York: New York University Press, 1968).

Thomas, Alexander, and Chess, Stella, *Temperament and Development* (New York: Brunner/Mazel, 1977).

Carey, William B., "Clinical Applications of Infant Temperament Measurements," *Journal of Pediatrics,* Vol. 81, 1972, pp. 823–28.

Coles, Robert, "Shrinking History, Part I," *The New York Review of Books,* February 22, 1973, pp. 20–21 (quote on parents).

Shaver, Benjamin A., "Maternal Personality and Early Adaptation as Related to Infantile Colic," Chapter 10 in *Psychological Aspects of a First Pregnancy and Early Postnatal Adaptation,* edited by P. Shereshefsky and J. Yarrow (New York: Raven Press., 1973), pp. 209–16 (report on colic).

Paradise, Jack L., "Maternal and Other Factors in the Etiology of Infantile Colic," *Journal of the American Medical Association,* Vol. 197, July 18, 1966, pp. 191–99 (report on colic).

Faber, Adele, and Mazlish, Elaine, *Liberated Parents, Liberated Children* (New York: Grosset & Dunlap, 1974).

Shaw, Charles R., *The Psychiatric Disorders of Childhood* (New York: Appleton-Century-Crofts, 1966). (Report on H. A. Newman and identical twins.)

Weinberger, Gerald, "Some Common Assumptions Underlying Traditional Child Psychotherapy: Fallacy and Reformulation," *Psychotherapy: Theory, Research and Practice,* Vol. 9, No. 2, Summer 1972, pp. 149–52.

Orlansky, Harold, "Infant Care and Personality," *Psychological Bulletin,* Vol. 46, 1949, p. 1.

Coughlan, Robert, "How to Survive Parenthood," *Life,* June 26, 1950, p. 112 (changing fashions in child care).

Spock, Benjamin M., "How Not to Bring Up a Bratty Child," *Redbook,* February 1974.

Conant, James B., *The Education of American Teachers* (New York: McGraw-Hill, 1963).

Koerner, James D., *The Miseducation of American Teachers* (Boston: Houghton Mifflin, 1963).

Noshpitz, Joseph D., "The Quiet Ones, The Noisy Ones," *Today's Education,* September 1971, pp. 24–30.

Stickney, Stonewall B., "Schools Are Our Community Mental Health Centers," *American Journal of Psychiatry,* Vol. 124, No. 10, April 1968, pp. 1407–14.

Brammer, Lawrence M., "The Counselor Is a Psychologist," *Personnel and Guidance Journal,* September 1968, pp. 4–8.

Winthrop, Henry, "Bad Faith in Counseling and Therapy," *Mental Hygiene,* Vol. 53, No. 3, July 1969, pp. 415–21.

CHAPTER IX

Janov, Arthur, *The Primal Scream* (New York: Putnam, 1970).

Janov, Arthur, *The Primal Revolution* (New York: Simon & Schuster, 1972).

Berkowitz, Leonard, "The Case for Bottling up Rage," *Psychology Today,* July 1973, p. 24.

Casriel, Daniel, *A Scream Away from Happiness* (New York: Grosset & Dunlap, 1972).

Berne, Eric, *Games People Play* (New York: Grove Press, 1964).

Harris, Thomas A., *I'm OK—You're OK: A Practical Guide to Transactional Analysis* (New York: Harper & Row, 1967).

Reich, Wilhelm, *The Discovery of the Orgone: The Function of Orgasm* (New York: Noonday Press, Farrar, Straus & Giroux, 1966).

Lowen, Alexander, *The Betrayal of the Body* (New York: Collier Books, 1967).

Maliver, Bruce L., *The Encounter Game* (New York: Stein & Day, 1973).

Fagan, Joan, and Shepherd, Irma Lee, eds., *Life Techniques in Gestalt Therapy* (New York: Perennial Library, Harper & Row, 1970).

Perls, Frederick; Hefferline, Ralph; and Goodman, Paul, *Gestalt Therapy* (New York: Delta Books, 1951).

Perls, Frederick S., *Gestalt Therapy Verbatim* (New York: Bantam Books, 1970).

Maslow, Abraham H., *Toward a Psychology of Being*, 2nd ed. (New York: Van Nostrand, 1968).

Schutz, William C., *Joy: Expanding Human Awareness* (New York: Grove Press, 1967).

Ruitenbeek, Hendrik M., *The New Group Therapies* (New York: Avon Books, 1970).

Beldoch, Michael, "The False Psychology of Encounter Groups," *Intellectual Digest,* October 1971, pp. 85–88. Reprinted from *Modern Occasions.*

Rogers, Carl, *On Encounter Groups* (New York: Harper & Row, 1970). (Several quotes by Rogers on Encounter.)

Lieberman, Morton A.; Yalom, Irvin D; and Miles, Matthew B., *Encounter Groups: First Facts* (New York: Basic Books, 1973). (Stanford study.)

Yalom, I. D., and Lieberman, M. A., "A Study of Encounter Group Casualties," *Archives of General Psychiatry,* Vol. 25, No. 1, 1971, pp. 16–30.

Peters, Joseph J., "Do Encounter Groups Hurt People?", *Psychotherapy: Theory, Research and Practice,* Vol. 10, No. 1, Spring 1973, pp. 33–35.

Siroka, Robert W.; Siroka, Ellen K.; and Schloss, Gilbert A., *Sensitivity Training and Group Encounter* (New York: Grosset & Dunlap, 1971).

Coffey, Hugh, "Encounter's Debt to Kurt Lewin," a review from the *Psychiatry and Social Science Review,* November 12, 1971, pp. 25–28.

"Sensitivity Training," Council on Mental Health, *Journal of the American Medical Association,* Vol. 217, No. 13, September 27, 1971, p. 1853.

Klaw, Spencer, "Management Psychologists Have Landed," *Fortune,* April 1970, p. 106.

Calame, Byron, "Sensitivity Training," *Wall Street Journal,* July 14, 1969.

Bry, Adelaide, *est: 60 Hours That Transform Your Life* (New York: Harper & Row, 1976).

Clarke, Gary, "*est* with an English Accent: A Look Inside the First London Training," *The Graduate Review,* an *est* publication, August 1977, pp. 1–7.

Glass, Leonard L.; Kirsch, Michael A.; and Parris, Frederick N., "Psychiatric Disturbances Associated with Erhard Seminars Training: A Report of Cases," *American Journal of Psychiatry,* Vol. 134, No. 3, March 1977, pp. 245–47.

Lilly, John C., *The Center of the Cyclone* (New York: Julian Press, 1972).

Karlines, Marvin, and Andrews, Lewis M., *Biofeedback: Turning on the Power of Your Mind* (Philadelphia: Lippincott, 1972).

Theodore X. Barber, ed., *Advances in Altered States of Consciousness and Human Potentialities,* Vol. 1 (New York: Psychological Dimensions, Inc., 1976), pp. 149–58. (Reprint of T. Mulholland's report on alpha "high.")

CHAPTER X

*Diagnostic and Statistical Manual, II,* American Psychiatric Association, Washington, D.C., 1968.

*Diagnostic and Statistical Manual, III, Draft,* American Psychiatric Association, Washington, D.C., April 15, 1977.

May, Rollo, *The Meaning of Anxiety,* rev. ed. (New York: Norton, 1977).

Miner, Gary D., "The Evidence for Genetic Components in the Neuroses," *Archives of General Psychiatry,* Vol. 29, July 1973, pp. 111–18. (Brown, Slater and twin studies.)

# Index

ABOUT THE AUTHOR

MARTIN L. GROSS is an author, editor, educator and social critic. Mr. Gross's two previous books, both published by Random House, are *The Brain Watchers* (1963) and *The Doctors* (1966).

*The Brain Watchers* was a critical study of psychological testing, which critic C. Northcote Parkinson called "a book that could hardly be bettered." *The Brain Watchers* led to hearings in the U.S. Congress, at which Mr. Gross was the leading witness.

*The Doctors,* a critical study of American medicine, was praised by many university physicians and angrily attacked by the American Medical Association. The book stimulated an ongoing debate on the efficiency and ethics of American medicine.

Mr. Gross is the author of over 100 magazine articles, which have appeared in major publications. His column "The Social Critic" was syndicated in metropolitan daily newspapers throughout the country. He is a member of the faculty of The New School For Social Research and an adjunct assistant professor of Social History at New York University. He is the recipient of awards from the National Education Association and American Heritage Foundation.

Mr. Gross was founder and editor of *Intellectual Digest* and is now editor-in-chief of a national magazine.